THE HAGUE
Odyssey

THE HAGUE
Odyssey

ISRAEL'S STRUGGLE FOR SECURITY ON THE
FRONT LINES OF TERRORISM AND HER BATTLE
FOR JUSTICE AT THE UNITED NATIONS

RICHARD D. HEIDEMAN

Bartleby Press
Washington • Baltimore

Published and distributed by:

Bartleby Press

PO Box 858
Savage, MD 20763
800-953-9929
www.bartlebythepublisher.com

Library of Congress Cataloging-in-Publication Data

Heideman, Richard D., author.
  The Hague odyssey: Israel's struggle for security on the front lines of terrorism and her battle for justice at the United Nations / Richard D. Heideman.
      pages cm
  Includes bibliographical references and index.
  ISBN 978-0-910155-99-1 (alk. paper)
  1. Arab-Israeli conflict--Law and legislation. 2. International Court of Justice. 3. Israel--Trials, litigation, etc. I. Title.
  KZ6795.A72.H45 2013
  956.04--dc23
                                                              2013010077

In memory of the victims of terrorism who have lost their lives as a result of heinous acts of murder caused by terrorists and their sponsors.

Contents

ACKNOWLEDGEMENTS   xiii

PREFACE   xv

INTRODUCTION   1

Chapter One: THE ARAB-ISRAELI CONFLICT AND
THE ROLE OF UNITED NATIONS   5

Chapter Two: THE VIOLENCE AND ATTEMPTS AT
ACHIEVING PEACE BETWEEN ISRAEL AND THE
ARAB PALESTINIANS   9

Peace, War and the Status of Diplomatic Relations • Past
Attempts at Peace • The Oslo Accords, the Gaza Security
Fence, the Wye River Accords and the Middle East Peace
Summit at Camp David • Failed Attempts at Peace • The
Second Intifada's Reign of Terror • A Missed Opportunity •
The Palestinian Authority and Terrorist Organizations • The
Second Intifada, the Mitchell Report, Historic Rose Garden
Speech by President George W. Bush and the Roadmap for
Peace in the Middle East • The Disengagement Plan • The
Failure of Leadership by Yasser Arafat and the Hopes for
His Successor • Implementing Israel's Disengagement from
Gaza • The Political Rise of Hamas as an Obstacle to Peace •
Quartet Envoy Tony Blair, Diplomacy and the Security Fence
• US Efforts to Improve Security • Continued Attacks from
Gaza—At the Center of the Ongoing Conflict • Gaza, the
Naval Blockade and Relations with Turkey • Hamas Efforts
to Destroy Peace Making in Spite of Efforts to Implement
the Roadmap • The Obama Administration's Efforts Toward

Peacemaking • Benjamin Netanyahu's Government and His
View of the Security Fence as a Necessary Means to Stopping
Terrorism

Chapter Three: THE HISTORY OF THE TERRORISM
PREVENTION SECURITY FENCE—ITS PURPOSE
AND STRUCTURE   61

The Meaning of the "Green Line" • Historical Origins of
the Terrorism Prevention Security Fence and the Debate
Surrounding its Construction • Construction of the Security
Fence • The Terrorism Prevention Security Fence Saves and
Protects Lives • The Israel-Jordan Security Fence has Helped
the Countries be Good Neighbors and has Helped Israel
Fulfill Her Obligation of Protecting Her Citizens • Terrorism
Must Not Be Allowed To Succeed

Chapter Four: THE IMPACT OF THE SECURITY FENCE
ON THE LIVES OF PALESTINIANS AND ISRAELIS   87

The Fence's Impact on Palestinians Living on the West Bank
• The Fence's Impact on Israeli Lives

Chapter Five: PROPAGANDA AND RED HERRINGS:
SEMANTICS, SPECTERS OF THE BERLIN WALL   99
AND APARTHEID

Semantic Debate: Fence, Wall and Separation Barrier •
Specter of the Berlin Wall • Specter of Apartheid

Chapter Six: JUDICIAL AND POLITICAL ACTIONS LEADING
UP TO THE ICJ OPINION   117

Proceedings Before the Israeli High Court of Justice •
Actions in the United Nations Security Council • The UN
Charter and The International Court of Justice • United
Nations General Assembly Referral of the Issue of the Fence
to the International Court of Justice

Chapter Seven: THE ADVISORY OPINION: SUM
AND SUBSTANCE   123

The Advisory Opinion • History of the Proceedings:
Paragraphs 1 through 12 • Questions of Jurisdiction:
Paragraphs 13 through 42 • Discretionary Power of the
Court to Exercise its Jurisdiction: Paragraphs 43 through
65 • Scope of Question Posed: Paragraphs 66 through
69 • Historical Background: Paragraphs 70 through 78

• Description of the Wall: Paragraphs 79 through 85 •
Applicable Rules and Principles of International Law:
Paragraphs 86 through 113 • United Nations Charter and
General Assembly Resolution 2625 (XXV): Paragraphs 87
through 88 • International Humanitarian Law: Paragraphs
89 through 101 • Human Rights Law: Paragraphs 102
through 113 • Violation of Relevant Rules: Paragraphs
114 through 142 • Impact on Right of Palestinian People
to Self-determination: Paragraphs 115 through 122 •
Relevant International Humanitarian Law and Human
Rights Instruments: Paragraphs 123 through 137 • Self-
defense and the State of Necessity Defense: Paragraphs
138 through 142 • Legal Consequences of the Violation:
Paragraphs 143 through 148 • Legal Consequences for
Israel: Paragraphs 149 through 154 • Legal Consequences
for States Other than Israel: Paragraphs 154 through 159 •
Legal Consequences for the United Nations: Paragraph 160
• General Context of the Conflict: Paragraphs 161 through
162 • Dispositif: Paragraph 163 • Judge Buergenthal's
Strong Dissent from the Advisory Opinion • The Separate
Opinions of the Other ICJ Judges

**Chapter Eight: LACK OF JURISDICTION FOR THE
INTERNATIONAL COURT TO ISSUE AN
ADVISORY OPINION**   **187**

Jurisdiction Lacking Because of Procedural Defects • The
Jurisdictional Grants of the ICJ Statute were Not Met •
A Jurisdictional Requirement Without Meaning? • The
Meaning of "Legal Question" within Realist/Idealist Debate
• The Textual Interpretations of "Legal Question" • There is
No Legal Question Because the Dispute Does Not Concern
Two States • There is No Legal Question Because the
Question was Legally Uncertain •Conclusion

**Chapter Nine: THE IMPROPRIETY AND DANGERS OF THE
INTERNATIONAL COURT OF JUSTICE'S ISSUANCE OF
THE ADVISORY OPINION**   **207**

The ICJ's Actions were Improper in Light of Its Judicial
Function • Compelling Reasons Not to Have Issued an
Advisory Opinion on Israel's Security Fence

Chapter Ten: ISSUES, QUESTIONS AND DANGERS   **239**

The Fourth Geneva Convention and the Israeli Terrorism

Prevention Security Fence • Israel's Inherent Right to Self-Defense and the ICJ's Interpretation of Self-Defense in the Advisory Opinion • The ICJ's Interpretation of Article 51 of the UN Charter in the Advisory Opinion on Israel's Security Fence • The Court's Historical Limitations on its Interpretation of Self-Defense • Israel's Self Defense—Within the UN Charter • Israel's Self-Defense—Beyond the UN Charter • Israel's Self-Defense in the Age of Terrorism • Israel's Security Fence is a Legal and Effective Measure of Self-Defense • Israel's Use of Land, Restriction on Movement and Rights to the Land through the Effluxion of Time

Chapter Eleven: OMISSIONS AND ERRORS EQUAL INJUSTICE   **253**

The Advisory Opinion Omitted Facts Regarding Palestinian Terrorist Attacks Against Israel • The Advisory Opinion Omitted Facts Regarding Israel's High Court of Justice Opinion on the Security Fence and the Role and Responsibility of the Israeli Judiciary's Continual Legal Review of the Security Fence • The *Beit Sourik Village Council* Opinion • The Effect of the *Beit Sourik* Opinion • The *Alfei Menashe* Opinion • Additional Israeli High Court Orders • The *Bil'in Village Council* Opinion • The Israeli High Court's Ongoing Role Overseeing the Route of Fence • Conclusion • The Advisory Opinion Omitted the Standard of Proportionality as a Counter Terrorism Measure • The Meaning of Proportionality • Proportionality and the International Court of Justice • The Proportionality Analysis in the Israeli High Court's *Beit Sourik* Decision • Conclusion • The Advisory Opinion Omitted Facts Regarding Other Countries' Fences and Barriers

Chapter Twelve: IN THE AFTERMATH OF THE ADVISORY OPINION   **277**

The UN Security Council, the General Assembly, UN Agencies and Israel • The Policies of the United States in the Aftermath of the ICJ's Advisory Opinion • The Measures Taken in the Aftermath of the ICJ Advisory Opinion Reflect a Reality in Which an Advisory Opinion is No Longer Just an Opinion • A Few Hopeful Signs that the Law-Abiding World Will Recognize Israel as a Respected Member and Acknowledge Her Right and Obligation to Defend Her Citizens

Chapter Thirteen: THE VICTIMS   296

    The Terrorism Prevention Security Fence Works: It is
    Necessary to Protect the Victims of the Future • More Must
    Be Done to Stop Terrorism

Chapter Fourteen: ISRAEL'S BATTLE FOR JUSTICE IN A
    DANGEROUS NEIGHBORHOOD   301

    Political Maneuvers to Delegitimize Israel Continue • Israel's
    Battle for Security on the Frontlines of Terror • Conclusion

ENDNOTES   307

INDEX   371

ABOUT THE AUTHOR   383

Acknowledgements

I have devoted a good part of my adult life advocating on behalf of victims of tragedy and acts of terrorism. Before I give thanks to the people who helped make this book possible, I would like to pay tribute to my parents, Marion and Ted Heideman and to my father in law, Max D. Greenberg, all of blessed memory, and to my mother in law, Esther Greenberg. Without their lifelong guidance and wisdom I may never have understood the meaning of true commitment.

I wish to express special thanks to my wife, Phyllis Greenberg Heideman and to our daughters, Stefanie, Elana and Ariana. They not only provide me with constant love, support and encouragement, but have worked tirelessly to help me complete this work.

My law partners, Noel J. Nudelman and Tracy Reichman Kalik, continually offered valued counsel, commentary and advice for this volume—as they do in all matters for our clients. It is a privilege to work together with them as we seek the pursuit of justice.

Without the immeasurable efforts of my legal assistant, Keyauna Chase Fogle, this book could not have been completed. In addition, I am grateful to all those who have worked diligently in the research and editing of *The Hague Odyssey*: Lauren Posten, Jacqueline Kaufman, Matthew Apfel and Faye Eisen. Finally, thanks to my publisher, Jeremy Kay, and the staff at Bartleby Press for their assistance in bringing this work to publication.

Preface

Every Nation-State has the inherent right to defend her people. The principle of self-defense has been a long-standing principle under international law and is enshrined in Article 51 of the UN Charter. Yet in this world of dangerous places, and living in a dangerous neighborhood, the State of Israel among all nations is held to a double standard at the United Nations and in world opinion. Steadfast in her obligation to defend her people, she has taken the necessary steps to do so, yet receives constant international criticism for protecting her citizens from violent attack.

At a plenum of Israel's parliament, the Knesset, Prime Minister Benjamin Netanyahu emphasized that this paradox which Israel faces is not only an obstacle to Israel's internal security, but also a targeted attack on Israel's very existence, stating "The international battle against Israel began in UN Durban Conference I, and continued in the ... ICJ advisory opinion against the security fence and in the Durban Conference II, as well as the Goldstone Report." Netanyahu emphasized that, "this is a comprehensive attack, not on a specific Israeli government but on the State of Israel."[1]

This systematic attack on Israel's sovereignty must be taken quite literally as a concerted and ongoing attack on the rights of the State of Israel as a nation-state of the world and as a serious active threat to Israel's overall security.

One of the major components of this ongoing attack on Israel has been the vitriolic politicization of Israel's construction of a terrorism prevention security fence built in direct response to the Second Intifada's repeated heinous and murderous attacks upon her population, cities and general welfare. The epicenter of this assault has been at the United Nations and reached feverous heights when, at the request of the Palestine Liberation Organization ("PLO"), and certain member states of the UN, the United Nations General Assembly ("UNGA" or "General Assembly") referred to the International Court of Justice ("ICJ") a request for an advisory opinion as to certain questions presented by the PLO and her governmental allies. The International Court of Justice sitting at The Hague, over Israel's objection, determined that it had the jurisdiction to issue an advisory opinion concerning Israel's construction of the barrier and subsequently issued a far-reaching advisory opinion. The International Court of Justice's highly politicized "advisory opinion" has largely redefined and restricted the legal mechanisms that could be available to countries under terrorist threat. It has also raised implications for Israel's borders and surely will be a future centerpiece of debate relating to the long elusive permanent peace between The State of Israel and the Palestinian people.

Prime Minister Benjamin Netanyahu further declared before the Joint Session of the US Congress in 2011, "The precise delineation of [a future Palestinian state's] borders must be negotiated. We will be very generous on the size of a future Palestinian state. But as President Obama said, the border will be different than the one that existed on June 4, 1967. Israel will not return to the indefensible lines of 1967."[2]

The construction of the fence and barrier designed to keep the terrorists out has regrettably caused hardship upon the lives of both Palestinians and Israelis living near the fence line and has resulted in much harsh criticism of Israel. However, when the issues are analyzed in context with applicable substantive law, free of political overtones, the reality becomes clear that Israel's terrorism prevention security fence has indeed saved lives—meeting an essential obligation of any country to its citizenry. For Israel, this responsibility carries special significance. As Netanyahu further declared on May 24, 2011 before the United States Congress, "As for Israel, if history has taught the Jewish people anything, it is that we must take calls for our destruction seriously. We are a nation that rose from the ashes of the Holocaust. When we say Never Again, we mean Never Again."[3]

Canadian Prime Minister Stephen Harper, a leading public voice on issues of human rights and respect for the rule of law, eloquently characterized the universal values Israel has portrayed in her struggle for freedom and democracy when he stated:

> All of my life, Israel has been a symbol—a symbol of the triumph of hope and faith. After 1945, our battered world desperately needed to be lifted out of post-war darkness and despair... It was the people who had suffered who most provided that inspiration. By their example, they led the world back to the light... Their pilgrimage was the culmination of a two-thousand-year-old dream; it is a tribute to the unquenchable human aspiration for freedom, and a testament to the indomitable spirit of the Jewish people...
>
> ...But the source of Israel's strength and success, in my view, is its commitment to the universal values of all civilized peoples: freedom, democracy, human rights and the rule of law....There will be many challenges along the way, but considering how far Israel has come in such a short time, in the face of such seemingly insurmountable odds, I can foresee no dark force, no matter how strong, that could succeed in dimming the light of freedom and democracy that shines from within Israel.[4]

When all is said and done, what is undeniable is that Israel is entitled, like every country, to live forever—in peace and security, free from terrorist attack. To deny her that right denies, at the minimum, basic principles of international law and the foundations upon which freedom, democracy and justice are built.

Introduction

A s a result of the ongoing terrorism against and murder of Israeli citizens, the State of Israel has over the past decade built a terrorism prevention security fence as a defensive measure designed to keep terrorists out of the state. Throughout its history but most dramatically since the commencement of the Second Intifada in late September 2000, Israel has endured an onslaught of violent terrorist attacks initiated by infiltrators—primarily Palestinians—funded, supported, aided, assisted and enabled by those who encourage and sponsor terror, leaving Israel's citizens and visitors murdered and maimed.

Under international law, Israel has both the right and the obligation to defend itself as a sovereign nation-state within recognized borders. Israel has repeatedly demonstrated its willingness to make concessions for peace with Egypt, Jordan and with the Palestinians at Madrid, at Oslo, at The White House, at Wye River, in the Hebron Accords, by approving the Roadmap, by completing its unilateral disengagement from the Gaza Strip, at Annapolis, in repeated statement at the United Nations and in public calls to the PLO for the parties to convene discussions on final status agreement core issues. However, the Palestinian record, in contrast, evidences a habitual retreat to terrorism and the threat of terrorism, employing the politics of fear and assault and making the construction of the security fence necessary for Israel to protect her people and those from throughout the world who visit Israel including Jerusalem and the holy places.

While the route of the security fence is a topic of dispute, the dramatic reduction in the number of terrorist attacks within Israel since the fence's construction is incontrovertible. In spite of this reduction and the proven reason for its necessity, Israel has been wrongly accused of intending to and committing an apartheid-like separation between Israel and the Palestinians in constructing the security fence zone between Israel and the Palestinian Territories.

Israel's High Court of Justice has considered the legal issues surrounding the building of the terrorism prevention security fence in cases brought by aggrieved Palestinian residents as well as human rights groups. In an extraordinary display of judicial independence and in the spirit of a true democracy, on June 30, 2004 the Israeli High Court of Justice, which is Israel's Supreme Court ("Israeli Court," "High Court," "Supreme Court" or "HCJ"), ordered that the security fence be rerouted. Subsequent Israeli High Court decisions, including the recent December 2012 decision, have also ordered modifications to the route of the barrier, mandating that the Israeli Defense Forces ("IDF") relocate portions of the fence and barriers.

Notwithstanding the Israeli High Court decision and without giving judicial deference to the opinion rendered by the highest court of the country, the State of Israel, with jurisdiction over the legal issues relating to the security fence, the International Court of Justice, sitting at the Hague, rendered an advisory opinion ten says later on July 9, 2004 acting on a request by resolution of the United Nations General Assembly regarding "the legal consequences arising from the construction of the wall being built by Israel..."[5] The advisory opinion was issued despite strong objections by Israel, the United States, and many other countries regarding the ICJ's acceptance of jurisdiction of the question referred to the Court.[6]

In essence, the advisory opinion, which is non-binding and lacks the force of law or of an enforceable Judgment, advised that Israel must cease construction of the fence, pay reparations to affected Palestinians and determined that the security fence was in violation of international and humanitarian law. The mere existence of the advisory opinion has inappropriately been and surely will continue to be cited as precedent and is likely to have a future detrimental effect on democratic processes, the negotiations between Palestinians and Israelis and will moreover likely have a negative impact on all UN member states in pursuit of effective means to protect their citizenry from terrorist attacks by infiltrators into their society.

The ICJ's issuance of the advisory opinion suffered from numerous procedural and substantive defects that cast a shadow on the Court's opinion. Firstly, the ICJ improperly exercised jurisdiction over the issue. Notably, the ICJ failed to justly acknowledge the waves of Palestinian terror which necessitated construction of the security fence in the first place or the repeated violations by the Palestinians of their agreements with Israel and of various UN resolutions. Most importantly, while emboldening Palestinian terror attacks threatened and committed under the guise of freedom fighting, the ICJ attempted in effect to eradicate Israel's right to self-defense, an inherent right recognized and codified in Article 51 of the UN Charter. As this author stated in his brief filed on behalf of the Foundation for Defense of Democracies ("FDD") with the Clerk of the International Court of Justice in opposition to the pending question before the ICJ, The State of Israel, as any other sovereign nation-state that is a member of the United Nations and the family of nations, is entitled and obligated to protect and defend her people.[7]

In addition, the question referred to the Court was rife with political determinations that have no place in a proper legal opinion, albeit advisory, prior to completion of the required and contemplated agreements resulting from direct negotiations between the parties to establish borders and resolve the other core issues in controversy between the parties. Inappropriately adopting the language of the question submitted to it by the United Nations General Assembly, the Court calls Israel's terrorism prevention security fence a wall (which is a concrete barrier for approximately five percent of its length and located mostly in strategically dangerous areas used by terrorist infiltrators) and uses terminology such as occupying power and occupied Palestinian territory that prejudge contested issues of international law.[8] The advisory opinion was issued without a full consideration of the legal history between the parties, the agreements between them and the truthful evidence existing on the ground; all the while ignoring the legal and factual context and justification for the essential need for the security fence considering the realities of the controversy and the murderous assaults launched upon Israel by the very terrorists which the security fence is designed to stop.

Since the advisory opinion's publication in the summer of 2004, the security fence has become a lightning rod for Israel's critics seeking to further demonize and delegitimize the very standing and existence of the Jewish state. These critics call the fence an apartheid wall and liken it to the Berlin Wall—wholly ignoring the fence's proven effectiveness in preventing suicide bombings and other deadly attacks. The opinion has been cited in numerous UN reports and referenced in committee meetings.[9] Indeed, on the fifth anniversary of its issuance, UN officials and the Palestine Liberation Organization and its Palestinian Authority called on Israel to tear down the wall in accordance with the advisory opinion.

Neither the UN General Assembly nor any country or organization has any authority to attempt to convert the advisory opinion to binding law or to seek its enforcement. Politicized attempts to do so fly in the face of due process and applicable international law. Ultimately, no ruling, resolution or even an advisory opinion of the International Court of Justice can interfere with a nation's rights and obligations to defend her citizens; nor any citizen's right and entitlement to be defended by her country.

CHAPTER ONE

The Arab-Israeli Conflict and The Role of United Nations

On November 29, 1947, the passage of General Assembly Resolution 181 set the stage for the emergence of two nations, one Jewish and one Arab, in the territory formerly subject to the British Mandate over Palestine ("Partition Resolution").[10] Israel accepted the resolution while the Arab world fiercely rejected it. Seven months later, on May 14, 1948, the British Mandate ended and the State of Israel declared its independence within the territory designated by Resolution 181. The same day that Israel declared its independence it was recognized as a government and independent state by the world's great powers and countries throughout the world committed to respecting and applauding the legal establishment of the State of Israel. However, Egypt, Jordan, Syria, Lebanon and Iraq, rejecting even the concept of the existence of the independent Jewish state, launched an immediate war of aggression against the newly created Jewish state of Israel. These combined powers were defeated in what is now termed Israel's War of Independence. Israel was subsequently admitted as a member-state to the body of the United Nations in 1949.

The UN Partition Resolution essentially divided into portions, one to be Jewish, and one Arab, land that was formerly the ancient home of the Jewish people in Judea and Samaria and including land that had come to be known as Palestinia including Trans-Jordan and lands previously occupied by the Ottoman Turks and others who had invaded and conquered the land over thousands of years.[11] The

Jewish people have resided in ancient Judea and Samaria for thousands of years with Jerusalem at the site of the First Temple, the Second Temple and a rich religious and cultural ancestral heritage. In adopting the Partition Resolution, the United Nations sought to secure and indeed guarantee for the Jewish people their rightful return to their ancient homeland, while respecting the rights of other peoples who had lived in the areas under the British Mandatory Period and who were living in the partitioned areas, including Jerusalem, at the time of the adoption of the UN Partition Resolution ("Resolution 181"). Despite Resolution 181's text and intent, no corresponding Arab nation arose. Instead, those portions of the land partitioned by the UN Resolution which was referred to as Palestine and in ancient Judea and Samaria that did not become part of Israel, which includes the West Bank and Gaza, became occupied during the War of Independence, first, by Iraq and then by Jordan.

Jordan annexed the West Bank in 1949 and remained in control of the West Bank until such time as King Hussein of Jordan unilaterally relinquished control over Trans-Jordan in 1988.[12] The ensuing period saw Israel develop a government, communities and cities, kibbutzim and moshavim and an exciting period of statehood building. Subsequently, Israel endured wars with her neighbors in 1956, 1967 and 1973 and vicious terrorist attacks upon Israelis both at home and abroad.

Prior to the 1967 Six Day War, Jerusalem was a divided city, with "west" Jerusalem under the control of Israel and "east" Jerusalem under the control of Jordan. In the 1967 Six Day War, Israel was attacked from all sides and pushed Egypt's armies out of the Sinai and back to Cairo, Syria's armies almost back to Damascus, after which it took control of the Golan Heights overlooking Israel's Sea of Galilee. Israel also pushed Jordan's armies back to Amman and out of the area of Jerusalem, the Jordan Valley, Judea and Samaria. Israel annexed Jerusalem, uniting the city, and subsequently endured another war in 1973, the Yom Kippur War.

Since 1967, Israel has administered the Palestinian Territories turning over selected areas to the Palestinian Authority ("PA"), an organization which was created by the Palestine Liberation Organization in accordance with various agreements reached during and following the Oslo Accords period in 1992-94 ("PA"), and subsequent agreements reached in the Wye River and Hebron Accords in 1998-99. Israel also unilaterally withdrew from Lebanon and subsequently from Gaza and has turned over to the Palestinian Authority security and other functions for certain areas within the West Bank and Gaza ("the Palestinian Territories") as Israel reached agreements or made unilateral or bilateral determinations that the PA was capable of providing and assuring Israel of security in those areas.

No other international issue has singularly preoccupied the United Nations more than the Arab-Israeli conflict. The conflict has been the subject of innumerable resolutions in both the Security Council and the General Assembly. Indeed, from 1964 to 1988, the UN Security Council passed 88 resolutions against Israel, the only democracy in the region, while the UN General Assembly passed more than 400 such resolutions against Israel.[13] It is shameful that during, for example, its 61st Session (2006-2007), the General Assembly enacted 22 anti-Israel resolutions and nary a single resolution on Sudan's genocide in Darfur.[14] Following that, during its 62nd Session (2007-2008), the General Assembly enacted 19 anti-Israel resolutions, typical of subsequent years.[15] In the 2012 session of the UN General Assembly, 22 anti-Israel resolutions were passed and only four addressing the rest of the world (1 each regarding Syria, Iran, North Korea and Burma), according to UN Watch. These anti-Israel resolutions do not count the additional resolutions enacted against Israel by the UN Human Rights Council or its predecessor UN Commission on Human Rights.

As the number of resolutions against Israel has continued to grow, it has become more and more clear that the UN which functions in the General Assembly on the basis of one country one vote is being used as a vehicle engineered by mostly non-democratic states, many of which have no diplomatic relations with Israel, and some of which maintain a formal state of war against Israel, to publicly hold up for ridicule the democratic State of Israel while covering up or excusing the violence and terrorism of its own regimes and authoritarian neighbors. This double standard prevents the UN from acting as a fair and impartial facilitator and makes it more difficult to resolve the ever-present issue of finding a lasting peace between the Arab Palestinians and the State of Israel. Moreover, in its attempt to appear impartial, the UN has applied a concept of "proportionality" — inappropriately equating the severity of attacks and the measure of a response.[16]

In the now heavily criticized and discredited Goldstone Report, adopted by the UN in 2009 and fully embraced by Israel's enemies, Israel was accused of war crimes due to its responsive attack on Hamas, a Foreign Terrorist Organization ("FTO") that has control in Gaza, and which repeatedly launched missiles into Israel, requiring a strong defensive counter assault by Israel. Israel's responsive actions in 2008 during Operation Cast Lead, and again in 2012 during Operation Pillar of Defense, were part of a concerted effort to put a stop to the dangerous continued launching of thousands of rockets fired from Gaza into Israel proper. Despite its subsequent retraction by Judge Goldstone, who has essentially said that if he knew then what he knows now he would not have issued the Goldstone Report at the UN, these libelous accusations have done significant damage to Israel's reputation, sanctioned by the UN and embraced by both country opponents and others who have fashionably taken to accusing Israel of human rights violations. Yet, in 2012, not one UN General Assembly resolution was passed against Hamas for its thousands of Gaza based terrorist missile launchings against the sovereign State of Israel.

Instead of constantly attacking Israel, without simultaneously addressing the necessity of Israel's responses to Palestinian terrorism, the United Nations has done a gross disservice to Israel, to the region and to humanity by its failure and refusal to hold Palestinian terrorist organizations operating within or under the often blind eye of the PLO and its PA responsible for their acts of murder, maiming and constant threat of terrorist attacks upon Israel. The UN would best serve the interests of peace and the affected parties by returning to its proper role as a constructive, impartial and thoughtful actor in pursuit of true peace and security as a means of solving the Arab-Israeli conflict.

The Violence and Attempts at Achieving Peace Between Israel and the Arab Palestinians

D espite the oft-stated stated desire among both the Arab Palestinians and the Israelis for coexistence and achieving a meaningful peace, violence between Israel and Arab Palestinians has been a fixture of the Arab Palestinian-Israeli relationship since Israel's independence in 1948. In recent years, terrorist violence has continued unabated upon Israel. From repeated rocket barrages emanating from Gaza and also those launched by Hezbollah based in Lebanon on Israel's northern border, and continuing through the recent November, 2012 heavy missile launchings from Gaza, to bus and suicide bombings in Jerusalem and elsewhere in Israel, various terrorist groups, including Hamas, Hezbollah, Palestinian Islamic Jihad and the Al-Aqsa Martyrs Brigade, continue to operate from bases/havens in and/or with the support of Iran, Lebanon, Syria, Gaza and the West Bank and from within areas that are under the responsibility of the Palestinian Authority, which was created by and is under the control of the Palestine Liberation Organization. Moreover, the heavy support of the Islamic Republic of Iran and the Syrian Arab Republic, each having been designated by the US Department of State as the worst sponsors of terrorism in the world, provided to Hamas, Palestinian Islamic Jihad and Hezbollah, including munitions and both short and long range heavy missiles, have continued to threaten Israel to this day and on many fronts.

These groups have a long standing and continuing single aim: to push the Israeli state into the sea through acts of heinous vio-

lence. Understandably, the Government of Israel views these terrorist groups and their operations as a threat to both the safety of all
Israelis and her visitors and the overall security of the nation. Israel
has not relied on defensive tactics alone in combating this threat to
its existence. Israel's military has taken both preemptive and reac-
tive actions within and upon Gaza, the West Bank and other areas
from which these terrorist threats emanate in an attempt to neutralize the ongoing threats and realities of attacks upon the Israeli
people and those visiting or doing business in the country.

Acts of violence committed by terrorist organizations within
Israel and Israel's actions to neutralize and respond to terrorist
threats have resulted in death and grave injury to Arab and Israeli
civilians alike. During and after the Second Intifada—70 percent of
Israelis killed during the period spanning September 2000 through
November 2006[17] were non-combatants.[18] Additionally, from September 2000 to September 2002 during the height of the Second
Intifada, almost 50 percent of Palestinian fatalities were combatants or non-combatants killed by Palestinians themselves.[19] The
lives lost in 2008 in Gaza and again in 2012 are tragic and were
surely avoidable but for the repeated rocket launches by Hamas
and other terrorist groups determined to attack Israel and in spite
of repeated ceasefires.

Although terrorism has been in the last decade officially rejected by the United Nations as a means of achieving political ends,
particularly when directed against civilians, the UN has failed or
refused to take actions to protect the Israeli people from terrorist
attacks. In Resolution 57/27 of January 15, 2003, the General Assembly reaffirmed its commitment in the Declaration on Measures to
Eliminate International Terrorism.[20]

Nevertheless, in spite of its adoption of this resolution and
declaration specifically condemning terrorism as criminal and unjustifiable, the United Nations has as a world body done essentially
nothing and has been indifferent and ineffectual in stopping terrorism directed toward Israel, Israelis and their allies, including the
United States. The unwillingness or inability of the Palestinians to
stop terrorism, blamed by many on the failure to achieve the jointly

pronounced goal of a two state solution to the Israeli-Palestinian conflict, has resulted in injury and death to thousands of innocent people while also causing an enormous disruption to people's lives. This constant state of siege has drained Israel's resources and also crippled Palestinian society as a whole.

The Quartet, consisting of the United Nations, the European Union, Russia and the United States ("Quartet") has failed in its efforts to achieve a peaceful solution and to stop the constant terrorist attacks emanating from those who deny and refuse to acknowledge Israel's right to exist as a sovereign nation-state. In reality, it is this failure to stop terrorism that truly continues to be the primary obstacle to peace between the Israeli and Palestinian peoples coupled with the failure and refusal of the Palestinian leadership to come together with the Israeli government to discuss and agree upon the final status issues contemplated in the Oslo Accords.

Peace, War and the Status of Diplomatic Relations

While the State of Israel has successfully entered into official peace agreements with two of its border states, Egypt and Jordan, to this day, a state of war continues to exist with Syria and Lebanon, Israel's other border states.[21] Other Arab and predominately Muslim led governments throughout the region have largely treated Israel as a pariah and some, like Iran as well as Iraq under Saddam Hussein and Libya under Moammar Gadhafi, have gone so far as to fund, sponsor and enable terrorism that targeted Israel and those who support a peaceful resolution of the Arab-Israeli conflict. Moreover, in terms of diplomatic relations throughout the international community, Israel has been unable to establish diplomatic relations with many countries; and others with whom diplomatic relations have been established have subsequently broken or suspended relations after the occurrence of various events. In addition, although Israel has been accepted into the Western European and Others Grouping at the United Nations ("WEOG"), she has been refused proper admission and participation in the United Nations' regional grouping to which Israel geographically belongs, thereby depriving her of any right to sit on the United Nations Security Council. All in all, Arab governments, for the most part, refuse to have diplomatic relations with Israel altogether, although many have promised relations if Israel agrees to the Arab Peace Initiative proposed in 2002 by Saudi Arabia.

Past Attempts at Peace

Despite attempts at mediation by the United States, other countries and the United Nations itself no lasting peace in the form of a final agreement has been achieved between the State of Israel and the Palestine Liberation Organization or the Palestinian Authority. Attempts at peace, however, whether genuine or not, and partial progress have been made by both sides resulting in some agreements but no final understanding on important core issues. As the Covenant of the PLO called for the destruction of Israel, an essential negotiating term was required by Israel before it reached its first agreement with the PLO, that the PLO renounce its intention to seek the destruction of Israel and formally acknowledge Israel's right to exist as a nation-state. On September 9, 1993, in a letter to Israeli Prime Minister Rabin, Yasser Arafat, who served as Chairman of the PLO, declared for the first time that the Palestine Liberation Organization recognized the right of the State of Israel to exist in peace and security. In exchange, Rabin declared that the State of Israel recognized the PLO as the representative of the Palestinian people ("Exchange of Letters").[22] Arafat, on behalf of the PLO had declared in 1988 the creation of the independent Palestinian state, recognized by many countries, but not by the United States, Israel nor most of their allies. The PLO was granted Observer status at the UN and on November 29, 2012 granted upgraded non-member state observer status at the UN similar to the status held by the Vatican.

In early 2013, by Executive Order, Mahmoud Abbas, President of the PA, changed the name of the PA to "the State of Palestine." However, although various governments have recognized Palestine as a state, the United States, Canada, Israel and various other countries have not done so, nor has the UN Security Council.

With the Exchange of Letters, Israel and the Palestinians proceeded to enter into the Oslo Accords and various agreements designed to achieve peace and recognition of formal sovereign statehood for the Palestinians to be accomplished through a process leading to what is referred to as "final status negotiations," where the end result is envisioned to include a resolution of the major open issues concerning security, borders, refugees, the status of Jerusalem and the formal creation of an internationally and UN recognized independent State of (Arab) Palestine. Following the Exchange of Letters, and pursuant to the Oslo process and agreements, the Palestinian Authority was created to assume responsibilities over certain areas of the Palestinian Territories, in accordance with the terms of the agreements. On April 26, 1996, the Palestinian National Authority formally approved and ratified Arafat's Exchange of Letters commitment.[23]

The Oslo Accords, the Gaza Security Fence, the Wye River Accords and the Middle East Peace Summit at Camp David

In 1992-94, as a result of the Madrid peace process and in order to protect against further terrorist threats and to set the stage for the eventual creation of a recognized Palestinian state, the late Israeli Prime Minister Yitzhak Rabin and the late Palestinian leader Yasser Arafat signed the Oslo Accords. During the negotiations leading to the Oslo Accords, Israel negotiated with the PLO and addressed Israel's administration of the areas that had been under Jordanian control.

Shortly after beginning the implementation of the Oslo Accords, Israel built a 60-kilometer security fence around the Gaza Strip.[24] This fence was of limited controversy, was seen for what it was: a security fence designed to keep people from Gaza out of Israel as a necessary protective measure against terrorist infiltrators and in the Agreement on The Gaza Strip and The Jericho Area, both Israel and the PLO agreed that, "as long as this Agreement is in force, the security fence erected by Israel around the Gaza Strip shall remain in place..."[25]

In 1998, the Wye River Accords were signed by Prime Minister Netanyahu during his first term, in the presence of President Clinton and by Chairman Arafat, who simultaneous served as Chairman of the PLO and President of the Palestinian Authority. The parties also subsequently signed the Hebron Accords, both of which were the first Israeli-Palestinian agreements since the Oslo Accords, and are the last formal agreements to have been signed between Israel and the Palestinians. Although the Wye River Accords were intended to implement the unfinished business of the Interim Agreement of September 28, 1995, most of the agreement's provisions remained in limbo due to the replacement of Prime Minister Netanyahu who was succeeded by the election of Prime Minister Ehud Barak, and the subsequent developments on the ground.

In 2000, Israeli Prime Minister Ehud Barak and Chairman Arafat, at the invitation of President Bill Clinton, convened at Camp David in an attempt to resolve most of the major open issues between the Israelis and the Palestinians. President Clinton expended significant efforts in an attempt to conclude his Presidency with achieving a full Middle East peace agreement between Israel and the Palestinians. Despite Barak's reported offer of the creation of a Palestinian state in approximately 96 percent of the West Bank and the whole of the Gaza Strip, with its capital in East Jerusalem, Arafat remained quite recalcitrant and steadfastly opposed a final peace agreement on the terms offered and much to the disappointment and surprise of President Clinton and Prime Minister Barak, flatly rejected the Israeli proposal. Arafat's insistence that millions of Palestinian refugees be given the right to "return" to lands within Israel proper effectively destroyed any possibility of achieving what many believe would have been an historic peace treaty between the Israelis and the Palestinians.

Failed Attempts at Peace

The disappointing outcome resulting from Arafat's refusal to reach a final peace agreement at Camp David in 2000 begs the question as to what were Arafat's real intentions for the Middle East Peace Summit in the first place. Why did he decline President Clinton's suggestions and the Israeli offers for establishment of a Palestinian State? Arafat's post-Camp David statements offer some telling clues.

On August 28, 2000, shortly after the failed summit, when Arafat essentially left President Clinton and Prime Minister Barak standing alone at Camp David, Arafat attended a meeting of the Al-Quds Committee in Agadir, Morocco.[26] The Al-Quds Committee is committed to the liberation of East Jerusalem, if not all Jerusalem.[27] At the event, Arafat described the return of Al-Quds (to be read here as Jerusalem) to its legitimate owner (to be read here as the Palestinians) as a red line in his negotiations at Camp David. Several leaders from moderate Arab states, including the Tunisian President, supported Arafat's East Jerusalem claim, thereby endorsing Arafat's refusal to achieve an agreement with the Government of Israel at Camp David.

During the period leading up to the Oslo Accords, control of certain lands, police responsibilities and governing and judicial functions were transferred from the Israelis to the Palestinians through direct negotiations. After the Oslo Accords, the PA's security services were established for the dual purposes of providing routine police functions by Palestinians for the Palestinian people as well as to serve as Palestinian border guards in areas where both Israeli and Palestinian guards had responsibilities, even though official borders had not and have not yet been established. For the most part, the Palestinian Authority has failed to meet its important obligations: it has largely failed to establish democratic law abiding institutions, it has largely failed to construct much needed schools using textbooks free of hate for Israel, has failed to fully establish highest standards health care facilities and has failed to develop a robust and stable economy, notwithstanding enormous aid provided by various foreign governments. The PA blames almost all its failures on Israel, its policies and its security presence within the West Bank. Most importantly, for Israel, the PLO and the PA have failed to thwart or prevent terror attacks targeted against Israel emanating from the West Bank and from Gaza.

The Second Intifada's Reign of Terror

Shortly after Arafat refused Israel's offer at Camp David in July 2000, the Palestinians initiated a new campaign of terror against the

State of Israel and all Israelis, thus commencing "the Second Inti-fada" or " civil uprising," a period marked by intense violence and heinous murder targeting Israelis, Americans and others visiting Is-rael.[28] The First Intifada occurred starting in 1987 and took countless lives as the PLO and its member organizations rained terror upon Israel as a means of accomplishing its political aims.

As a result of the Second Intifada, Israeli citizens endured a particularly lethal and steady barrage of heinous terrorist strikes and attacks. The form of attack varied in method, location and tar-get. All throughout Israel, there were bombings and rocket and mortar attacks, as well as bombings of buses, restaurants, shopping centers, hotels, synagogues and other public and private places. The attackers, most often men and women wearing bombs strapped to their bodies, detonated their explosives with the goal of killing and injuring as many Israelis and Americans as possible, thereby achieving martyrdom in dying for the Palestinian cause of seeking independent statehood. These bombings have come to be known as "suicide bombings" or sometimes, and perhaps more aptly, as "ho-micide bombings." The Israeli High Court described the difficult security situation:

> Israel's fight is complex. Together with other means, the Palestin-ians use guided human bombs. These suicide bombers reach every place that Israelis can be found (within the boundaries of the State of Israel and in the Jewish communities in Judea and Samaria and the Gaza Strip). They sow destruction and spill blood in the cities and towns. The forces fighting against Israel are terrorists: they are not members of a regular army; they do not wear uniforms; they hide among the civilian Palestinian population in the territories, including inside holy sites; they are supported by part of the civil-ian population, and by their families and relatives.[29]

During the Second Intifada, the Palestinian terrorist organi-zations, which long have promoted terrorism as a negotiating tool against Israel, escalated their activities and expressly sought (and continue to seek) to destroy Israel, all the while posturing behind slogans like "end the occupation." That these terrorists plead their case through violence and murder in Israel, and by launching rock-ets from Gaza, while simultaneously through political and legal maneuvering before the United Nations and the world, is not only offensive but is also an affront to the fundamental principles and values upon which international law and the foundational principles of the United Nations itself are grounded.

From the beginning of the Second Intifada through April of 2004 when the Israeli High Court first took up the issue of Israel's security fence, more than 10,000 attacks were carried out in Israel and the surrounding territories. These attacks claimed the lives of more than 1,000 Israeli citizens, residents and visitors, and injured more than 6,000.[30]

Even though Palestinian citizens have suffered greatly as well, certain of their leaders have continued to encourage members of their own population, including children, to threaten, commit or provide cover for these terrorist attacks. Despite repeated calls by countries such as the United States for peace and constructive PA leadership, the Palestinian Authority has historically sanctioned or turned a blind eye to this terrorism, heralding the attackers and continuing to provide a friendly base for terrorist organizations within Palestinian territories.

A Missed Opportunity

Yasser Arafat, himself an early terrorist who largely failed to achieve peace during his lifetime, clearly missed the opportunity for the Palestinian people to establish universally recognized statehood in 2000 and then resorted back to sponsoring terrorist attacks upon Israel during the Second Intifada. His death on November 11, 2004 which some have claimed to have been caused by a suspected poisoning, resulting in the 2012 exhumation of his body for forensic testing, seemingly offered a new opportunity to build a foundation for the Palestinian people grounded, not in terror, but in international legitimacy. Many hoped that his passing and the emergence of new leadership would usher in a new era of relations between Palestinians and Israelis. Arafat's death may have signaled a subtle shift in the role of terrorism as a hallmark of the PA, if only to the extent that terrorist attacks decreased in the immediate months following his death.[31]

Yet, terrorist entities continued to find an outstretched hand of support and even protection from the PLO and the PA. Arafat's aide and successor as head of the PA, Mahmoud Abbas, who publicly expressed his willingness to work for a new détente with Israel has largely failed or refused to do so. Abbas blames his failures to achieve peace upon actions of the Israeli government. Moreover, presumably in the hope that it would morph into a political group and disarm its military wing, Abbas permitted the terrorist group HAMAS, the Islamic Resistance Movement ("Hamas"), to participate in the January 2006 PA legislative elections.[32] Little progress was made in ending the violence, however, and Hamas, which gained political and de facto control of Gaza, and has retained and solidified its control over Gaza, not only never disarmed but has at every turn been belligerent toward Israel and has pronounced its intention and commitment to freeing all of Israel for the benefit of the Palestinian people; essentially meaning that it is committed to removing Israel from the map and has and continues to refuse to recognize Israel's status as a sovereign nation state. The ongoing and continuing conflict between the Palestinians and Israel has cost lives and wreaked havoc upon persons and property. During the Second Intifada and between the period of September 27, 2000 and January 1, 2005, 1,010 Israelis were killed in the course of terrorist attacks, of which, 764 (or 76 percent) were non-combatants. During the same period, 3,179 Palestinians died as a result of Israeli incursions, of which, 1,099 (or 35 percent) were non-combatants killed by Israeli actions and 406 (or 13 percent) were killed by actions of the Palestinians. During the time period, almost 50 percent of Palestinians killed were combatants or were killed by their own side while almost 80 percent of Israeli fatalities have been civilians.[33]

The Palestinian Authority has been basically either unwilling or unable to curb these terrorist acts from the West Bank, or from Gaza, and has largely failed, or refused, to put a stop to the suicide bombings and other acts of terror and murder perpetrated or attempted upon Israeli civilians, a government minister, the military, police and members of the border patrol, necessarily leaving it to the Israelis to provide for their own self defense. Terrorism and the threat of terrorism as a means of expression continue to be the norm emanating from the Palestinian territories. Various terrorist organizations are permitted to operate freely within the Palestinian territories including Hamas, Palestinian Islamic Jihad and other groups including the Al Aqsa Martyrs Brigade, the armed wing of Fatah, which controls the PLO and the PA. Palestinian textbooks teach hatred and leaders encourage and/or fail to stop attempted suicide bombings by children and young people who were trained to see martyrdom as an honorable destiny. Within the Palestinian territories, democracy in all meaningful forms has been largely non-existent, elections have rarely been held, objections to Palestinian leadership repressed and a state of essential lawlessness and quasi dictatorship has long existed, although circumstances and accomplishments in the economy and selected governmental functions have improved in the West Bank in more recent years under Palestinian Prime Minister Salam Fayyad.

Even today, Palestinian textbooks, media, religious sermons, and social discourse are full of hatred toward Jews and Israel. In September and November 2012, President Abbas of the Palestinian Authority repeated his vitriolic attacks on Israel at the United Nations. Everything wrong in Palestinian society appears to be blamed on Israel rather than on Palestinian leadership failures. Despite billions of dollars in foreign aid given to the Palestinian Authority, many Palestinians continue to live in squalor, with little or no hope for the future. Allegations abound about the misappropriation of foreign aid money by Yasser Arafat and others during his lifetime and evidence continues to accumulate on the funneling of foreign aid to those who support and conduct or have conducted terrorist acts, including admitted payments by the Palestinian Authority to convicted Palestinian terrorists who are prisoners held in Israeli jails.

Since the Second Intifada, the Israeli government has responded in numerous ways to these acts of violence:

    (a) as a security measure, it has intermittently re-taken control of certain of the Palestinian territories and asserted military presence in place of the Palestinian Authority police;

(b) it has targeted terrorist leaders in Gaza and arrested, deported, or killed them;

(c) it has attempted to weaken the terrorist infrastructure, physically and financially; and

(d) it has largely sealed off ground access to Israel from both Gaza and the West Bank.

Unfortunately, most of the cooperative progress that was made between the State of Israel and the Palestinian Authority during the Oslo Accords process has been halted since 2000. Joint efforts at regional economic development, education, health care, democracy building, society building and integration of infrastructure have largely come to a grinding halt. The Palestinian people, the Israeli people, and their respective joint businesses, have suffered greatly as a result of the ongoing state of affairs. The Israeli economy has thrived; the Palestinian economy has recently shown some growth but only in certain areas. Few joint economic development or joint business efforts exist between Israel and Palestinians. The number of Palestinian workers in Israel has decreased over time. Official Palestinian Authority actions have created and encouraged boycotts of Israeli products produced in areas which the PA deems to be in the West Bank and beyond the pre-1967 border lines that existed between Israel and trans-Jordan. Palestinians have launched coordinated efforts throughout the world designed to turn attitudes, organizations, business people, governments and the UN itself against Israel.

Despite efforts by the United States, Russia, the European Union and many other governments, as well as the Quartet under the leadership of former UK Prime Minister Tony Blair the significant progress necessary for successful Palestinian economy, democracy, and society building has not been achieved to date. Nor has resolution of the serious open issues between the parties been achieved. Hope continues that PA President Abbas would agree to return to direct negotiations and a meaningful peace process. Abbas' refusal to engage in a renewal of direct negotiations with Israel is largely based upon his demand that Israel must cease ongoing and planned construction in the cities, town and settlements located on the West Bank and in East Jerusalem. This is a precondition to which Prime Minister Netanyahu will not agree.

Terrorist organizations in the Palestinian Territories have been continually funded and supported by Iran, Syria, Saudi Arabia and other sources. The Arab-Palestinian-Israeli conflict has continued to fester in spite of the United Nations adoption of the Roadmap to achieve peace under the vision of there being two states, one Jewish and one Arab, living side by side in peace and security. Although terrorist organizations such as Hamas, Palestinian Islamic Jihad, Al Aqsa Martyrs Brigade, Hezbollah and others have been branded as outlaws and as Foreign Terrorist Organizations, they have continued to thrive. Since the commencement of the Second Intifada, steps have been taken to stop the terrorists' sources of funding in order to force them out of business. The determination of Iran, in conjunction with Syria, to continue to arm and supply, fund and support terrorist activities against Israel has been largely tolerated by most of the world.

The Palestinian Authority and Terrorist Organizations

The Palestinian Authority has not taken the necessary steps to dismantle terrorist organizations or to stop attempts at murderous attacks against the Israeli people. It is indeed questionable whether they are capable of doing so or simply have no resolve in convincing terrorist organizations within the Palestinian Territories such as Hamas, Palestinian Islamic Jihad and others to stop launching rockets or planning, conducting and supporting suicide bombings and other acts of terrorism. Through the Al-Aqsa Martyrs Brigade, which is responsible for numerous suicide bombings and other acts of terrorism, Fatah and the Palestinian Authority embraced and/or did not stop the use of terrorism as a matter of policy or strategic choice.

Some claim that the Palestinian Authority cannot stop terrorism without rebuilding and rearming its own police and security services. The Israelis have been loath to permit rearmament because of the historic proliferation of weapons throughout the Palestinian territories and the use of those weapons against the citizens of Israel. Nonetheless, Israel has in recent years cooperated with the Palestinian Authority, the United States and Jordan in the training and equipping of Palestinian police in the hope that properly trained police officers would be able to achieve security in the Palestinian territories for both the Palestinian Authority and Israel. Accordingly, Israel periodically authorizes shipments of armored vehicles, rifles and ammunition to President Abbas' pro-Fatah police to assist in Palestinian operations against armed militants in the West Bank.[34] Gaza, under the control of Hamas, however, is another matter as terrorists from Gaza have long continued to launch rockets into Israel, killing, injuring and threatening Israeli society.

The world has encouraged the Palestinian Authority to undertake major democracy-building steps and to change the way it has done business. The position of PA Prime Minister was established during the Second Intifada as an attempt to gain some control over Arafat's terrorist-supporting leadership approaches in 2002. The first Palestinian Prime Minister, Mahmoud Abbas (also known as Abu Mazen), was installed and subsequently received by President George W. Bush and other world leaders, with a goal that terrorism would be curbed and direct negotiations could resume. Abbas resigned in 2003 without any significant accomplishments. A new Prime Minister, Ahmed Queria, was installed and there was hope that he would provide the needed leadership. Subsequently, it was Prime Minister Salam Fayyad who brought a degree of stability and transparency to the economy and society, but whose political strength is seen as marginalized by other factions.

Notwithstanding the successes or failure of political leadership and pressures from other governments, both Israel and Arab Palestinians have intermittently made moves to achieve peace. However, to date, these efforts have not resulted in a permanent or even a lasting peace. Dreams have been dashed, people have died and true peace has remained elusive largely as a result of terrorist attacks upon Israel which have repeatedly caused Israel to either respond with force or simply conclude that it did not have a reliable negotiating partner with whom it could reach a lasting peace agreement.

The Second Intifada, the Mitchell Report, Historic Rose Garden Speech by President George W. Bush and the Roadmap for Peace in the Middle East

The investigative committee of the Middle East Peace Summit, at a meeting convened to determine the continuing cause of violence in the Middle East particularly during the raging Second Intifada, produced the Mitchell Report. Summit participants—the United States, Israel, Egypt, the Palestinian Authority, Jordan, the European Union and the United Nations—directed the investigative committee through its chair, former US Senator George Mitchell, to investigate "the events of the past several weeks and how to prevent their recurrence."[35] After a lengthy and intensive investigation, the Mitchell Report recognized that the central obstacle to any peaceful coexistence between Israel and Arab Palestinians is the ongoing violence:

> The . . . overriding concern of those in the region with whom we spoke is to end the violence and to return to the process of shaping a sustainable peace. . .

> With widespread violence, both sides have resorted to portrayals of each other in hostile stereotypes. This cycle cannot be easily broken. Without considerable determination and readiness to compromise, the rebuilding of trust will be impossible.

> Cessation of Violence: Since 1991, the parties have consistently committed themselves, in all their agreements, to the path of nonviolence. To stop the violence now, the PA and GOI need not "reinvent the wheel." Rather they should take immediate steps to end the violence, reaffirm their mutual commitments, and resume negotiations.[36]

The Mitchell Report also found that:

> Despite their long history and close proximity, some Israelis and Palestinians seem not to fully appreciate each other's concerns. Some Israelis appear not to comprehend the humiliation and frustration that Palestinians must endure every day as a result of living with the continuing effects of occupation, sustained by the presence of Israeli military forces and settlements in their midst, or the determination of the Palestinians to achieve independence and genuine self-determination. Some Palestinians appear not to comprehend the extent to which terrorism creates fear among the Israeli people and undermines their belief in the possibility of co-

existence, or the determination of the GOI to do whatever is necessary to protect its people.

Fear, hate, anger, and frustration have risen on both sides. The greatest danger of all is that the culture of peace, nurtured over the past decade is being shattered. In its place there is a growing sense of futility and despair, and a growing resort to violence.[37]

Following the publication of the Mitchell Report, in a historic Rose Garden speech on June 24, 2002, President George W. Bush outlined a vision of two states, Israel and Palestine, living side by side in security and peace. This vision, which became embodied in the "Roadmap for Peace in the Middle East" was drawn from the international community's long-standing desire to effect a just and comprehensive resolution to the lingering conflict. Following President Bush's vision, the "Roadmap" became an internationally sanctioned and monitored agreement and process for the creation of a viable Palestinian state alongside a secure state of Israel.

The Roadmap states:

a two state solution to the Israeli-Palestinian conflict will only be achieved through an end to violence and terrorism.

Further, Phase I of the Roadmap requires:

the Palestinians to immediately undertake an unconditional cessation of violence. Such actions should be accompanied by supportive measures undertaken by Israel [in part by making] efforts on [the] ground to disrupt and restrain individuals and groups conducting and planning violent attacks on Israelis anywhere.[38]

Although the Palestinians originally agreed to adhere to the Roadmap and to engage in negotiations with Israel the Palestinian Observers in April 2003 publicly rejected the concept of the Roadmap. Terrorist attacks upon Israel continued inside Israel, in the West Bank and in Gaza. A State Department convoy was attacked and blown up in October 2003 by terrorists operating near and under the watchful eye of the Palestinian security post in Gaza. This attack targeted, maimed and killed US State Department officials delivering Fulbright scholarships in Gaza. Efforts by the US Department of State to stop the terrorism failed and attacks continued unabated.

On November 19, 2003 pursuant to Security Council Resolution 1515, the parties agreed to and adopted what officially became known as the "Roadmap for Peace in the Middle East" as the mechanism whereby they would formulate a lasting peaceful co-existence.

In its fight against terrorism, Israel faces an unjust equation. To Israel human life is sacred and killing is abhorrent. Yet many Palestinians praise suicide bombers and vicious killers as heroes and martyrs of the Palestinian cause. While the international community has not hesitated to recognize the ongoing violence, it largely ignores or flat-out dismisses this nihilistic and alarming fundamental disregard for the value of human life. Until there is an end to this inhuman logic and tragedy, Israel has no choice but to do whatever is necessary to protect her citizens.

The Disengagement Plan

In April 2004, Israeli Prime Minister Sharon formally announced a Disengagement Plan for Israel to unconditionally withdraw from Gaza.

The unilateral disengagement plan strongly illustrated Israel's dedication to peace. As one of the plan's many aims, the evacuation of the Gaza Strip was ordered to "reduce friction with the Palestinian population" and to create a "potential for improvement in the Palestinian economy and living conditions."[39] Further, Israel vowed "when there is evidence from the Palestinian side of its willingness, capability and implementation in practice of the fight against terrorism and the institution of reform as required by the Roadmap, it will be possible to return to the track of negotiation and dialogue."[40] In spite of the withdrawal, however, terrorists in Gaza have continued their missile attacks upon Israel, resulting in major armed responses by Israel in 2008 and again in November 2012.

Terrorism remains a serious threat to the safety and security of all people in the region and particularly to Israel. Everyone agrees that this untenable situation cannot continue. The world, and the United Nations itself, however, have largely given lip service in pledging its support to improve the situation on the ground so that negotiations can resume and lead to a satisfactory conclusion. Israel, in accordance with UN Security Council resolutions, has put forth clear conditions to the resumption of negotiations focused on central issues: the cessation of terrorist acts against the Israeli people and that there be no preconditions to such negotiations. The PA set forth its conditions to the resumption of negotiations, also focused on central issues: the withdrawal by Israel from the West Bank and Gaza and demands that Israel cease settlement building on the West Bank and in East Jerusalem. As none of these conditions have yet been met by the parties, negotiations have remained stalled for a prolonged period of time. Notwithstanding the fact that Sharon's Disengagement Plan was a unilateral effort to curb the cycle of violence and begin movement towards a reality where peace and negotiations would have become a real possibility, it has not occurred.

The Disengagement Plan itself received worldwide support. Notably, at its June 2004 meeting in Sea Island, Georgia, USA, the leaders of the Group of Eight emphatically endorsed the plan and hoped that it would:

> Stimulate progress towards peace in the region, the realization of Palestinian national aspirations and the achievement of our common objective of two states, Israel and a viable, democratic sovereign and contiguous Palestine, living side-by-side in peace and security.[41]

In further support, UN Secretary-General Kofi Annan pledged the United Nation's assistance in its implementation.[42] Israel's Knesset overwhelming approved the Disengagement Plan in October 2004 and it was thereafter put into effect, turning Gaza over to the Palestinian Authority to govern.

The Failure of Leadership by Yasser Arafat and the Hopes for His Successor

Subsequent to Knesset approval of the Disengagement Plan, Yasser Arafat died on November 11, 2004. He was on the one hand revered by many as the father of the revolution designed to liberate Palestine from the Israelis; while on the other hand seen as a failed leader who missed opportunity after opportunity to become a statesman and a true leader. He largely failed during his lifetime to build a positive future for his people. Years later, mystery surrounds his life and death, his assets and his legacy. He is entombed in the PA controlled city of Ramallah located on the West Bank of the Jordan River.

Following his death and despite the overwhelming belief by Israelis that they still lacked a Palestinian partner in their quest for peace, Israel continued to adhere to the Disengagement Plan.[43] It remains to be seen whether Arafat, who made the legitimization of terrorism under the guise of freedom-fighting the hallmark of his regime, merely represented what could possibly be a larger problem. Palestinian leaders often agree to do one thing with the Israelis, and say so in English, but speak to their own population in Arabic, espousing different intentions.[44] For instance, after signing the Oslo Accord and recognizing Israel as a State, the PA continued to publish school textbooks with maps that omitted Israel and mentioning her only as an occupying power.

Notwithstanding this history, immediately upon Arafat's death, Israel expressed its willingness to facilitate renewed negotiations. Israel refrained from initiating new military action in the disputed territories, reduced roadblocks, made outreach efforts to begin discussions and expressed its readiness to coordinate its withdrawal from Gaza with Palestinian leadership.[45] Dan Gillerman, Israeli Ambassador to the UN, emphasized the historic opportunity for a change in leadership that could lead to peace with Israel. Terje Roed-Larsen, the former Secretary General's Special Coordinator for the Middle East Peace Process, echoed this sentiment in his final briefing to the UN Security Council stating, "the extent and success of coordination in [the] recent days [since Arafat's death] is reminiscent of earlier, happier days, and might herald a new beginning – a new beginning that would come not because of President Arafat's passing, but in spite of the very difficult situation."[46]

Nevertheless, PA President Mahmoud Abbas, while espousing the end of the intifada and halting terrorism, referred to Israel as "the Zionist enemy," a term he has continued to use.[47] In the months after Arafat's death, however, Palestinian terror attacks significantly decreased,[48] which led US Secretary of State Colin Powell to reaffirm the United States' dedication to resolving the conflict. He made it clear that if the new Palestinian President "shows a real commitment to end terror, I think he will find an Israeli partner ready to work with him, and he will certainly find the international community and especially the United States ready to play an important role."[49]

On January 25, 2005, signaling an important change in the direction of peace, militant Palestinian groups agreed to assist President Abbas in working toward a cease-fire with Israel by temporarily refraining from initiating attacks.[50] Then, in February, Prime Minister Sharon and President Abbas pledged "that all Palestinians will stop all acts of violence against all Israelis everywhere . . . and Israel will cease all its military activity against all Palestinians anywhere."[51] Although the agreement did not have the force of a formal cease-fire, it was a hopeful sign. As then Prime Minister Sharon stated at the summit:

> We do hope we will have a new era, which will make a real change that will be a proper, solid basis for new relations between us. I am absolutely determined to implement the disengagement plan, which I have initiated. This was initiated as a unilateral step by ourselves, but if a real change actually comes about from the Palestinian side, then disengagement can bring about peace and act as a new launching point for coordinated and successful plan.[52]

Prime Minister Sharon further called on the leaders of all Arab countries to work together in this effort:

> Let us hold hands, let us get together and bring about a new atmosphere of openness and tolerance. Today, we can stem the flood of radicals who could otherwise allow us all to be swept away in a whirlpool of bloodletting and violence. I do hope that we are able to say to the peoples of the Middle East there are the initial, the first glows of light of hope here. I hope for all of us that we will be able to live in liberty, in hope, prosperity and peace.
>
> May we all be worthy of this great opportunity which has presented itself to us.[53]

President Abbas echoed the desire for a peaceful resolution of the Palestinian/Israeli conflict and for international collaboration to work toward this end.

> And also I assert our interest in respecting all our obligations and implementing all our commitments. And will save no effort whatever to protect this newborn opportunity of peace that is provided through what we have already declared here today. We hope that

our brothers in the Arab Republic of Egypt and the Hashemite Kingdom of Jordan, we hope that they will continue their good efforts as well as we hope that the quartet, the international quartet, will resume its responsibilities to achieve acceleration of progress on the Palestinian/Israeli with reviving a peace process, as well, on the Syrian and Lebanese track as -- tracks as one . . . .

We look forward to that day and hoping it will come as soon as possible in order that the language of negotiations will replace the language of bullets and cannons and in which neighborhood and livelihood will prevail instead of the war; and in order to provide our grandsons and our future generations, Palestinian and Israelis, a different tomorrow, a promising tomorrow.

This is a new opportunity. A new opportunity of peace is won today in the city of peace. Let us all pledge to protect this opportunity in order to see that the wish of peace becomes a true and daily fact in this region.[54]

US Secretary of State Condoleezza Rice called the meeting "the most promising moment for progress between Palestinians and Israelis in recent years."[55] On February 21, 2005, President George W. Bush reiterated this sentiment in a speech before European leaders, stating "Our greatest opportunity, and our immediate goal, is peace in the Middle East," adding that "settlement of the conflict between Israelis and Palestinians is now within reach."[56] Additionally, President Bush called on Arab states to "end incitement in their own media, cut off public and private funding for terrorism, stop their support for extremist education, and establish normal relations with Israel."[57]

Unfortunately, despite his 2005 promises for change, President Abbas has been unwilling or unable to fully unite the Palestinian people under his leadership and act upon his stated goals. He was able, however, to gain the support of Hamas for his 2012 bid at the United Nations for upgraded status. Yasser Arafat on the other hand, although extremely controversial, was in retrospect more capable of attempting to seek unity among disparate Palestinian groups and an oft-divided Palestinian public.

Dismantling the terrorist infrastructure and reaching a peaceful resolution to this longstanding and violent conflict will surely require successful implementation of the Roadmap, which cannot be achieved through unilateral actions by Israel alone. Success requires firm positive action by PA leadership under Mr. Abbas and his successors. Achieving peace will require affirmative Palestinian participation that demonstrates a true commitment to reaching a peaceful resolution, a resolve that was clearly lacking during Arafat's tenure and which has continued to be lacking under Abbas, who has preferred the international stage at the United Nations over face to face negotiations with Israel to discuss the core open issues between the Palestinians and Israel. Arafat was rarely able to bring himself over the line for real peace, to do more than shake hands and participate in photo opportunities; to, as it has been said, take off his kafiya which was seen by many as a signature symbol of warrior rather than statesman; and to become a leader willing to and capable of negotiating the difficult final status issues which are agreed upon preconditions for the ultimate establishment of a universally recognized Arab State of Palestine. Such accomplishments were within his grasp had he been able or willing to exercise strong leadership. His people would have followed him, applauded him and heralded him for having taken bold steps leading to a better future for all Palestinians. However, while Arafat understood that peace could only be achieved when the Palestinian people fully committed to stop the violence, Arafat himself was unwilling to take the necessary steps to do so. Moreover, to delegitimize terrorism and reach a successful resolution, terrorist attacks must be thoroughly investigated, rocket launchings from Gaza must be stopped and terrorists must be prosecuted to the fullest extent of the law. Under the leadership of Yasser Arafat, these essential elements were never fulfilled, nor have they been accomplished by Abu Mazen.

Implementing Israel's Disengagement from Gaza

The unilateral Disengagement Plan was envisioned as a means of leaving the problems and future of Gaza to the Palestinian Authority rather than continuing the responsibility for security, economy and administration resting with the Israelis. It was also in the hope and anticipation that the people of Gaza could and would build prosperity, free of Israeli presence inside Gaza and that the disengagement would lead to a better future for all. Unfortunately, even after seven years, the hopes for a positive future for the Palestinians in Gaza have still not been realized.

On February 20, 2005, Prime Minister Sharon and Israeli Defense Minister Shaul Mofaz signed orders implementing the Disengagement Plan.[58] These orders contemplated an evacuation beginning on June 20, 2005 of all 21 Israeli settlements in the Gaza Strip and four on the West Bank.[59] Accepting the difficulties inherent in the decision to pull out of the contested areas, Prime Minister Sharon expressed Israel's continued dedication to peace in a speech before the Conference of Presidents of Major American Jewish Organizations. He acknowledged that with the "Government decision, Israel proved that it is willing to make painful compromises and take great steps towards achieving peace."[60]

Dissenters to the pullout, including Israel's then Minister of Jerusalem Affairs, Natan Sharansky, expressed concern that Israel was compromising too much:

> It is a dramatic and far-reaching step which is being taken on a unilateral basis, without linking it to any concession on the other side... I believe that every step in a peace process, if it is to succeed, must be connected to democratic reform in the Palestinian Authority.[61]

Prime Minister Sharon, however, reiterated Israel's commitment to defending her people against the ongoing threat of terrorist attacks, stating:

> For a genuine and real peace, we are willing to make many painful compromises. But there is one thing we are not willing to make any compromise on, not now and not in the future. That is when it comes to the security of Israeli citizens and the security of the state of Israel . . . We hope that our neighbors will also have the courage to take bold steps. If each party takes the necessary steps, then a peaceful Middle East is a real possibility for the future. And I believe that we can realize this future.[62]

Israel moved swiftly to implement the Disengagement Plan, issuing two decrees in March 2005 prohibiting the relocation of Israeli citizens into the Gaza Strip and the West Bank communities of Sanur, Homesh, Ganim and Kadim.[63] Next, control of the West Bank city of Tulkarem was turned over to Palestinian security forces.[64]

The agreement implementing this evacuation also contemplated a future transfer of control over Bethlehem and Ramallah.[65]

The members of the UN Security Council released a statement at the early stages of the Disengagement expressing their support for the Plan and commitment to the Roadmap. The statement read:

> The members of the Security Council believe that successful dis-engagement can be the first step toward a resumption of the peace process. They reiterate their call upon both parties, in close coop-eration with the Quartet, to ensure continued progress in the full implementation of the Roadmap and relevant Security Council resolutions towards the creation of an independent, viable, demo-cratic and sovereign State of Palestine living side by side with Israel in peace and security.[66]

By September 12, 2006, the Israeli Defense Forces ("IDF") had completed the evacuation of over 8,500 civilians and all military forces from the Gaza Strip including the border area with Egypt known as the Philadelphi corridor.[67] After Israel's 38-year presence in the Gaza Strip, Maj. Gen. Yishayahu Gavish took the final formal as IDF commander in the Gaza Strip and signed a declaration stating the end of military rule.[68]

The pullout proved to be an extremely painful process for Israelis. It required vast amounts of restraint by soldiers who, in the name of peace with the Palestinian population, fought back their own tears and dragged protesting settlers, prayer books in hand, from their synagogues.[69] The IDF's actions have been praised as a triumph of democracy and the rule of law insofar as the majority of soldiers dutifully carried out their orders to evacuate the settlements and the majority of settlers vacated peacefully. Businesses, fertile fields and buildings, greenhouses and opportunities were turned over to the Palestinians.

With the departure of Israelis from the Gaza Strip, "full responsibility for events occurring in the Gaza Strip and for thwarting terrorist attacks was now in the hands of the Palestinian Authority and its apparatuses."[70] Khan Yunis Mayor Osama al-Farra toured Neve Dekalim soon after the pullout and admitted to the daunting task before the PA, stating, "In the past, we complained that we could not do the work. Now we must do everything possible to develop the land, without the excuse of Israel or the settlements."[71] President George W. Bush, recognizing the prospects for a peaceful future while also noting the magnitude of the task before the PA, proclaimed that the "opportunity rests with the Palestinian people to show that they can govern themselves in a peaceful way."[72] Calling upon

Arab nations to take responsibility for developing a Palestinian economy, he said, "Now is the time for people to step up."[73]

Despite the fact that, overall, 70 percent of Israelis favored the plan at the time, the issue of disengagement brought up intense controversy within Israeli society. During the summer of 2005, many Israelis publicly demonstrated their opposition to disengagement with speeches, political commercials and rallies. One rally in the Gaza Strip settlement of Neve Dekalim drew tens of thousands of protesters.

Benjamin Netanyahu, Finance Minister of Israel at the time, opposed implementation of Sharon's Disengagement Plan. Prior to cabinet ratification of the first phase on August 7, 2005, Netanyahu announced his resignation from the cabinet. "There is a way to achieve peace and security," he said, "but a unilateral withdrawal under fire and with nothing in return is certainly not the way."[74] Netanyahu called the pullout "an irresponsible step which will endanger Israel's security, split the people, institute the principle of return to the 1967 borders, and in the future, endanger Jerusalem as well."[75]

Prime Minister Sharon, on the other hand, continued to stress his commitment to the Disengagement and to implementing the Roadmap, calling the period immediately following the withdrawal from Gaza the "pre-Roadmap phase." He made sure to note, however, that future Israeli concessions would not be unilateral and must correspond with Palestinian efforts at peace.[76] "To enter the Roadmap," he said, "there should be a full cessation of terror hostilities and incitement. The Palestinian Authority should dismantle the terrorist organizations, collect their weapons and implement serious reforms in [the] security [services]."[77] Before the UN General Assembly, he underscored Israel's right to self-defense, stating:

> I am among those who believe that it is possible to reach a fair compromise and coexistence in good neighborly relations between Jews and Arabs. However, I must emphasize one fact: there will be no compromise on the right of the state of Israel to exist as a Jewish state, with defensible borders, in full security and without threats of terror.[78]

Dismantling the terrorist infrastructure was an obligation of the PLO and the Palestinian Authority under the Roadmap. In his speech, Sharon referred to the need to dismantle Hamas, an increasingly powerful terrorist group with ties to Iran as well as to the Hezbollah terrorist group.

Unfortunately, even as Israel put the Disengagement Plan into action, Palestinian terrorists continued their assault. During the pullout, a Qassam rocket was fired. Although no one was injured, it highlighted the unilateral nature of Israel's efforts. While speaking to officers, soldiers and military reporters at a makeshift military base, Israeli Defense Minister Shaul Mofaz conveyed a hopeful sentiment despite the rocket attack and called on Palestinians to "enforce law and order in the Gaza Strip and establish a different reality."[79] He said:

> I hope [the Palestinian Authority realizes] that Israel has made a very significant, painful and historic step in order to give hope for a new reality that would bring us to coexistence and peace . . . Today 38 years of Israeli presence of Gaza have ended. I am full of hope that when the gates of Gaza reopen, they will be gates of peace.[80]

Much to the dismay of most, post-disengagement Gaza has been marked by lawlessness, civil unrest and violence. PA security forces, for instance, failed to intervene in Gaza, when Moussa Arafat, Abbas' adviser and the cousin and former head of military intelligence to Yasser Arafat, was dragged into the street and murdered by dozens of armed men following a 30-minute long gun battle between his security guards and Arafat's attackers.[81] Displaying the PA's lack of control, gunmen from terrorist groups set up checkpoints in Gaza in an attempt to control looters, a job that should have been reserved for Palestinian security forces.[82] Concerned about the fragmented Palestinian security structure, the Quartet released a statement underscoring the "continued importance of comprehensive reform of the Palestinian security forces."[83]

Prime Minister Sharon's call to dismantle Hamas went unheeded as its power and influence grew. Senior Hamas leader Mahmoud Al-Zahar vowed to continue terrorist activities despite Israel's withdrawal, stating, "In the long term Israel will disappear from the face of the earth."[84] The continued popularity of Hamas was evident from the development of the women's military wing, whose members partake in weapons training and the spread of propaganda. The commander of the women's unit of the Hamas military wing echoed Al-Zahar's sentiment, warning that if Israel did not withdraw from the entire West Bank and Jerusalem "of their own will, they will be defeated and [all that will be left of them] will be the remains of corpses."[85] Evidently, as women and mothers, their goal was to spread the "message to educate [their children] to jihad, which [they consider to be] a sacred duty that cannot be neglected."[86]

Palestinian leader Abbas, although purporting to commit to the Roadmap, instead has continued to ignore it. He expressed trepidation at the suggestion that he disassemble the terrorist groups and went even further to legitimize the terrorists by signing an agreement with both Hamas and Islamic Jihad, subsequently allowing them to participate in the PA's legislative elections.[87] In the days following Israel's withdrawal from the Gaza Strip, the situation escalated toward anarchy. Mere hours after Abbas pledged to restore order, tens of thousands of Hamas members gathered for a rally in Gaza City.[88] Synagogues were desecrated, the greenhouses turned over to the Palestinians were destroyed and looting was widespread. Moreover, on September 14, 2005, amidst reports of rampant smuggling of assault rifles and pistols into Gaza from Egypt by Palestinian gunrunners, Hamas militants blasted a hole in the Gaza wall making it even easier for Palestinians to illegally enter Egypt.[89] Despite the agreement between Egypt and the PA to regulate the Philadelphi Corridor, the border remained extraordinarily porous, allowing the smuggling of weapons by jihadists into Gaza and Israel from Egypt.

Nevertheless, Israel continued to voice its support for Palestinian leader Mahmoud Abbas' authority. Israel's Foreign Minister Silvan Shalom explained, "Israel is taking great pains to ensure that Palestinian leader Mahmoud Abbas is given every opportunity to establish his authority. We seek to ensure conditions which will benefit the Palestinian people, without posing a security threat to Israel."[90]

As parliamentary elections approached in January 2006, however, Hamas gained momentum daily, capitalizing on the pullout by holding several parades all within a week.[91] Meanwhile, Abbas failed to appear in public, addressing his people only once by television.[92] During a public Palestinian celebration being held in the ruins of a Jewish settlement, Abbas sent an aide as his representative while Hamas' top leader, Mahmoud Al-Zahar, participated in the festivities.[93] Residents of Gaza noticed. One was quoted as saying that Abbas "is living in an isolated island in Gaza, with no way [for his people] to see him or talk to him and when he talks to us he uses the TV screens like he is addressing foreigners."[94] While proclamations of impending stability among Palestinians are not uncommon, they are often grossly exaggerated. For example, even as gun-toting militants exercised unbridled freedom in the Gaza Strip after the Disengagement, Abbas astonished listeners by announcing that Gaza was under "complete control."[95]

Prime Minister Sharon's decision to pull out of Gaza was admired by supporters and critics alike. During a dinner in Washington commemorating 350 years of American Jewish life, President George W. Bush praised Sharon in a speech, calling him "a man of courage; he's a man of peace."[96] At the Republican Jewish Coalition's 20th Anniversary Luncheon, President Bush told coalition members "the United States of America is firmly committed to defending the security and the well-being of our ally, Israel."[97] As he recalled a 1998 trip to Israel he took as Governor of Texas where he met with then-Cabinet member Ariel Sharon, President Bush, calling Prime Minster Sharon his "partner in peace," articulated his "strong impression" of the Israeli people as those who "not only want to defend themselves, but how much they love democracy, that democracy is a critical part of their existence." At the same time, President Bush recognized how critically important it was for the PA to gain control and assert its authority before the US moved forward with the peace plan. During a meeting with Prime Minister Sharon on the same day that Hamas militants broke through the Gaza wall, President Bush said that Palestinians must first ensure "quiet, security and proper governance" before the US moved forward with the peace plan.[98]

Expressing similar sentiments, representatives of the Quartet at the UN, including US Secretary of State Condoleezza Rice, commended "the political courage of Prime Minister Sharon and . . . the Israeli government, its armed forces and its police for the smooth and professional execution of the operation" and called the pullout a "brave and historic decision [which] should open a new chapter on the path to peace in the region."[99] They recognized that "Israel has gone beyond its obligations under the first phase of the Roadmap" and called for the PA to "maintain law and order and dismantle terrorist capabilities and infrastructure."[100]

Indeed, Sharon's manifest dedication to the Disengagement Plan induced even Israel's most outspoken critics to take note of Israel's commitment to peace. French President Jacques Chirac, only months after personally paying homage to Yasser Arafat as he lived out his final days in a Paris hospital, invited Prime Minister Sharon to Paris to strengthen France's relationship with Israel. While there, he praised the Disengagement Plan, calling it "determined and courageous."[101] Additionally, on September 1, 2005, Khurshid Kasuri, the Foreign Minister of Pakistan, met with Israel's Deputy Prime Minister and Minister of Foreign Affairs, Silvan Shalom, in the first ever high-level talks recognized by the two countries.[102] While addressing the UN General Assembly on 20 September 2005, Shalom recognized the positive effects of Israel's Disengagement Plan. His optimism over the potential for new relationships was apparent when he said:

> Israel's contacts with Arab and Muslim states are growing, at a rate never seen before. Countries – like Pakistan and others – who in the past refused to acknowledge our shared humanity, today are extending their hand in friendship and recognition. Relations with

key Muslim states such as Turkey are flourishing, while our peaceful ties with both Egypt and Jordan, are improving all the time. . .

Here in New York this week, I have had the honor of meeting with more than ten of my colleagues from the Arab and Muslim world, a number unthinkable, even two years ago. These meetings have been open and friendly, as befits meetings between countries which have no conflict – neither over territory nor economy. Israel welcomes this new readiness for contact, and we encourage our neighbors to build on the foundations that we are now laying.[103]

The Political Rise of Hamas as an Obstacle to Peace

On January 26, 2006, the Islamic Resistance Movement aka HAMAS ("Hamas"), although designated as a Foreign Terrorist Organization ("FTO") by the US and other governments, won a large majority in the Palestinian Legislative Council elections garnering 74 of 132 seats, while Fatah, the ruling party at the time, took 45 seats.[104] Notwithstanding Hamas' pronounced dedication to a Holy War against Israel and its continued threats to persist in carrying out terrorist attacks against Israel's citizens, Palestinians implored Israel not to intervene in their January 2006 legislative election.[105] Palestinian negotiator Saeb Erekat said "I urge the Israelis to stay out of our elections and our internal affairs, and not to put their noses in this . . . Our election will be a turning point toward political pluralism and toward maintaining law and order."[106]

However, the Palestinians seemingly well intended push for democratic elections created a situation in which neither the Quartet nor Israel were willing to pursue further negotiations with the Hamas-led Gaza based government. When Hamas took power, the Bush Administration, along with the Quartet members (Russia, the European Union, and the United Nations) ("the Quartet") and Israel, responded by terminating contact with and assistance to the PA. The US and other states immediately conditioned continued diplomatic and economic relations with the Palestinian Authority (including aid) on Hamas' disavowing terrorism, recognizing Israel, and accepting all previous Israeli-Palestinian agreements.[107] Notwithstanding the ramifications of its policies, to this day, Hamas has refused to take those steps or make those pronouncements.

In early April 2006, the US and the EU announced they would stop assistance to the Hamas-led PA government but that humanitarian aid would continue to flow through international and non-governmental organizations (NGOs).[108] Elliott Abrams, former Deputy National Security Advisor to President Bush's National Security Council, noted, in hindsight, that, "theoretically, there is no reason that a Palestinian state cannot be democratic, peaceful and also Islamist. But practically speaking, this is very unlikely, given all the trends in the Muslim world."[109] His remarks were prophetic, given the subsequent developments in Egypt, the Arab Spring and resultant instability in the region.

In June 2006, Israel began Operation Summer Rains. Israel re-entered the Gaza Strip in an attempt to recover its kidnapped Israeli soldier, Gilad Shalit, and to put a stop to the heavy bombardment of Qassam rocket fire, launched from Gaza into Israel, that Israel had endured for months. Shalit remained in Hamas hands for five more years until Israeli Prime Minister Benjamin Netanyahu, serving his second term, concluded an agreement for his release in exchange for more than one thousand convicted terrorists.

The conflict between Israel and Palestinian militants in the Gaza Strip became regional on July 12, 2006. In a surprise attack in the north, Hezbollah launched a barrage of rocket attacks and captured and later killed two Israeli soldiers along the Israeli-Lebanese border. In what has come to be known as the Second Lebanon War, Israel responded with air strikes against suspected Hezbollah targets in Lebanon while Hezbollah launched multiple rocket attacks against cities and towns in northern Israel. Israel was forced to mount full-scale ground operations in Lebanon to push Hezbollah forces away from Israel's border and north of the Litani River. Hezbollah, also a designated Foreign Terrorist Organization, had amassed weapons and missiles from Iran and Syria; controlled much of Lebanon, including its government; and implanted gun and missile launching placements in civilian areas. Israel's responsive attacks hit emplacements in Beirut and elsewhere in Lebanon in an attempt to put a stop to Hezbollah capabilities and terrorist attacks. While this was going on, Hamas and other Palestinian militant groups continued their fight with the Israeli military in Gaza. The UN Security Council issued Resolution 1701 calling for a permanent ceasefire between Israel and Lebanon, and a UN brokered deal went into effect on August 14, 2006.[110]

On November 26, 2006, after five months of fighting in Gaza, Israel and the Palestinians reached another cease-fire.[111] Prior to Israel's departure from Gaza, most of the rockets had been aimed at Jewish settlements in Gaza. After Israel's departure, over a thousand rockets were directed into Israel itself.[112] The truce lasted only a few short months. Subsequently in 2008 and again in 2012 Israel responded with full force as a result of torrents of Hamas rockets.

The end of 2006 saw many armed clashes between supporters of Fatah and Hamas, as the PA government could no longer pay its employees and living conditions deteriorated.[113] Lawlessness increased as the fighting increased between supporters and opponents of the Hamas-led government. "The well-armed Palestinian security forces, manned largely by Fatah opponents of the government . . . repeatedly confronted the Hamas military wing and other armed groups loyal to government."[114] In December 2006, the US Congress passed the Palestinian Anti-Terrorism Act of 2006 (P.L. 109-446), to tighten existing restrictions on aid to the Palestinians.[115] The Act:

> Bars aid to the Hamas-led Palestinian government unless, among other things, it acknowledges Israel's right to exist and adheres to all previous international agreements and understandings. It exempts funds for humanitarian aid and democracy promotion. It also provides $20 million to establish a fund promoting Palestinian democracy and Israeli-Palestinian peace. The law limits the PA's representation in the United States as well as US contact with Palestinian officials.[116]

In February 2007, Fatah and Hamas agreed to the "Mecca Accord," where both agreed to form a national unity government, share power, and work towards the stated goals of ending rising violence and an international aid embargo.[117] In a brutal coup in June 2007, Hamas forces took control of the Gaza Strip from Fatah and the Palestinian security services and established a radical Islamic entity in the Gaza Strip. They largely operate separate from, but still formally a part of the Palestinian Authority, which remains based on the West Bank headed by Fatah and President Mahmoud Abbas.[118] The coup signaled a fundamental change in Hamas' status since control over the Gaza Strip made Hamas responsible for the lives of the Gaza Strip's 1,400,000 residents.[119]

Since the 2006 victory of Hamas, in the opinion of some, "Gaza has emerged as the seat of Palestinian political authority."[120] This switch of power, with Hamas having control in Gaza, could not have come at a more inopportune time. As "foreign donors, who cut off aid following its election, [demanded] that [Palestine] renounce its founding charter and recognize Israel," Hamas and its uncompromising intent and design to destroy Israel wrapped itself with government authority.[121] In the 12 months following the coup and Gaza take-over, Hamas fired close to 4,300 rockets and mortar shells from Gaza into Israel, killing four Israelis.[122] This continuous barrage, in addition to Hamas' disavowal of the November 2006 ceasefire, and their amassing and launching of missiles obtained via smuggling through tunnels from Egypt, forced Israel to launch Operation Cast Lead in December 2008, and continuing to be under constant missile attack from Gaza. During the period November 14-20, 2012 alone, according to the IDF, 1102 rockets were launched from Gaza into Israel, of which 7 were long range and more than half were medium range, resulting in Israel's Operation Pillar of Defense response in November 2012.

Quartet Envoy Tony Blair, Diplomacy and the Security Fence

The international Quartet of Middle East Peacemakers established in Madrid, Spain in 2002, is a group of four nations and international bodies – the United States, Russia, the European Union, and the UN – whose mission is to work towards a peace agreement between Israel and the Palestinians.[123] In June 2007, Tony Blair ended his 10-year tenure as British prime minister and accepted the position as the Quartet's Special Envoy to the Middle East.[124] His role as Special Envoy has largely focused primarily on developing the Palestinian economy for future statehood. The Quartet, in its statement on Blair's appointment as Special Envoy, directed him to "help create viable and lasting government institutions representing all Palestinians, a robust economy, and a climate of law and order for the Palestinian people."[125] Specifically, the Quartet mandated Blair to:

(1) Mobilize international assistance to the Palestinians, working closely with donors and existing coordination bodies;

(2) Help to identify, and secure appropriate international support in addressing, the institutional governance needs of the Palestinian state, focusing as a matter of urgency on the rule of law;

(3) Develop plans to promote Palestinian economic development, including private sector partnerships, building on previously agreed frameworks, especially concerning access and movement; and

(4) Liaise with other countries as appropriate in support of the agreed Quartet objectives.[126]

In implementing this mandate, Blair was required to "work closely with the Palestinian Authority government" for the purpose of developing "a multi-year agenda for institutional and economic development." [127]

In November of 2007, Special Envoy Tony Blair, Palestinian Prime Minister Fayyad and Israel's Minister of Defense and former Prime Minister Ehud Barak reaffirmed their "commitment to revive the Palestinian economy and to improve living standards."[128] Following a trilateral meeting held in Jerusalem, Blair announced four projects: (1) the construction of an agro-industrial park in Jericho; (2) an emergency sewage treatment project in north Gaza; (3) the development of industrial zones, particularly in the area of Tarqumiya; and (4) tourism projects for both the Palestinian and Israeli sectors.[129]

In December 2007, Blair co-chaired a conference in Paris to raise funds for the Palestinian people. The conference, convened at the request of Palestinian President Abbas, included nearly 90 countries and international organizations that pledged $7.4 billion over the course of three years for the development of a Palestinian state.[130] The amount of donations exceeded Palestinian expectations and Blair, pleased with the outcome and the potential ramifications, announced, "Paris now sets in motion the Palestinian state-building... It means we have a chance to do it."[131] Following Blair's announcement of the four projects and the conference, the Quartet praised the efforts of the Government of Israel and the Palestinian Authority, giving its "strong support."[132]

In May 2008, the Palestinian Investment Conference, a forum to discuss investment opportunities and build partnerships between the Palestinian and international business communities, was held in Bethlehem. Tony Blair was a key backer. He then went on to organize a June conference in Berlin where 242 million dollars was committed "to bolster the Palestinian police and justice system to help pave the way to a viable state."[133] The money was to be distributed to the PA over a span of three years and was aimed to increase police forces, rebuild destroyed courthouses and train judges.

While peace-making per se is not part of the Quartet appointment mandate of Prime Minister Blair, his office has attempted to improve coordination on security matters between the world powers, the Palestinians and the Israelis.

Blair refuses to "simply just...give up" on talks of peace.[134] When asked about how the December 2008 Operation Cast Lead affected his job as peace envoy, he reaffirmed his commitment, saying he'll "be back in business again" as long as three elements – "a credible political negotiation for a two-state solution; a program of major change on the West Bank, and an easing of the blockade in Gaza" – are achieved.[135] During even the most violent periods when Blair opposed talks with Hamas because of its rocket fire at Israel, Blair supported "humanitarian help in its broadest sense" going into Gaza, "not just food and fuel but also help in rebuilding infrastructure and houses."[136] And when Israel allowed 12 million dollars to be transferred into Gaza, he "welcomed... the decision" and called for "larger and more predictable transfers of cash on a monthly basis."[137] Following Operation Cast Lead, at a donor's conference in Sharm el-Sheikh, Blair continued his efforts on behalf of Gaza, getting donors to pledge "$4.4 billion in aid to the Palestinians for reconstruction in Gaza."[138]

As for the Quartet's stance on the security fence, they acknowledge that the barrier is intended to be a temporary barrier. The Quartet has expressed concern about the impact the route of the fence has on Palestinian life.[139] In 2004 the Quartet reaffirmed this position, taking note of the ICJ advisory opinion and urging the Government of Israel to take "positive action."[140] Blair has continued his efforts to reach a peace agreement. Even when negotiations appear to be at a standstill, Quartet Envoys and Blair meet with both parties. In December 2011, Blair met in Jerusalem with both parties separately and stressed the "Quartet Principles and… the important objective of a direct exchange between the parties without delays or preconditions."[141] Again in April 2012, the Quartet reaffirmed its commitment to the Quartet Principles. It called upon the international community to help to contribute 1.1 billion in assistance to help Palestine meet its financial obligations. It called upon the Palestinian Authority to "continue to make every effort to improve law and order, to fight violent extremism and to end incitement."[142]

US Efforts to Improve Security

The United States has been repeatedly involved in attempting to improve and protect Israel's security and to achieve a peaceful resolution between Israel and the Palestinian Authority. After the disengagement, in an attempt to restart the peace process, President Bush convened the Annapolis Conference in Annapolis, Maryland in November 2007. Subsequently, General James L. Jones, a retired four-star general and former NATO commander, was appointed to serve as the Bush administration's Special Envoy for Middle East Security. Assisted by Lieutenant General Keith Dayton, the US Security Coordinator, and Lieutenant General William Fraser III, Jones' mission was to "work with Israelis and Palestinians on the full range of security issues . . . strengthen security for both sides . . . [and] engage with key countries to support Middle East security."[143] General Dayton's mission was to help "the Palestinian Authority … build and rationalize its security forces."[144] General Fraser was charged with monitoring and verifying Palestinian and Israeli compliance with the Roadmap.

To carry out his mission, General Jones set up an Israeli-Palestinian security model in the West Bank town of Jenin to organize training for Palestinian police and funding for development projects. General Dayton led the US plan "to train Palestinian paramilitary forces and deploy them . . . in West Bank cities to keep order." Beginning in 2007, Dayton organized training for Palestinian security forces in Jordan and by December 2008, around 1,100 Palestinians had graduated from the US-directed training program, with another 1,000 on track to do the same.[145] In what was called the "Jenin Initiative" General Jones' team capitalized on the new security by funding new schools, clinics and other development projects.[146] On March 17, 2009, the Presidential Guard Training Center, funded by "$10.1 million of State Department assistance," formally opened in Jericho. The center boasted a training capacity of 700 officers and enlisted men and was the "first of several construction projects meant to improve PA security forces in the West Bank through funding from the US Bureau of International Narcotics and Law Enforcement Affairs."[147]

With the help of General Jones, the US effort appeared to improve the security situation in Jenin. Amos Gilad, the head of the Israeli Defense Ministry's Diplomatic-Security Bureau, recognized the progress in a November 2008 interview when he said that Palestinian Authority forces are "working more effectively than in the past, in Jenin . . . there's certainly an improvement."[148] There were many instances of improvement, such as the PA forces' crack down on Jenin's criminal gangs, in one instance staging a raid on an Islamic Jihad cell in nearby Qabatiya.[149]

There have been vast improvements in Jenin although terrorist murders have taken place, including that of an Israeli whose family founded the Freedom Theater in Jenin. He was gunned down outside the theater, another symbolic strike at peaceful cooperation in the Palestinian Territories. PA Security Forces have largely restored order to what was once a central hub for suicide bombers. Much of this improvement can be credited to General Jones, who has been praised as "bringing clarity to a messy situation" and for successfully "forc[ing] all of the different parts of the US government to work together to make Jenin a model of economic hope, despite a very dreary past, and so far, so good."[150] General Jones was later appointed as President Barack Obama's National Security Advisor. General Dayton has also been praised for his excellent security team training programs which will hopefully bear fruit in the future as Palestinian security services become better able to control the situation within the West Bank, providing normal police and civil order functions.

Continued Attacks from Gaza — At the Center of the Ongoing Conflict

Since 2001, the number of rocket attacks and mortar shellfire towards Israel from Gaza has steadily increased, reaching high levels and becoming "the Palestinian terrorist organizations' preferred form of attack."[151] Rocket and mortar shell fire have had "devastating effect[s] on the daily life and sense of security of the 200,000 western Negev residents."[152] In 2006, Palestinians fired 1,726 crude rockets from Gaza and 946 rocket hits were identified in Israeli territory. The attacks killed two Israelis and left 163 wounded.[153] In 2007, 896 rocket hits were identified in Israeli territory.[154] In 2008, 1,571 rockets and 1,531 mortar bombs, fired from the Gaza Strip, struck southern Israel.[155] Compared to 2001 through 2005, the years before the disengagement, the period from 2006 to 2008 brought a "substantial increase in rocket fire" as well as a "significant increase in the amount of mortar shell fire."[156]

During the 2008-2012 time period, little changed in Gaza. Hamas rocket attacks escalated. Egypt largely failed to stop the smuggling of weapons. Abbas pledged but was unable to secure a united government between Fatah and Hamas although there were repeated discussions and meetings hosted in Egypt, with predictions and pronouncements of the future formation of a unity government between Fatah and Hamas. In January 2013, Egyptian President Morsi hosted unity discussions between Mahmoud Abbas of the Fatah controlled Palestinian Authority and Khaled Meshal of Hamas. Even in a unity government is established, Hamas has made it clear that its military wing will continue attacks upon Israel.

Gaza, the Naval Blockade and Relations with Turkey

Gaza has continued under a naval blockade by Israel, which remains determined to stop the smuggling of weapons into Gaza by land, air or sea. While Israel was unable to get Egypt to seal the tunnels through which munitions were moved into Gaza, it was largely successful in stopping deliveries by boat. A casualty of the blockade, however, has been the previously strong and growing relationship between Israel and Turkey. Although the relationship had been suffering after Erdogan became the Turkish Prime Minister, it had not exploded until Israel stopped a flotilla which left a Turkish port on May 22, 2010 headed to Gaza. The *Mavi Marmara* was determined to break the naval blockade. While the flotilla claimed to be carrying supplies and humanitarian goods, the Israelis believed it to be carrying terrorists and weapons. Israeli forces stopped the boat and boarded it by helicopters; as the Israeli soldiers boarded they were attacked and responded with force. Nine Turkish citizens were killed. Israel had warned the ship not to sail into waters near the Gaza Strip in circumvention of Israel's naval blockade of the coastal strip. Their doing so, and the subsequent on-board battle resulted in a public break in Turkish-Israel relations.

IDF personnel are presently being tried in absentia on war crimes charges in Turkey. According to a *Jerusalem Post* report on December 18, 2012, the criminal court case is proceeding against former IDF Chief of Staff Lt.-Gen Gabi Ashkenazi and other Israeli military leaders. The charges reportedly include manslaughter, causing bodily harm, deprivation of freedom, plundering, damage to property and illegal confiscation of property. The Israeli government ordered a complete investigation into the matter, resulting in significant evidence about the terrorist organization IHH which organized the flotilla and the vicious attack on the IDF soldiers as they boarded the ship. At the commencement of the trial in Turkey, the IHH launched a series of anti-Israel hate demonstrations including photographs comparing Israel to Hitler. The Turkish government has taken no steps to curb IHH activities or to hold IHH responsible.

The issue of restoring good relations with Turkey nevertheless remains on the agenda of the Netanyahu government. During his trip to Israel, President Obama facilitated a teleconference with Turkish Prime Minister Erdogan and Israeli Prime Minister Netanyahu in the hopes of thawing the chill between the two U.S. allies. Netanyahu expressed a diplomatic apology for the "operational errors" in the Mavi Marmara incident that resulted in the death of Turkish citizens and pledged compensation. To date, however, the once-friendly relations between these two nations have not been restored.

Hamas Efforts to Destroy Peace Making in Spite of Efforts to Implement the Roadmap

At the Annapolis Conference, Prime Minister Ehud Olmert, who succeeded Prime Minister Sharon, and President Mahmud Abbas had reached a "Joint Understanding" which consisted of a twosided agreement in which they would launch continuous bilateral negotiations in an "effort to conclude a peace treaty by the end of 2008 and to simultaneously implement the moribund 2003 Performance-Based Road Map to a Permanent Two-State Solution to the Israeli-Palestinian Conflict." [157]

One year later in November of 2008, the Quartet met in Sharm el-Sheikh, Egypt to keep the Annapolis conference momentum going and to reaffirm their backing of Israeli and Palestinian negotiations toward a two state solution. The Quartet Statement read, in part:

> The parties remained committed to implementation of their respective obligations under the Performance-Based Roadmap to a Permanent Two-State Solution to the Israeli-Palestinian Conflict and to the agreed mechanism for monitoring and judging Roadmap implementation and that, unless otherwise agreed by the parties, implementation of the future peace treaty will be subject to implementation of the Roadmap, as judged by the United States.[158]

On December 16, 2008, the United Nations Security Council adopted Resolution 1850 endorsing for the first time the Quartet principles and the Annapolis process. It had been nearly five years since the UN Security Council had last passed a resolution addressing the Israeli-Palestinian conflict. In Resolution 1850, the Security Council:

1. *Declare[d]* its support for the negotiations initiated at Annapolis, Maryland, on 27 November 2007 and its commitment to the irreversibility of the bilateral negotiations;
2. *Support[ed]* the parties' agreed principles for the bilateral nego-

tiating process and their determined efforts to reach their goal of concluding a peace treaty resolving all outstanding issues, including all core issues, without exception, which confirm the seriousness of the Annapolis process;

3. *Call[ed] on* both parties to fulfill their obligations under the Performance-Based Roadmap, as stated in their Annapolis Joint Understanding, and refrain from any steps that could undermine confidence or prejudice the outcome of negotiations;

4. *Call[ed] on* all States and international organizations to contribute to an atmosphere conducive to negotiations and to support the Palestinian government that is committed to the Quartet principles and the Arab Peace Initiative and respects the commitments of the Palestine Liberation Organization, to assist in the development of the Palestinian economy, to maximize the resources available to the Palestinian Authority, and to contribute to the Palestinian institution-building programme in preparation for statehood;

5. *Urge[d]* an intensification of diplomatic efforts to foster in parallel with progress in the bilateral process mutual recognition and peaceful coexistence between all States in the region in the context of achieving a comprehensive, just and lasting peace in the Middle East;

6. *Welcome*[d] the Quartet's consideration, in consultation with the parties, of an international meeting in Moscow in 2009;

7. *Decide[d]* to remain seized of the matter.[159]

Israeli Foreign Minister Tzipi Livni reacted positively to the resolution, stating:

Today's Security Council resolution constitutes international endorsement for the Annapolis process in keeping with the guiding principles established by the parties, namely: direct bilateral negotiations between the parties, without international intervention, and according to the principle that nothing is agreed until everything is agreed, a commitment to the Quartet principles - recognizing Israel, ending terror and accepting former agreements - as well as conditioning implementation of any future agreement on the implementation of the Road Map. The Security Council's clear support is a vote of confidence in the process Israel is advancing with the legitimate Palestinian leadership, that has no substitute, and that confirms that with sensible leadership it is possible to harness the international community to support Israel's interests and the interests of advancing genuine peace.[160]

Condoleezza Rice voiced her support saying that the international community was now on record in believing that the Annapolis process—"bilateral negotiations toward a two-state solution, a comprehensive solution, and the various principles of Annapolis and what the parties have established since then – " is now irreversible.[161] She reminded everyone that, "Annapolis ... is not just a top-down—that is negotiated process toward the solution of two states, but also a bottom-up process of Roadmap obligations and of improving life for the Palestinian people on the ground."[162] When President Bush met with Mahmoud Abbas on December 19, 2008, he expressed similar sentiments, noting that he was "pleased ... that the UN Security Council passed a resolution which confirms that the bilateral negotiation process is irreversible . . . and it's a path to a Palestinian state and a path to peace in the Middle East."[163]

Israel's efforts to move towards a negotiated peace and the agreements she undertakes do not compromise her duty to protect her citizens. It is a basic human right to live in a safe and secure environment that is based on law and order and is safe and free from terrorist acts.

Following President Bush's meeting with Mahmoud Abbas, again dooming the peace process Hamas declared that it would not extend its six-month ceasefire with Israel. In the prior decade, Israel suffered over 10,000 attempted rocket attacks coming from Gaza. Hamas' sudden disavowal of the ceasefire and the subsequent increased barrage of deadly rocket fire from Gaza forced Israel's hand and the Israeli military launched Operation Cast Lead on December 27, 2008. These terrorist attacks again stopped negotiations between the Israelis and Palestinians as the Bush administration concluded and President Barack Obama prepared to take office for his first term.

Foreign Minister Livni summed up Israel's position when she said:

> It is important to understand that Israel withdrew from the Gaza Strip a few years ago in order to create a vision of peace ... The Gaza Strip should have been the beginning of a Palestinian state, . . . but instead of the creation of something that gives hope to the Palestinian people, as well as to the Israeli people, Hamas took control, after a coup against Abu Mazen and his group, and has been abusing the situation in order to target Israel.[164]

Reiterating Israel's right to self-defense, she noted that:

"Israel is under ongoing attack from these terrorist organizations. Israel withdrew from the Gaza Strip. Israel wants to live in peace but there are certain things that nobody can accept. No state in the world would have accepted the fact that its citizens are being targeted and children cannot go to school or to kindergartens because of these terrorists."[165]

President Bush, voicing his support, reaffirmed his view that Israel has a right to defend itself in light of the attacks emanating from Gaza:

"I understand Israel's desire to protect itself and that the situation now taking place in Gaza was caused by Hamas....instead of caring about the people of Gaza, Hamas decided to use Gaza to launch rockets to kill innocent Israelis. And Israel has obviously decided to protect herself and her people."[166]

Operation Cast Lead lasted for 22 days of fighting in Gaza and concluded with a unilateral declaration by Israel to hold its fire. Throughout the operation, the IDF made sure to provide as much humanitarian aid to the residents of Gaza as it was able to deliver. This included helping with the delivery of 1,511 trucks carrying 37,162 tons.[167] The IDF also made sure to avoid or limit harm to the Palestinian population in Gaza as much as possible, while still combating the constant barrage of rocket and mortar fire from Hamas.[168] Hamas, on the other hand, did nothing to prevent Israeli civilian casualties.

Following Hamas' declaration and the launch of Operation Cast Lead, the UN Security Council adopted Resolution 1860 on January 8, 2009, which called for an "immediate, durable and fully respected ceasefire, leading to the full withdrawal of Israeli forces from Gaza."[169]

Israeli Ambassador to the United Nations Gabriela Shalev responded sharply to the resolution, stressing that "eight years of continuous rocket attacks by the Hamas terrorist organization, Hamas' refusal to extend the period of calm, and its smuggling of weapons during this period, left Israel with no choice but to act in self defense."[170] US Secretary of State Condoleezza Rice agreed with Ambassador Shalev's assertion when, following the resolution, she said, "the United States recognizes the right of Israel, like other states, to exercise its right of self-defense."[171] Similarly, when asked prior to his inauguration about his view regarding the Gaza conflict,

President-elect Barack Obama said, "I think that's a basic principle of any country is that they've got to protect their citizens."[172]

Bolstering its support of Israel's right to self-defense, on January 16, 2009, the United States entered into a "Memorandum of Understanding" with Israel that dealt with "Prevention of the Supply of Arms and Related Material to Terrorist Groups."[173] In further support, on March 13, 2009, representatives of nine countries (Canada, Denmark, France, Germany, Italy, Netherlands, Norway, the United Kingdom, and the United States) signed an agreement on a "program of action in response to concerns over continued smuggling of weapons into Gaza."[174] Yet the stream of weapons into Gaza has never stopped. Missiles launched by Hamas and Palestinian Islamic Jihad from Gaza against Israel have never stopped. Although the Gaza security fence has been largely effective in stopping infiltrators from entering Israel, it has neither stopped those entering Israel from Egypt, where a security fence is in the process of being built, nor has it stopped Hamas and other terrorist organizations from launching missiles over the fence into the sovereign state of Israel.

In October of 2011, Israeli Prime Minister Netanyahu secured the release of kidnapped soldier Gilad Shalit in exchange for the release of more than 1000 convicted Palestinian terrorist prisoners, many of whom were released into Gaza. This agreement was accomplished in the hopes that it would not only bring home Israel's soldier to his family and meet Palestinian demands for prisoner releases, but also to lead to wider talks between the Israel government and the Palestinian Authority. However, President Abbas repeatedly refused to return to the negotiating table, after the election of President Obama and the election in Israel of Prime Minister Netanyahu to his second term, repeatedly citing Israel's construction activities in settlements and East Jerusalem. Moreover, hopes for a long term peace remained dashed as Hamas continued to launch rockets upon Israel from Gaza. During the November 2012 Hamas attacks on Israel, many missiles landed not only in the South, but for the first time in the environs of Tel Aviv and Jerusalem, causing Israel to respond with a surgical strike killing the head of Hamas' military wing and subsequently flying sorties over Gaza in an attempt to destroy Hamas missile and munitions emplacements. Egypt, headed by Hosni Mubarak for thirty years and now headed by Mohammed Morsi, in conjunction with the intense personal effort of US Secretary of State Hillary Clinton, the active support of President Barrack Obama and the personal involvement and consent of Israeli Prime Minister Benjamin Netanyahu, achieved a cease fire agreement in December 2012 between Hamas and Israel. However, even after the cease fire went into effect, Hamas has continued to launch rockets on Israeli targets although December 2012 and January 2013 have been basically quiet between Gaza and Israel; only time will tell how long that condition will hold.

The Obama Administration's Efforts Toward Peacemaking

Shortly after entering the Presidency in 2009, President Obama said, "The United States strongly supports the goal of two states, Israel and Palestine, living side by side in peace and security. We must reject the use of terror, and recognize that Israel's security concerns are legitimate."[175] Then again, during his May 18, 2009 press conference with Prime Minister Benjamin Netanyahu at the White House, President Obama reaffirmed his administration's support stating, "It is in US national security interests to assure that Israel's security as an independent Jewish state is maintained."[176] He stressed the need for a two-state solution based on peace and security in line with the Roadmap.

Middle East researcher and writer Robert Satloff, Executive Director of the Washington Institute, summed up the administration's commitment when he commented that, at the time, Obama may have signaled "the resurrection of the Roadmap as a point of reference for progress in Israeli-Palestinian relations" because there were specific references in his speech that "referred… to the phase-one requirements to which each side committed itself: for the Palestinians, action on security, counterterrorism, and incitement; for the Israelis, action on settlement activity."[177]

As the President commenced his second term in office, peace in the Middle East is a topic priority of the White House and of new Secretary of State John Kerry. During the President's first term and in an attempt to move back to the negotiating table with the Palestinians, Prime Minister Benjamin Netanyahu agreed to impose a ten-month freeze on certain construction projects on the West Bank. However, the Palestinians rebuked the attempt at negotiations and for the remainder of President Obama's first term President Abbas steadfastly continued to refuse to reenter into direct negotiations with the Israelis, notwithstanding the efforts of the Obama administration and Prime Minister Netanyahu's repeated invitations, suggestions and proposals to reconvene direct negotiations between the parties.

In March 2010, the administration proposed:

(1) the cancelation of the approval of the housing units in Ramat Shlomo,

(2) a freeze on all Jewish construction in eastern Jerusalem,

(3) a gesture to the Palestinians such as the release of Palestinian prisoners held in Israeli prisons and

(4) the agreement by Israel to conduct all substantive issues such as the partition of Jerusalem through indirect, Obama administration-mediated negotiations with the Palestinians.

On May 19, 2011, President Obama called on Israel to return to negotiations based upon pre-1967 borders, albeit with mutually agreed land swaps.[178] The President made it clear that the negotiated border should be "different from the one that existed on June 4, 1967."[179] Prime Minister Netanyahu was warmly received in a bipartisan show of solidarity with Israel by the United States Congress and said during his address to a Joint Session of Congress:

> The vast majority of the 650,000 Israelis who live beyond the 1967 lines reside in neighborhoods and suburbs of Jerusalem and greater Tel Aviv.
>
> Now, these areas are densely populated, but they're geographically quite small. And under any realistic peace agreement these areas, as well as other places of critical strategic and national importance, will be incorporated into the final borders of Israel.
>
> The status of the settlements will be decided only in negotiations. But we must also be honest. So I'm saying today something that should be said publicly by all those who are serious about peace: In any real peace agreement, in any peace agreement that ends the

conflict, some settlements will end up beyond Israel's borders.

Now, the precise delineation of those borders must be negotiated. We'll be generous about the size of the future Palestinian state. But as President Obama said, the border will be different than the one that existed on June 4th, 1967. Israel will not return to the indefensible boundaries of 1967.[180]

In November 2012 President Obama and Secretary of State Hillary Clinton stood strongly with Israel in responding to Israel's right to defend herself from Hamas rockets launched from Gaza. They also joined with Israel in joint opposition to Abbas' unilateral efforts to achieve upgraded non-member state observer status at the UN, although this was approved by the UN General Assembly on November 29, 2012. The President reiterated this support during his State of the Union Address in February 2013 when he said, "Our iron-clad commitment—and I mean iron-clad—to Israel's security has meant the closest military cooperation between our two countries in history."[181]

Now into his second term, President Obama made a brief, long-anticipated visit to Israel. He met in Jerusalem with Prime Minister Netanyahu and President Shimon Peres and then traveled to Ramallah to meet President Mahmoud Abbas. Both sides felt encouraged by his comments.

The President Obama made one final stop in Jordan where he met with King Abdullah II. The main focus was the growing problem of Syrian refugees escaping from the civil war. In addition to overwhelming aid agencies and refugee camps, there are fears that extremists and terrorists would take advantage of the chaos to destabilize Jordan.

Benjamin Netanyahu's Government and His View of the Security Fence as a Necessary Means to Stopping Terrorism

Prime Minister Benjamin Netanyahu was sworn in for his second term as Prime Minister of Israel on March 31, 2009 to lead Israel's 32nd government.[182] Netanyahu continued a strong proponent of building the security fence and a critic of the ICJ's advisory opinion, remaining committed to his July 2004 New York Times article, where he responded to the ICJ advisory opinion

> While the advisory finding by the International Court of Justice last
> week that Israel's barrier in the West Bank is illegal may be cheered
> by the terrorists who would kill Israeli civilians, it does not change
> the fact that none of the arguments against the security fence have
> any merit.[183]

Netanyahu highlighted three points, emphasizing that, (1) "Israel is
not building the fence on territory that under international law can
be properly called 'Palestinian land,'" and "this dispute is to be resolved by a negotiated peace that provides Israel with secure and
recognized boundaries," (2) "the fence is not a permanent political
border but a temporary security barrier," and (3) "despite what some
have argued, fences have proven highly effective against terrorism."[184] Netanyahu further indicated that, should peace be achieved,
the security fence may be moved or even dismantled. Specifically,
he indicated that if a compromise is reached "with a future Palestinian leadership committed to peace that requires adjustments to the
fence, those changes will be made. And if that peace proves genuine
and lasting, there will be no reason for a fence at all."[185] He bashed
the ICJ's prioritization of Palestinian quality of life issues over the
need to protect Israelis from murder:

> Instead of placing Palestinian terrorists and those who send them
> on trial, the United Nations-sponsored international court placed
> the Jewish state in the dock, on the charge that Israel is harming the
> Palestinians' quality of life. But saving lives is more important than
> preserving the quality of life. Quality of life is always amenable to
> improvement. Death is permanent. The Palestinians complain that
> their children are late to school because of the fence. But too many
> of our children never get to school—they are blown to pieces by ter-
> rorists who pass into Israel where there is still no fence.[186]

Sharply critical of the ICJ opinion, he concluded with, "The court's
decision makes a mockery of Israel's right to defend itself, the government of Israel will ignore it. Israel will never sacrifice Jewish life
on the debased altar of 'international justice.'"[187]

Five years later, in a Knesset session on July 22, 2009, Netanyahu
addressed the question of dismantling the security fence:

> I hear people saying that since there is quiet, the fence can be torn
> down. My friends, the opposite is true. Because we have the fence,
> there is quiet. And that is of course in addition to IDF operations, and

I must cautiously add, there is also a degree of improvement in the operations of the Palestinian security apparatuses, and we commend this.[188]

Calling the security fence "a critical component of Israel's security"[189] Netanyahu told those at the meeting that "the separation fence will remain in place and will not be dismantled." This remark was likely in response to Israeli media reports indicating the Palestinian Authority had pressed the United States to demand that the Israelis remove the security fence.

Frustrated with the constant attacks on Israel consistent with his long-held and voiced belief that the true danger to the world was not Israel but Iran, speaking at the American-Israel Public Affairs Committee ("AIPAC") Policy Conference in May 2009, Netanyahu stressed that a nuclear capable Iran posed grave danger to the peoples in the Middle East. Moreover, he voiced his willingness to resume peace talks with the Palestinians immediately "without any delay and without any preconditions."[190] He proposed a triple track toward peace based on politics, security, and economy:

The political track means that we are prepared to resume peace negotiations without any delay and without any preconditions–the sooner the better. The security track means that we want to continue the cooperation with the program led by General Dayton, in cooperation with the Jordanians and with the Palestinian Authority to strengthen the security apparatus of the Palestinians. This is something we believe in and something that I think we can advance in a joint effort. The economic track means that we are prepared to work together to remove as many obstacles as we can to the advancement of the Palestinian economy. We want to work with the Palestinian Authority on this track, not as a substitute for political negotiations, but as a boost to them. I want to see Palestinian youngsters knowing that they have a future. I want them not to be hostage to a cult of death and despair and hate. I want them to have jobs. I want them to have career paths. I want them to know that they can provide for their families. This means that we can give them a future of hope, a future that means that there is prosperity for all. And this has proved to be successful in advancing a political peace in many parts of the world.[191]

Netanyahu stressed that two requirements for a final peace agreement with the Palestinians were 1) Israeli security and 2) Palestinian recognition of Israel as a Jewish state. That very same day, Hamas' political leader, Khaled Meshal, vowed that "Hamas would not recognize Israel's right to exist," announcing that any recognition "was an error committed in negotiations held by Fatah leaders with Jerusalem over the course of the Oslo Accords."[192] Meshal has repeatedly reconfirmed the refusal of Hamas to honor peace agreements between the PLO and Israel; and has repeatedly vowed to continue its attacks with a goal of liberating all of Palestine.

Following his May 2009 meeting with President Obama, Netanyahu reiterated his continued goal. "I want to make it clear that we don't want to govern the Palestinians. We want to live in peace with them. We want them to govern themselves, absent a handful of powers that could endanger the state of Israel."[193] He noted that:

> If we resume negotiations, as we plan to do, then I think that the Palestinians will have to recognize Israel as a Jewish state; will have to also enable Israel to have the means to defend itself. And if those conditions are met, Israel's security conditions are met, and there's recognition of Israel's legitimacy, its permanent legitimacy, then I think we can envision an arrangement where Palestinians and Israelis live side by side in dignity, in security, and in peace.[194]

Robert Satloff has argued that the difference between President Obama's 'two-state solution' formula and Prime Minister Netanyahu's goal of living 'side by side' in 'security and peace' "is more rhetorical than substantive."[195] The more significant potential divergence, he goes on to argue, is between "the Roadmap and Annapolis models of peacemaking."[196] Making a distinction between the Roadmap and Annapolis, Israeli Foreign Minister Avigdor Lieberman stated that Israel was not bound by the Annapolis process, but would pursue peace based on the Roadmap. Addressing the non-binding nature of the Annapolis Conference, he said, that "the Annapolis Conference...has no validity... The Israeli government never ratified Annapolis, nor did the Knesset."[197] Deputy Foreign Minister Ayalon supported Lieberman's view, saying that:

> An interim agreement with the Palestinians is totally unrealistic. Under no circumstances will Israel withdraw from additional territories in the West Bank in the current reality, since any land we will cede will almost immediately be taken over by Hamas. These territories will become Hamastan and the Palestinian Authority will collapse.[198]

Delivering a major and significant foreign policy address at Bar Ilan University in June, 2009, Prime Minister Netanyahu publicly and directly addressed a two-state solution to the Israeli-Palestinian conflict:

> We do not want to rule over them, we do not want to govern their lives, we do not want to impose either our flag or our culture on them... In my vision of peace, in this small land of ours, two peoples live freely, side-by-side, in amity and mutual respect. Each will have its own flag, its own national anthem, its own government. Neither will threaten the security or survival of the other.[199]

He pointedly called on the Palestinians to resume negotiations, stating, "I turn to you, our Palestinian neighbors, led by the Palestinian Authority, and I say: Let's begin negotiations immediately without preconditions."[200]

His statements about Palestinian statehood continued:

> It is impossible to expect us to agree in advance to the principle of a Palestinian state without assurances that this state will be demilitarized... If we receive this guarantee regarding demilitarization and Israel's security needs, and if the Palestinians recognize Israel as the state of the Jewish people, then we will be ready in a future peace agreement to reach a solution where a demilitarized Palestinian state exists alongside the Jewish state.[201]

Netanyahu stressed the importance of Palestinian and Arab recognition of Israel's right to exist as a Jewish homeland, stating that "a fundamental prerequisite for ending the conflict is a public, binding and unequivocal Palestinian recognition of Israel as the nation-state of the Jewish people."[202] He rejected any right of return for Palestinian refugees to Israel and argued that "justice and logic demand that the Palestinian refugee problem be solved outside Israel's borders."[203]

Focusing on security as his prime concern for Israel and the Jewish people, before the Joint Session of Congress in 2011, Prime Minister Netanyahu stated,

> I believe that, with creativity and with good will, a solution can be found. So this is the peace I plan to forge with a Palestinian partner committed to peace. But you know very well that in the Middle East, the only peace that will hold is the peace you can defend. So peace must be anchored in security...Solid security arrangements on the ground are necessary not only to protect the peace; they're

necessary to protect Israel in case the peace unravels, because in our unstable region, no one can guarantee that our peace partners today will be there tomorrow.[204]

Netanyahu followed Abbas in addressing the opening of the UN General Assembly in September 2011. President Abbas had called upon the United Nations to grant full UN membership for Palestine, asserting his effort at a unilateral declaration of statehood. Prime Minister Netanyahu stated, "We've both just flown thousands of miles to New York. Now we're in the same city. We're in the same building. So let's meet here today in the United Nations. Who's there to stop us? What is there to stop us? If we genuinely want peace, what is there to stop us from meeting today and beginning peace negotiations," publicly calling upon President Abbas to meet him while in New York for direct discussions.[205] As he received no response to his invitation, the meeting never occurred.

At the September 2012 opening of the UN General Assembly, Prime Minister Netanyahu again made his views clear, stating "We have to sit together, negotiate together and reach a mutual compromise, in which a demilitarized Palestinian state recognizes the one and only Jewish State."[206]

Netanyahu's repeated calls for direct negotiations without preconditions have continually been rejected by Abbas, who refuses to enter into negotiations with the Israeli government until Israel ceases construction in the settlements and in East Jerusalem.

On November 29, 2012, the United Nations granted the PLO upgraded status from observer to non-member state observer status. Although opposed by the US, Israel and other countries who voted no or abstained, the resolution passed with 138 countries voting in favor. Abbas had hinted prior to the vote that if approved, he was prepared to return to the negotiating table with Israel. However, he has not done so and there is no indication he will do so in the near future. He also threatened that if approved, the PLO would consider seeking status with other international bodies, such as the International Criminal Court, where they could seek to bring charges against Israel for war crimes and crimes against humanity including charges arising out of the existence of Israel's terrorism prevention security fence.

CHAPTER THREE:
The History of the Terrorism Prevention Security Fence—Its Purpose and Structure

The Government of Israel responded to the renewed terrorism of the Second Intifada with both defensive and offensive measures. Following a series of military operations that proved insufficient as a means to ending the terrorist siege, a Ministers' Committee on National Security considered steps that were intended to prevent additional terror acts and deter potential terrorists.

Those measures, unfortunately, also proved inadequate. In 2003, after years of rejecting the concept of erecting a barrier between Israel and the West Bank, Israel determined that it must establish a terrorism prevention security fence that would serve as an impediment to terrorists attempting to enter Israel. The fence would run near, though not exactly along, the "Green Line" between Israel and the Palestinian territories.[207] In deciding to build the fence, Israel publicly stated that it was building the fence solely for security purposes, in keeping with its obligation to protect its people and its right to defend itself.

The Security Fence, as a whole, consists mostly of (1) an electronic fence to detect infiltration attempts; (2) a trench-like obstacle surrounding the fence to prevent vehicles from breaking through; and (3) an internal delaying fence,[208] which includes taller concrete walls and barriers to prevent gun and stone throwing attacks. In urban areas where space is limited, concrete walls have been built, which account for approximately five percent of the entire security fence project.[209] However, it is this portion that has gained most international attention.

The Israeli government has made clear that the terrorism prevention security fence is a temporary defensive measure and has pledged to remove the structure once the PA proves its willingness and ability to curb the campaign of terror.[210] Since her founding, Israel has basically refrained from establishing a fixed borderline, fences or barriers between herself and her neighbors, except for security purposes or pursuant to agreements reached between Israel and her neighbors. In keeping with this stance, the sole purpose of the security fence is to prevent terrorism, intending no effect on the political or legal status of any disputed land.

According to Col. (Res.) Danny Tirza, the Israeli military official responsible for mapping out the route of the security fence, if the route remained as planned, "at the end of the project there will be fewer than 7,000 people with Palestinian IDs on the Israeli side of the fence [in addition to Jerusalemites], but there will be a lot of Israelis living east of the fence."[211] Israel vowed, when approving the construction of the fence, to make "every effort to minimize, to the extent possible the disturbances to the daily lives of the Palestinians due to the construction of the obstacle."[212] In fact, because of the increased security the fence provides, "the number of Israeli troops in Palestinian towns has been significantly reduced."[213] Moreover, many Palestinian towns appear to have benefited economically from the presence of the fence, owing to the reduction in Israeli incursions. For the first time in years, residents were able to re-open their businesses and provide for their families, as the reduction in troops also signaled the end of restrictions such as curfews.

Criticism of Israel's efforts to protect its citizens from brazen and bloody acts of terror continues to stun Israel. Some in the international community have used the image of the security fence, particularly the concrete barriers, to promote the misconception that Israel is unilaterally establishing permanent borders between Israel and the Palestinians. Others have used the images to argue that Israel is creating an apartheid-type separation between peoples. Israel has repeatedly publicly denied these allegations, making it clear that the terrorism prevention security fence is just that: a protective, defensive, terrorism prevention fence and not a border. Israel has repeatedly clarified that upon the completion of final status negotiations with the Palestinian Authority, in accordance with the Roadmap, Israel will relocate the security fence to be on or within the agreed upon borders between the State of Israel and the State of (Arab) Palestine.

Israel's willingness to relocate a security fence if and when a final settlement is reached is evident by its history of following through on its commitments, *i.e.*, the agreement to withdraw from Sinai in 1975, the relocation of a security fence as part of the peace treaty with Jordan in 1994, the relocation of a terrorism prevention fence and withdrawal of Israeli troops from Lebanon and the extension of a comprehensive peace offer to the Palestinian Authority at Camp David in August 2000. The security fence's sole purpose is to prevent further bloodshed of Israeli citizens and others visiting or doing business in Israel. If a final settlement is reached, and if the PA properly exercises its policing obligations and functions, and if Israel will have no further need to defend itself from those residing in the West Bank, the purpose of the security fence will presumably no longer exist. Whether those conditions will be met, however, remains to be seen.

The Meaning of the "Green Line"

The route of the terrorism prevention security fence has been routinely criticized over the fact that it was constructed, in certain areas, east of the Green Line, treated as a demarcation line. This criticism, however, disregards the historical significance of the Green Line and its lack of legal standing in determining territorial boundaries. Israeli Minister of Internal Security, Uzi Landau framed the relevance of the Green Line to territorial boundaries as follows:

> We are sometimes asked: Can't you build the fence on the Green Line? Why should you go into Palestinian areas? My answer is that we are building it in our own areas. Judea and Samaria is ours. That is our homeland. The Palestinians don't like it. They say it's theirs. Fine, let's sit and negotiate. There is a dispute over this? What do people throughout the world do? They sit and negotiate.[214]

The Israeli Government understands that the Green Line has no official boundary status. The Armistice Agreement that established the Green Line's location explicitly stated that "it is not to be construed in any sense as a political or territorial boundary and is delineated without prejudice to rights, claims and positions of either Party to the Armistice as regards ultimate settlement of the Palestine question."[215]

The sole importance of the Green Line is that it marks the area under Israeli Military Administration. Viewing the Green Line as a presumptive border between Israel and a Palestinian state neglects all existing agreements and attempts to prejudice the outcome of future negotiations. Israel continues to reiterate that the Green Line has no official status. Any accusations that Israel is annexing that land are unfounded.

The Green Line arose from the 1949 Armistice Agreement between Israel and Jordan that, in its pursuit to end hostilities between the two countries, established the "Armistice Demarcation Line" ("Green Line"), now known as the Green Line. Following the 1947 Partition Plan, Israel's Declaration of Independence in 1948 and the ensuing Israeli War of Independence, the Armistice Agreement between Israel and Jordan made clear that "the Armistice Demarcation Lines [or Green Line] defined in articles V and VI of this Agreement are agreed upon by the Parties without prejudice to future territorial settlements or boundary lines or to claims of either Party relating thereto."[216] Territory west of the Armistice Demarcation Line was sovereign Israeli territory while the land to its east was Jordanian.

Israel's decisive victories at the end of the 1967 Six Day War resulted in Israeli control of the West Bank, territory east of the Green Line that was formerly Jordanian. The UN General Assembly, however, refrained from calling the captured land east of the Green Line as "occupied Jordanian [or occupied Egyptian] territory" because most states, including Arab states, "had not recognized the West Bank as Jordanian territory [and Egypt had not even claimed sovereignty over the Gaza Strip]."[217] The fact that Jordan previously had physical control over the West Bank was insufficient to consider the territory "occupied Jordanian territory." Yet, today the area has become referred to as occupied Palestinia territory.

As a result of its peace agreement, Jordan and Israel have officially accepted borders – borders that, because of the Green Line's lack of legal validity, were not binding as permanent boundaries. As international law professor Robbie Sabel notes:

> In accordance with international law, international boundaries survive the demise of the treaties that established them. This, however, is not true of ... armistice demarcation lines. The temporary nature of ... armistice line[s] is such that their validity expires with the expiration of the ... armistice. Therefore, formally, there is no longer any legal validity to the [Armistice Demarcation Lines]."[218]

The location of the Armistice Demarcation Line, or Green Line, was logically drawn to reflect the best way to end hostilities. Still today, although not officially or legally recognized borders, the Green Line separates sovereign Israeli territory from her neighbors in areas in which there is no formal agreement. This line, however, does not carry with it any legal or binding political boundary implications.

Critics of Israel's placement of the Security Fence, when questioning why the fence is not on the Green Line, conveniently forget the history and purpose of the Green Line. They impose an importance and significance to it that just does not exist. However, the inaccurate but repeated use of the Green Line as an indication of a boundary has potential lasting affects, presumably contributing to the ICJ's characterization of the land east of the Green Line as "occupied Palestinian territory." Considering that prior to 1976, the UN refused to call the Israeli captured land east of the Green Line, "occupied Jordanian territory," even when it was previously physically occupied by Jordan, it is grossly inconsistent to today call land east of the Green Line, "occupied Palestinian territory," since at no point in time has there been a Palestinian state with clear and recognized borders, an essential requirement in international law for statehood.

In its *Beit Sourik* decision, the Israeli High Court rejected claims that the fence should have been built on the Green Line precisely because it would mean that political considerations would dictate the route of the fence rather than security considerations. "It is the security perspective—and not the political one—which must examine the route on its security merits alone, without regard for the location of the Green Line."[219] The Council for Peace and Security, a nonpartisan Israeli non-profit organization comprised of experts on security, stressed to the court that the route of the fence should be based on security concerns.[220] Critics who wrongly accuse Israel of having annexed the land within the terrorism prevention security fence should refresh themselves on the history of the Green Line and pay closer attention to Israel's stated purposes for the fence.

Historical Origins of the Terrorism Prevention Security Fence and the Debate Surrounding its Construction

The wave of violence during the Second Intifada was what ultimately fueled the momentum that led to the construction of the terrorism prevention security fence, although the initial idea of geographically separating Israelis and Palestinians pre-dates the State of Israel and has transcended party lines.[221] In 1917, the British government issued the Balfour Declaration calling for a renewed national homeland for the Jewish people in Palestine. In 1937, the British government's Peel Commission Report on Palestine recommended partition of Palestine. In 1947, as the British Mandatory period ended, the UN partition resolution called for the establishment of an Arab state and a Jewish state in the geographic areas which were historically ancient Jewish lands known as Judea and Samaria, parts of which became known as Palestine. During its quest for statehood, Jewish groups created the Palestine National Fund to build the Jewish state, raising monies for tree planting, infrastructure and defense. Some wonder why those who declared the creation of the independent state of Israel didn't call it Palestine. Instead, calling the new Jewish state "The State of Israel" left the opportunity for the Arab state to become whatever name they would select, today being known as "The State of Palestine." This distinction is more than that represented by a name as it has allowed the Palestinians to point to the geographical area called Palestine, including the ancient Jewish lands of Judea and Samaria, and to claim that the entire area is all Palestinian. The belief that all Israel must be removed and the land of all Palestine restored to the Palestinian people totally discounts history, ancestry, geography and the UN Partition Resolution. Moreover, Palestinian textbooks, teachings, logos, songs, tv programs and speeches by leaders often portray a map without any reference to Israel. Based upon this revisionist philosophy, Palestinian terrorists often believe they are acting to liberate their national homeland in all of Palestine, not in a partitioned Palestine, and accordingly feel justified in crossing into Israel to commit their "justified" terrorist attacks. As more generations have been taught to believe this revisionist history, the need for the security fence has become more pronounced.

The late Yitzhak Rabin has been called "the intellectual father of the current fence."[222] Prior to his election as Prime Minister in 1992, he stated that "Israel must 'take Gaza out of Tel Aviv'—that is, create two distinct entities, so the two populations could avoid what he called 'chikuch' (friction)."[223] The notion of a physical separation played a significant part in his decision to sign the Oslo Accords more than a year later, because his "imagining [of] a physical, complementary mechanism for peace" appeased his skepticism over the truthfulness of Yasser Arafat's promises.[224] In October of 1994, after a series of violent attacks against Israeli civilians, Rabin stated that "we have to decide on separation as a philosophy. There has to be a clear border. Without a border demarcating the lines, whoever wants to swallow 1.8 million Arabs will just bring greater support for Hamas."[225] Thus, in early 1995, Prime Minister Rabin established the Shahal Commission. The committee, headed by police minister Moshe Shahal, was charged with exploring the possibility of constructing a security barrier to separate Israelis and Palestinians and making susequent recommendations.

The concept of constructing the security fence around Gaza coincided with Israel's handover of control under the Oslo Accords. However, as to the possibility of building a separate security barrier between Israel and the West Bank, not only was the idea long rejected, but the "idea of disengagement soon receded . . . and the recommendations of the Shahal Commission died along with Rabin in November 1995."[226] Rabin's successor, Shimon Peres, who later not only served as Prime Minister, but as Foreign Minister and subsequently as Israel's President said that he "feared that it would impede Israeli-Palestinian economic integration, which he viewed as the key to peace."[227] After Benjamin Netanyahu was first elected Prime Minister in 1998, he declined to implement the Commission's recommendations because of "opposition inside his own Likud Party, mostly settlers."[228]

When Ehud Barak was elected Prime Minister in 1999, the Israeli public had already taken to believing that the Palestinians would not abide by their security commitments under the Oslo Accords. Prime Minister Barak vowed "to build 'a physical separation between the two sides" before "the Camp David summit in the summer of 2000."[229] Barak announced that, in addition to being good for Israel, a physical barrier would be "essential to the Palestinian nation in order to foster its national identity and independence, without being dependent on the State of Israel."[230] The border lines that Prime Minster Barak offered at Camp David played a large role in determining the lines utilized at the time the route of the security fence was ultimately constructed and is believed to bear a strikingly similarity in location.

Elected Prime Minister in February of 2001 after the start of the Second Intifada, Ariel Sharon initially opposed the construction of a barrier. He believed "that a fence would create a de facto Palestinian state in the West Bank and would mean abandoning those settlements that ended up on the wrong side."[231] Failure of the Camp David Summit in August 2000 and the subsequent eruption of violence during the Second Intifada beginning in late September 2000 began to persuade the Israeli public that construction of a terrorism prevention security fence was necessary. As Israel suffered suicide attack after suicide attack, public opinion forced Sharon to change his views. The number of terror acts increased: in March 2002, 139 people were murdered in one month.[232] According to Tel Aviv University's Steinmetz Center, by October of 2003, support for the separation barrier among Israeli Jews had grown to 83 percent.[233] The Israeli public,

> Pressed the government to build a barrier between Israelis and Palestinians, and although the government didn't want to do it, out of concern that any line on the ground would have a political mean-

ing in future negotiations, it was forced by public opinion to build the fence.[234]

Additionally, Prime Minister Sharon felt pressure from the heads of the security services, who insisted that without the fence, the Israeli military and security forces would be "unable to provide Israelis with adequate protection from Palestinian terror attacks."[235] In response to public and internal pressure, the Israeli government ordered the Israeli military to "find a route for the fence between Israel and the West Bank that would stop the terror but would not be a political border."[236] It is important to note that, in all the governmental decisions:

> It was emphasized that the line the army was building was only a security line and it would not be the line for future negotiations. The line of the fence is not going to set the borders of Israel. We understand that at the end of the day the only line will be the one agreed upon by the two sides.[237]

Construction of the Security Fence

On April 14, 2002, in an effort to improve "the framework of fighting terror," the Ministers' Committee on National Security tasked the IDF and the police with "preventing the passage of Palestinians into the State of Israel."[238] The decision to construct a barrier in regions found to be "most vulnerable to the passage of terrorists into Israel" was a temporary solution, agreed upon only after all other options failed. Prior to the decision, the IDF had tried many other security measures. However, as cited in the *Beit Sourik* decision "Despite all these measures, the terror did not come to an end. The attacks did not cease. Innocent people paid with both life and limb. This is the background behind the decision to construct the separation fence."[239] In its initial phase, the fence was referred to as the "Seam Line."

On June 23, 2002, the Committee met to review Stage 1 of the "Seamline Area" Program. The goal of Stage 1 was to prevent terrorist "infiltration into the north of the country, the center of the country and the Jerusalem area."[240] In approving Stage 1, the High Court reiterated that:

> Approval of the security fences and obstacles in the "Seamline

Area" and in Greater Jerusalem [is] for the purpose of preventing
the penetration of terrorists from the area of Judea and Samaria
into Israel.... [and] the fence, like the other obstacles, is a security
measure. Its construction does not mark a national border or any
other border.[241]

The fence was to "begin in the area of the Salam village adjacent to
the Meggido junction and continue until the trans-Samaria road"
and it included a barrier in the Jerusalem area.[242]

In December, the Prime Minister and the Minister of Defense
approved stage 2 of the Seam Line, which would run from "Salam
village east to the Jordan River, 60 km [about 37 miles] long, and
an extension, a few kilometers long, from Mount Avner (adjacent
to El-Mouteelah village) in the Southern Gilboa range to the village of Tayseer."[243] It was not until September of 2003 that the Ministers' Committee on National Security decided to construct Stage
3 of the Seam Line security fence in the Greater Jerusalem area
(except in the Ma'aleh Adumim area.) In explaining its decision as
to Stage 3 and 4, the Committee again highlighted "the importance
of the "Seamline Area" ... emphasiz[ing] the security need for the
obstacle in the "Seamline Area" and in "Greater Jerusalem."[244] The
Committee, understanding the delicacy of the imposition as well
as the need for balance between Israeli security and Palestinian
interests, made sure to impose safeguards aimed to protect Palestinian interests:

- The obstacle that will be erected pursuant to this decision, like
  other segments of the obstacle in the "Seamline Area," is a security measure for the prevention of terror attacks and does not
  mark a national border or any other border.
- Local changes, either of the location of the obstacle or of its implementation, will be brought before the Minister of Defense and
  the Prime Minister for approval.
- The Prime Minister, the Minister of Defense, and the Finance
  Minister shall calculate the budget necessary for implementation of this decision as well as its financial schedule. The com-
  putation shall be brought before the government for approval.
- In this framework, additional immediate security steps for the
  defense of Israelis in Judea and Samaria during the period of
  construction of the obstacle in the "Seamline Area" shall be
  agreed upon.
- During the planning, every effort shall be made to minimize, to

> the extent possible, the disturbances to the daily lives of the Pal-
> estinians due to the construction of the obstacle.

The Committee's decision reflected an understanding and sensitiv-
ity of the delicacy of the project and the importance of balance, see-
ing as, "The location of this fence… stands at the heart of the dispute
between the parties.[245]

Danny Tirza, a retired army colonel in the Israel Defense Force
(IDF), was the main designer for the location route of the fence. The
need for balance and delicacy was imparted on him when given
the job. "The main thing the government told me," he said "was to
include as many Israelis inside the fence and leave as many Palestinians outside… The idea was to do it with balance."[246] The IDF was
responsible for designing the map of the fence and patrolling most
of it. The border police, however, patrolled Jerusalem. During the
design phase, the IDF did its best to accommodate the needs of the
Palestinians without sacrificing security. The Israeli military went
out into the West Bank with commanders and village leaders to discuss the route. Reflecting on the planning and designing phase, Col.
Tirza said:

> We tried to negotiate with people on the ground. Most of the time
> when the Palestinians asked for changes, we tried to accommodate
> them. But, we couldn't change the route just because they preferred
> that the fence cross their neighbor's land or if they wanted a change
> that was not secure….
>
> … We tried to balance security needs and the rights of people on
> the ground. It was not only where to put the fence, but when to
> [construct] it. [The Palestinians] would ask us to wait for the agri-
> cultural season to be over, and sometimes we would. We would ne-
> gotiate with people to move drainage pipes. We tried to minimize
> the damage to people on the ground.[247]

Simply put, one of the central goals during the security fence's
planning phase was to create a fence location that was the least restrictive as possible to the Palestinians without sacrificing security.
The IDF, working with the Israeli Civil Administration of Judea
and Samaria, consulted with regional Palestinian officials to ensure
that access to essential community locations like schools and religious institutions was not cut off.[248] The Israeli Civil Administration "would talk with the regional Palestinian Authority officials in

places where people wanted access to a school or access from one village to another. We had to know what was going on in the areas, beyond the maps."[249] For example, in Azariya, the Israeli military received a request to include more than a dozen Christian monasteries that sit outside the Jerusalem city limits on the Israeli side. All of the requests were accommodated.[250]

In 2004, the *Beit Sourik* case was brought to Israel's High Court contesting the legality of constructing the barrier and asserting that the barrier "illegally infringed on the rights of the Palestinian inhabitants."[251] Addressing the legality of construction, the court held that, under "the principles of the Israeli administrative law" and "provisions of public international law... established principally in" the Hague Conventions, the barrier was legal because its construction was solely for security purposes.[252] Addressing whether the barrier infringed on Palestinian rights, the court highlighted the need for balance, stating that an "occupied population must be in proportion to the security benefits."[253] The court ordered the IDF to reroute a 30 km portion of the existing and planned barrier.

The High Court ordered the IDF "to give greater weight to the daily life of the Palestinians," instructing them to balance security needs against the rights of the residents in the area so as to "minimize disruption of their lives."[254] At the time of the ruling, the military had already built 145 kilometers (about 90 miles) of the security fence. To implement the court order, the military changed the route of the fence in some places. In others, it altered "the procedures that enable people to cross from one side of the fence to the other."[255] For instance, to address the location of the route, the military "tried to build as far as possible from urban Palestinian centers . . . as the High Court said it's not just about proximity to the Palestinians but also how they feel in their houses."[256]

Additionally, the military implemented a procedural safeguard that gave Palestinian villagers more time to request changes in the route.[257] Another change in procedure that improved access for the Palestinians was the IDF's decision to "have fewer gates but have them continuously open from morning to evening so farmers and agricultural workers could come and go."[258]

As of August 2012 the Israeli Supreme Court ordered that the fence be rerouted six separate times, only two of which have yet to be completed.[259] On December 13, 2012, the Israeli High Court of Justice urged Israeli defense officials to reroute part of the West Bank security barrier planned for construction on farmland belonging to Battir village. According to the *Jerusalem Post*, the justices noted that only a 500 meter long section was under dispute in Battir, known for its terraced agricultural fields, some of which are believed to go back to biblical times.[260] The High Court said, "In light of the unique character of the region in question, it would be worthy for security officials to do some more thinking especially about what type of divider and security arrangements to employ in the problematic section." The article, attributed to Reuters, concluded "IDF Col. Ofer Hindi argued for the security benefits of the planned section by saying that two villagers were jailed in 2008 for planning to bomb the railway that runs by Battir." According to *Haaretz*, "Citing fear of armed Palestinian infiltrators who have struck inside Israel since 2000, the Defense Ministry plans to fortify a fence protecting the train line at Battir with a wall.[261] Quoting Col. Hindi, the article continued "The area is also an access point for Palestinians seeking to work illegally in Israel, and whom the military regards as security threats." The military continues to negotiate the route of the security fence and defers to the Israeli Supreme Court's judgment on the most appropriate route.[262]

In designing and constructing the security fence's route, Israel attempted to avoid creating enclaves wherever possible. An enclave "is an area closed on all sides where you need to cross using a checkpoint."[263] Col. Tirza recalled showing Prime Minister Sharon the map of the fence, and since they both "believed that neither Palestinians nor Israelis should live in enclaves," in 2005, "the map was changed so there would be no enclaves."[264] Since that time, because of Israeli Supreme Court orders and differing considerations, the map has undergone many changes and the fence has been rerouted.

Israel has also made great efforts to ensure Palestinian accessibility by building roads and passageways. In Qalqilya, the military removed the eastern checkpoint to open access to Nablus and constructed an underground passageway under the road to Alfei Menashe to provide access to villagers living south of Qalqilya.[265] The military also constructed a new road under Road #45 connecting Bir Naballah and Ramallah. Between Bir Naballah and the western villages, the IDF built a road with a tunnel without checkpoints close to one mile long.[266] More recently, the IDF "resum[ed] work on separate roads for Israelis and Palestinians between Jerusalem and the West Bank settlement of Ma'aleh Adumim."[267]

In 2011, a gate was opened in East Jerusalem's Shoafat neighborhood.[268] Tirza admits the new terminals are expensive but are beneficial to the people who have to cross them.[269] In Jerusalem, the terminal is still manned by military border police, but there are "hopes that will change in the coming years."[270] As of July 2012, 80 designated gates were opened to provide access through the barrier, all of which are manned by civilians who reportedly have provided good quality of service.[271] Taking together the massive road and gate construction Israel has developed, one can see the initial Israeli goal of fencing out the terrorists largely come to fruition. Seen differently, a UN update in 2011 pointed out:

> You get a picture of Israel erecting, at enormous expense, a major system of roads and checkpoints that would allow for the total separation of Palestinians and Israelis while also enabling the construction of Mevasseret Adumim, a neighborhood that would connect Ma'aleh Adumim to Jerusalem.[272]

The reasons for the security fence are obvious when considering the history of Route 443 which also demonstrates the level of difficulty the IDF faced in achieving a balance between security and Palestinian interests. Route 443 is the main highway that connects the Modi'in communities and the Tel Aviv area to Jerusalem and the West Bank settlements. It also serves as a secondary highway to the highway between Tel Aviv and Jerusalem, which is often crowded. Beginning in October 2000 and due to an increasing number of terror attacks Palestinians were limited in access to Route 443.[273] In 2002, following the sixth fatality on or near Route 443 in two years, a ban was unofficially declared that limited Palestinian access to a relatively small number who obtained permits.[274]

Brig.-Gen. Noam Tivon, the commander of the Judea and Samaria Division of the IDF, underscored how increasingly difficult it had become to protect Israelis on Route 443. It was a major security concern, "not only because Israelis driving on it could easily be the target of drive-by shootings, ambushes, rocks and firebombs but because it included many side roads leading directly into Israel."[275] The decision to ban Palestinian access was not done lightly, only once "the entire length of Highway 443 has been the target of many such attacks," did the IDF decide that "only by isolating the road can we protect Israel from suicide attacks or booby-trapped vehicles."[276]

In the midst of dealing with ongoing terror attacks, the IDF has and continues to make efforts to balance security with Palestinian interests. Col. Tirza noted how important it was to not create enclaves when he said "we ha[ve] to consider the 47,000 Palestinians living west of the road, and we will have to find ways to defend this road without creating enclaves."[277] In 2007 and 2008, to accommodate the needs of the Palestinians without Route 443 access, the IDF built three separate roads, which are referred to as "fabric of life" roads. The roads provided villages south of Route 443 free access to Ramallah and Israel constructed "a new road to Ramallah and an underground road to the north. These people should not live in enclaves."[278] In March 2008, the Israeli High Court issued a decision "call[ing] on the army to give a progress report . . . on its efforts to build separate roads and take other steps for the Palestinians to compensate them for being barred from Highway 443."[279]

In December 2009, in response to a petition by Palestinian residents, the Israeli High Court of Justice ruled that the IDF must open the road to Palestinians. In light of the ruling, the IDF increased security measures on Route 443 through checkpoints and roadblocks.[280] The ruling, however, did not give specifics on how to implement the order. Because of the difficulty in implementing the order and the safety concerns involved, route 443 has yet to be opened to Palestinians. In August 2010, in preparation for allowing Palestinian access, the IDF banned Israelis from entering certain Palestinian villages and roads near route 443.

Prime Minister Netanyahu may in the future reassess the security fence's location vis-à-vis Road 443 and take a position different from previous governments' views. It is believed that "Netanyahu thinks the right thing to do is to put the fence north of Road 443 and make the area south of the road be on the Israeli side of the fence (within the Seam Zone)."[281] Netanyahu originally described these plans while leader of the Opposition and during his January 22, 2005 speech at The Herzliya Conference, Israel's premier public policy and national security conference.[282]

Recent years have seen a major slowdown in IDF construction. According to the state comptroller at the time, almost all work related to the fence had been halted from 2007 to 2009.[283] As of March 2009, there still remained "four huge gaps in the fence in addition to dozens of small ones alongside passageways lacking security measures."[284] Facing strong opposition from the United States, Israel stopped work "on the fingers"—enclaves east of the Green Line that are to have included large settlement blocs such as Ariel, Kedumim, Karnei Shomron and Ma'aleh Adumim. The military, prior to its halt in construction, had closed up many of the "holes" that would have been openings to these "fingers;" however, large gaps still remained, in particular in the southern outskirts of Jerusalem, in the Etzion bloc and in the Judean Desert.[285] "Between Gilo in south Jerusalem and Gush Etzion, "tens of kilometers of barrier" were suspended pending decisions on petitions before the Israeli High Court.[286] By August 2009, Israel had spent about NIS 9.5 billion, or nearly 7.75 billion dollars[287] on its security fence, but only around 300 miles of the planned 500-mile fence were completed.[288]

From March 2009 to July 2012, only one of the four large gaps had been finished, leaving "three large gaps along the Green Line, and the majority of the big blocs—Gush Etzion, Ma'aleh Adumim and Ariel-Kedumim—are outside the barrier that has been built."[289] The consequences of these delays are far reaching, according to sources as, interestingly, "access to Jerusalem from the direction of Bethlehem is relatively easy—for commuters and terrorists both."[290]

The level of security in the Golan Heights on the Syrian border was not a cause for significant concern until the recent upheaval in Syria which has already taken more than 60,000 lives. In September

2012, following a period of turmoil in Syria, the IDF launched an "unprecedented operation" to ensure that the barrier on the border built 40 years prior remains impenetrable. This "facelift" will include "setting up a new fence, deploying an advanced alert system to replace the old one and significantly improve the Combat Intelligence Collection Corps' observations layout."[291] The upgrade is predicted to cost Israel close to NIS six million per kilometer.[292]

The Netanyahu government has not set a target date for completing the fence. Defense Ministry spokesman Shlomo Dror has "blamed both the High Court and budget problems for the delays in completing the fence in the areas of Ma'aleh Adumim, Gush Etzion, the Ariel and Kedumim fingers, as well as the South Hebron Hills."[293] According to Tirza in 2009, there were three primary reasons for the stall in construction: fence budget cuts resulting from military recovery efforts following the Second Lebanon War in 2006, the disputed political nature of the gap areas and fence-related decisions still pending before the Israeli High Court.[294] In Tirza's opinion, the most urgent gap in the fence to be constructed is near Gush Etzion, where the military has been working slowly on problems on the ground and legal cases are pending.[295]

Col. (ret.) Shaul Arieli, a senior member of the Council for Peace and Security, has argued that the fence project suffers from a lack of public interest.[296] In 2009, Arieli told *Haaretz* "exorbitant sums of money have been pumped into infrastructure and fences that were supposed to follow a route that was impossible to complete."[297] He believes "the desire to include more territory within the confines of the fence than is practically possible has resulted in a situation where the settlement blocs are left outside of the fence while other blocs remain vulnerable and do not receive protection."[298] He warns that if building is not resumed to close the gaps in Israel's security fence, "Israel is soon liable to find itself in another wave of Palestinian terrorism and violence."[299]

Israel's terrorism prevention security fence, which has materially reduced entry into Israel by Palestinian terrorists, is not a closed loop and entry is possible for those determined to achieve access. Detection methods, however, have increased and enhanced surveillance, intelligence and quality police work has assisted Israel in largely stopping the dangers to its population from terrorist infiltrators. Fear, however, continues to exist that a future flare-up between Israel and the PA in the West Bank will bring a renewal of increased acts of terrorism inside Israel and the areas populated by Israel in the towns and villages that make up settlements and outposts constructed since 1967.

The majority of the ongoing construction involves rerouting pursuant to High Court of Justice decisions. Rerouting took place in June 2011 in Bil'in and is also currently underway around the Tulkarm community of Khirbet Jubara.[300] In Bil'in where there once stood a high voltage fence where the "IDF had in the past fired tear gas and rubber bullets at rioters," there now stands a concrete wall along a different route.[301] Although it took the IDF two years to provide the court with an acceptable route, the one finally approved will cost Israel NIS 30 million. The route redesign came as a relief to Palestinians in Bil'in who have held Friday protests since the Bil'in fence was constructed in 2005. IDF Brigade commander Col. Sa'ar Tzur, when asked about whether the Bil'in protests will continue, answered yes. Without giving additional details, he asserted that the protests will continue despite the fact that "for a long time this has not been a political or diplomatic issue," because the protesters "'get money from foreign funders... teenagers were being paid to participate in the demonstrations."[302] Whether the protesters continue or not, the High Court's ruling to reroute the fence is the final word on where the barrier will be located.

When it is completed, the security fence will be "726 kilometers long [about 450 miles]" and will likely cost more than 12 billion shekels in total, with additional costs for operations and regular maintenance. By July 2011, 61.8 percent of the barrier had been completed, with 8.2 percent under construction and 30 percent planned but not yet constructed.[303] As of July 2012, 62.1 percent of the barrier was completed, 8 percent was under construction, and 29.9 percent was planned but not yet constructed.[304] By then, Israel had spent more than NIS 11 billion, with maintenance costing close to NIS 1 billion a year.[305]

The Terrorism Prevention Security Fence Saves and Protects Lives

Thus far, the terrorism prevention security fence has served its purpose. The number of suicide bombings and mass killing attacks within Israel has decreased significantly since the peak in 2002. Compared to the four in 2006 and the 55 in 2002, there were only two suicide bombings from 2007 to 2008; one in Eilat in 2007 and another carried out in 2008 in Dimona.[306] What is more, no suicide bombings originated from Judea and Samaria in 2007."[307] Maj. Gil Limon, legal adviser for Judea and Samaria and responsible for security affairs from 2002 to 2005, noted: "the purpose of the fence was to prevent unsupervised and illegal entry into Israel, and it has been very effective. Nothing else can stop suicide bombings."[308]

Fortunately there has been a "sharp decline in the number of terrorist attacks perpetrated in Israel since the construction of the security fence."[309] Although the fence is not yet complete, the number of attacks on Israel per month reportedly decreased from an average of 26 per year to just three in the year after the first segment of the fence was built, even though the number of attempted attacks remains high.[310]

Dan Gillerman, Israel's Ambassador to the UN, addressed the General Assembly on July 16' 2004 noted "there has been a dramatic reduction of over 90 percent in successful terrorist attacks which can be attributed directly to the security fence"[311] What is more, the human costs have diminished. For example, from August 2003 to September 2004, when the first portion of the fence between Salem and Elkana was completed, there was an 84 percent decrease in Israelis killed in terror attacks.[312]

Prior to the Samaria section of the security fence, which was constructed from April to December 2002, 17 suicide attacks were committed within Israel by terrorists who infiltrated from Samaria (northern West Bank). After the construction of the Samaria section, in 2003, there were only 5 attacks by terrorists infiltrating from Samaria. By contrast, in Judea—which has no security fence—from April to December 2002, there were 10 suicide attacks by terrorists infiltrating from Judea. This continued into 2003, which saw 11 attacks by suicide terrorists infiltrating from Judea.[313] Likewise in the unprotected city of Beer Sheva in August 2004, 16 Israelis were killed and more than 100 were wounded in twin suicide bombings. These bombings served as a "grim reminder" of the important purpose of the security fence.[314] As one study by Hillel Frisch reported, "The victims of the [Beer Sheva] attacks had the misfortune to be living in a part of the country that is not yet protected by this life-saving barrier."[315]

From the outset, Israel's goal has been to reduce Palestinian violence against the Israeli population. The terrorism prevention security fence, as demonstrated above, has been a primary factor in helping to achieve this goal. Measuring the success of the security fence should also take into consideration the possible alternatives that could have been implemented to achieve Israel's goal of reducing Palestinian violence. The fence, as a defensive measure, should be compared to the offensive measures Israel could have implemented to reduce the violence such as "targeted killings, penetration into "enemy territory" on search and surprise missions, and... massive onslaughts and temporary conquest of areas in which terrorist infrastructure has taken root."[316] In light of the consequences that would have resulted from these alternative measures, the inconveniences inflicted by the fence's construction and location appear slight.

Hillel Frisch, an expert on Palestinian and Islamic politics, institutions and military strategies, has examined the effectiveness of the security fence as a defensive measure versus the offensive alternatives in achieving Israel's goal of reduced violence.[317]

Frisch used three tests to measure the fence's effectiveness. The first test compared the number of wounded and fatalities from June 2002 to August 2003—when Israel launched two large offensives before completion of the fence—with the number of wounded and fatalities as against a similar period after the fence was completed. Using the stretch between Salem (north) to Elkana (south), Frisch found that casualties reduced from 274 deaths during the Israeli offensive period to 107 right before fence completion, a 61.5 percent reduction.[318] In the alternative two periods after the obstacle was

built, the casualty number declined from 107 to 42, a 60.1 percent reduction. The reduction of wounded between the compared periods
was a 57 percent reduction compared to a 76.4 percent reduction
with the barrier.[319] Analyzing the first test's results, Frisch concluded
that the "continuous decline of fatalities and wounded in all four
periods suggests the importance of both measures, yet since the
decline in the latter two periods cannot be attributed totally to the
fence, it would suggest the primacy of offensive moves."[320]

Frisch's second, "more rigorous" test compared casualties
within the Green Line before and after fence completion with casualties in Judea and Samaria during the same period. If casualty
reduction in Israel proper is greater, then the fence as a defensive
measure is vindicated as an effective defensive measure.[321] Frisch
found that the casualty reduction was, in fact, higher in the West
Bank, there was a 61.5 percent decline in deaths and a 67.1 percent
decline in wounded, than in Israel proper, which had 67.1 percent
and 56.2 percent respectively.[322] While this suggests that "offensive
measures were indeed [more] effective [than defensive measures]
in reducing terrorism," the increase in West Bank casualties after
the fence completion, versus the continuous reduction of casualties
within Israel proper, suggests that the terrorists sought the path of
least resistance when deciding where to strike.[323]

This substitution theory, that terrorists will strike in areas that
are easier to reach, was confirmed with the findings of the third
test, which compared casualties within the Green Line parallel to
the fence to the areas where the fence had yet to be built. Fatalities
declined by more than half in areas with the fence and doubled in
areas where the fence had yet to be constructed. Clearly the fence
was an "impediment the terrorist organizations wanted to avoid."[324]

Frisch's findings suggest that while past offensive measures
have had greater results, the study also shows the importance of the
fence as a "supplemental measure in achieving greater security."[325]
Again, the findings show that the fence is an "impediment the terrorist organizations wanted to avoid."[326] The findings also demonstrate that the substitution theory applies to the means of violence
as well. With the fence construction, penetration became more diffi-

cult and, according to Frisch, "Palestinian ballistic and mortar activity," being "poor substitutes compared to other means of violence the Palestinians have pursued at least when measured by fatalities," indeed have "increased significantly."[327] A meaningful point that must be taken from the study is that terrorists will continue to try and "circumvent the fence,"[328] and when the fence is fully constructed, there will no longer be a path of least resistance available. One can speculate that when this happens, the casualty numbers overall from before completion to after completion will reflect the full effectiveness of the fence as an appropriate and necessary defensive measure.

Despite the propaganda disseminated by Palestinians and anti-Israel organizations, Israel's terrorism prevention security fence has sharply decreased the number of suicide bombings and terrorist attacks that are attempted and completed within Israel. Even the Palestinian terrorists themselves have acknowledged the security fence's effectiveness. In a March 2008 interview with Qatari newspaper *Al-Sharq*, Palestinian Islamic Jihad leader Ramadan Abdallah Shalah admitted that during the second intifada, the change in form of terrorist tactics, from suicide bombing to rocket attacks, was attributable to the existence of the terrorism prevention security fence. He acknowledged that Israel had found ways to protect itself against suicide bombings.

> "For example, they built a separation fence in the West Bank," "We do not deny that it limits the ability of the resistance [i.e., the terrorist organizations] to arrive deep within [Israeli territory] to carry out suicide bombing attacks, but the resistance has not surrendered or become helpless, and is looking for other ways to cope with the requirements of every stage [of the intifada] . . .[329]

This was not the first time Ramadan Abdallah Shalah admitted to the fence's effectiveness. On Hezbollah's "Al-Manar" television in November 2006, Shalah also acknowledged that although Palestinian terrorists did not intend to abandon suicide bombings, "the separation fence ... is an obstacle to the resistance and if it were not there, the situation would be entirely different."[330] Additionally, the deputy chairman of Hamas' political bureau in Damascus, Mousa Abu Marzouq, was asked while in Egypt in 2007 why the number of suicide bombings had decreased since the Hamas government came to power. He said "[carrying out] such attacks are made difficult by the security fence and the gates surrounding West Bank residents."[331]

While the security fence has proven effective in decreasing the number of suicide bombings within Israel, terrorist mass killing strikes and other attempted terror attacks against Israelis continue. In 2008, there was an increase in the number of mass-killing attacks, including the suicide bombing in Dimona, the shooting attack at Mercaz Ha'Rav Yeshiva in Jerusalem and attacks at border crossings, settlements, and military targets near the security fence on the West Bank and in Gaza.[332] In late 2008, the IDF noted a considerable increase in attempts to place explosive devices on the Gaza Strip security fence.[333] Rocket attacks and mortar shellfire from Gaza also increased and has continued to bombard Israel in large numbers, as evidenced by the November 2012 Operation Pillar of Defense response by Israel to the more than 1500 rockets launched from Gaza into Israel. These methods of attack have become the Palestinian terrorist organizations favored method.[334] In November 2012, the first bus bombing in a number of years occurred in Tel Aviv, injuring more than 30 people, perpetrated by a terrorist attacker in response to Israel's air strikes in Gaza in Israel's attempt to stop the launching of rockets from Gaza.

Hillel Frisch noted in his study discussed earlier that:

> The IDF, on the military strategic level, would be well advised to regard the fence as a supplementary measure only in achieving security whose value in the long run will continuously depreciate in the face of Palestinian attempts to circumvent it by other means.[335]

Hopefully, however, this depreciation in effectiveness will only continue until the planned route of the barrier has been fully constructed. The decrease in the number of suicide bombings indicates that the security fence has been effective in preventing certain types of attacks. Nonetheless, the high level of attacks and attempted attacks in general indicate that the need for preventative security measures, including the security fence, has not diminished since Palestinian terrorists bent on the destruction of Israel continue to utilize new methods to attack Israelis, Americans and anyone who visit Israel or reside in the towns and villages that comprise the settlements.

The terrorism prevention security fence has been an effective method of containing violence against Arabs and Israelis alike. As a legitimate security measure, the fence will continue to help end terror and restore calm—steps necessary for renewing the peace process.

The security fence is also effective because it reduces the amount of offensive counter-terrorism measures Israel is currently forced to use to protect its citizens; measures such as military re-occupation of areas handed over to the PA during or pursuant to and since the Oslo Accords or the imposition of curfews, checkpoints and roadblocks that impede the free movement of Palestinian civilians.

In public statements, the Israeli government and the Palestinian Authority each proclaim their willingness to pursue peace. This goal will only be achieved when terrorist acts stop, democracy building continues and the political process and direct negotiations between the State of Israel and the Palestinian Authority resume. Until that time, Israel has no choice but to exercise its right to protect itself in meeting its obligation to protect its people.

The Israel-Jordan Security Fence has Helped the Countries be Good Neighbors and has Helped Israel Fulfill Her Obligation of Protecting Her Citizens

Security fences have proven effective in preventing some, but not all, types of terrorist attacks. Following the 1994 Jordan-Israeli peace treaty, Israel's border with Jordan is one example of a fence that has proven its effectiveness in furthering peaceful border state relations. The Gaza security fence has also been widely effective in preventing suicide bombers from infiltrating into Israel. This success is a major reason for Gaza militants' shift in their means of attack toward mortars and rockets. Indeed, since the Gaza fence was rebuilt in 2001, Israel has suffered a barrage of more than 10,000 mortar and rocket launches.

Security fences are not fail proof and do not protect against all forms of attack against civilians. This fact, however, does not in any way diminish the legitimacy of constructing a security fence to help prevent forms of lethal attack against a State's citizens. Nation-states have the right and obligation to take affirmative steps to protect their citizens from attack by infiltrating terrorists, a danger that Israel rarely experiences on its border with Jordan, established pursuant to its permanent peace agreement.

Israel's experience with Jordan is a prime example of how, in some circumstances, fences can make good neighbors. Israel's border with Jordan has been Israel's most peaceful border. Much, but not all, of the 148-mile border between Israel and Jordan is fenced "with a double fence with a patrol road between the fences."[336] Areas around the shore of the Dead Sea are not fenced. The border fence "runs in some parts along the actual border, but in most sections, it fences in farmland that belongs to Israel."[337] A good fence not only prevents violence, it also has the ability to improve relationships. For instance, in March 2004, Israel and Jordan took part in a joint project that took down a section of the fence between the Dead Sea and the Red Sea to build a joint desert scientific research center called the "Bridging the Rift" center. The Israeli-Jordanian fence has been rerouted just as the West Bank terrorism prevention fence has been rerouted since its initial construction. As a result of the 1994 Jordan-Israeli peace treaty, Israel moved some areas and lines of its fences to comply with the terms of the treaty. Israel has repeatedly said it will follow this precedent of moving its security fence should the Israelis and Palestinians come to an agreement on border issues at some future date.

Israel first erected the Gaza security fence shortly after the implementation of the Oslo Accords. Palestinian militants destroyed much of the fence during the Second Intifada. From December 2000 to June 2001, Israel rebuilt the Gaza fence[338] and following Israel's disengagement from Gaza in the summer of 2005, the Gaza security fence took on increased security significance.

While the Gaza fence has not stopped mortar or rocket fire into Israel, like other effective security fences it has decreased the number of suicide bombings and other attacks within Israel. The Gaza fence has proven to be an effective means of self-defense despite its inability to prevent all attacks. Likewise, while the West Bank terrorism prevention security fence will not stop all attacks against Israel, its lack of total prevention does not diminish the fact that the security fence is a most important and proven Israeli self-defense measure. So long as Israel continues to be attacked by its neighbors—whether it is by state actors or terrorists— Israel has an affirmative duty under the UN Charter to enact measures to protect its inhabitants.

Terrorism Must Not Be Allowed To Succeed

Palestinian terrorist organizations pursue goals incompatible with both the UN Charter and the Roadmap's vision of the establishment of a universally recognized and fully democratic Palestinian State. Radical Islamic Palestinian terrorist groups and radical Islamic terrorists worldwide are strengthened wherever and whenever terrorism is viewed as a successful tool and tactic to achieve political means and goals. People who are genuinely committed to freedom for Palestinians to live in a peaceful and independent state also should wish for freedom for Israelis to live free from violence and terror. Freedom, as a universal value, means that Palestinian terrorism cannot be allowed to succeed. The terrorism prevention security fence represents a non-violent and effective defensive measure that hinders terrorists in pursuit of their violent and hateful objectives. Such an outcome is good for Israelis and good for Palestinians: in a world of escalating global terrorism, it is good for the world.

CHAPTER FOUR

The Impact of the Security Fence on the Lives of Palestinians and Israelis

There is no question that the security fence provides an important defense against terrorist attacks. At the same time, however, it is also undeniable that it impacts the lives of Palestinians living on the West Bank and Israeli citizens alike.

Israel recognizes that the fence has caused many Palestinians and some Israelis certain hardships and inconvenience. Israel's High Court has ruled on several occasions to reroute the fence in order to diminish the fence's negative impact. The Israeli government, even as it insists that the fence must be erected and maintained to combat terrorism, acknowledges that Israel must be "sensitive to the hardship faced by those Palestinians whose everyday life is impacted by the construction of the fence, and [the Israeli government] is working to find practical solutions to the problems arising in the field."[339] Their stated aim is to:

> Balance the imperative to protect innocent lives from terror with the humanitarian needs of the local Palestinian population. Israel's government realizes that the construction of the Security Fence can introduce hardship into the lives of innocent Palestinians and regrets those hardships. All attempts to minimize such problems have been and will continue to be made.[340]

The Fence's Impact on Palestinians Living on the West Bank

1. Restrictions on Movement

The fence has impacted Palestinians by limiting movement

between Israel and the West Bank and, in certain areas, within the West Bank. In October 2003, the Israeli military ordered "the area between the first section of the barrier to be constructed and the Green Line a closed military area."[341] The order refers to this area as the "Seam Area," and mandates that "no person shall enter or stay in the seam area" and that "a person found in the seam area shall be obligated to leave it immediately."[342] This restriction does not apply to Israeli citizens, either Jewish or Arab. Since the order was issued, Palestinian residents of the West Bank have "been subject to a permit system in order to reach their land west of the barrier."[343] The Israeli human rights organization, B'Tselem, has stated that "the permits system has resulted in hundreds of Palestinians being prohibited from enjoying the benefits of their private property or from their right to work and support their families."[344] They report that "Palestinian travel in the West Bank is now an exception, which must be justified to the Israeli authorities, and almost every trip entails uncertainty, friction with soldiers, much waiting, and often great expense."[345]

In B'Tselem's view, "the geographic division of the West Bank has far-reaching implications on every aspect of Palestinian life."[346] The security fence and the permit system have "greatly reduced movement between East Jerusalem and the rest of the West Bank."[347] In sections near Jerusalem, "the barrier runs inside the municipal border and separates a few densely populated Palestinian neighborhoods—the Shu'afat refugee camp, new 'Anata, Kafr 'Aqab, andal-Walajah—with their 55,000 residents, from the rest of the city." [348] Consequently, B'Tselem notes that "the residents of these neighborhoods have difficulty gaining access to services, schools, workplaces, and other places in Jerusalem, although under Israeli law they are entitled to access."[349]

Israel has acknowledged that the fence makes daily life difficult for local Palestinians in certain areas. They have, however, "[tried] to find solutions to alleviate these hardships."[350] The government reiterates that:

> If one considers the difficulties of daily routine, as compared to the real and immediate threat faced by Israeli citizens from suicide bombers, it cannot be clearly stated that the Palestinians' right to

freedom of movement must take precedence over the right of Israelis to live, or the duty of the Israeli government to protect them
from becoming the next victims of Palestinian terrorism.[351]

Israel has set priorities and "saving lives must come first."[352]

Israel argues that the security fence's gates allow for freedom
of movement and access for law-abiding residents and cites the approximately 40 agricultural gates and school passages that have
been constructed to ease access for farmers to their fields and passage of students to their schools.[353] Moreover, Israel has rerouted the
fence multiple times to improve Palestinian movement. In the area
of Rachel's Tomb (near Bethlehem), the route was changed to reduce
the number of Palestinian homes included in the area west of the
fence. An underground passage between the village of Habla and
the city of Qalqilya (in Samaria) was constructed to ease movement
between the two areas. Additional adjustments in the fence route
are anticipated[354] and once completed the security fence should
eliminate the necessity for most Israeli checkpoints and other internal hindrances on transportation in the populated Palestinian areas.
When Israel controls entrance to its population centers the "Israel
Defense Forces (IDF) will have less need or incentive to monitor traf-
fic within the populated Palestinian areas."[355]

2. Land and Property

Running roughly along the Green Line, the security fence de-
viates in many parts and necessarily cuts through both public and
private property. An "order of seizure" is issued by the Commander
of the IDF when private land must be used for the fence's construction.[356] The Israeli High Court has "found no defect in the process
of issuing the orders of seizure... or in the process of granting the
opportunity to appeal them."[357] Explaining the order of seizure process and the protections within, the Court said:

> Pursuant to standard procedure, every land owner whose land
> is seized will receive compensation for the use of his land. After
> the order of seizure is signed, it is brought to the attention of the
> public, and the proper liaison body of the Palestinian Authority is
> contacted. An announcement is relayed to the residents, and each
> interested party is invited to participate in a survey of the area af-
> fected by the order of seizure, in order to present the planned

location of the fence. A few days after the order is issued, a survey is taken of the area, with the participation of the landowners, in order to point out the land which is about to be seized. After the survey, a one week leave is granted to the landowners, so that they may submit an appeal to the military commander. The substance of the appeals is examined. Where it is possible, an attempt is made to reach understandings with the landowners. If the appeal is denied, leave of one additional week is given to the landowner, so that he may petition the High Court of Justice.[358]

The Court noted that when property is seized "the military commander must consider the needs of the local population" and if this precondition is met, then the order of seizure process satisfies all procedural due process rights.[359] Once the needs of the local population are considered, the Court says "there is no doubt that the military commander is authorized to take possession of land in areas under his control."[360]

B'Tselem, however, believes that the barrier's construction severely impinges on property rights because "it limits access to private property, and the construction itself entails the taking of tens of thousands of dunams of private land and the destruction of agricultural property, such as trees, greenhouses, and irrigation systems."[361] Additionally, B'Tselem notes that "in most cases, the barrier's route runs right alongside the... built-up area[s] of villages [situated between the barrier and the Green Line], and often surrounds the village on three sides, blocking any possibility of urban development and breaching the residents' planning rights."[362]

Palestinian farmers have complained that they do not have adequate access to their agricultural lands. B'Tselem takes the position that "Palestinians wanting to continue to farm their land must go to the District Coordinating Offices [DCO] and other offices, time after time, to obtain certification of land registration, to submit a request for permit, and to check on the status of the request."[363] B'Tselem notes that the permits are valid for only two weeks, which requires frequent renewals.[364] Further, B'Tselem claims "Palestinians who are denied access to their land, [different than landowners whose property is expropriated], are not entitled to any compensation for the resulting loss of income."[365]

Access to agricultural land is a legitimate concern and Israel has taken many steps to ensure that Palestinian property rights are protected when Palestinian land is procured during the fence's construction. Israel has responded to such property complaints:

> In building the fence, preference is given to using public land. When there is no other choice, the fence is built on private land. Even in these cases, every effort is made to avoid building on cultivated land. The private land is not expropriated from its owners, yet remains the property of the original owners, who are eligible to receive one-time compensation for its seizure, as well as annual payment for its use. To date, dozens of requests for compensation and payment have been received.[366]

Israel's Ministry of Defense has also attempted to answer criticisms:

> An attempt has been made to avoid separating landowners from their lands. In circumstances where such a separation is unavoidable, agricultural gates have been built, which allow the farmers to cross into their land. These gates are manned and operated by the IDF. The functionality of the gates is coordinated with the local population in each area. In the future with the issue of new smart cards, access to the lands through the agricultural gates will not require military presence.[367]

The High Court has also addressed the legality of procuring property. In the *Beit Sourik* case, Israel said, "the power to seize land for the obstacle is a consequence of the natural right of the State of Israel to defend herself against threats from outside her borders."[368] Israel's High Court agreed, concluding that:

> The infringement of property rights is insufficient, in and of itself, to take away the authority to build it. It is permitted, by the international law applicable to an area under belligerent occupation, to take possession of an individual's land in order to erect the separation fence upon it, on the condition that this is necessitated by military needs. To the extent that construction of the fence is a military necessity, it is permitted, therefore, by international law.[369]

The High Court also took up the issue of the legality of the route of the fence and Palestinian property. It stated that the fence's route must be proportionate and proportionality is tested on a case-by-case basis for each individual section of the fence. In *Beit Sourik*, for example, the Court found that the "relationship between the injury to the local inhabitants and the security benefit from the construction of the separation fence along the route, as determined by the military commander, is not proportionate."[370]

3. Health and Medical Services

Unfortunately, restrictions on movement have sometimes affected a Palestinian's ability to quickly receive medical care. In 2005, a trio of French, Israeli and Palestinian medical organizations issued a position paper on the fence's impact on Palestinian health and access to medical services:

> Patients from the West Bank and Jerusalem are facing increasing difficulties to access services in hospitals and primary health care centers. The prolonged waiting time at gates and checkpoints associated with the Wall has extended the delays for ambulances to reach the patients and then the hospital in case of emergency. 26 fixed primary health care clinics have been isolated by the Wall from the rest of the health care system. Half of the doctors working in these clinics are delayed in reaching their work place or denied access. For 200,000 Palestinians, regular access to hospitals, specialists, laboratory services and other secondary and tertiary health care has been disrupted.[371]

Another report, prepared in 2005 by the Health, Development, Information and Policy Institute in Ramallah also discussed the state of Palestinian healthcare in the period following completion of the fence's first phase:

> Rapid and effective emergency care is becoming increasingly inaccessible, particularly in the north western Jenin enclave 1 and south of Qalqiliya enclaves 6 and 9. [Neighborhoods] north and south of Qalqiliya lack health facilities and along the First Phase seven communities with 3,950 inhabitants have no access to health care facilities inside their [neighborhoods]. . . Access to preventive services is severely impeded, especially prenatal and post-natal care. In the absence of appropriate home deliveries and movement restrictions, the rate of delivery complications has increased. . . . Screening services are minimal in all isolated clinics, with the Tulkarem area being the worst affected. . . . Access to medication is becoming a significant problem in Jenin, south of Qalqiliya and villages around Jerusalem. . . . Access to specialty services is highly restricted.[372]

There have been numerous reports of Palestinian individuals who have had difficulties getting to needed medical services because of the fence and its related bureaucracy. For instance, in Azzun Atma, a village near Qalqiliya encircled by the security fence, pregnant Palestinian women "prefer to take up residence outside of the town in the later stages of their pregnancy for fear that they will be prevented from crossing the fence to get to the local hospital when they go into labor."[373] This is partly because the checkpoint separating Azzun Atma from the rest of the West Bank is not manned at night, resulting in the possibility of going into labor without being able to reach a local hospital.[374]

Access to medical care by both Israelis and Palestinians at such outstanding medical institutions as Hadassah Hospital located in Jerusalem is renowned and available without regard to religion, race, nationality or other such factors.

4. Commerce and the Economy

The security fence is claimed by the Palestinians to have impeded the flow of goods and workers, increased transportation costs and increased the time it takes to get Palestinian goods to the market. Palestinian Ministry of National Economy senior policy advisor Saad Kahtib has said, "economic actors are restricted in their ability to move internally as well as externally."[375] According to Kahtib, the restrictions on free movement have increased the cost of transportation "to as much as 30 to 50 percent of the overall cost of the products."[376]

Kahtib noted that before the Second Intifada began in September 2000, 120,000 Palestinians were legally employed in agriculture and construction. The number of workers was even larger if taking into account the number of illegal workers that commuted into Israel. By 2004, the number of legal workers had reduced to between 4000-5000 Palestinians.[377] While it is sad, indeed, that these Palestinian workers no longer have jobs in Israel, it must be noted that there is neither a legal nor any other obligation of Israel to provide work or benefits for persons who are not citizens of Israel. Moreover, the Palestinian economy under the PA has failed to develop sufficiently to absorb these workers within the West Bank, a fact that cannot be blamed wholly on the existence of the security fence.

Agriculture has always been an important part of the Palestinian economy in the West Bank. Since the security fence's construction, however, B'Tselem takes the position that "thousands of families living east of the barrier are separated from their farmland situated west of the barrier, impairing their ability to earn a living."[378] They claim that this is in addition to the thousands of olive trees and fruit trees that they assert have been uprooted to make way for the fence. They also claim that shepherding has been affected as well since land can be cut off from its water wells. Khalid Jaber, spokesperson at the Palestinian Ministry of Agriculture, has said that "some farmers have been cut off from their land and do not have unimpeded access to their and livestock" because of "restrictions of movement inside the territories as well as the closure of crossing points between Israel and the PA."[379] According to Kahtib, "farm produce and other perishable items cannot be quickly and easily traded, and the general population's physical access to food is extremely problematical."[380] He noted that, "agricultural products are the most severely hit, since they are perishable."[381] While Israel welcomed Palestinian workers prior to the Second Intifada open access became impossible in light of new security requirements. Israel encourages trade and commerce between Israel and all her neighbors, including from the Palestinian territories, but finds relatively few willing partners. Israel's view is that regional economic development will help all people; and it seeks to enhance mutual commerce and economic development between Israel and the Palestinians.

5. Fabric of Life

The Israeli High Court, in its opinion in the *Beit Sourik* case, recognized that "the injury caused by the Separation Fence is not restricted to the lands of the inhabitants or to their access to these lands. The injury is of far wider scope. It is the fabric of life of the entire population."[382] The Court ordered the military to balance military necessity with humanitarian considerations. In response, the Israeli government said "the matrix of civilian bonds and ties- economic, educational, medical etc, between Palestinian villages and cities has been thoroughly examined as well as the way they were affected by the construction of the Security Fence."[383] It highlights this point, stating "any modifications in both the route and the construction of the fence were undertaken for humanitarian considerations, many of these at a financial and operational detriment to the Israeli government."[384]

For Palestinians who have been affected by the presence of the security fence and who direct their complaints to Israel, one must also ask why they have not put public pressure on the Palestine Liberation Organization and the Palestinian Authority to take the necessary steps to assure security and to prevent ongoing terrorist activity.

The Fence's Impact on Israeli Lives

1. Israeli Jews and Arabs Living West of the Fence

Israeli Jews and Israeli Arabs alike have benefitted from the increased security provided by the fence. They can board buses without the constant fear of a suicide bombing. They can go to restaurants, shopping malls and outdoor markets without hesitation. And they can send their children to school without fearing the unimaginable.

Israelis clearly support the fence as a means of defense against terror. A study of Israeli public opinion concerning national security found support for construction of the fence to be overwhelming, reporting "it is hard to find any issue in Israel about which there is so wide a consensus."[385] This "immense support" has remained solid over time.[386] When Israelis were asked whether "you agree or disagree with the construction of a fence between us and the Palestinians," 80 percent agreed with the statement in 2004, 82 percent in 2005, 79 percent in 2006, and 76 percent in 2007."[387] Little has changed in the ensuing years with support for the fence continuing at high numbers, particularly in the context of the attacks by Hamas from Gaza in 2008 and continuing through 2012, repeated attempts by Palestinians to infiltrate Israel for terrorist purposes and the terrorist attack upon a public bus in Tel Aviv in November 2012.

This renewed sense of security has also had positive ramifications for the Israeli economy. Some Arab-Israeli communities, especially those neighboring Palestinian villages, have reported "a spike in both security and economic activity, as Arabs who once hauled back millions of shekels worth of wares from Jenin now shop locally." [388] Umm el-Fahm City Manager Tawfiq Karaman was quoted as saying "God be blessed, the fence ended the parade of terrorists through this city and gave us an economic boom and increased security."[389] Prior to the fence's construction, Umm el-Fahm residents had complained, "Palestinians casually filtering through from the territories had harassed schoolgirls, stolen cars, and even snatched laundry."[390] The mayor of the city, Sheikh Abdel Rahman Mahajaneh, has admitted that he, too, feels like the fence has benefitted the community; however, it is to be noted that he has been sharply criticized for this admission.[391]

The movement of Palestinian populations has caused unintended consequences for Israel's demography. For instance, according to a 2004 study by The Jerusalem Institute for Israel Studies, it appears that the existence of the fence is "inducing many residents of East Jerusalem (who hold Israeli ID cards) to return to the city from rented accommodations outside the Jerusalem area of jurisdiction for fear of losing their rights."[392] Along the same lines, the *Washington Post* reported that "many of the 250,000 Palestinian who are residents of East Jerusalem, but not Israeli citizens, are ... concerned about losing access to Israeli services such as medical care and social security if their neighborhoods became part of a Palestinian state."[393] Daniel Seidemann, an Israeli lawyer opposed to the fence, has explained this activity saying, "Palestinians cannot allow themselves to be trapped on the Palestinian side of the wall lest they be plummeted into poverty. They are culturally, politically and religiously tied to the West Bank, but economically connected to Israel."[394]

An increasing number of Palestinian residents of East Jerusalem are moving into predominantly Jewish neighborhoods such as French Hill or Pisgat Zeev— areas that are considered illegal Israeli settlements by Palestinian officials.[395] Linda Gradstein reports in the *Washington Post* that if "one of the goals of the wall was to maintain a Jewish majority in Jerusalem," then the result presents a contradiction because "the barrier is now encouraging Palestinians to move into mainly Jewish areas.[396] Such an effect is incompatible with "the Israeli policy of maintaining the demographic balance [at a ratio of 70:30] between Jews and Arabs in Jerusalem."[397] Lt. Col. (Ret.) Amir Cheshin, former adviser on Arab affairs to Mayor Teddy Kollek, commented on Palestinian movement, noting that:

> The Arab population, while being restrained by the Israeli establishment from building legally, engages in illegal construction within the city [of Jerusalem]. Thousands are moving to the West Bank areas adjacent to Jerusalem, while keeping their Israeli identity cards. According to estimates, the numerical ratio within the municipal bounds in the year 2020 will be 69 percent Jews versus 31 percent Arabs.[398]

Within Israel, people who are legal citizens are free to live where they choose, without regard to race, creed, color, gender, religion or national origin.

2. Israeli Jews Living East of the Fence

Large blocs of villages, towns, cities and community settlements exist outside of the security fence's boundary. One such community is Ariel, one of Israel's biggest cities still referred to by some as a "settlement." Ariel, with a significant population, well developed services and a college that has grown so large and well respected that it has recently been approved by the Israeli government for an upgrade to University status (subject to resolution of an appeal being taken by other Israeli Universities), has a fence surrounding the community, but it is not connected to the main route of the barrier.[399] When Benjamin Netanyahu took office for his second term, the late Ariel Mayor Ron Nachman had expressed hope. He urged Netanyahu to connect Ariel's fence with the main fence "instead of dithering as past Israeli leaders have done."[400]

The issue of the extension or connection of the security fence to the large block area of Ariel remains controversial[401] with some believing it has less to do with security and more to do with dividing Israel and setting borders for a sovereign Palestinian state. As Danny Dayan, Chairman of the Yesha Council, asserted, "It is evident that the fence is a tool designed to castrate the Jewish existence beyond the fence and not a tool to maintain security."[402] He sees the fence's positive contribution to be a "demand for houses in settlements to the west of the fence, even when they are beyond the Green Line (such as Alfei Menashe); it is easy to sell them and easy to populate them."[403] Indeed, an investigation by the *Marker*, the Israeli business daily, in February 2006 revealed that the value of dwellings east of the fence had gone down 10-15 percent while the prices of dwellings in settlements west of the barrier and far from hostile Palestinian villages stayed stable.[404]

Analysis by Haaretz based on Israeli Interior Ministry data concluded, "while only 48 of the 122 settlements in the West Bank are situated to the west of the separation fence route, these settlements house the vast majority of settlers,"[405] with 76.2 percent of all settlers, or 209,716, residing in these settlements."[406] Settlement population growth outside the area protected by the fence has decreased since the fence's construction. Prior to construction, from 1994 to 2000, the population grew by 15,913 individuals and from 2000 to 2004 it grew by only 10,126.[407]

As meaningful peace negotiations between Israel and the PA have remained stalled due to President Abbas' precondition that Israel stop construction in all parts of the West Bank, including the towns, villages and settlement communities populated by Israelis for decades as well as in East Jerusalem, it is clear that in spite of improvements in the Palestinian economy in such areas as Ramallah, the Palestinian economy has grown at a dramatically slower rate than Israel's economy. It is also clear that the impact of the fence on the lines of both Palestinians and Israelis is a much less disturbing impact than that caused by the death and destruction resulting from acts of terrorism.

Propaganda and Red Herrings: Semantics, Specters of the Berlin Wall and Apartheid

Semantic Debate: Fence, Wall and Separation Barrier

The debate about what to call the structure Israel has constructed reflects the same pattern of politicization as the Arab-Israeli conflict itself. In the ongoing war of words, it has been called a "linguistic skirmish," since "at almost every point of contention in the Mideast conflict there is a new mini-vocabulary," and advocates on both sides vehemently protest when their coined terminology is not used.[408] Ruvik Rosenthal, writer of a language column for the Israeli newspaper *Maariv* and author of several books on language, has commented that "language is absolutely part of the conflict, not only between us and the Palestinians, but inside Israeli society."[409]

The language of the security barrier is no different. Professor Tami Amanda Jacoby wrote:

> In uncontested political contexts, a fence or a wall may be completely benign, unremarkable and even mundane, hardly ever noticed by anybody and with no meaning attached to it beyond the immediate and technical purpose for which it was built... In such a violently disputed space as Israel/Palestine, however, geography is decidedly political... Beyond the immediate entity, a barrier is a "meaning structure" that has political, economic, social, cultural, and even existential effects on the broader course of political events.[410]

The various terms for the terrorism prevention security fence/barrier/wall reflect an assortment of physical descriptions, functional descriptions and political narratives.

The barrier's advocates refer to it as Israel's anti-terrorist fence, security fence, terror prevention fence, seam zone, seam line, separation fence and security barrier, along with other related variations. The terms heard most frequently in Hebrew are *gader* (fence) and *gader ha'hafrada* (separation fence). The Government of Israel refers to the program of building the barrier as *Merhav Ha'Tefer* (The Seam Zone). The barrier's advocates who call the barrier a fence support their position by highlighting that more than 95 percent of the barrier is physically a fence, therefore "fence" is the most appropriate physical descriptor. They add functional descriptions to emphasize the barrier's purposes of preventing terrorist infiltration and providing a defensive means of security. The left-leaning Israeli media and the Israeli High Court use the term "separation fence." This terminology avoids security considerations and reflects the lessening of the conflict as well as the recognition of two neighboring states in the future."[411]

Opponents to the barrier call it a wall, a separation wall or, for those wishing to paint Israel as an apartheid racist state, an "apartheid" wall. Some Palestinians refer to it as *jidar al-fasl al-'unsuri* (Arabic for racist segregation wall). Although less than five percent of the actual barrier consists of a wall, the walled areas are often in highly populated urban areas that are more visible to Israelis and journalists that most likely receive greater media coverage.[412] The term "wall" implies a non-temporary measure with nefarious purposes such as oppression, control and segregation. Moreover, the term "wall" summons the negative imagery of the Berlin Wall, implying that just as the people of Berlin caused that wall to be dismantled, the same fate will befall Israel's barrier.[413] Surely, the "mere mention of wall is an act of terminological solidarity with the Palestinians."[414] The use of the term "separation barrier" conjures an apartheid-like forced separation of races and builds upon the myths of the old, discredited but still popular among Israel's enemies, the accusatory "Zionism is Racism" anti-Israel campaign at the United Nations. More noteworthy is that "Apartheid wall" is the official term put forward by the Palestinian National Authority ("PNA") and the PNA Ministry of Foreign Affairs (though the latter uses other terms as well).[415] It is worth noting that Palestinian diplomats do not usually use the term apartheid wall when speaking to foreign audiences, instead employing different terminology such as "separation wall," or just "wall."[416] Oftentimes, Palestinian diplomats, including Arafat during his lifetime and Abu Mazen today, use different words when they speak English for foreign consumption than they do in Arabic for their domestic audience. On the other hand, official Israeli usage remains fairly consistent regardless of language spoken or how or where it is used.[417]

Those who seek neutrality or at least the semblance thereof employ the term "barrier, " which has become favored by journalists as well as in diplomatic circles, "albeit with opportunities for 'side-taking' adjectives inserted before or after the word." In Israel, the use of "security barrier" or "separation barrier," denotes whether one leans to the right or to the left in the political spectrum, with security used more by the political right and separation more by the political left. It is interesting that the adjective "separation" is "now occasionally acceptable to the Palestinian official diplomatic position [vis-à-vis the US and the I.C.J.], but only together with 'wall'."[418] The term "separation barrier," however, still evokes in the mind the separation of apartheid and is not deemed to be a neutral term.

The copious innuendos and assumptions that are evoked also depend upon what terms are used and exemplifies why this semantic issue is so contentious. It has been suggested that since news organizations have struggled to find a "description that is both accurate and that doesn't raise charges of bias,"[419] they should "simply inform news consumers about the semantics debate, and let them decide."[420] The specific term chosen by world organizations, leaders and politicians is oftentimes a political statement, reflecting an individual or country's view of the fence.[421] Indeed, these public statements are also scrutinized to determine the extent to which they may reflect political moments or lessons learned after reflection on the use of one term or another. For example, at a July 2003 White House event with PA President Mahmoud Abbas, President Bush criticized the "wall snaking through the West Bank."[422] With Mr. Sharon as his companion, he said, "the fence is a sensitive issue."[423]

UN Secretary-General Kofi Annan has shown similar sensitivities. In a January 11, 2005 letter addressed to the General Assembly, he consistently used the term wall, but added in a footnote "the term used in the present letter, 'the wall,' is the one employed by the General Assembly."[424] Annan's decision has been analyzed as "not only a case of conscious term selection, but also a recognition that other terms exist, from which 'the wall' was chosen."[425]

The UN General Assembly has consistently used the term "wall," however there has been a shift in terms used by member states at the UN. A study analyzing the various terminologies found that:

> In October 2003, most of the Council's members used 'separation wall' and 'the wall.' In an isolated cluster, the Palestinians used the term 'expansionist wall,' together with Yemen, Sudan, and the Organization of Islamic Conferences. Israel and Germany were the only countries using 'security fence.' The official UN term . . . is 'the barrier'; the US and the U.K. refer to 'the fence' (though the US representative mentions 'wall' as well); the E.U., represented by Italy, employs 'separation wall.' Among the more poignant terms are the Palestinian 'bantunstan walls,' the Iranian 'racist wall' and the Saudi Arabian 'racist wall of separation.'[426]

The same study also found that "in July 2005... the term 'barrier' [became] more popular, and the clustering around terms [represented] a sharper geographical division." That is:

> the countries that cluster around 'separation wall' are mostly Middle Eastern, including the Palestinian representative. Europe clusters around 'barrier'; other members speak of 'the wall.' The US representative refrained from mentioning the structure. Israel is persistent yet alone in employing 'security fence.' A few Arab countries continue to use such terms as the 'colonial separation wall' (Syria), 'expansionist wall' (Kuwait) and 'wall of injustice' (Sudan). 'Apartheid wall' is introduced to the space by the Organization of Islamic Conferences (and not employed by the Palestinians). Following the same analytical angle of seeking non-mentions (as applied to the media space), here again we found that 'fence' is rejected by all of the Council's members (except for Israel), 'wall' is rejected by the 'West,' and adjectives other than 'separation' are less popular.[427]

In light of how consistently certain parties have come to use certain terms, it seems obvious that when the ICJ used the term "wall" in its advisory opinion on the legality of the "wall" in the "occupied Palestinian territory," the UN General Assembly in framing the question, and the Court itself were both clearly favoring the Palestinian side."[428] Rather than using the more neutral term "barrier," which was used in the Secretary-General's report, the ICJ stated in paragraph 67 that it had "chosen to use the terminology employed by the General Assembly" in its request for the advisory opinion. For what it's worth, the Court admitted that the word had connotations beyond a strict physical description, noting "the 'wall' in question is a complex construction, so that that term cannot be understood in a limited physical sense."[429] The Court added, "the other terms used, either by Israel ("fence") or by the Secretary-General ("barrier"), are no more accurate if understood in the physical sense."[430]

Specter of the Berlin Wall

The image of the Berlin Wall and the political repression and deprivation of liberty associated with it have undoubtedly colored many critics' perceptions of Israel's security fence. Israel addressed this perception in its submission to the ICJ:

> The use of the term "wall" in the resolution requesting an opinion is neither happenstance nor oversight. It reflects a calculated media campaign to raise pejorative connotations in the mind of the Court of great concrete constructions of separation as the Berlin Wall, intended to stop people escaping from tyranny.[431]

According to the Germans themselves, "The Berlin Wall was the symbol of German division, of the GDR leadership's contempt for human rights and basic freedoms, and of the confrontation between two political systems after the end of the Second World War."[432]

The German Democratic Republic (East Germany) (GDR), a Soviet bloc communist country in the post-Nazi era, began building the Berlin Wall in August of 1961. The roughly 96-mile wall sealed off West Berlin and was constructed to prevent vast numbers of East Germans from emigrating to West Germany. Unlike any other security barrier, the focus of the Berlin Wall, with its 302 watchtowers, was "directed inward, against the country's own population."[433] That is, the GDR used the Berlin Wall to stop East German citizens from lawfully leaving East Germany.

In contrast, the Israeli security fence was built to keep terrorists with murderous intent out of Israel. A comparison of the UN and the ICJ's treatment of the ill-intentioned Berlin Wall with how the Israeli security fence has been dealt with brings to light some serious neutrality concerns. For, even with the Soviet veto-power within the United Nations Security Council at the time, there was neither a UN resolution condemning the Berlin Wall nor any ICJ advisory opinion questioning its legality.

Israel's Ministry of Foreign Affairs made the following distinction between the two very different barriers:

> The Berlin Wall was designed by the Communist regime of East Germany to solidify and perpetuate the division of the city by keeping the German citizens of "East Berlin"— who sought only freedom and contacts with their German brethren in "West Berlin" — locked in. . . .

> In stark contrast, Israel is building the anti-terrorist fence for only one purpose – to keep Palestinian terrorists, who wish to murder and maim Israeli citizens, out. Israel, a democratic society, is building the fence to protect its citizens from deadly attack, not from peaceful contacts with the other side. [434]

Former German Interior Minister Otto Schily expressed support for this point of view when he said, "those who draw comparisons with the Berlin Wall are wrong, because [the terrorism prevention security fence] does not shut people in and deprive them of their freedom. Its purpose is to protect Israel from the terrorists."[435]After noting that the fence was built after many other failed attempts to prevent terrorists from entering Israel, Minister Schily acknowledged that it was "understandable that Israel should erect a protective barrier, which furthermore has shown it works, and I think that the criticism is far from reality."[436] In addressing the semantics of what to call the fence, he said that the terrorism prevention security fence should be referred to as what it is–a "fence"–and not a "wall" as it is often called in Germany and other nations.[437]

Specter of Apartheid

Haunting the security fence debate, much like the Berlin Wall analogy, is the specter of apartheid. In Afrikaans, the term "Apartheid," coined in the 1930's, means "apartness." The policy of institutionalized racial separateness, however, has its origins in the 17th century white settlement of South Africa. This policy, by categorizing people who reside within one country into racially-defined groups, limited the rights of all non-whites within the country and maintained the white minority in power.

Apartheid has been successfully eliminated in South Africa; it has become a potent code word to describe the powerful pressures of boycotts and sanctions which can be brought to bear against nations who discriminate against their own people. It has also been used pervasively as a diplomatic slur against Israel throughout the debate over the fence.[438] Indeed, "Israel-is-an-apartheid state" is the mantra of the current generation of anti-Semites and opponents of Israel, supplanting the defamatory 'Zionism is Racism' slogan. It does not take much imagination to posit that the proponents of the "Zionism is Racism" myth will continue to seek to criminalize the security fence as an apartheid wall, in what can only be described as a perversion of the meaning of human rights.

This new rhetoric was spotlighted in September 2001 at the United Nations World Conference against Racism, Racial Discrimination, Xenophobia and Related Intolerance held in Durban, South Africa. At that time, this author served as Chairman of the Conference of Presidents of Major American Jewish Organizations United Nations Committee, as President of B'nai B'rith International and as Head of Delegation to the Durban Conference and witnessed first-hand the hatred toward Israel and the Jewish People on the very grounds of the United Nations Conference. The Durban Conference has been described as an "unprecedented anti-Semitic hate fest in the course of which the apartheid stigma was viciously stamped upon Israel,"[439] This characterization was even admitted to by the South African hosts of the conference. The significance of Durban is that it resulted in a

> spin that turned the human rights cause against itself, disingenuously creating congruence between anti-Semitism and support of human rights. Anti-Semitism postured as anti-racism, and Israel was demonized as South Africa's successor apartheid state![440]

In April 2009, the United Nations Durban Review Conference (aka Durban II) was held in Geneva. Much like the Durban Conference itself, the Durban Review Conference was "meant to address those human rights issues and their violators." However, the Durban Review Conference quickly became an anti-Israel summit[441] held on the official grounds of the United Nations in Geneva. The United States, Israel, Canada, Italy, Holland, Germany, Australia and New Zealand all boycotted the conference.

This author also served as Head of Delegation at the Durban Review Conference and addressed the assembly delegates from the same podium occupied a day or two earlier by Iranian President Mahmoud Ahmadinejad. Iran's public language toward Israel in tandem with its sponsorship of terrorist attacks, terrorists and foreign terrorist organizations, and its promise to annihilate Israel must be taken as seriously by the rest of the world as it is by Israel. It is actually quite unbelievable that UN diplomatic protocol permitted Ahmadinejad, a Holocaust denier who has called for the total annihilation of Israel to have a featured role at a UN sponsored human rights conference. At the Durban Review Conference, Ahmadinejad gave a virulently anti-Israel speech, stating "Governments must be encouraged and supported in their fights at eradicating this barbaric racism . . . Efforts must be made to put an end to Zionism."[442] Ahmadinejad didn't stop there. He went on to say, "World Zionism personifies racism that falsely resorts to religions and abuses religious sentiments to hide its hatred and ugly face."[443] It is no surprise that the delegates from 23 European Union nations and other accredited organizational delegates led by this author walked out on his speech citing "Ahmadinejad's blatantly racist and anti-Israel language as the reason."[444] UN Secretary-General Ban Ki-Moon responded to the speech: "I deplore the use of this platform by the Iranian president to accuse, divide and even incite."[445] Ban Ki-Moon concluded by pressing UN members to "turn away from such a message in both form and substance."[446]

That the president of the world's worst state sponsor of terrorism, whose anti-Jewish, anti-Zionist, anti-Israeli and anti-Semitic rhetoric includes repeated public calls for the destruction of Israel, is given a venue at the United Nations to preach hatred is grossly unacceptable. Somehow Ahmadinejad gets away with it, is applauded by many of those remaining in the audience even though it is incomprehensible that he was allowed to spew his venom at a UN sponsored conference against racism. This very fact demonstrates the biased attitude toward Israel practiced to varying degrees at the United Nations itself and is a further backdrop for understanding the UN General Assembly vote seeking the advisory opinion on the legality of Israel's "wall" between Israel and the West Bank.

The argument that Israel's security fence constitutes apartheid generally takes three forms. One argument compares the security fence to the actual practices and policies of South Africa's specific Apartheid regime, the second compares the fence to the crime of apartheid outlawed by international law and the third argument asserts broad sweeping generalizations in which all types of unfair treatment resulting from the fence automatically constitutes apartheid. As discussed below, all of these arguments are groundless.

(1) An Inappropriate Comparison to the Actual Practices and Policies of South Africa's Specific Apartheid Regime

Israel's construction of a security fence significantly differs from South African apartheid measures "in its rationale, its goals, its effect, and its historical context."[447]

In regards to racism, the Israeli government has stated, "the conflict between Palestinians and Israelis is not a racial one, nor a domestic one, but, in fact, a national-territorial conflict between two distinct peoples."[448] According to Gideon Shimoni, professor emeritus of Hebrew University, in South Africa, "the essence of the [apartheid] struggle was for a *shared* civic society and for individual equality, whereas, the Israel-Arab conflict was and remains in essence a struggle between two nationalist aspirations for self-determination in the same territory."[449] South African apartheid was about skin color. As one South African writer has commented, apartheid, as "applied to Israel [is a] joke: for proof of that, just look at a crowd of Israeli Jews and their gradations in skin-colour from the "blackest" to the "whitest."[450] He noted further that Palestinians are not oppressed on racial grounds as Arabs, but rather, they are "competitors . . . in a national/religious conflict for land."[451]

In addition to the goal of limiting the rights of the non-white population, an explicit goal of apartheid was actual racial separation through the creation of ten independent homelands, or "Bantustans," on about 14 percent of South Africa's land area for the South African blacks which were allocated to them and on which they were permitted to live. Four of these impoverished homelands were proclaimed but never recognized internationally.

In contrast, the security fence was built to prevent terrorist access to Israel and not to create borders or separation. As testament to this, one need only understand that 20 percent of Israel's population consists of citizens of Palestinian Arab descent who enjoy the same rights and status as all other Israeli citizens.[452] Moreover, the security fence is not inherently designed to separate people of different races from each other within the same country, as was the case in South Africa.

It is true that the security fence prevents access to Israel and certain areas within the West Bank by those living outside the fence. This restriction of movement is not ideal but it has proven to be one of the only effective means of stopping terrorist attacks. The Israeli government has reiterated its number one goal time and time again.

> Israel is basically interested in contacts between Israelis and Palestinians. The only reason that Palestinians have in recent years been restricted from entering into Israel is because of their terrorist attacks against Israelis, attacks that escalated every time Israel tried to relax restrictions.[453]

The official policy of apartheid was to exclude people of color from the political process and eventually, through the creation of homelands, to strip all black South Africans of their citizenship. In comparison, Palestinians in the West Bank were never citizens of Israel and are highly unlikely to ever become citizens of Israel. As noted before, Israeli citizens of Palestinian Arab descent make up roughly 20 percent of Israel's population and enjoy equal rights and freedoms under Israeli law.[454] They can and do participate in the political process and oftentimes elect representatives to the Knesset (Israel's Parliament) from a number of political parties, some of whom become very outspoken in the true spirit of free speech and democracy.

It has been estimated that "between 1950 and 1986, about 1.5 million Africans were forcibly removed from 'white' cities to rural reservations."[455] Neither Israel nor its security fence forcibly transfers populations.

It is noteworthy that blacks in South Africa, whether they lived in *Bantustans* or not, did not seek the destruction of South Africa. Rather, their goal was to remove by peaceful means the apartheid system and the parties that created and supported it.[456] In contrast, polls have consistently shown and continue to demonstrate that a majority of Palestinians in the territories dispute the right of Israel to even exist. Despite this enmity, the State of Israel has been clear that it does "not wish to rule the Palestinians and accepts in principle the establishment of a Palestinian state, provided that it not be a terrorist state and that it exists in peace alongside Israel."[457]

Apartheid's purpose for creating South African tribal homelands was an effort to force a permanent international status on the lands, and their black population.[458] This goal is completely dissimilar from the goal of the security fence which, as the Israeli government has frequently repeated, is to create "a temporary defensive measure, not a border," where the "inconveniences caused by the fence are reversible."[459]

There has also been a misguided attempt by some to continue to regard the colonialism inherent in South African apartheid as similar to the situation in Israel. This linkage is false, unfair and reflects neither history nor reality. Israel's people are not colonizers. They were refugees with a deep, historical and continuous connection to the land, committed to the reestablishment of a national Jewish homeland in the ancient land of Israel. "In contrast to the white settlers (Afrikans, English, and others) who created Johannesburg and Pretoria,"[460] Zionism and the movement to re-establish a national homeland for the Jewish people is not premised upon colonialism but upon return of the Jewish people to their ancestral lands. The core of the issue between the Arabs and the Jews is a clash of competing national and religious aspirations coupled with a desire by each to live in the areas of their respective, but historically different, ancestral roots. The Jewish people have resided in the areas of Judea and Samaria in ancient Israel for thousands of years. The Palestinians, in asserting their own historical claims, seek to fully deny the

ancient historical ties of the Jewish people, notwithstanding historical and archaeological undisputed proof of ancient Jewish culture,
civilization, religious and community life.

(2) A Wrongful Comparison to the Crime of Apartheid Outlawed by International Law

Critics of the security fence often wrongfully argue that Israel
violates international law outlawing the crime of apartheid. This
law encompasses the specific practices of the South African regime,
yet is broader and not limited to those South African practices.

The real purpose of those who choose to refer to Israel's security fence as an apartheid wall allegedly designed to illegally separate
Israelis from Palestinians is in an attempt to label Israel as an apartheid, racist, criminal state acting in violation of international law
and thus entitling aggrieved persons to bring charges against Israel,
Israelis, the IDF and others who assisted in designing or constructing the "wall" to be held accountable to the International Criminal
Court. They may also seek remedies in courts of other countries
which are determined to press the public policy position of investi-
gating or charging people under the banner of war crimes or crimes
against humanity. It is part of the continuing attempt and design
to malign, weaken, slander and demonize Israel, ostensibly for the
purpose of forcing Israel to withdraw from the West Bank and "end
the occupation" without requiring a final status negotiated agreement on the core issues including security, borders, refugees and
Jerusalem that continue to exist between Israel and the Palestinians.

Article 5 of the 2002 Rome Statute of the International Criminal
Court makes "the crime of apartheid" a crime against humanity for
which the International Criminal Court has jurisdiction. Article 7,
paragraph 2, section (h) provides a definition: "'The crime of apartheid' means inhumane acts of a character similar to those referred to
in paragraph 1, committed in the context of an institutionalized regime of systematic oppression and domination by one racial group
over any other racial group or groups and committed with the intention of maintaining that regime."

A number of countries, including the United States and Israel,
have decided not to be parties to the International Criminal Court

and thus have no legal obligations to answer to the Court. The ICC can only exercise jurisdiction in three ways: (1) If the accused is a citizen of a state party to the Court, (2) if the alleged crime took place on territory of a state party to the Court or (3) if the UN Security Council referred the situation to the Court. Since Israel is not a party, it is only subject to the jurisdiction of the International Criminal Court upon a referral from the UN Security Council. However, that will not prevent the PLO/PA (should it be determined to have the standing to do so under the second jurisdictional condition above as a result of its recently upgraded "non member state observer status" at the UN) from attempting to initiate charges against Israel or Israelis before the Court for acts which it will claim to have occurred within their "territory as a state party" and in violation of international law. The stage is already set for this assault by the PLO/PA upon Israel notwithstanding the fact that the (a) issue of the "territory" of the PA/PLO is disputed and (b) Israeli policy on the West Bank, including the security fence, does not meet the definition of apartheid under the 2002 Rome Statute. While the Palestinians on the West Bank surely suffer unfortunate hardships and burdens, they do not endure "inhumane acts" rising to the level of "crimes against humanity," although Israel will surely be accused of these crimes. It is worth noting that Israel's own High Court has ordered the Israeli military to consider the direct and indirect impact of the security fence on the lives of Palestinians on the West Bank and to minimize hardships when feasible. The High Court continues to monitor issues relating to the fence. The Israeli High Court of Justice, with its deep regard for human rights and humanitarian issues, surely does not and will not tolerate "inhumane acts" by the government of Israel or the IDF.

The "inhumane acts of a character similar to those referred to in paragraph 1" are crimes such as murder, extermination, and enslavement. Israel's security fence is not an "institutionalized regime of systematic oppression and domination." Rather, it is a means of securing Israel against Palestinian terrorists emanating from the West Bank. Most importantly, the security fence, its presence, functions or its administration do not involve domination by one racial group over any other racial group. Israeli citizens are different than Palestinians in the West Bank by virtue of their legal citizenship, not their race or racial segregation.

The International Convention on the Suppression and Punishment of the Crime of Apartheid (ICSPCA) outlaws apartheid. Neither the United States nor Israel has signed the ICSPCA. Article 1, paragraph 1 states:

> The States Parties to the present Convention declare that apartheid is a crime against humanity and that inhuman acts resulting from the policies and practices of apartheid and similar policies and practices of racial segregation and discrimination, as defined in article II of the Convention, are crimes violating the principles of international law, in particular the purposes and principles of the Charter of the United Nations, and constituting a serious threat to international peace and security.[461]

Article 2, paragraph 1 defines the term apartheid:

> For the purpose of the present Convention, the term "the crime of apartheid", which shall include similar policies and practices of racial segregation and discrimination as practiced in southern Africa, shall apply to the following inhuman acts committed for the purpose of establishing and maintaining domination by one racial group of persons over any other racial group of persons and systematically oppressing them:
>
> (a) Denial to a member or members of a racial group or groups of the right to life and liberty of person:
>
> (i) By murder of members of a racial group or groups;
>
> (ii) By the infliction upon the members of a racial group or groups of serious bodily or mental harm, by the infringement of their freedom or dignity, or by subjecting them to torture or to cruel, inhuman or degrading treatment or punishment;
>
> (iii) By arbitrary arrest and illegal imprisonment of the members of a racial group or groups;
>
> (b) Deliberate imposition on a racial group or groups of living conditions calculated to cause its or their physical destruction in whole or in part;
>
> (c) Any legislative measures and other measures calculated to prevent a racial group or groups from participation in the political, social, economic and cultural life of the country and the deliberate creation of conditions preventing the full development of such a group or groups, in particular by denying to members of a racial group or groups basic human rights and freedoms, including the right to work, the right to form recognized trade unions, the

right to education, the right to leave and to return to their country, the right to a nationality, the right to freedom of movement and residence, the right to freedom of opinion and expression, and the right to freedom of peaceful assembly and association;

(d) Any measures including legislative measures, designed to divide the population along racial lines by the creation of separate reserves and ghettos for the members of a racial group or groups, the prohibition of mixed marriages among members of various racial groups, the expropriation of landed property belonging to a racial group or groups or to members thereof;

(e) Exploitation of the labour of the members of a racial group or groups, in particular by submitting them to forced labour;

(f) Persecution of organizations and persons, by depriving them of fundamental rights and freedoms, because they oppose apartheid.[462]

Even if Israel were subject to the ICSPCA, Israel's security fence and its administration would not violate the International Convention. But that is not to say that Israel would not be accused of such violations notwithstanding the fact that Israel's policies toward Palestinians in the West Bank are not based on race or racial segregation, but simply on the fact that Palestinians are not Israeli citizens and that Israel has the right to determine for itself policies and practices that protect its citizens from infiltrators seeking to enter its country to harm its citizens. The clear and stated purpose of the security fence is to prevent terrorist infiltration from the West Bank, not to "establish or and maintain domination" or "systematically oppress them." While Palestinians endure hardships because of the security fence, those hardships do not rise to the level of apartheid under international law.

The reality of the situation is not apartheid but rather is a concerted response by Israel, who suffers from Palestinian terrorist attacks that originate on the West Bank and Gaza. Therefore, Israel is forced to protect its citizens—Jewish citizens and Arab citizens alike—from terrorism perpetrated by non-Israeli citizens from the West Bank and Gaza.

(3) Broad Sweeping Generalizations and Wrong Headed Accusations that All Types of Unfair Treatment Necessarily Constitute Apartheid

According to Gideon Shimoni, opponents of Israel who call

the security fence an apartheid wall or accuse Israel of apartheid, "give that term a meaning so broad that it is deprived of its original significance."[463] This incorrect labeling creates a "disingenuous transform[ation] of the term 'apartheid' from the description of a singular historical phenomenon in a particular time and place—South Africa from about 1948 to 1994—into a generic concept."[464] Apartheid has been obscured and hijacked, much like the term "holocaust," has been taken to use by those desiring to emphasize a human tragedy, although the Holocaust is unique in all of history and should not be misapplied to other historical events. This incorrect labeling masks the racism fundamental to apartheid and the one place where it took place, South Africa."[465]

"Apartheid wall" is a term that South African-born Benjamin Pogrund calls "a debasement of the word for the sake of slick propaganda."[466] It allows opponents of Israel the ability to label any Israeli policy or action as apartheid. This removes the natural inclination of a person to want to fully comprehend a situation before he or she makes a judgment about it. Pogrund argues that apartheid is a "lazy label for the complexities of the Middle East conflict" and it is only used because "if it can be made to stick, then Israel can be made to appear to be as vile as was apartheid South Africa and seeking its destruction can be presented to the world as an equally moral cause."[467]

Israel is a democratic state committed to the rule of law with a vibrant free press and an independent judiciary. It is these institutions themselves that work to safeguard the rights of Israeli citizens and Palestinians within the West Bank and work to ensure that no government policy of apartheid could possibly survive democratic scrutiny.

Israeli society has numerous racial, ethnic, religious and linguistic components and it struggles to protect the rights of its diverse citizenry. But, like virtually every other country in the world, Israeli society is not fully immune from what some like to point out as acts appearing to have characteristics of racial or ethnic discrimination. In this context, there is criticism about the security fence and its impact on the Palestinian population, particularly in and around Jerusalem.[468]

Jewish-Israeli citizens from Arab countries and from Ethiopia have claimed "they do not receive the same educational or career opportunities afforded to Jews of European origin... and that their native cultures and traditions are not respected."[469]

No one contests the fact that Palestinians in the West Bank bear certain hardships and burdens due to the presence of the security fence. Like other democratic countries faced with the threat of terrorism, the Israeli government chose to take necessary preventive measures against terror, which included the construction of the security fence. It is unfortunate that it was necessary to build the security fence in the West Bank and often near Palestinian population centers, but its route was determined based on the locations from where the wave of suicide bombings and other terrorist attacks or terrorist infiltrations emanated. However, it is obvious that the mere existence of the security fence does not reach to the level of "crimes against humanity," and certainly is not apartheid.

Exaggerating Palestinian hardship and holding Palestinians out as victims of claimed Israeli illegalities by virtue of the existence security fence does not serve the interests of the Palestinian people nor of the pursuit of peace. Such conduct demeans the pride of the Palestinian people. By classifying themselves as victims of Israeli acts serves to damage efforts to build self respect and the societal infrastructure needed for building a vibrant society.

It is important to note that Israel is not unique among democracies which confront claims of discrimination at some point. In Israel, just like in other democracies, those who suffer racial or ethnic discrimination have recourse through different legal and political remedies within the court system, the democratic process, and the media. The Israeli High Court has received numerous Palestinian petitions claiming unfair treatment and increased burdens associated with the security fence and its establishment. The High Court has issued multiple significant decisions on the fence.[470] Israeli media, in addition to many non-governmental organizations, broadcasts to the world the impact the fence has had on Palestinians. The Israeli democratic system has shown that it is capable of self-reflection, self-criticism and taking strong corrective actions to right wrongs.

It is able to withstand both public and legal scrutiny and constantly strives to right its course when the reality strays from its democratic principles. Rhetoric aside, one cannot honestly characterize Israel as an apartheid regime or its security fence as a means of intended apartheid.

And, does it really need to be said that Israelis come in every size, shape and color? Or that they are followers of and believers in different religions ... and some in no religion at all? To call the State of Israel and her people violators of "apartheid" is without merit or legal foundation and is slanderous, libelous and presumptively actionable in its own right.

CHAPTER SIX

Judicial and Political Actions Leading Up to the ICJ Opinion

Proceedings Before the Israeli High Court of Justice

Palestinian, Israeli and international human rights groups have filed numerous petitions in the Israeli justice system, which raise fence-related legal issues.

The High Court's *Beit Sourik* opinion on June 30, 2004 was its seminal ruling addressing the legality of the fence.[471] There have been many other petitions and rulings since that initial ruling. For example, in 2003 and 2004, two human rights groups, HaMoked: Center for the Defence of the Individual ("HaMoked") and the Association for Civil Rights in Israel ("ACRI"), filed separate petitions to Israel's High Court of Justice seeking a declaration that the permit system that regulates residency in the Seam Zone area infringes on the rights of Palestinian residents.[472] The Court consolidated the two petitions. After two responses by the State of Israel in 2006 and 2009, the second of which stated that Israel was taking additional steps to improve the "fabric of life" in the Seam Zone area, the Court dismissed the petitions in 2011 and left the permit regime intact.

Additionally, ACRI filed a petition in 2003 seeking injunctive relief against the IDF to keep the fence's access points continuously open to Palestinian residents, vehicles and agricultural equipment.[473] The High Court of Justice agreed to review the issue and the following year the High Court issued an order *nisi*, obligating the IDF to justify the limited access and explain the lack of more reasonable hours of access.[474] The IDF was ordered to provide the

High Court with justification and explanation for its actions within 20 days.[475]

The Israeli High Court has frequently determined the legality of actions taken by the Government of Israel and the IDF in the Palestinian territories.[476] They have routinely taken bold measures to uphold the human rights and civil liberties of Palestinians, even in times of major combat. Indeed, as Justice William Brennan of the United States Supreme Court once observed:

> It may well be Israel . . .that provides the best hope for building a jurisprudence that can protect civil liberties against the demands of national security . . .The nations of the world, faced with sudden threats to their own security, will look to Israel's experience in handling its continuing security crisis and may well find in that experience that expertise to reject security claims that Israel has exposed as baseless and the courage to preserve the civil liberties that Israel has preserved without detriment to its security.[477]

The Government of Israel necessarily reviews the route of the terrorism prevention fence in light of the Israeli High Court findings that routinely and rigorously assess the legality of issues raised concerning the fence.

Actions in the United Nations Security Council

When the UN Security Council, the ultimate UN authority, adopted Resolution 1515 in November 2003, "Roadmap for Peace in the Middle East" (or "Roadmap"), it acknowledged that "a two state solution to the Israeli-Palestinian conflict will only be achieved through an end to violence and terrorism."[478] Israel had already pledged its commitment to the Roadmap, noting that only the Roadmap's "process—that sets out mutual rights and mutual obligations—can achieve real results."[479]

In the resolution, the Security Council demanded "an immediate cessation of all acts of violence, including all acts of terrorism, provocation, incitement, and destruction" and reiterated its "vision of two States, Israel and Palestine, living side by side within secure and recognized borders." This resolution followed the path originally outlined by President George W. Bush in his Rose Garden speech of June 24, 2002 given at the height of the Second

Intifada. The Roadmap was subsequently adopted by Israel, the Palestinian Authority, the Quartet and the UN Security Council which was an important step towards the goal of achieving peace between the Palestinians and Israel because it provided both parties with a UN Security Council sanctioned means to govern their own final status negotiations. However, not long thereafter, the UN General Assembly, without the approval of the UN Security Council, referred to the UN's own International Court of Justice the request for an advisory opinion as to the legality of Israel's terrorism prevention security fence, which it termed a wall, thereby inflaming the situation rather than solving it and placing the ICJ in the center of the controversy.

The UN Charter and The International Court of Justice

In 1945, the UN Charter established the International Court of Justice as "the principal judicial organ of the United Nations."[480] Since its beginning, the court has heard many varied cases. The Court under UN procedures consists of fifteen judges selected by the UN and who are to be "independent" and "elected regardless of their nationality." The current composition of the Court as of February 2013 includes judges from China, France, Brazil, Japan, Somalia, Italy, Mexico, Morocco, New Zealand, Russia, Uganda, India, Slovakia, the United Kingdom and the United States. The International Court of Justice has two roles. For one, it settles legal disputes, *i.e.,* "contentious cases," between adversarial states, where the ruling is legally binding. In making its decisions, the Court is required to rely on the following sources of international law in descending priority:

(a) international conventions, whether general or particular, establishing rules expressly recognized by the contesting states;

(b) international custom, as evidence of a general practice accepted as law;

(c) the general principles of law recognized by civilized nations;

(d) subject to the provisions of Article 59, judicial decisions and the teachings of the most highly qualified publicists of the various nations, as subsidiary means for the determination of rules of law.[481]

The ICJ's second role consists of its authority to issue advisory opinions. An advisory opinion is a non-binding legal interpretation where "no parties [are] to be bound within the meaning of Article 59 of the Statute of the Court."[482] It was meant to be a way in which UN agencies could seek the court's help in resolving complex legal issues. Advisory opinions have often been controversial because the question is presented to the ICJ as an indirect way of bringing what is really a contentious issue before the court.

Judicial advisory opinions exist in various countries and are governed by the rules of construction, interpretation and application of the country specific analysis as well as the application of international law to the extent permitted by that country. However, since the non-binding nature of an advisory opinion conflicts with the inherent influence of a decided judicial opinion, some nations prohibit their courts from issuing advisory opinions. They are also prohibited "on the ground that it distorts the true function of a court of law, which is to render binding decisions on disputes."[483] For example, the United States federal judiciary is fully prohibited from issuing advisory opinions although certain states allow their state judiciary to issue advisory opinions on particular topics. By contrast, other nations have legal systems that allow the executive to request judicial advisory opinions. In the United Kingdom, the Judicial Committee of the Privy Council may issue advisory opinions by request.

United Nations General Assembly Referral of the Issue of the Fence to the International Court of Justice

Under Resolution 377 A (V), known as "Uniting for Peace," the General Assembly can call an emergency special session within 24 hours if a "lack of unanimity of the permanent members, [makes the Security Council fail] to exercise its primary responsibility for the maintenance of international peace and security."[484] In March of 1997, under the "Uniting for Peace" resolution procedures, following a request from the permanent representative of Qatar, the General Assembly called the 10th Emergency Special Session to address "Illegal Israeli actions in Occupied East Jerusalem and the rest of the Occupied Palestinian Territory."[485] What is distinct about the 10th Emergency Special Session is that is has been adjourned and resumed a multitude of times since it was convened. In fact, since 1997, there have been more than 13 separate and subsequent meetings, each one recessed and reconvened, while sitting under the aegis of and as a part of the continuing 10th Emergency Special Session.

The UN Charter directs the General Assembly to refer all international peace and security issues that require UN action to the Security Council. In 2003, despite the fact that there were petitions pending for review before the Israeli High Court and further despite the fact that the Security Council remained "seized of the matter," as evidenced by its adoption during the previous month of the Resolution approving the Roadmap, the General Assembly circumvented the Security Council's authority and requested an advisory opinion from the ICJ. The General Assembly, at the request of the Palestine Liberation Organization, as a UN Observer, and governments sitting at the UN on its behalf and in violation of its charter, introduced Resolution A/RES/ES-10/14, which asked for an advisory opinion on the key question before us:

> What are the legal consequences arising from the construction of the wall being built by Israel, the occupying Power, in the Occupied Palestinian Territory, including in and around East Jerusalem, as described in the report of the Secretary-General, considering the rules and principles of international law, including the Fourth Geneva Convention of 1949, and relevant Security Council and General Assembly resolutions?[486]

Resolution A/RES/ES-10/14 (A/ES-10/L.16) was passed on December 8, 2003 just three weeks after the Security Council approved its Roadmap resolution. The General Assembly's request for an advisory opinion on Israel's security fence violated the UN Charter that grants the Security Council the authority to be the only body able to act on matters of "international peace and security." By bypassing the procedure called for in the Charter, the General Assembly requested action without the legal authority to do so, impeding the

Roadmap and the interfering with key issues to be negotiated by the parties themselves regarding the Israeli-Palestinian relationship.

Although the measure to refer this advisory opinion to the ICJ garnered the requisite two-thirds of those member states voting and present, it failed to receive an absolute majority of the 191 member states at the UN. The voting results were 90 in favor, 8 against, with 74 abstentions, including most of Europe. Numerous countries failed to even appear to vote on the issue.

Subsequent to the vote referring the request for an advisory opinion to the International Court of Justice, Israel and other countries strongly objected to and contested the right of the ICJ to exercise jurisdiction over the issue. Israel and other countries refused to appear before the International Court of Justice and Israel filed a written statement with attachments essentially contesting the court's jurisdiction. Other countries filed briefs, pro and con both on the jurisdictional issues and on the substantive question before the Court. As noted, this author filed a brief with the Clerk of Court on behalf of the Foundation for Defense of Democracies, a 501(c)3 non profit, nongovernmental organization. The brief, as filed, can be found posted at www.hnklaw.com. The essential argument of the brief was that The State of Israel, as any other nation-state in the world, has the right and obligation to take such actions as are necessary to protect and defend her people.

CHAPTER SEVEN

The Advisory Opinion: Sum and Substance

The Advisory Opinion

On July 9, 2004, roughly nine months after the UN General Assembly passed the resolution requesting an advisory opinion, the ICJ delivered its advisory opinion on the *Legal Consequences of the Construction of a Wall in the Occupied Palestinian Territory*.[487]

After briefly recounting the history of the proceedings, the 71-page document began with a discussion of jurisdiction and whether the ICJ has discretionary power to exercise its authority. The opinion goes on to discuss the scope of the question posed, the historical background of the wall's construction including a physical description of the barrier[488] and analysis of the relevant rules and principles of international law including the United Nations Charter, General Assembly Resolution 2625, international humanitarian law and human rights law.

Ultimately, the ICJ determined in the opinion of the court that Israel violated international law, concluding that the "wall" severely impedes the Palestinian right to self-determination. The opinion advises that Israel breached various obligations under the applicable provisions of international humanitarian law and human rights instruments. With regard to Israel's self-defense argument under Article 51 of the United Nations Charter, the Court essentially without commenting on the substance of the issues regarding the danger to Israel's citizenry from Palestinian terrorist attacks, rejected the self-defense argument.[489] It advised that Israel's justification for the wall and its use as self-defense against the constant threat of terrorist attacks was not justifiable because the terrorist attacks originated within a territory over which Israel exercises control. The Court rejected the argument of necessity under customary international law, saying that it did not find the wall's construction to be the sole means available to protect Israel. Thus, the Court advised the construction of the wall and its "associated regime" are contrary, in its view, to international law.

As to the legal consequences of Israel's construction of the wall, the Court advised that Israel must stop violating its international obligations, stop construction of the wall, dismantle it and nullify any related laws or regulations. The Court also advised that Israel make reparations to Palestinians for damages caused by the fence and its construction. The ICJ advised the international community that all states were required to not recognize the illegal situation resulting from construction of the wall and further advised that states could not render aid or assistance in maintaining the situation created by its construction. The opinion advised the United Nations to consider further action to end the "illegal situation" resulting from the wall.

Finally, the Court urged Israel and the Palestinians to abide by their obligations under international humanitarian law, implement all relevant Security Council resolutions in good faith (particularly resolutions 242 (1967) and 338 (1973)), and follow the path toward peace under the Roadmap. The Court recognized that additional efforts are necessary to encourage a negotiated solution to the outstanding problems and to encourage the establishment of a Palestinian State, with peace and security, for all in the region.

History of the Proceedings: Paragraphs 1 through 12

The advisory opinion's preliminary section, paragraphs 1 through 12, recounts the history of the proceedings. The Court was composed of fifteen judges: President Shi Jiuyong (China); Vice-President Raymond Ranjeva (Madagascar); Gilbert Guillaume (France), Abdul G. Koroma (Sierra Leone), Vladlen Stepanovich

Vereshchetin (Russian Federation), Dame Rosalyn Higgins (United Kingdom), Gonzalo Parra-Aranguren (Venezuela), Pieter H. Kooijmans (Netherlands), Francisco Rezek (Brazil), Awn Shawkat Al-Khasawneh (Jordan), Thomas Buergenthal (USA), Nabil Elaraby (Egypt), Hisashi Owada (Japan), Bruno Simma (Germany), and Peter Tomka (Slovakia).

The Court advisory opinion preliminarily restated General Assembly Resolution ES-10/14 and the question it posed:

> What are the legal consequences arising from the construction of the wall being built by Israel, the occupying Power, in the Occupied Palestinian Territory, including in and around East Jerusalem, as described in the report of the Secretary-General, considering the rules and principles of international law, including the Fourth Geneva Convention of 1949, and relevant Security Council and General Assembly resolutions?[490]

After receiving the General Assembly request for the Advisory Opinion, on December 10, 2003 the ICJ Registrar notified all states as parties entitled to appear before the Court of the General Assembly's request for an advisory opinion. In response, the Government of Israel raised a number of issues with the Court by letter the following day. While reserving Israel's position with respect to the proceedings, Israel argued that the Court should not "entertain the advisory opinion request for reasons of jurisdiction and admissibility" and noted its concern with "the negative effect of pending proceedings on any activities aimed at facilitating negotiations between the parties as envisaged by the "Road Map.""[491] Israel also noted that to "adequately, or fairly" address the seriousness of the question, the length of preparation for written statements should be months, not weeks.[492]

On December 19th, eight days after receiving Israel's letter explaining the need for substantial time to prepare, the Court ordered the UN and Member States to submit their written statements by January 30, 2004. Noting that the UN and Member States were likely to provide relevant information on "all aspects raised by the question submitted to the Court," it allowed their submissions in addition to a submission from the Palestine Liberation Organization ("Palestine"), notwithstanding its observer organization status.[493] The League of

Arab States and the Organization of the Islamic Conference were also allowed to submit written statements. Pursuant to Article 65, paragraph 2, the Secretary-General of the United Nations submitted a dossier of documents relevant to the question to the Court.

Prior to submission of its written statement on January 30, 2004, Israel sent the Court two letters, one on December 31st and a confidential one on January 15th, which raised additional concerns over the Court's composition and ICJ Judge Elaraby's role in the Emergency Special Session that instigated the General Assembly's request for the advisory opinion. The Court dismissed Israel's concerns, deciding that Israel's reasons were not enough to preclude Judge Elaraby from sitting on the panel.

Many states and organizations filed written statements on January 30th.[494] Israel refused to directly present evidence at the oral hearings but did submit a 246-page written statementwherein it reasserted its position on "the jurisdiction of the Court and the propriety of any response by it on the substance of the request" without addressing "the legality of the fence, legal consequences that flow from it or other matters pertaining to the question of substance presented to the Court."[495] Israel noted that it "considers that the Court does not have jurisdiction to entertain the request and that, even were it to have jurisdiction, it should not respond to the requested opinion."[496]

From February 23rd to the 25th, the Court held public hearings so Member States and Palestine could make oral statements. The ICJ heard oral statements by representatives of Palestine (6 statements), South Africa (2), Algeria (1), Saudi Arabia (1), Bangladesh (1), Belize (1), Cuba (1), Indonesia (1), Jordan (2), Madagascar (1), Malaysia (1), Senegal (1), Sudan (1), League of Arab States (1), and the Organization of the Islamic Conference (1).[497]

Questions of Jurisdiction: Paragraphs 13 through 42

Jurisdiction is defined as the power and authority granted to a judge or court to hear and make a pronouncement on legal matters to ultimately administer justice. In paragraphs 13 through 42, the ICJ analyzed whether it was within its jurisdiction to issue the advisory opinion requested by the General Assembly.

The court wrongly found itself competent to give the advisory opinion. To be competent, the Court stated "it is... a precondition of the Court's competence that the advisory opinion be requested by an organ duly authorized to seek it under the Charter [and] that it be requested on a legal question."[498] The Court erroneously concluded that the General Assembly, which sought the advisory opinion, was competent to make the request under Article 96, paragraph 1, of the United Nations Charter, which provides, "The General Assembly or the Security Council may request the International Court of Justice to give an advisory opinion on any legal question."[499]

As to whether the request met the second precondition of being a "legal question," the Court noted that the "present case" is within its jurisdiction because it falls within the situation where "the Court has sometimes in the past given certain indications as to the relationship between the question, the subject of a request for an advisory opinion and the activities of the General Assembly."[500] In plain language, this means that the Court determined it can opine on the subject of a request, even if it is not a "legal question" per se, if the subject of the request falls within the authorized activities of the General Assembly. The Court noted that the General Assembly, under Article 10, is competent over "'any questions or any matters' within the scope of the Charter" and, under Article 11, paragraph 2, is specifically competent over "'questions relating to the maintenance of international peace and security'... and [can] make recommendations under certain conditions."[501] Since the "Assembly, in its resolution ES-10/12 on April 25, 1997, "considered [the question of the construction of the wall in the Occupied Palestinian Territory as constituting] a threat to international peace and security," the subject of the General Assembly's request is an authorized activity upon which the ICJ can, therefore, opine.[502]

(1) The ICJ's Response to the Contention that the General Assembly Acted *Ultra Vires* under the Charter when it Requested an Advisory Opinion

It was alleged before the ICJ that the General Assembly went beyond the powers granted to it under the Charter when it adopted

resolution ES-10/14 requesting an advisory opinion on the legal consequences of the construction of the wall.

Article 24 of the United Nations Charter grants the Security
Council with "primary responsibility for the maintenance of international peace and security." This responsibility, however, is not
necessarily exclusive, and under Article 14, the General Assembly
may also "recommend measures for the peaceful adjustment of various situations."[503] This Article 14 authority to recommend measures
can only be comprised if the Security Council is already addressing
the dispute or situation. Under Article 12, the Charter instructs that:

> While the Security Council is exercising in respect of any dispute
> or situation the functions assigned to it in the present Charter,
> the General Assembly shall not make any recommendation with
> regard to that dispute or situation unless the Security Council so
> requests.[504]

On November 19, 2003, the Security Council unanimously approved resolution 1515, adopting the Roadmap for Peace between
Israel and the Palestinians as official UN policy. The resolution endorses a permanent two-state solution and calls on both sides to
implement their obligations under the Roadmap. It did not specifically mention the construction of the wall. Nineteen days later, on
December 8, 2003, the General Assembly met in the Tenth Emergency Special Session and adopted resolution ES-10/14 requesting
the ICJ issue an advisory opinion on the legality of the construction
of the "wall."

Israel argued that the General Assembly violated the Charter
by requesting an advisory opinion since the Security Council, in
implementing the Roadmap, was already "exercising in respect of
any dispute or situation the functions assigned to it."[505] The ICJ dismissed the argument.

The ICJ posited that the General Assembly's request for an advisory opinion was not, in itself, a prohibited "recommendation"
on a "dispute or situation" that the Security Council was addressing. The irony is clear. While the ICJ is correct in stating that the
request, "in itself," was not a "recommendation," the entire purpose
of the request was to get an ICJ recommendation that, "in itself,"
was on the very "dispute or situation" the Security Council was

already addressing, i.e. of which the Security Council was seized the Arab-Palestinian-Israeli conflict. The ICJ's explanation for why Article 14 was not violated uses linguistic loopholes and completely disregards the purpose behind Article 14's prohibition on certain recommendations.

Additionally, the Court examined the legality of the General Assembly's action adopting resolution ES-10/14, in relation to its proximity to the Security Council's resolution 1515, and concluded that the "accepted practice of the General Assembly [in adopting a resolution on a subject that the Security Council is also addressing], as it has evolved, is consistent with Article 12, paragraph 1, of the Charter."[506] To support its conclusion, the Court explained that the "interpretation of Article 12 has evolved" from its initial interpretation, that "the Assembly could not make a recommendation on a question… while the matter remained on the Council's agenda," to an interpretation of Article 12 that allows "the General Assembly and the Security Council to deal in parallel with the same matter concerning the maintenance of international peace and security."[507]

It is important to keep the text and purpose of Article 14 in mind when evaluating the ICJ's faulty reasoning and conclusion. Article 14 is clear on what it prohibits:

> While the Security Council is exercising in respect of any dispute or situation the functions assigned to it in the present Charter, the General Assembly shall not make any recommendation with regard to that dispute or situation unless the Security Council so requests.[508]

A plain reading of the above prohibition against the General Assembly making any recommendation with regard to a dispute that is before the Security Council is clear on its face. However, to support the Court's inappropriate validation of this new interpretation of Article 14 that allows the two bodies to "deal in parallel with the same matter," the ICJ referred to two past situations where the General Assembly made recommendations while the matter was still on the Council's agenda. It cites General Assembly "recommendations in the matter of Congo … and the Portuguese colonies… [to highlight that] those cases still appeared on the Council's agenda."[509] The crippling fact the ICJ glosses over, however, is that although the cases were still on the Security Council's agenda, "the Council [had not] adopted any recent resolution[s] concerning them." Additionally, the ICJ cited the UN Legal Counsel's interpretation of the words in Article 14, that the Security Council "is exercising the functions," to mean "is exercising the functions at this moment."[510]

The evidence used to support Article 14's supposed evolution consisted of two matters in the 1960's and a Legal Counsel interpretation adding "at this moment." With this scant support as its foundation, the ICJ reached the conclusion that the words, "while the Security Council is exercising… the General Assembly shall not make any recommendation," should be interpreted as meaning "the General Assembly and the Security Council [can] deal in parallel with the same matter." As the Security Council's resolution 1515 was nineteen merely days before the UNGA resolution, it raises the serious questions that if the passage of, nineteen days is enough time passed to presume that the Security Council is no longer exercising its "primary responsibility" to maintain "international peace and security," over the Arab-Palestinian-Israeli conflict then it is clear that the General Assembly's present power far surpasses the level the framers of the UN Charter ever intended. Moreover, the Security Council Resolution adopting the Roadmap clearly envisioned ongoing and additional actions and involvement of the Security Council, making it clear that the Security Council was then exercising the functions relating to maintaining international peace and security at the time the General Assembly inappropriately intervened.

(2) The ICJ's Response to the Contention that the Request for an Advisory Opinion Did Not Meet the Conditions of Resolution 377 A (V)

Next, the Court addressed the contention that the request for the advisory opinion did not fulfill the "essential conditions under which the Tenth Emergency Special Session was convened and has continued to act."[511] UN General Assembly Resolution 377 A (V) is known as the "Uniting for Peace Resolution" of November 3, 1950. It was proposed by the United States as a way to bypass the USSR's veto in the Security Council.[512] Resolution 377 A (V) states:

if the Security Council, because of lack of unanimity of the permanent

members, fails to exercise its primary responsibility for the maintenance of international peace and security in any case where there
appears to be a threat to the peace, breach of the peace, or act of
aggression, the General Assembly shall consider the matter immediately with a view to making appropriate recommendations to
Members for collective measures . . .[513]

The Court explained that there are two conditions that must be met
before the General Assembly can follow the procedures set forth in
Resolution 377 A (V). For one, the Security Council must, because of
at least one negative vote of a permanent member, fail to exercise its
responsibility of addressing the threat to the peace. Secondly, there
must be an actual threat to the peace. If both conditions are met, the
General Assembly has the authority to call an Emergency Special
Session to address the threat.

The ICJ quickly dismissed any notion that the conditions were
not met. Opponents argued that the first condition was not met because the Security Council was never seized of the specific matter of
requesting an advisory opinion. In response, the Court stated that
the Security Council's rejection of the draft resolution on the wall
which came before it on October 14, 2003 initiated the procedure set
forth in Resolution 377 A (V) and since the Council did not reconsider the resolution from October 20th to December 8th, the General
Assembly was justified in calling the Emergency Meeting to properly seize the issue.[514]

Incredibly, the Court makes no mention of the Security Council's resolution 1515, adopted between those dates, on November 19th,
after the time the draft resolution on the wall came before it on October 14th, which directly addresses the Palestinian–Israeli conflict by
officially putting the backing of the UN behind the Roadmap, almost
as if that Security Council action carried no weight or relevancy to
the request for the advisory opinion. The Security Council action on
November 19th should have been deemed to have encompassed all
issues relating to maintaining peace and security between the Israel
and the Palestinians. However, the ICJ's decision to treat resolution
1515 as an issue separate from and unrelated to the fence, rather than
the singular question of the legality of the "wall" being a part of the
larger issue covered by resolution 1515 was a glaring departure from

court practice and precedent, interpreting resolution 1515's silence on the specific issue of the wall as the Council's lack of consideration, an interpretation which makes no sense, since the issue of the wall clearly is within the issues to be determined by the Roadmap, the very subject of resolution 1515. By blindly interpreting out of resolution 1515 any Council consideration of the wall's construction, the Court validated the Assembly's request for an advisory opinion, thereby circuitously justifying its issuance of its own opinion and inappropriately injecting itself into matters within Security Council purview.

Moreover, the Court dismissed the unique 'rolling' character of the Emergency Special Session stating that the fact that the Session was convened in April 1997, close to seven years prior is irrelevant and, "namely the fact of its having been... reconvened 11 times since then, [does not have] any relevance with regard to the validity of the request by the General Assembly."[515] The ICJ analysis on that issue is somewhat inane. Comparing the situation to another situation during the 1980's where an emergency session was reconvened four times, the court reiterated that the "validity of resolutions or decisions of the Assembly adopted under such circumstances was never disputed."[516] The Court does not address the significant difference between the situations nor does it address the Assembly's use of the 377 A (V) emergency procedures as a free pass to gain more authority than the UN Charter ever intended. Furthermore, the Court considered that:

> While it may not have been originally contemplated that it would be appropriate for the General Assembly to hold simultaneous emergency and regular sessions, no rule of the Organization has been identified which would be thereby violated, so as to render invalid the resolution adopting the present request for an advisory opinion.[517]

The ICJ's analysis and interpretation of the General Assembly's authority is another example of how the ICJ reinterpreted the UN Charter to self-validate its ability to give its own advisory opinion.

(3) The ICJ's Response to the Contention that the Request Did Not Ask for an Opinion on a Legal Question

Next, the Court addressed the contention that the advisory

opinion request was "not on a 'legal question' within the meaning of Article 96, paragraph 1, of the Charter and Article 65, paragraph 1, of the Statute of the Court."[518] Opponents argued that to be a legal question and appropriate for ICJ review, it must be "reasonably specific" so that the ICJ can "determine with reasonably certainty the legal meaning of the question asked."[519] To support the contention that the request was not a legal question because of its lack of "reasonably certainty [of] the legal meaning," opponents argued first that all interpretations of the question of the "legal consequences" lead to a course of action that is precluded for the Court. Secondly, opponents argued that the request was not a legal question because it is "not of a 'legal' character because of its imprecision and abstract nature."[520]

The Court quickly dismissed both arguments. First, addressing the effect of the lack of clarity on the "legal nature" of the question, the Court points out that a lack of clarity does not diminish its legal nature or the Court's jurisdiction, noting: "rather, such uncertainty will require clarification in interpretation, and such necessary clarifications of interpretation have frequently been given by the court."[521] The Court explained its procedure for processing a request and noted that many past occasions required the Court to "broaden, interpret and even reformulate the questions put."[522] Applying its established procedure to the case at hand, the court said, "in the present instance, the Court will only have to do what it has often done in the past, namely 'identify the existing principles and rules, interpret them and apply them.'"[523]

Interpreting the question asked, the Court clarified the request and explained that since it was asked about the "legal consequences," it must determine whether the construction of the wall does or does not breach international law. If so, the Court noted that upon whom those consequences fall is not an "abstract one" and it "would be for the Court to determine for whom any such consequences arise."[524] In sum, while there may be various interpretations of the question, the Court's ability to interpret the question as it sees fit is a longstanding precedent and has no effect on whether the question is considered a 'legal question' upon which an advisory opinion can be rendered.

To conclude the jurisdictional issues, the Court responded to the assertion that the issue before it was really a political question. The Court acknowledged the political aspects of the issue but insisted that this was the case in "so many questions which arise in international life" and this fact did not "deprive [the request] of its character as a legal question [nor] deprive the Court of a competence expressly conferred on it by its Statute."[525] The Court noted:

> The political nature of the motives which may be said to have inspired the request and the political implications that the opinion given might have are of no relevance in the establishment of its jurisdiction to give such an opinion... [and there is] no element in the present proceedings which could lead it to conclude otherwise.[526]

Discretionary Power of the Court to Exercise its Jurisdiction: Paragraphs 43 through 65

Having concluded that it had jurisdiction to hear the question and issue an advisory opinion, the Court moved to analysis as to whether it was proper for it to do so under the circumstances. The Court reflected on its role as "the principal judicial organ of the United Nations"[527] and went on to explain that its "discretionary power to decline to give an advisory opinion[,] even if the conditions of jurisdiction are met,"[528] should only be exercised, "consistent [with] jurisprudence," for "compelling reasons" and "in principle, should not be refused."[529]

To highlight the weight the Court places on its role as the "principal judicial organ of the United Nations," the Court noted that it has never declined a request for an advisory opinion and its predecessor, the Permanent Court of International Justice, only declined once and that was solely because it lacked jurisdiction, "not on considerations of judicial propriety."[530]

Opponents argued that there were "specific aspects" of the General Assembly's request that were compelling enough to make the exercise of ICJ jurisdiction "improper and inconsistent with the Court's judicial function."[531] For one, Israel's "lack of consent" as a member-state affected party and the fact that the case "concerns a contentious matter between Israel and Palestine," means that issuance of an advisory opinion would violate the principle that "a State is not obliged to allow its disputes to be submitted to judicial settlement without its consent."[532] Essentially, Israel wanted the Court to decline the question based on the Permanent Court of International Justice's precedent in *Status of Eastern Carelia* where:

> The question directly concerned an already existing dispute, one of the States parties to which was neither a party to the Statute of the Permanent Court nor a Member of the League of Nations, objected to the proceedings, and refused to take part in any way.[533]

The Court dismissed this contention by differentiating between its role in giving an advisory opinion versus its role in a contentious case. It noted that "lack of consent to the Court's contentious jurisdiction by interested States has no bearing on the Court's jurisdiction to give an advisory opinion"[534] since an advisory opinion is requested by the United Nations, "the organ which is entitled to request it," in order to obtain "enlightenment as to the course of action it should take."[535] It is not given to a state and it is not legally binding. The Court declared further that it is judicially proper for it to give an opinion, "which the General Assembly deems of assistance to it for the proper exercise of its functions," and since "the opinion is requested on a question which is of particularly acute concern to the United Nations," then "the Court… cannot… decline to give an opinion [on the ground of lack of consent.]"[536]

The Court pointed out that, like in the *Western Sahara* case, the legal controversy arose during UN proceedings and not independently out of bilateral relations between the two parties. The Court did not accept the view that "the General Assembly's request can be regarded as only a bilateral matter between Israel and Palestine." Instead, the United Nations has "powers and responsibilities… in questions relating to international peace and security" and "a permanent responsibility towards the question of Palestine until the question is resolved."[537] The Court concluded, "the opinion is… one which is located in a much broader frame of reference than a bilateral dispute."[538] Under these circumstances, the Court did not view the giving of an advisory opinion to have the effect of circumventing the principle of consent to judicial settlement.

Next, the Court rejected the argument that an advisory opinion on the wall "could impede a political, negotiated solution to the

Israeli-Palestinian conflict" and, more importantly, undermine the Roadmap process, explaining that it has considered and rejected such arguments in the past. The Court referenced its advisory opinion on *Legality of the Threat or Use of Nuclear Weapons* where a similar contention was raised and explained that an ICJ advisory opinion is a "matter of appreciation," meaning "no matter what might be its conclusions in any opinion it might give, they would have relevance for the continuing debate on the matter in the General Assembly and would present an additional element in the negotiations on the matter." In essence, the Court discredits the possibility that its advisory opinion could adversely affect disarmament negotiations, concluding that it has "heard contrary positions advanced and there are no evident criteria by which it can prefer one assessment to another."[539]

The ICJ recognized the Roadmap as a negotiating framework but questioned, "what influence the Court's opinion might have on those negotiations" and concluded that it "cannot regard this factor as a compelling reason to decline to exercise its jurisdiction."[540] In sum, since both sides have differing views on how the advisory opinion might affect future negotiations, and determining that it should not decline to exercise its jurisdiction, the court found that it should proceed to give an advisory opinion and that there was no reason to give more weight to one side's assessment over the other, effectively nullifying any credible points on either side.

The Court further rejected the argument that it should decline to give an advisory opinion because the construction of the wall was "only one aspect of the Israeli-Palestinian conflict, which could not be properly addressed in the present proceedings."[541] It reiterated that:

> The question that the General Assembly has chosen to ask of the Court is confined to the legal consequences of the construction of the wall, and the Court would only examine other issues to the extent that they might be necessary to its consideration of the question put to it.[542]

Another argument rejected by the Court was that the Court "does not have at its disposal the requisite facts and evidence to enable it to reach its conclusion" on the legal consequences of the wall and "if the Court decided to give the requested opinion, it would be forced to speculate about essential facts… [which in this case] cannot be elucidated without hearing all parties to the conflict… and [therefore] make assumptions about arguments of law" based on speculation.[543] Israel argued that, for the Court to determine the legal consequences of the wall, it must also know the facts surrounding "the nature and scope of the security threat to which the wall is intended to respond,… the effectiveness of that response, and… the impact of the construction for the Palestinians."[544] The Court summarily dismissed the need for this knowledge because obtaining it, "would already be difficult in a contentious case… [and] would be further complicated in an advisory proceeding," in part because Israel "alone possesses much of the necessary information and has stated that it chooses not to address the merits."[545]

To validate its conclusion that certain facts need not be known for the Court to render an advisory opinion, the Court explained "whether the evidence available to it is sufficient to give an advisory opinion must be decided in each particular instance."[546] In this case, the Court pointed out that it had at its disposal:

> The report of the Secretary-General, as well as a voluminous dossier submitted by him to the Court, comprising not only detailed information on the route of the wall but also on its humanitarian and socio-economic impact on the Palestinian population… The Secretary-General's… written statement updating his report, which supplemented the information contained therein… [and] numerous other participants have submitted to the Court written statements which contain information relevant to a response to the question put by the General Assembly.[547]

In addition, the Court had Israel's Written Statement, which:

> Although limited to issues of jurisdiction and judicial propriety, contained observations on other matters, including Israel's concerns in terms of security, and was accompanied by corresponding annexes; many other documents issued by the Israeli Government on those matters are in the public domain.[548]

Therefore, the Court concluded that it had sufficient information and evidence to allow it to give the advisory opinion requested.

Advisory opinions are meant to help clarify what future actions a UN organ, agency or consenting state can legally take to address a certain situation. Another argument put forth to the Court for declining to give the requested opinion was that the opinion "would lack any useful purpose" since the General Assembly had already "declared the construction of the wall to be illegal and... determined the legal consequences by demanding that Israel stop and reverse its construction."[549] Additionally, the General Assembly "never made it clear how it intended to use the opinion."[550]

The Court glossed over the important point that, at the time of the request, the General Assembly had already pronounced its decision on what the appropriate future action should be: that is, that Israel must stop construction. The Court supports its decision to give the opinion by bringing up general principles surrounding advisory opinions and the role of the Court, stating that the opinion is only meant to "guide the United Nations in respect of its own action" and "furnish... the elements of law necessary for them in their action,... the General Assembly has the right to decide for itself on the usefulness of an opinion in the light of its own needs."[551]

In sum, the Court explains away the significant concerns raised by objecting parties. It refuses to address why the General Assembly seems to be requesting a legal opinion in hindsight of its action. Further, it ignores what little importance the advisory opinion might have on the General Assembly, particularly in light of the fact that the Security Council was seized of the matter and the General Assembly should therefore have no role in the issue unless the Security Council failed or refused to act.

Additionally, the Court concluded as irrelevant the fact that the General Assembly did not make it clear what the purpose was for the request itself. The Court refused to speculate on what the purpose may be, noting that it "considers that the General Assembly has not yet determined all the possible consequences of its own resolution."[552] The Court said its "task [is] to determine in a comprehensive manner the legal consequences of the construction of the wall, while the General Assembly—and the Security Council—may then draw conclusions from the Court's findings."[553] Its response blatantly ignores the fact that the General Assembly had already concluded the legal consequences of the construction even before it made the request, setting the stage for the Court to essentially impose its validation on the General Assembly, its opinion on the Security Council and its pronouncements for consumption in the court of public opinion.

The Court wrote a strongly worded rejection of Israel's contention that "Palestine, given its responsibility for acts of violence against Israel and its population which the wall is aimed at addressing, cannot seek from the Court a remedy for a situation resulting from its own wrongdoing."[554] Invoking the legal maxim "*nullus commodum capere potest de sua injuria propria*," meaning "no one shall take advantage of his own wrong," Israel argued "good faith and the principle of 'clean hands' provide a compelling reason that should lead the Court to refuse the General Assembly's request."[555] The Court dismissed this argument as not pertinent, reiterating that the General Assembly itself, not a state or other entity, such as the Palestinian Authority, requested and will be given the advisory opinion.

The Court concluded that asserting jurisdiction to render an advisory opinion was proper and rather than determining that there was no compelling reason to issue its opinion it determined that there existed no compelling reason to exercise its discretion to decline to give an opinion.

Scope of Question Posed: Paragraphs 66 through 69

The Court addressed what term(s) it would use in the advisory opinion when referring to the "complex construction." After noting "the other terms used, either by Israel ("fence") or by the Secretary-General ("barrier") are no more accurate [than the term "wall"] if understood in the physical sense," the Court decided to use the General Assembly's terminology and call the construction a "wall."[556]

The Court went on to state that it would only consider the General Assembly's question as asking about the legal consequences of the wall that has or will be constructed on land "in the Occupied Palestinian Territory, including in and around East Jerusalem." It would not examine those parts of the wall built on the territory of Israel itself.

The Court explained that in order to properly answer the question as to the legal consequences of the wall, it must first determine whether the law breaches international law. In so doing, the Court determined that it must analyze the status of the territory on which the wall has been constructed and determine what law applies that may or may not be breached. Only then, the Court said, could it determine whether the law had been breached.

Historical Background: Paragraphs 70 through 78

The Court continued its advisory opinion with its own version of a brief historical background of the conflict meant to explain its reasons for concluding that the territory in question is "occupied Palestinian territory" and that Israel is the occupying power. The Court's analysis was thus:

Following the end of World War I, "a class 'A' Mandate for Palestine was entrusted to Great Britain," pursuant to Article 22 of the Covenant of the League of Nations which read:

> Certain communities formerly belonging to the Turkish Empire have reached a stage of development where their existence as independent nations can be provisionally recognized, subject to the rendering of administrative advice and assistance by a Mandatory until such time as they are able to stand alone.[557]

To explain the general purpose behind mandates, the Court referred to its *International Status of South West Africa* advisory opinion that said, "The Mandate was created, in the interest of the inhabitants of the territory, and of humanity in general, as an international institution with an international object—a sacred trust of civilization."[558] According to the Court, when considering the Mandate, "two principles were considered to be of paramount importance: the principle of non-annexation and the principle that the well-being and development of . . . peoples [not yet able to govern themselves] form[ed] 'a sacred trust of civilization.' "[559]

The territorial boundaries for the British Mandate "were laid down by various instruments, in particular on the eastern border by a British memorandum of 16 September 1922 and an Anglo-Transjordanian Treaty of 20 February 1928."[560] Then in 1947, the United Kingdom announced that it would completely evacuate the mandated territory by May of 1948. At the same time, in November of 1947, the General Assembly adopted resolution 181 (II) that called for a "Plan of Partition" of the territory "between two independent States, one Arab, the other Jewish, as well as the creation of a special international regime for the City of Jerusalem."[561] The Plan of Partition was never implemented. The Arab states and Palestinians rejected the plan as being "unbalanced." On May 14, 1948, Israel declared its independence and armed conflict subsequently broke out between Israel and the Arab states.

In November of 1948, the Security Council concluded in resolution 62 that "an armistice shall be established in all sectors of Palestine."[562] Mediation led to general armistice agreements between Israel and neighboring states. One of such agreements, between Israel and Jordan, established an armistice demarcation line, now known as the "Green Line," between Israeli and Arab forces. Israel and Jordan agreed that the Article V and VI provisions of the agreement would not be "interpreted as prejudicing, in any sense, an ultimate political settlement between the Parties" including "future territorial settlements or boundary lines or to claims of either Party relating thereto."[563]

As a result of the Six Day War in 1967, "Israeli forces occupied all the territories which had constituted Palestine under British Mandate (including those known as the West Bank, lying to the east of the Green Line)."[564] Shortly after, the Security Council adopted resolution 242, reiterating the principle that a state cannot acquire territory through war but also setting out the right of states to respect for and acknowledgement of the sovereignty, territorial integrity and political independence of every State in the area and their right to live in peace within secure and recognized boundaries free from threats or acts of force. The resolution called for the "[w]ithdrawal of Israel armed forces from territories occupied in the recent conflict" and Israel's "[t]ermination of all claims or states of belligerency."[565] In 1994, Israel and Jordan signed a peace treaty that established the "administrative boundary" "between the two States 'with reference to the boundary definition under the Mandate as is shown in Annex I(a) . . . without prejudice to the status of any territories that came under Israeli military government control in 1967."'[566]

Following 1967, the Security Council condemned Israeli attempts to change the status of Jerusalem and, in 1971, formally did so in resolution 298. Then in resolution 478, adopted in 1980, the Security Council concluded that Israel's establishment of Jerusalem as its capital was a violation of international law. Since 1993, Israel and the Palestine Liberation Organization have signed a number of agreements binding both parties to various obligations, some of which "required Israel to transfer to Palestinian authorities certain powers and responsibilities exercised in the Occupied Palestinian Territory by its military authorities and civil administration."[567]

The Court continued with a note on what it considers "occupied territory" under customary international law, asserting that "territory is considered occupied when it is actually placed under the authority of the hostile army, and the occupation extends only to the territory where such authority has been established and can be exercised."[568] Applying its definition of "occupied" to the advisory opinion's territory in question, the Court concluded that:

> Under customary international law...the territories situated between the Green Line and the former eastern boundary of Palestine under the Mandate were occupied by Israel in 1967 during the armed conflict between Israel and Jordan...[And are] therefore occupied territories in which Israel had the status of occupying Power. Subsequent events in these territories . . . have done nothing to alter this situation. All these territories including (East Jerusalem) remain occupied territories and Israel has continued to have the status of occupying Power.[569]

Description of the Wall: Paragraphs 79 through 85

The Court relied on the Secretary General's report and its supplement to describe the construction and work associated with the wall. In July of 2001, the Israeli Cabinet approved for the first time a plan to halt infiltration from the West Bank. On April 14, 2002, the Cabinet, "adopted a decision for the construction of works, forming what Israel describes as a 'security fence,' 80 kilometres in length, in three areas of the West Bank."[570] Then in June, the first phase was approved for construction in the West Bank (including East Jerusalem.) In August, the Cabinet adopted the route of the fence to be completed in Phase A, "with a view to the construction of a complex 123 kilometres long in the northern West Bank, running from the Salem checkpoint (north of Jenin) to the settlement at Elkana."[571] Then in December, Phase B was approved, which "entailed a stretch of some 40 kilometres running east from the Salem checkpoint towards Beth Shean along the northern part of the Green Line as far as the Jordan Valley."[572] A full route was approved on October 1, 2003, "which, according to the report of the Secretary-General, 'will form one continuous line stretching 720 kilometres along the West Bank.'"[573]

The Court referred to the Israeli Ministry of Defense website for information on Phases C and D, which had a map showing for Phase C, "a continuous section... encompassing a number of large settlements [that] will link the north-western end of the 'security fence' built around Jerusalem with the southern point of Phase A construction at Elkana."[574] The same map also indicated that for Phase D, "the 'security fence' will run for 115 kilometres from the Har Gilo settlement near Jerusalem to the Carmel settlement southeast of Hebron."[575]

The Court referred to the Secretary-General's report when it discussed the status of the different phases of construction and the details pertaining to the direction and length of the different routes, the number of Palestinians and Israelis living in those areas, and the estimated dates for completion. The Court did note that, "the Israeli Government has explained that the routes and timetable as described above are subject to modification."[576] For instance, "In February 2004 . . . an 8-kilometre section near the town of Baqa al-Sharqiya was demolished, and the planned length of the wall appears to have been slightly reduced."[577]

The Court described the physical nature of the construction that was reported in the Secretary-General's report and Written Statement, consisting of:

    (1) a fence with electronic sensors;
    (2) a ditch (up to 4 metres deep);
    (3) a two-lane asphalt patrol road;

(4) a trace road (a strip of sand smoothed to detect footprints) running parallel to the fence;

(5) a stack of six coils of barbed wire marking the perimeter of the
complex.[578]

Noting the amount of concrete wall in the construction, the Court
stated that the concrete wall was "generally found where Palestinian population centres are close to or abut Israel (such as near Qalqiliya and Tulkarm or in parts of Jerusalem)" and, at the time of the
Secretary-General's report, 8.5 kilometres, out of the approximately
180 kilometres of the complex completed or under construction,
was concrete wall.[579]

The Court compared the wall's position in relation to the Green
Line, saying:

> In its northernmost part, the wall as completed or under construc-
> tion barely deviates from the Green Line. It nevertheless lies within
> occupied territories for most of its course. The works deviate more
> than 7.5 kilometres from the Green Line in certain places to encom-
> pass settlements, while encircling Palestinian population areas. A
> stretch of 1 to 2 kilometres west of Tulkarm appears to run on the
> Israeli side of the Green Line. Elsewhere, on the other hand, the
> planned route would deviate eastward by up to 22 kilometres. In
> the case of Jerusalem, the existing works and the planned route lie
> well beyond the Green Line and even in some cases beyond the
> eastern municipal boundary of Jerusalem as fixed by Israel. . . .
> On the basis of that route, approximately 975 square kilometres
> (or 16.6 per cent of the West Bank) would . . . lie between the Green
> Line and the wall.[580]

The Court also took note of the people living in those areas:

> The area [between the Green Line and the wall] is stated to be home
> to 237,000 Palestinians. If the full wall were completed as planned,
> another 160,000 Palestinians would live in almost completely encir-
> cled communities, described as enclaves in the report. As a result of
> the planned route, nearly 320,000 Israeli settlers (of whom 178,000
> in East Jerusalem) would be living in the area between the Green
> Line and the wall.[581]

The Court next turned its attention to the new administrative
regime that the Israelis created to accompany the wall's construction
and the limited accessibility. In October of 2003, the Israeli Defense
Forces ordered the area between the Green Line and the "wall," to
be a "Closed Area" in which "residents of this area may no lon-

ger remain in it, nor may non-residents enter it, unless holding a permit or identity card issued by the Israeli authorities."[582] On the other hand, "Israeli citizens, Israeli permanent residents and those eligible to immigrate to Israel in accordance with the Law of Return may remain in, or move freely to, from and within the Closed Area without a permit." Addressing accessibility to the Closed Area, the Court noted that entry and "exit from the Closed Area can only be made through access gates, which are opened infrequently and for short periods."[583]

Applicable Rules and Principles of International Law: Paragraphs 86 through 113

From paragraph 86 through paragraph 113, the advisory opinion explained the Court's determination of "the rules and principles of international law which are relevant in assessing the legality of the measures taken by Israel." The rules and principles discussed were derived from the United Nations Charter, other treaties, customary international law and relevant General Assembly and Security Council resolutions. The Court mentioned that Israel expressed doubts on the applicability of certain rules. The Court considered Israel's contentions within the paragraphs.

United Nations Charter and General Assembly Resolution 2625 (XXV): Paragraphs 87 through 88

The Court applied international rules and principles on the use of force, territorial acquisition, and self-determination. As a preliminary matter, the Court provides Article 2, paragraph 4, of the United Nations Charter that prohibits UN members from using or threatening to use force against "the territorial integrity or political independence of any State, or in any other manner inconsistent with the Purposes of the United Nations."[584] The Court referenced General Assembly resolution 2625, entitled "Declaration on Principles of International Law concerning Friendly Relations and Co-operation among States" and adopted on October 24, 1970, that reflects the international principle that "no territorial acquisition resulting from the threat or use of force shall be recognized as legal."[585] The rules espoused in both the UN Charter and resolution 2625 reflect principles of customary law.

The Court went on to note that this principle of self-determination, found in the UN Charter and resolution 2625, is also a right under customary international law regardless of whether the territory is self-governing or not. The Court explained that this right of all people to self-determination is the "sacred trust" the Covenant of the League of Nations refers to in Article 22, paragraph 1.[586] International law, both customary and law defined by international agreements and treaties, requires states to respect and promote the realization of this *erga omnes*, a right towards all.[587]

International Humanitarian Law: Paragraphs 89 through 101

The Court went on to discuss what principles of international law were applicable. It noted preliminarily that Israel was not a party to the Fourth Hague Convention of 1907. However, the Convention and the Hague Regulations annexed to it were found by the Court and by the International Military Tribunal of Nuremburg as "recognised by all civilised nations, and were regarded as being declaratory of the laws and customs of war," and as such, are now customary international law.[588] Additionally, the Court observed that Israel was a willing party to the Fourth Geneva Convention, and pursuant to the Convention's Article 154, it was supplementary to the Hague Regulations Sections II and III. Section III of the Regulations concern "Military authority over the territory of the hostile State."[589]

The Court then addressed Israel's contention that the Fourth Geneva Convention does not legally apply to the Occupied Palestinian Territory. The Geneva Convention relative to the Protection of civilian Persons in the time of War, commonly referred to as the Fourth Geneva Convention, is one of the four treaties of the Geneva Convention. Israel supports its position that the Convention does not apply to the Occupied Palestinian Territories by pointing out "the lack of recognition of the territory as sovereign prior to its annexation by Jordan and Egypt" plus the fact that it is "not a territory of a High Contracting Party as required by the Convention."[590] Israel, on the other hand, ratified and is a High Contracting Party to the Fourth Geneva Convention. Jordan is also party to the Convention.

To begin its support of its conclusion that the Occupied Palestinian Territory is subject to the Fourth Geneva Convention, the Court noted that "the Palestinian Liberation Movement in the name of the 'State of Palestine'" requested on June 14, 1989 "'to accede' *inter alia* to the Fourth Geneva Convention," and that "Switzerland, as a depositary State, considered the unilateral undertaking valid" but concluded that it '[was] not—as a depositary—in a position to decide whether' 'the request... can be considered as an instrument of accession.'"[591]

The Court went on to examine the text of the Fourth Geneva Convention's Article 2 to evaluate its applicability. Article 2 reads:

> In addition to the provisions which shall be implemented in peacetime, the present Convention shall apply to all cases of declared war or of any other armed conflict which may arise between two or more of the High Contracting Parties, even if the state of war is not recognized by one of them.

> The Convention shall also apply to all cases of partial or total occupation of the territory of a High Contracting Party, even if the said occupation meets with no armed resistance.

> Although one of the Powers in conflict may not be a party to the present Convention, the Powers who are parties thereto shall remain bound by it in their mutual relations. They (are) bound by the Convention in relation to the said Power, if the latter shall furthermore be accepts and applies the provisions thereof.[592]

The foundation of Israel's argument that the Fourth Geneva Convention does not apply is derived from the second paragraph of Article 2. Israel asserted that the text "the Convention shall also apply to all cases of partial or total occupation of the territory of a High Contracting Party" shows the inapplicability of the Convention to the Occupied Palestinian Territory, since it is not a High Contracting Party. This argument flows from the idea that only a party that has willingly subjected itself to the rules of the Convention should get the benefits and protections the treaty provides. It follows to ask why the Palestine Liberation Organization which is deemed not subject to the other requirements of the Convention, should be entitled to the privileges and protections the Convention provides to its parties.

Jordan, Israel admitted, was a party to the Fourth Geneva Convention at the time that armed conflict broke out between the nations in 1967. However, regarding the current land in question, Israel argued, being the "territories occupied by Israel subsequent to that conflict [did not fall previously] under Jordanian sovereignty."[593]

The Court and "the great majority of other participants in the proceedings" disagreed, with the Court noting, "the Fourth Geneva Convention is applicable to those territories pursuant to Article 2, paragraph 1, whether or not Jordan had any rights in respect thereof prior to 1967."[594]

The Court went on to explain that customary international law provides that "a treaty must be interpreted in good faith in accordance with the ordinary meaning to be given to its terms in their context and in the light of its object and purpose."[595] Interpreting the first paragraph of Article 2 of the Fourth Geneva Convention, the Court said the "Convention is applicable when two conditions are fulfilled: that there exists an armed conflict (whether or not a state of war has been recognized); and that the conflict has arisen between two contracting parties."[596] Using this interpretive approach, it went on to explain that the aim of the second paragraph of Article 2 "is not to restrict the scope of application of the Convention, as defined by the first paragraph, by excluding therefrom territories not falling under the sovereignty of one of the contracting parties" but rather "it is directed simply to making it clear that, even if occupation effected during the conflict met no armed resistance, the Convention is still applicable."[597] Therefore, if there exists an armed conflict, here, between Israel and Jordan, and the conflict is between two contracting parties, here, Israel and Jordan, then "the Convention applies… in any territory occupied in the course of the conflict by one of the contracting parties."[598]

The Court explained that this interpretation reflects the intention of the "drafters… to guarantee the protection of civilians in time of war, regardless of the status of the occupied territories, as is shown by Article 47 of the Convention."[599] The Court cited the Convention's *travaux preparatoires* or official records to confirm this interpretation where:

> The Conference of Government Experts convened... for the purpose of preparing the new Geneva Convention: recommended that these conventions be applicable to any armed conflict "whether [it] is or is not recognized as a state of war by the parties" and "in cases of occupation of territories in the absence of any state of war.[600]

The Court noted that the parties to the Fourth Geneva Convention approved this interpretation "at their Conference on 15 July 1999" and moreover, on December 5, 2001, the High Contracting Parties, referring in particular to Article 1, once again reaffirmed the "applicability of the Fourth Geneva Convention to the Occupied Palestinian Territory, including East Jerusalem."[601]

The Court went on to validate its interpretation by giving examples of past situations where the General Assembly took a position that led to the same effect. The Court cited to multiple resolutions for the General Assembly.[602] Additionally, the Security Council has, on various occasions, pressed the parties to comply with the Geneva Conventions.[603] In resolution 237 (1967), the Security Council stressed that "all the obligations of the Geneva Convention relative to the Treatment of Prisoners of War . . . should be complied with by the parties involved in the conflict."[604] Likewise, the Court noted, in resolution 271 (1969), the Security Council called upon "Israel scrupulously to observe the provisions of the Geneva Conventions and international law governing military occupation."[605] The Court concluded:

> In view of the foregoing, the Court considers that the Fourth Geneva Convention is applicable in any occupied territory in the event of an armed conflict arising between two or more High Contracting Parties. Israel and Jordan were parties to that Convention when the 1967 armed conflict broke out. The Court accordingly finds that that Convention is applicable in the Palestinian territories which before the conflict lay to the east of the Green Line and which, during that conflict, were occupied by Israel, there being no need for any enquiry into the precise prior status of those territories.[606]

Human Rights Law: Paragraphs 102 through 113

The Court continued its advisory opinion by discussing human rights law and the applicability of human rights instruments to the Occupied Palestinian Territory. Israel contended that certain international human rights conventions to which Israel is a party do not apply within the territories. The particular human rights conventions at issue were two international Covenants, the International Covenant on Civil and Political Rights and the International Covenant on Economic, Social and Cultural Rights, and the Convention on the Rights of the Child. Israel argued "humanitarian law is the protection granted in a conflict situation such as the one in the West Bank and Gaza Strip, whereas human rights treaties were intended for the protection of citizens from their own Government in times of peace."[607]

The first of these issues the Court considered was the relationship between international humanitarian law and human rights law and whether human rights law, as Israel asserted, does not apply during armed conflict. Reiterating its position taken in a previous advisory opinion, the Court stated, "the protection of the International Covenant of Civil and Political Rights does not cease in times of war... In principle, the right not arbitrarily to be deprived of one's life applies also in hostilities."[608] In effect, protections from human rights Covenants still apply during armed conflict, even if certain provisions "may be derogated from in a time of national emergency. Respect for the right to life is not, however, such a provision."[609]

The Court continued that since human rights law does apply during armed conflict, three possible situations exist: "some rights may be exclusively matters of international humanitarian law; others may be exclusively matters of human rights law; yet others may be matters of both these branches of international law."[610]

To address whether the Covenants at issue apply only to the territories of a State party to the Covenant or whether they also apply to land outside the territory of a State party that is subject to the State's jurisdiction, the Court considered each Covenant individually. The Court first looked at the International Covenant on Civil and Political Rights and rejected Israel's argument that it did not apply beyond its territory to the situation in the occupied territories. Article 2, paragraph 1 of the Covenant defines its scope:

> Each State Party to the present Covenant undertakes to respect and to ensure to all individuals within its territory and subject to its jurisdiction the rights recognized in the present Covenant, without distinction of any kind, such as race, colour, sex, language, religion, political or other opinion, national or social origin, property, birth or other status.[611]

Interpreting the language to mean that the Covenant applies to the Occupied Palestinian Territory, the Court observed that, "while the jurisdiction of States is primarily territorial, it may sometimes be exercised outside the national territory."[612] Moreover, "considering the object and purpose of the International Covenant on Civil and Political Rights, it would seem natural that, even when such is the case, States parties to the Covenant should be bound to comply with its provisions."[613]

To support its conclusion that the Covenant applied, the Court looked at the past practice of the Human Rights Committee and the Covenant's *travaux preparatoires*. The Court observed that the Human Rights Committee's practice constantly followed this interpretation and additionally, had found the "Covenant applicable where the State exercises its jurisdiction on foreign territory."[614] The Covenant's *travaux preparatoires* confirm this interpretation, reasoning that the drafters "did not intend to allow States to escape from their obligations when they exercise jurisdiction outside their national territory."[615] Noting Israel's consistent position opposing application to the Occupied Palestinian Territory, the Court concluded the "International Covenant on Civil and Political Rights is applicable in respect of acts done by a State in the exercise of its jurisdiction outside its own territory."[616]

The Court then considered the applicability of the International Covenant on Economic, Social and Cultural Rights and concluded, despite the fact that it "contains no provision on its scope of application," that "it applies both to territories over which a State party has sovereignty and to those over which that State exercises territorial jurisdiction."[617] Since the occupied territories have been subject to Israel's territorial jurisdiction as the occupying power for over 37 years, "Israel is bound by the provisions of the International Covenant on Economic, Social and Cultural Rights."[618] The Court further noted that Israel "is under an obligation not to raise any obstacle to the exercise of such rights in those fields where competence has been transferred to Palestinian authorities."[619]

The Court also found the Convention on the Rights of the Child of November 20, 1989 applicable to the territories.

Violation of Relevant Rules: Paragraphs 114 through 142

The Court determined next "whether the construction of the wall has violated those rules and principles" set forth above.

Impact on Right of Palestinian People to Self-determination: Paragraphs 115 through 122

Annex II of the Secretary-General's report, entitled "Summary Legal Position of the Palestine Liberation Organization," contended that the wall prevents the right of the Palestinian people to self-determination. "The construction of the Barrier is an attempt to annex the territory contrary to international law' and 'the de facto annexation of land interferes with the territorial sovereignty and consequently with the right of the Palestinians to self-determination.'"[620] Written statements to the Court argued that "'the route of the wall is designed to change the demographic composition of the Occupied Palestinian Territory, including East Jerusalem, by reinforcing the Israeli settlements' illegally established on the Occupied Palestinian Territory."[621] It was further argued "the wall aimed at 'reducing and parceling out the territorial sphere over which the Palestinian people are entitled to exercise their right of self-determination.'"[622] Based on these assertions, opponents to the wall argued that the Palestinian people's "territorial sphere," in which they have the right to self-determination, was severed by the construction of the wall. Further, their inability to self-determine "constitutes a violation of the legal principle prohibiting the acquisition of territory by the use of force."[623]

Israel argued that the wall is a "temporary measure" whose sole purpose is "to enable it effectively to combat terrorist attacks launched from the West Bank."[624] It emphasized that the fence "does not annex territories to the State of Israel" and reiterated that Israel is "ready and able, at tremendous cost, to adjust or dismantle a fence if so required as part of a political settlement."[625] Israel's Permanent Representative restated this position before the General Assembly when he said:

> As soon as the terror ends, the fence will no longer be necessary. The fence is not a border and has no political significance. It does not change the legal status of the territory in any way.[626]

The Court went on to discuss what the General Assembly and Security Council referred to, with regard to Palestine, as the "customary rule of 'the inadmissibility of the acquisition of territory by war.'"[627] The Security Council, in accordance with this rule, adopted resolution 242 (1967) on November 22, 1967 that called for peace in the Middle East by:

> (i) Withdrawal of Israel armed forces from territories occupied in the recent conflict;
>
> (ii) Termination of all claims or states of belligerency and respect for and acknowledgement of the sovereignty, territorial integrity and political independence of every State in the area and their right to live in peace within secure and recognized boundaries free from threats or acts of force.[628]

The Court added that the Security Council has condemned Israel's measures to change the status of Jerusalem "on this same basis."

The Court stated that the existence of a 'Palestinian people' is no longer a questionable issue. Israel recognized their existence first in 1993 in an Exchange of Letters where the Israeli Prime Minister informed Yasser Arafat "in the light of [Arafat's] commitments, 'the Government of Israel has decided to recognize the PLO as the representative of the Palestinian people."[629] Additionally, the September 1995 Israeli-Palestinian Interim Agreement on the West Bank and the Gaza Strip "refers a number of times to the Palestinian people and its 'legitimate rights.'"[630] The Court interpreted the "legitimate rights" that Israel recognizes to include the right to self-determination, "as the General Assembly has moreover recognized on a number of occasions."[631]

The Court then addressed the Israeli settlements in the Occupied Palestinian Territory. Noting that "the wall's sinuous route has been traced in such a way to include within that area the great majority of the Israeli settlements in the Occupied Palestinian Territory (including East Jerusalem),"[632] the Court advises that the Israeli settlements in the territory have been established in violation of international law. The Court refers to Article 49, paragraph 6, of the Fourth Geneva Convention, which says: "The Occupying Power shall not deport or transfer parts of its own civilian population into the territory it occupies," including "any measures taken by an occupying Power in order to organize or encourage transfers of parts of its own population into the occupied territory."[633] Israel, the Court stated, has, since 1997, "conducted a policy and developed practices involving the establishment of settlements in the Occupied Palestinian Territory, contrary to the terms of Article 49, paragraph 6."[634] The Court recounted the Security Council's view that the Israeli settlement policy and practices "have no legal validity" and referenced a past Security Council resolution that called upon Israel, as the occupying Power, to "abide scrupulously" by the Fourth Geneva Convention and "to rescind its previous measures and to desist from taking any action which would result in changing the legal status and geographical nature and materially affecting the demographic composition of the Arab territories occupied since 1967, including Jerusalem and, in particular, not to transfer parts of its own civilian population into the occupied Arab territories."[635]

The Court disregarded all assurances Israel repeatedly stated, claiming that it could not dismiss fears that the route "will prejudge the future frontier between Israel and Palestine, and the fear that Israel may integrate the settlements and their means of access."[636] The Court concluded on this point that it considered the wall and its "associated regime" to create a 'fait accompli' since it could become permanent, which would be "tantamount to *de facto* annexation."[637] The Court set forth its view that past Israeli measures with regard to Jerusalem and the settlements were illegal and that the wall's construction risks further alterations to the Occupied Palestinian Territory's demographic composition while also contributing to the "departure of Palestinian populations from certain areas."[638]

Thus, the construction, "along with measures taken previously... severely impedes the exercise by the Palestinian people of its right to self-determination, and is therefore a breach of Israel's obligation to respect that right."[639]

The Court displayed an utter disregard for Israel's assertions on the terrorism prevention security needs of Israel, the reasons for the fence as a security deterrent, pledges that the fence was not a border but a security fence, and that it would indeed be moved upon achieving an agreement between the parties. The Court pointed out that Israel has recognized the existence of the Palestinian people. A distinction between people and land must be made as this does not automatically mean that the land on which the Palestinians reside is theirs today without question, particularly considering the Jewish people's thousands of years of historical presence in its ancient lands. The Court, in its ultimate conclusion, advises that the parties themselves must negotiate final status issues, including borders.

Relevant International Humanitarian Law and Human Rights Instruments: Paragraphs 123 through 137

The next section of the advisory opinion discussed particular provisions of international humanitarian law and human rights instruments and whether they apply to Israel's construction of the wall. The Court again referred to the Secretary-General's report and other submissions to support its opinion that Israel violated the specified instruments.

The Court began by describing various provisions of human rights instruments and explaining their applicability. Beginning with the Hague Regulations of 1907, the Court noted that Section III, which deals with military authority in occupied territories, was applicable in the West Bank. Section III includes Articles 43, 46 and 52, all of which the Court asserted are applicable to the Occupied Palestinian Territory. These articles impose duties on occupants:

> Article 43 imposes a duty on the occupant to "take all measures within his power to restore, and, as far as possible, to insure public order and life, respecting the laws in force in the country". Article 46 adds that private property must be "respected" and that it cannot "be confiscated". Lastly, Article 52 authorizes, within certain

limits, requisitions in kind and services for the needs of the army of occupation.[540]

The Court further discussed the Fourth Geneva Convention and its applicable provisions. In the Court's view, since military operations that led to the occupation were over, only Article 6, paragraph 3 provisions, which apply throughout the entire period of occupation, were applicable to the occupied territory. Article 47 states that "protected persons" within an occupied territory will not be deprived of the benefits of the Geneva Convention because of such occupation. Nor will the occupation "change the institutions or government of the said territory, nor by any agreement concluded between the authorities of the occupied territories and the Occupying Power, nor by any annexation by the latter of the whole or part of the occupied territory."[541]

Article 49 of the Fourth Geneva Convention covers "individual or mass forcible transfers, as well as deportations of protected persons from occupied territory."[542] It allows evacuation if security or imperative military reasons demand and prohibits detainment of protected persons where they are exposed to dangers of war unless the reasons above are present. Lastly, "the Occupying Power shall not deport or transfer parts of its own civilian population into the territory it occupies."[543]

Article 52 of the Fourth Geneva Convention prevents interference with the right of a worker to request intervention by the Protecting Power. It also prohibits any measures meant to create unemployment or measures meant to restrict work opportunities in an occupied territory, for the purpose of getting the worker to work for the Occupying Power.

Article 53 of the Fourth Geneva Convention prohibits the Occupying Power from destroying real or personal property owned individually or collectively by private individuals, the state, or organizations, unless military operations make the destruction absolutely necessary.

Article 59 of the Fourth Geneva Convention requires the Occupying Power to help and facilitate relief schemes if necessary.

The Court discussed the relevancy of the International Covenant on Civil and Political Rights. It noted that in October of 1991, Israel derogated from Article 9, which deals with the "right to liberty and security of person and lays down the rules applicable in cases of arrest or detention."[644] The Court advised that other articles, the relevant ones being Article 17, paragraph 1 and Article 12, paragraph 1, are applicable on both Israeli territory and on the Occupied Palestinian Territory. Article 17 reads, "No one shall be subjected to arbitrary or unlawful interference with his privacy, family, home or correspondence, nor to unlawful attacks on his honour and reputation."[645] Article 12 states that "Everyone lawfully within the territory of a state shall, within that territory, have the right to liberty of movement and freedom to choose his residence."[646]

The Court then discussed the importance of various human rights instruments that give "specific guarantees of access to the Christian, Jewish and Islamic Holy Places,"[647] noting that the 1949 General Armistice Agreement and the 1994 Peace Treaty guaranteed freedom of access to Holy Places both east and west of the Green Line.

The last human rights instruments discussed were the International Covenant on Economic, Social and Cultural Rights and the United Nations Convention on the Rights of the Child. The relevant provisions of the International Covenant on Economic, Social and Cultural Rights were:

> the right to work (Arts. 6 and 7); protection and assistance accorded to the family and to children and young persons (Art. 10); the right to an adequate standard of living, including adequate food, clothing and housing;, and the right "to be free from hunger" (Art. 11); the right to health (Art. 12); the right to education (Arts. 13 and 14).[648]

The Convention on the Rights of the Child has similar provisions in Articles 16, 24, 27 and 28.

The Court then considered "the information submitted to the Court, particularly the report of the Secretary-General" to determine what rights were violated and what duties were not met. The Court advised that the wall's construction "led to the destruction or requisition of properties under conditions" that violate Article 46 and 52 of the Hague Regulations and Article 53 of the Fourth Geneva Convention.[649]

With regards to the rights of the inhabitants of the Occupied Palestinian Territory to move freely under the International Covenant on Civil and Political Rights, the Court advised that "the establishment of a closed area between the Green Line and the wall itself and the creation of enclaves have... imposed substantial restrictions on the freedom of movement of the inhabitants."[650]

The Court also advised as to "serious repercussions for agricultural production, as is attested by a number of sources." It referred to the Special Rapporteur on the Right to Food of the United Nations Commission on Human Rights for evidence that the wall "cuts off Palestinians from their agricultural lands, wells and means of subsistence."[651] The Court noted that many inhabitants were restricted from accessing fertile Palestinian land located on the Israeli side of the wall, as well as "some of the most important water wells in the region."[652] The Court reflected on the destruction of property and the impositions on the right to work, noting "many fruit and olive trees have been destroyed in the course of building the barrier."[653]

In addition to the impositions on the inhabitants' right to work, move around freely, and have an adequate standard of living, the Court advised further that the wall "led to increasing difficulties for the population concerned regarding access to health services, educational establishments and primary sources of water" as "attested by a number of different information sources."[654] The Court continued to give examples of how the wall's construction violates the provisions mentioned, repeating the Special Rapporteur's observation that "with the fence/wall cutting communities off from their land and water without other means of subsistence, many of the Palestinians living in these areas will be forced to leave."[655] Thus, the Court concluded, the "wall would effectively deprive a significant number of Palestinians of the 'freedom to choose their residence'" in violation of the International Covenant on Civil and Political Rights. The Court also stated that many Palestinians have already been compelled to leave, which will continue as the wall is being built. The Court observed that this occurrence, in addition to the establishment of Israeli settlements, is "tending to alter the demographic composition" of the Territories. Concluding its synopsis, the Court said:

> To sum up, the Court is of the opinion that the construction of the wall and its associated regime impede the liberty of movement of the inhabitants of the Occupied Palestinian Territory (with the exception of Israeli citizens and those assimilated thereto) as guaranteed under Article 12, paragraph 1, of the International Covenant on Civil and Political Rights. They also impede the exercise by the persons concerned of the right to work, to health, to education and to an adequate standard of living as proclaimed in the International Covenant on Economic, Social and Cultural Rights and in the United Nations Convention on the Rights of the Child. Lastly, the construction of the wall and its associated regime, by contributing to the demographic changes referred to in paragraphs 122 and 133 above, contravene Article 49, paragraph 6, of the Fourth Geneva Convention and the Security Council resolutions cited in paragraph 120 above.[656]

The Court completed its analysis by addressing possible exceptions that would allow the construction of the wall, concluding that none of the exceptions applied, in its view. The Court acknowledged that some of the "applicable international humanitarian law contains provisions enabling account to be taken of military exigencies in certain circumstances." However, "neither Article 46 of the Hague Regulations of 1907 nor Article 47 of the Fourth Geneva Convention contain any qualifying provision of this type."[657] And, the Court analyzed, while the Fourth Geneva Convention provides an exception for security concerns or imperative military reasons, the exception does not apply to the Convention's prohibition against deporting or transferring parts of an Occupied Power's own civilian population into the territories it occupies, which is the case of the Occupied Palestinian Territory.

While Article 53 concerning the destruction of personal property has an exception to allow destruction "where such destruction is rendered absolutely necessary by military operations," the Court was "not convinced that the destructions carried out contrary to the prohibition in Article 53 of the Fourth Geneva Convention were rendered absolutely necessary by military operations."[658] The Court explained its view that even though Israel legitimately derogated from Article 9 of the Covenant, relating to the right to freedom and security of person"[659] in its communication to the Secretary-General of the United Nations on October 3, 1991, wherein Israel stated in part, "Since its establishment, the State of Israel has been the victim of continuous threats and attacks on its very existence as well as on the life and property of its citizens. These have taken the form of threats of war, of actual armed attacks, and campaigns of terrorism resulting in the murder of and injury to human beings. In view of the above, the State of Emergency which was proclaimed in May 1948 has remained in force ever since;" as to the remaining provisions, the Court advised that Israel is still "bound to respect all the other provisions of that instrument."

The Court acknowledged that certain provisions of human rights conventions also have clauses qualifying rights. Article 17 of the International Covenant on Civil and Political Rights has no such qualifier. Article 12, however, provides that restrictions on movement are illegal "except those which are provided by law, are necessary to protect national security, public order (*ordre public*), public health or morals or the rights and freedoms of others, and are consistent with the other rights recognized in the present Covenant."[660] This is a very high standard and based on the information available to it the Court advised that these conditions "are not met in the present instance."[661]

The Court was not convinced that the "specific course Israel has chosen for the wall was necessary to attain its security objectives."[662] It concluded that the wall:

> Gravely infringe a number of rights of Palestinians…and the infringements resulting from that route cannot be justified by military exigencies or by the requirements of national security or public order. The construction of such a wall accordingly constitutes breaches by Israel of various of its obligations under the applicable international humanitarian law and human rights instruments.[663]

Self-defense and the State of Necessity Defense: Paragraphs 138 through 142

The next argument the Court addressed was Israel's argument that the construction of the barrier was legal based on Israel's inherent right to self-defense and because there existed a state of necessity. Israel asserted that Article 51 of the UN Charter allowed the construction of the wall as self-defense since an "armed attack occur[ed] against [Israel,] a Member of the United Nations."[664] The Court considered this assertion and the point made by Israel's Permanent Representative to the UN in the General Assembly on October 20, 2003 that past Security Council resolutions have recognized "the right of States to use force in self-defense against terrorist attacks, and therefore surely recognize the right to use non-forcible measures to that end."[665]

The Court did not agree. The Court confirmed that Article 51 "recognizes the existence of an inherent right of self-defense in the case of armed attack by one State against another State." Here, however, Article 51 did not apply because "Israel does not claim that the attacks against it are imputable to a foreign State."[666] The Court, on the one hand giving the Palestinians, a non-state actor the right of access to the Court, denied to Israel protections of Article 51 on the grounds that Israel did not claim the attacks are imputable to a foreign State (because Palestine was not a State). The Palestinians were thus permitted by the Court to have it both ways, while Israel was denied its objections on all grounds.

The Court concluded that Israel could not invoke the Security Council resolutions since the situations contemplated by the resolutions were "different" than this situation since Israel has control over the territory and "the threat which it regards as justifying the construction of the wall originates within, and not outside, that territory."[667] The Court bluntly and wrongly concluded that "Article 51 of the Charter has no relevance in this case."

The Court next considered whether Israel could rely on customary international law's state of necessity defense, "which would preclude the wrongfulness of the construction of the wall" and justify Israel's violation of the previously mentioned treaties.[668] The Court brought up the possibility of this defense because, as mentioned previously, some of the conventions at issue included qualifying clauses or provisions for derogation. The Court answers the question in the negative, stating that the question was already answered in the case of the *Gabcikovo-Nagymaros Project*

(Hungary/Slovakia) where the Court explained that the state of necessity "can only be accepted on an exceptional basis,… can only be invoked under certain strictly defined conditions which must be cumulatively satisfied… and the State concerned [cannot be] the sole judge of whether those conditions have been met."[669] One such condition previously recognized by the Court was that the act challenged be "the only way for the State to safeguard an essential interest against a grave and imminent peril."[670] The Court advised that this condition was not met, stating that it was "not convinced that the construction of the wall along the route chosen was the only means to safeguard the interests of Israel against the peril which it has invoked as justification for that construction." The Court further wrongly said the "measures taken are bound nonetheless to remain in conformity with applicable international law" and the "wrongfulness of the construction of the wall" cannot be saved by Israel's claim of self-defense nor state of necessity.

In the advisory opinion's only substantive acknowledgement of the terrorism and violence suffered by Israeli citizens, the Court noted that "the fact remains that Israel has to face numerous indiscriminate and deadly acts of violence against its civilian population. *It has the right, and indeed the duty, to respond in order to protect the life of its citizens* (emphasis added)."[671] This is perhaps the most important and reality-based relevant statement in the entire opinion, making it clear that Israel has "the right, and indeed the duty, to respond in order to protect the life of its citizens."

Notwithstanding that important acknowledgment, in the illogical opinion of the court, Israel cannot assert self-defense under Article 51 because the territory from which the terrorism originates is not a State and because Israel has tried to maintain control over the non-State land from which the terrorism originates. Also, the Court believed, Israel cannot claim that there is a state of necessity because the Court incredulously did not view the terrorism Israeli citizens have faced as sufficient enough to warrant Israel's decision to construct a barrier to safeguard its citizens by fencing out the terrorists. The construction of the barrier is not narrowly tailored enough, in the wrongheaded view of the Court to be considered as providing an "essential interest against a grave and imminent peril." Notwithstanding years of suicide bombings and terrorist attacks upon and within Israel, perpetrated by Palestinian terrorists who were entering Israel unabated until the construction of the very security fence at issue before the Court, the Court advised that Israel's fence violated various principles of international law. In reality it's almost as if the Court reached its advisory conclusions without regards to the condition of the facts on the ground, and only in reliance upon biased reports prepared by various arms of the UN, the PLO/PA and her Arab country supporters for their own self serving purposes.

Legal Consequences of the Violation: Paragraphs 143 through 148

Having concluded that Israel's construction of the barrier is a violation of various international obligations, the Court turned to the legal consequences of the violation for Israel, other States, and for the United Nations. In paragraphs 144 through 148, the Court provided the contentions raised by the participants in the proceedings in their written and oral observations. The Court noted that many participants contended that Israel's actions have legal consequences not only on Israel, but also on other States and the United Nations. The Court also noted that Israel presented no arguments addressing possible legal consequences.

Legal Consequences for Israel: Paragraphs 149 through 154

The Court addressed its view as to the legal consequences for Israel resulting from the wall's construction and its associated regime. First that it must comply with its obligations under international humanitarian law and international human rights law, such as its obligation to respect the "right of the Palestinian people to self-determination."[672] It also "must ensure freedom of access to the Holy Places that came under its control following the 1967 War."[673]

The Court next observed that Israel is obligated to "put an end to the violation of its international obligations flowing from the construction of the wall in the Occupied Palestinian Territory."[674] The Court outlined the well-established principle in international law that a state responsible for a legally determined wrongful act is obligated to put an end to that act.[675] In the Court's view, Israel is obligated to "cease forthwith the works of construction of the wall being built by it in the Occupied Palestinian Territory, including in and around East Jerusalem."[676] This cessation includes dismantling "those parts of that structure situated within the Occupied Palestinian Territory, including in and around East Jerusalem."[677] Additionally, the Court opined that the government of Israel must repeal or render ineffective "all legislative and regulatory acts adopted with a view to [the wall's] construction, and to the establishment of its associated regime" unless the acts provide for "compensation or other forms of reparation for the Palestinian population [since they] may continue to be relevant for compliance by Israel with its obligations."[678]

The Court also observed that Israel must "make reparation for the damage caused to all the natural or legal persons concerned" since the wall's construction requisitioned and destroyed "homes, businesses and other agricultural holdings.[679] The Court used the Permanent Court of International Justice's explanation of how to make reparations under customary law, stating:

> Reparation must, as far as possible, wipe out all the consequences of the illegal act and reestablish the situation which would, in all probability, have existed if that act had not been committed. Restitution in kind, or, if this is not possible, payment of a sum corresponding to the value which a restitution in kind would bear; the award, if need be, of damages for loss sustained which would not be covered by restitution in kind or payment in place of it— such are the principles which should serve to determine the amount of compensation due for an act contrary to international law.[680]

The Court observed that Israel's reparations obligated it to "return the land, orchards, olive groves and other immovable property seized from any natural or legal person for purposes of construction of the wall in the Occupied Palestinian Territory."[681] If returning the property ends up being materially impossible, the Court said that Israel must then "compensate the persons in question for the damage suffered."[682] Additionally, it must "compensate... all natural or legal persons having suffered any form of material damage as a result of the wall's construction."[683]

Legal Consequences for States Other than Israel: Paragraphs 154 through 159

Widening its advisory opinion, the Court continued its discussion of legal consequences by addressing the legal consequences the Court would impose on other states that result from Israel's internationally wrongful acts. The Court noted that many of the obligations violated by Israel are obligations *erga omnes*: obligations that, "by their very nature, [are] 'the concern of all States.'"[684] The rights involved in this situation are important enough that "all States can be held to have a legal interest in their protection."[685] The Court explained that the obligations *erga omnes* that Israel violated include the "obligation to respect the right of the Palestinian people to self-determination" in addition to obligations that were violated under international humanitarian law.

First addressing the obligation of other States to respect the right of Palestinians to self-determination, the Court viewed a people's right to self-determination as an "irreproachable" right with an *erga omnes* character, having evolved from the UN Charter and from UN practice.[686] Additionally, the obligation of other States to respect this right is also expressed in General Assembly resolution 2625 (XXV), which obliges states to promote the "realization of the principle of equal rights and self-determination of peoples."[687]

The Court then addressed the obligations of other States under international humanitarian law. The Court noted that many of the rules governing armed conflict "constitute intransgressible principles of international customary law"[688] that all States, "whether or not they have ratified the conventions that contain them," are obligated to because they are "so fundamental to the respect of the human person and 'elementary considerations of humanity.'"[689]

The Court noted further that every state that is a signee of the Fourth Geneva Convention, whether or not it is a party to a specific conflict, is also "under an obligation to ensure that the requirements of the instruments in question are complied with."[690]

The Court advised that the character and importance of the rights and obligations involved subjected every State to the "obligation not to recognize the illegal situation resulting from the construction of the wall in the Occupied Palestinian Territory, including in and around East Jerusalem... situation created by such construction."[691] This did not end the obligations of other States. States, while making sure to comply with the UN Charter and international law, must also "see to it that any impediment, resulting from the construction of the wall, to the exercise by the Palestinian people of its right to self-determination is brought to an end."[692] The Court concluded its analysis by providing the particular obligations for States who are a party to the 1949 Geneva Convention Relative to the Protection of Civilian Persons in Time of War. These States are also under an obligation to "ensure compliance by Israel with international humanitarian law as embodied in that Convention."[693]

Legal Consequences for the United Nations: Paragraph 160

The Court advised that the United Nations, "especially the General Assembly and the Security Council," should consider what further action by them is necessary to "bring to an end the illegal situation resulting from the construction of the wall and the associated regime, taking due account of the present advisory opinion."[694]

General Context of the Conflict: Paragraphs 161 through 162

As a last note, the Court expressed its concern with the Arab-Palestinian-Israeli Conflict and emphasized the "urgent necessity for the United Nations as a whole to redouble its efforts to bring the Israeli-Palestinian conflict, which continues to pose a threat to international peace and security, to a speedy conclusion, thereby establishing a just and lasting peace in the region."[695]

The Court recognized that the construction of the barrier must be placed within a more general context. Noting the "succession of armed conflicts, acts of indiscriminate violence and repressive measures on the former mandated territory" that have existed in the territory since 1947, the Court reminded the General Assembly that "both Israel and Palestine are under an obligation scrupulously to observe the rules of international humanitarian law, one of the paramount purposes of which is to protect civilian life."[696] In the Court's view, "this tragic situation can be brought to an end only through implementation in good faith of all relevant Security Council resolutions, in particular resolutions 242 (1967) and 338 (1973)," and more recently, resolution 1515 (2003), the "Roadmap, which it clearly applied to the situation."[697] It is indeed disturbing that the Court, in its conclusion of its legal arguments, referenced the very political issues and applicable UN resolutions that are at the root of disagreements between the parties, requiring the direct negotiations envisaged by the Roadmap adopted by the parties and the UN itself in 2003; but filed to acknowledge that the adoption by the Security Council of the Roadmap should have itself precluded any review of the question presented by the Court. The Court further concluded with an urgent call to the General Assembly, emphasizing:

> the need for these efforts to be encouraged with a view to achieving as soon as possible, on the basis of international law, a negotiated solution to the outstanding problems and the establishment of a Palestinian State, existing side by side with Israel and its other neighbours, with peace and security for all in the region.[698]

It is further beyond comprehension that the Court disregarded its obligation to decline to advise on political question issues yet called for a "negotiated solution," a political question settlement, if you will, something the PLO and the Palestinian Authority have been unwilling to sit down and discuss with the Israelis for many years. Essentially, the Court's advice rewarded the Palestinians while invoking a political process to achieve implementation of the very peace and security that is within the sole purview of the Security Council. The illogical approach, evaluation and conclusion is outrageous, but typical, of the attitudes of the United Nations and its organizations towards the State of Israel and all matters involving the Arab-Palestinian-Israeli Conflict.

Dispositif: Paragraph 163

To conclude, the Court voted in the following way to issue its advisory opinion: [699]

The Court,

(1) Unanimously:

Finds that it has jurisdiction to give the advisory opinion requested;

(2) By fourteen votes to one:

Decides to comply with the request for an advisory opinion;[700]

(3) *Replies* in the following manner to the question put by the General Assembly:

:A. By fourteen votes to one

The construction of the wall being built by Israel, the occupying Power, in the Occupied Palestinian Territory, including in and around East Jerusalem, and its associated ;regime, are contrary to international law[701]

:B. By fourteen votes to one

Israel is under an obligation to terminate its breaches of international law; it is under an obligation to cease forthwith the works of construction of the wall being built in the Occupied Palestinian Territory, including in and around East Jerusalem, to dismantle forthwith the structure therein situated, and to repeal or render ineffective forthwith all legislative and regulatory acts relating thereto, in accordance with paragraph 151 of this Opinion;[702]

:C. By fourteen votes to one

Israel is under an obligation to make reparation for all damage caused by the construction of the wall in the Occupied Palestinian Territory, including in and around East Jerusalem;[703]

:D. By thirteen votes to two

All States are under an obligation not to recognize the illegal situation resulting from the construction of the wall and not to render aid or assistance in maintaining the situation created by such construction; all States parties to the Fourth Geneva Convention relative to the

Protection of Civilian Persons in Time of War of 12 August 1949 have in addition the obligation, while respecting the United Nations Charter and international law, to ensure compliance by Israel with international humanitarian law as embodied in that Convention;[704]

:E. By fourteen votes to one

The United Nations, and especially the General Assembly and the Security Council, should consider what further action is required to bring to an end the illegal situation resulting from the construction of the wall and the associated regime, taking due account of the present Advisory Opinion.[705]

Judge Buergenthal's Strong Dissent from the Advisory Opinion

Judge Thomas Buergenthal of the United States was the sole dissenting judge and primary voice of reason and applicability of the rule of law and due process on all issues of the advisory opinion. It is well known that at the United Nations, the rule is one nation one vote. Accordingly, at the United Nations, Israel always loses by the substantial majorities against her. Similarly, the ICJ panel consists of fifteen judges from different countries. And therefore, not only did Israel lose on this vote but she can expect to lose on future votes of the International Court of Justice where politics rules, bias is the norm and outcomes are predetermined.

Justice Buergenthal was the only judge to express any real understanding as to the plight of Israel being forced to respond to the terrorist attacks upon her people. In a blistering opinion, he dissented from the Court's decision to hear the case based on his view that "the Court should have exercised its discretion and declined to render the requested advisory opinion."[706] Judge Buergenthal felt "compelled to vote against the Court's findings on the merits" because he believed that "the Court did not have before it the requisite factual bases for its sweeping findings."[707] Judge Buergenthal was guided by the Court's explanation as to when it should decline to give an advisory opinion in Western Sahara, noting:

> The critical question in determining whether or not to exercise its discretion in acting on an advisory opinion request is 'whether the Court has before it sufficient information and evidence to enable it to arrive at a judicial conclusion upon any disputed questions of fact the determination of which is necessary for it to give an opinion in conditions compatible with its judicial character.'[708]

He believed that "the absence in this case of the requisite information and evidence vitiates the Court's findings on the merits."[709]

He made it clear that his declination did not reflect his views regarding the "serious questions" the construction of the wall raise under international law, noting that he believed that legal consequences do arise from the wall's construction and he agreed with parts of the advisory opinion. For example, he agreed with the Court's conclusion that "international humanitarian law, including the Fourth Geneva Convention, and international human rights law are applicable to the Occupied Palestinian Territory and must there be faithfully complied with by Israel."[710] He also agreed that any defense against terrorism must "conform to all applicable rules of international law."[711] He took strong issue with the Court's dismissal of Israel's right, under international law, to self-defense, for, "if applicable and legitimately invoked... [it] would preclude any wrongfulness" by Israel.[712]

For Judge Buergenthal, many of the Court's conclusions were "not legally well founded" because the Court did not "have before it [nor seek] to ascertain all relevant facts bearing directly on... Israel's legitimate right of self-defense, military necessity and security needs."[713] He cited Article 21 of the International Law Commission's Articles on Responsibility of States for Internationally Wrongful Acts to explain why the Court must first ascertain all relevant facts before it can conclude "that the right of legitimate or inherent self-defense is not applicable."[714] Article 21 states, "the wrongfulness of an act of a State is precluded if the act constitutes a lawful measure of self-defense taken in conformity with the Charter of the United Nations."[715]

To Judge Buergenthal, whether Israel's right to self-defense is invoked depended on:

> An examination of the nature and scope of the deadly terrorist

attacks to which Israel proper is being subjected from across the Green Line and the extent to which the construction of the wall, in whole or in part, is a necessary and proportionate response to these attacks.[716]

To determine whether the right to self-defense is invoked, the Court must "examine the facts" and how they related to the "specific segments of the wall, [Israel's] defensive needs and related topographical considerations."[717]

After examining the facts the Court had before it, Judge Buergenthal concluded that the Court was not given enough information to conclude that Israel's legitimate right to self-defense did not apply – for if it did apply – it would nullify many of the Court's conclusions. "The dossier provided the Court by the United Nations on which the Court to a large extent bases its findings barely touches on" any of the facts that must be known for the Court to reach the conclusion it did.[718] Because of this absence of facts, Judge Buergenthal strongly disagreed with the Court's "sweeping conclusion[s] that the wall as a whole... violates international humanitarian law and international human rights law" and that it "severely impedes the...Palestinian people of its right to self-determination."[719]

After explaining why the Court should not have given the advisory opinion, Judge Buergenthal went on to repudiate the substantive reasons the Court gave for rendering the right of self-defense inapplicable. Pointing out that the Court looked solely to Article 51 of the UN Charter, he took issue with the Court's conclusion that Article 51 is irrelevant for two reasons.

First, attacking the Court's conclusion that Article 51 did not apply because the attacks are not "imputable to a foreign State," he noted that the "United Nations Charter, in affirming the inherent right of self-defense, does not make its exercise dependent upon an armed attack by another State."[720] Instead, the text reiterates the inherent right of UN Members to self-defense "if an armed attack occurs," making no mention of where the armed attack must derive from.[721]

To further support his assertion that the right to self-defense is not limited only to actions against States, he recalled past Security Council resolutions that have made it clear that "international terrorism constitutes a threat to international peace and security."[722] Noting that past Security Council resolutions have invoked the right of self-defense to combat terrorism, he pointed out that the resolutions never "limit[ed] their application to terrorist attacks by State actors only, nor was an assumption to that effect implicit in these resolutions. In fact, the contrary appears to have been the case."[723]

Second, whether Israel exercised "control" over the Occupied Palestinian Territory is irrelevant to a proper assessment of the legitimacy of Israel's self-defense claim under Article 51. Here, Judge Buergenthal countered the Court's assertion that self-defense must be aimed at an outside threat. The judge strongly noted the contradiction within the Court's assertion that Israel has no right to self-defense because the threats originate from within the territory under its control, questioning what "the concept of 'control' means given the attacks to which Israel is subjected" originate from territory under its "control."[724] Further, if the Court considered the Green Line as "delimiting the dividing line," then the attacks do originate from territory outside of Israel proper. And if this is the case, "to determine whether or not the construction of the wall, in whole or in part, by Israel meets that test, [meaning Israel's claim that the wall is necessary for self-defense,] all relevant facts bearing on issues of necessity and proportionality must be analyzed."[725] The judge criticized "the Court's formalistic approach to the right of self-defense," asserting that it "enables it to avoid addressing the very issues that are at the heart of this case."[726]

Moreover, in reaching the conclusion that Israel violated humanitarian and human rights laws, Judge Buergenthal made it clear that the Court failed "to address any facts or evidence specifically rebutting Israel's claim of military exigencies or requirements of national security."[727] The Court barely addressed the "summaries of Israel's position on this subject... which contradict or cast doubt on the material the Court claims to rely on."[728] Instead, Buergenthal stated the Court filled this section of the opinion with evidence of the "suffering the wall has caused" and "extensive quotations of the relevant legal provisions."[729] Absent, however, were references to the suffering of the Israeli people as a result of the terrorist incursions and attacks which the wall, itself, was designed to prevent. Judge Buergenthal concluded that the Court's analysis "lack[ed]... an examination of the facts that might show why the alleged defenses of military exigencies, national security or public order are not applicable to the wall as a whole or to the individual segments of its route."[730]

Judge Buergenthal aptly observed that certain international humanitarian laws have no provisions for some of the exceptions that could be raised, such as military exigencies. He addresses Article 46 of the Hague Regulations, which requires respect for private property, and Paragraph 6 of Article 49 of the Fourth Geneva Convention, which prohibits the transfer of an Occupying Power's own population into the territory it occupies. With regard to Article 46. Judge Buergenthal stated that "while these Israeli submissions are not necessarily determinative of the matter," Israel's asserted position that addresses the subject of private property should at least be recognized and reviewed by the Court.[731] Buergenthal opined that disregarding Israel's assertions, that "there is no change in ownership of the land; compensation is available for use of land, crop yield or damage to the land; residents can petition the Supreme Court to halt or alter construction and there is no change in resident status," diminishes the legitimacy of the Court's own legal analysis.[732] Regarding the Court's determination that Israel violated Article 49, paragraph 6, the Judge agreed.

Regarding the assertion that Israel chose not to participate and provide sufficient evidence on its behalf and thus, the Court was justified to rely exclusively on the insufficient evidence within the UN reports, Judge Buergenthal was emphatic in relation to Israel's right not to participate in the proceedings:

> This proposition would be valid if, instead of dealing with an advisory opinion request, the Court had before it a contentious case where each party has the burden of proving its claims. But that is not the rule applicable to advisory opinion proceedings which have no parties. Once the Court recognized that Israel's consent to these proceedings was not necessary since the case was not bought against it and Israel was not a party to it, Israel had no legal obligation to participate in these proceedings or to adduce evidence

supporting its claim regarding the legality of the wall. While I have my own views on whether it was wise for Israel not to produce the requisite information, this is not an issue for me to decide. The fact remains that it did not have that obligation. The Court may therefore not draw any adverse evidentiary conclusions from Israel's failure to supply it or assume, without itself fully enquiring into the matter, that the information and evidence before it is sufficient to support each and every one of its sweeping legal conclusions.[733]

The Separate Opinions of the Other ICJ Judges

Judges Koroma, Higgins, Kooijmans, Al-Khasawneh, Elaraby and Owada all wrote separate opinions. The following summarizes their separate opinions to the extent that they elucidated, distinguished, criticized or added some argument to the advisory opinion. Arguments made separately that largely agreed with the advisory opinion are not discussed.

1. Jurisdiction

Although Judge Rosalyn Higgins of the United Kingdom agreed that it was within the Court's jurisdiction to issue the advisory opinion, she thought that the question of discretion made "matters... not as straightforward as the Court suggests."[734] She recognized that those parties seeking the opinion sought to draw similarities to the *Namibia* case.[735] She said this "misconceived analogy" was incorrect for several reasons. For one, "there was already, at the time of the request for an opinion... a series of Court Opinions on South West Africa which made clear what were South Africa's legal obligations."[736] Additionally, "all the legal obligations as mandatory Power" lay with South West Africa, none were on the South-West Africa People's Organization (SWAPO). [737]

In the present case, in contrast, "it is the General Assembly, and not the Court, which has made any prior pronouncements in respect of legality."[738] She added that this situation is also different than how "matters stood as regards Namibia in 1971" since the Israeli-Palestinian conflict is the "larger intractable problem (of which the wall may be seen as an element.)"[739] Also, unlike the *Namibia* situation where South Africa held all of the legal obligations, this situation "cannot be regarded as one in which one party alone has been already classified by a court as the legal wrongdoer; where it is for it alone to act to restore a situation of legality; and where from the perspective of legal obligation there is nothing remaining for the other 'party' to do."[740]

Judge Higgins also addressed the issue of a party's consent to jurisdiction in a situation where "the legal interests of a United Nations Member [is] the subject of that advice."[741] She clarified the principle in the *Western Sahara* case, saying "the Court did not… suggest that the consent principle to the settlement of disputes in advisory opinions had now lost all relevance for all who are United Nations Members."[742] Rather, the Court was saying that "*other factors* had to be considered to see if propriety is met in giving an advisory opinion" when a UN Member's legal interests are involved.[743]

Judge Higgins addressed these "other factors," or "conditions," that should be met stating one as being when "a United Nations Member: 'could not validly object, to the General Assembly's exercise of its powers to deal with the decolonization of a non-self-governing territory and to seek an opinion on questions relevant to the exercise of those powers.'"[744] Here, this is met since the UN has had a "long-standing special institutional interest in the dispute."[745] Another condition that the judge believes must be met is that the objective of the request must be "to obtain from the Court an opinion which the General Assembly deems of assistance to it for the proper exercise of its functions concerning the decolonization of the territory."[746] Here, the request for the opinion was not to "secure advice on the Assembly's decolonization duties [as in *Sahara*], but later, on the basis of our Opinion, to exercise powers over the dispute or controversy."[747] Recognizing that this is the reverse circumstance than in *Western Sahara*, she noted her concern, stating "the Court has not dealt with this point at all in that part of its Opinion on propriety. Indeed, it is strikingly silent on the matter, avoiding mention of [quotations from the Sahara case] and any response as to their application to the present case."[748] She cautioned about the consequences of the Court's silence, noting, "this Opinion by its very silence essentially revises, rather than applies, the existing case law."[749]

Judge Hisashi Owada of Japan asserted that the Court should

scrupulously examine the particular circumstances of each case to determine if it is "*proper* as a matter of judicial policy for the Court... to exercise jurisdiction in the concrete context of the case."[750] Here, a particular circumstance that should be considered is the "implication of the existence of a bilateral dispute in the subject-matter of the request for an advisory opinion"[751] and while a bilateral dispute should not automatically end jurisdiction, it "should be a factor to be taken into account."[752]

Judge Owada pronounced his belief that the intricacies of the present case make "the approach of applying the principles drawn from the past precedents automatically to the present situation... not quite warranted."[753] In the judge's view, the:

> Court had drawn too facile an analogy between the present case and the past cases of advisory opinion and especially the case concerning *Legal Consequences for States of the Continued Presence of South Africa in Namibia (South West Africa)* notwithstanding Security Council Resolution 276 (1970), Advisory Opinion.[754]

Recognizing that in the present case it is undeniable that there existed an underlying legal controversy or dispute between the parties, Judge Owada suggested that:

> The critical test for judicial propriety in exercising jurisdiction of the Court . . . should lie, not in whether the request is related to a concrete legal controversy or dispute in existence, but in whether 'to give a reply would have *the effect of circumventing the principle that a State is not obliged to allow its disputes to be submitted to judicial settlement without its consent.*[755]

Applying this test to the present case, the judge said the Court should make sure that any advisory opinion it gives is not "tantamount to adjudicating on the very subject-matter of the underlying concrete bilateral dispute that currently undoubtedly exists between Israel and Palestine."[756]

To conclude, he reiterated that the existence of a bilateral dispute should be a factor to consider when deciding whether to render an advisory opinion. He also re-emphasized his second contention that if a bilateral dispute does exist: the Court should make sure to:

> Focus its task on offering its objective findings of law to the extent necessary and useful to the requesting organ, the General Assembly, in carrying out its functions relating to this question, rather

than adjudicating on the subject-matter of the dispute between the parties concerned.[757]

While addressing jurisdictional issues, Judge Pieter Kooijmans of the Netherlands addressed the Court's acceptance of the General Assembly's use of one Security Council veto as evidence to determine that the Council was no longer exercising its functions under Article 12, Paragraph 1. He noted his concern with the Court's view that Resolution 377 A (V), the Uniting for Peace Resolution, only affected the authority relationship between the General Assembly and Security Council procedurally. He felt that the Uniting for Peace Resolution reflected the substantive change in relationship between the two organs and that the Court should have dealt more directly with the effect of the resolution on the Court's jurisdiction in the instant case. He believed that the resolution explained why the General Assembly's request for an advisory opinion, resolution ES-10/14, did not contravene the Article 12, Paragraph 1 prohibition that the General Assembly not make a recommendation while the Security Council is exercising its functions.

Judge Kooijmans commented on the Court's interpretation that the Uniting for Peace Resolution was "merely in relation to its procedural requirement" and he believed that the resolution had a "more substantive effect, namely with regard to the interpretation of the relationship between the competences of the Security Council and the General Assembly respectively."[758] This substantive effect is on the interpretation of Article 12, Paragraph 1's condition that "that the Assembly shall not make a recommendation" on a dispute or situation "*while* the Security Council is exercising its functions in respect of such dispute or situation."[759]

The judge believed that the resolution helped codify the General Assembly's actual practice when dealing with a situation where one Permanent Member of the Security Council casts a veto preventing a decision from being reached. He said that the resolution exhibits the General Assembly's practice of interpreting its authority to believe that "if a veto cast by a permanent member prevents the Security Council from taking a decision, the latter is no longer considered to be exercising its functions within the meaning of Article

12, paragraph 1."[760] Following this interpretation, the judge stated that at the time the Security Council voted on a resolution dealing with the construction of the wall and a veto was cast, the conclusion should have been reached "that the Security Council was no longer exercising its functions under the Charter with respect to the construction of the wall."[761]

While Judge Kooijmans agreed with the Court that there was already a developed practice between the General Assembly and the Security Council that enabled the organs "to deal in parallel with the same matter concerning the maintenance of international peace and security," he voiced doubts over,

> Whether a resolution of the character of [the General Assembly's resolution that demanded Israel to stop and reverse the walls construction,] resolution ES-10/13 (which beyond any doubt is a recommendation in the sense of Article 12, paragraph 1) could have been lawfully adopted by the Assembly,... if the Security Council had been considering the specific issue of the construction of the wall without yet having taken a decision."

He noted that the Court's "conclusion that resolution ES-10/14 did not contravene Article 12, paragraph 1, of the Charter cannot be dissociated from the effect resolution 377 A (V) has had on the interpretation of that provision."[762]

Judge Kooijmans also addressed whether giving the opinion was judicially proper. He felt "considerable hesitation" about the propriety of giving an opinion, and was concerned over "whether the Court would not be unduly politicized by giving the requested advisory opinion, thereby undermining its ability to contribute to global security and to respect for the rule of law."[763] The issue of politicization of the Court by Judge Kooijmans was an important and persuasive point. His chief concern was with the Court's dismissal of the argument that the Assembly was not clear on what use it would make of the opinion. He equated this case to the *Namibia* case and noted:

> The purpose of the request for an advisory opinion was in that case 'above all to obtain from the Court a reply such that States would find themselves under obligation to bring bear on South Africa pressure...' [Judge Petren] called this a reversal of the natural distribution of roles as between the principal judicial organ and the

political organ of the United Nations since, instead of asking the Court its opinion on a legal question in order to deduce the political consequences following from it, the opposite was done.[764]

He noted that the request was not "legally neutral" and that there was significant difference between "analyzing from a judicial viewpoint what the purpose of the request is," which he felt the Court should have done, and "substituting the Court's assessment of the usefulness of the opinion for that of the organ requesting it," which is what the Court did.[765]

The judge concluded with his view that with regard to judicial propriety, for the opinion not to be precluded, the Court was "duty bound to reconsider the content of the request in order to uphold its judicial dignity."[766] Judge Kooijmans believed the Court did meet this duty but it should not have done so "by assuming what the Assembly 'necessarily' must have assumed, something it evidently did not."[767]

2. History and Context

Judge Higgins criticized the Court for stating that it is aware that the question arises out the larger context of the Israeli-Palestinian conflict and that it "would take this circumstance carefully into account," noting that "it never does so."[768] She pointed out that there is "nothing in the remainder of the Opinion that can be said to cover this point."[769] Moreover, she found the Court's recollection of the 'history' in paragraphs 71-76 as "neither balanced nor satisfactory" and regretted the fact that "a balanced opinion, made so by recalling the obligations incumbent upon all concerned" was never achieved.[770] In her view, the Court should have done much more to avoid "the huge imbalance that necessarily flows from being invited to look at only 'part of a greater whole'" because it did not do enough to then "take that circumstance 'carefully into account.'"[771]

Judge Higgins believed that, in the *dispositif*, the Court should have called upon both parties "to act in accordance with international humanitarian law" and should have "reminded both parties not only of their substantive obligations under international law... but also of the procedural obligation to move forward simultaneously."[772]

Lastly, using important language, she noted that the Court should have taken the opportunity to reiterate:

> What regrettably today apparently needs constant reaffirmation even among international lawyers, namely, that the protection of civilians remains an intransgressible obligation of humanitarian law, not only for the occupier but equally for those seeking to liberate themselves from occupation.[773]

Judge Nabil Elaraby of Egypt, in an effort to give history and context, offered a historical survey meant to "serve... as the background to understanding the legal status of the Palestinian Territory" and also to highlight "the special and continuing responsibility of the General Assembly."[774] Among other things, Judge Elaraby believed that "*Israel's contractual undertakings* to respect the territorial integrity of the territory, and to withdraw from the occupied territories" must be examined.[775]

Judge Kooijmans believed that "the Court could and should have given more explicit attention to the general context of the request in its Opinion."[776]

3. Human Rights Law and Humanitarian Law

Judge Higgins did not agree with "several of the [Court's] stepping stones" nor "its handling of the source materials" in reaching its 'generalized' finding in the *dispositive* that the construction of the wall and its associated regime are contrary to international law.[777] She believed that to be more balanced in its analysis, the Court should have "shown not only which provisions Israel has violated, but also which it has not."[778] She noted that, in her opinion, the advisory opinion should have "contained a detailed analysis, by reference to the texts, the voluminous academic literature and the facts at the Court's disposal, as to *which* of [the proposed applicable provisions of humanitarian law] is correct" since "such an approach would have followed the tradition of using advisory opinions as an opportunity to elaborate and develop international law."[779]

Judge Elaraby concurred with the Court's reasoning and conclusions but felt obligated to "elaborate on the prolonged occupation, the scope and limitations of the principle of military necessity, the grave breaches of international humanitarian law; and the right to self-determination."[780] He went on to note that both Israelis and Palestinians have been subjected to "untold sufferings" but noted that "the fact that occupation is met by armed resistance cannot be used as a pretext to disregard fundamental human rights in the occupied territory."[781] He stated that the only "viable prescription" to end the "grave violations" of humanitarian law is for Israel to end the occupation. He noted that "breaches by both sides of the fundamental rules of humanitarian law reside in 'the illegality of the Israeli occupation regime itself.' Occupation, as an illegal and temporary situation, is at the heart of the whole problem."[782]

4. Right to Self-Determination

Judge Higgins did not believe that the wall should be seen as an impediment to the Palestinian right to self-determination. In her view, the Court was "quite detached from reality" when it found "that it is the wall that presents a 'serious impediment' to the exercise of this right."[783] To the judge, the real impediment is Israel and the Palestinians' "apparent inability and/or unwillingness" to both, at the same time "secure the necessary conditions—,... for Israel to withdraw from Arab occupied territory and for Palestine to provide the conditions to allow Israel to feel secure in so doing."[784]

Judge Kooijmans appropriately opined that "it would have been better if the Court had... left issues of self-determination to this political process," which is "embodied… in the Roadmap.[785]

5. Self Defense

As to self-defense, Judge Higgins disagreed with the Court's conclusion that Article 51 limits the availability of self-defense to only being against another State, stating, "nothing in the text of Article 51 . . . stipulates that self-defence is available only when an armed attack is made by a State."[786] She explained that the Court's finding was a qualification that resulted from the Court's determination in *Military and Paramilitary Activities in and against Nicaragua*.[787] In that case, the Court held that "military action by irregulars" which, "because of its scale and effects, would have been classified as an armed attack . . . had it been carried out by regular armed forces" may "constitute an armed attack if these were sent by or on behalf of the State."[788]

Judge Higgins was not persuaded by the Court's view that it is not an armed attack by one State against another if "the uses of force emanate from occupied territory.'"[789] She did not understand how the Court could conclude that "an occupying Power loses the right to defend its own civilian citizens at home if the attacks emanate from the occupied territory" when the territory has not been annexed "and is certainly 'other than' Israel."[790] Judge Higgins quite appropriately noted the inconsistencies in the Court's reasoning when she questioned how "Palestine cannot be sufficiently an international entity to be invited to these proceedings, and to benefit from humanitarian law, but not sufficiently an international entity for the prohibition of armed attack on others to be applicable."[791] She concluded that this reasoning by the Court is "formalism of an unevenhanded sort."[792] That was putting it mildly.

Judge Higgins curiously explained that her decision to vote for paragraph 3(a) of the *dispositive* was because she "remained unconvinced that non-forcible measures (such as the building of a wall) fall within self-defence under Article 51 of the Charter as that provision is normally understood."[793] She further believed that even if the building of the wall were an "act of self-defense, properly so called, it would need to be justified as necessary and proportionate."[794] And although the wall has admittedly decreased attacks against Israelis, Judge Higgins believed that "the necessity and proportionality for the particular route selected, with its attendant hardships for Palestinians uninvolved in these attacks, has not been explained."[795]

Judge Owada defended the Court's dismissal of Israel's self-defense arguments and the Court's conclusion that, "in light of the materials before it," it was "not convinced" that the construction of the wall "along the route chosen was the only means to safeguard the interests of Israel against the peril which it has invoked as justification for that construction."[796] The judge felt that the Court's lack of in-depth analysis of this point was sufficient since the "material available has not included an elaboration on this point" and, as such, "the Court has found no other way for responding to this situation."[797] The judge concluded that "an in-depth effort *could* have been made by the Court, *proprio motu*, to ascertain the validity of this argument… and to present an objective picture surrounding the construction of the wall in its entirety, on the basis of which to assess the merits of the contention of Israel" and, for Judge Owada, this was sufficient.[798]

Judge Kooijmans argued that the Court did not directly address Israel's self-defense argument since it dismissed it as not falling within Article 51. The Judge explained that Israel's contention relied on Security Council resolutions 1368 (2001) and 1373 (2001), both of which were adopted after the terrorist attacks of September 11, 2001. The Judge felt the Court's reasoning was lacking because, while the Court only addressed self-defense under Article 51, "resolutions 1368 and 1373 recognize the inherent right of individual or collective self-defence without making any reference to an armed attack by a State."[799] Kooijmans went on to note that the Security Council has included terrorism, without any pre-condition that it originates from a State, as "a threat to international peace and security which authorizes it to act under Article 51."[800] Therefore, Judge Kooijmans appropriately attacked the Court's reasoning, which did not include "this new element" of Article 51 that allows self-defense if against acts of international terrorism, as incomplete. The judge felt that "the Court has regrettably by-passed this new element, the legal implications of which cannot as yet be assessed but which marks undeniably a new approach to the concept of self-defense."[801]

6. Legal Consequences for Israel, Other States, and the UN

Judge Kooijmans voted against subparagraph (3)(D) of the *dispositif* that gave the Court's findings on the obligations of other States. He explained that he did not know whether "the scope given by the Court" to Article 1 of the Geneva Convention, which reads "the High Contracting Parties undertake to respect and to *ensure respect* for the present Convention in all circumstances" is "correct as a statement of positive law."[802] The judge felt that the Court did not give any argument in its reasoning for concluding that "this Article imposes obligations on third States not party to a conflict."[803]

He did not understand how there could be a positive obligation on States to not recognize an illegal situation. In explaining his confusion he said:

> I have great difficulty, however, in understanding what the duty not to recognize an illegal fact involves. What are the individual addressees... supposed to do in order to comply with this obligation? The duty not to recognize amounts, therefore, in my view to an obligation without real substance.[804]

Being unable "to see what kind of positive action, resulting from this obligation, may be expected from individual States," Judge Kooijmans felt compelled to vote against this particular finding.[805]

Although she voted with the Court, Judge Higgins did not think that the consequences the Court specified flowing from the identified violations of international law have any relation "with the concept of *erga omnes*."[806] She agreed that there are certain rights in which, by reason of their importance 'all states have a legal interest in their protection,'" but she felt that this concept "has nothing to do with imposing substantive obligations on third parties to a case."[807]

7. Other Issues

Judge Higgins concluded with a comment on the amount of information the Court considered and the lack of information provided by Israel. She said that, "information provided directly by Israel has only been very partial."[808] In addition, she was concerned that "it is not clear whether [the Court] availed itself of other data in the public domain." Nevertheless, asserting that the "Court's findings of law are notably general in character," she chose to support the opinion because of the "significant negative impact" that "cannot be excused on the grounds of military necessity" and because Israel did not explain why the route selected is derived from Israel's "legitimate security needs."[809]

Judge Owada likewise expressed reservations as to the amount of material the Court considered, noting "what seems to be wanting, however, is the material explaining the Israeli side of the picture, especially in the context of why and how the construction of the wall as it is actually planned and implemented is necessary and appropriate."[810] He explained that the lack of information made the Court's finding regarding the argument that the wall was constructed to combat terrorism qualified with, *"from the material available to it,"*[811] meaning, it was less of a "rebuttal of the arguments of Israel on the basis of the material that might have been made available by Israel" and more so an admission, in effect, of "the fact that elaborate material on this point from the Israeli side is not available."[812] To conclude, he connected the Court's lack of information to the importance of fairness, saying that:

> [The Court,] once deciding to exercise jurisdiction in this case, should be extremely careful not only in ensuring the objective fairness in the result, but in seeing to it that the Court is seen to maintain fairness throughout the proceedings, whatever the final conclusion that we come to may be in the end.[813]

Both Judge Elaraby and Judge Koroma had additional comments for the Court's opinion on the construction of the wall and annexation of the territory. Judge Elaraby felt that the Court's fear that the wall could become permanent "should have been reflected in the *dispositif* with an affirmation that the Occupied Palestinian Territory cannot be annexed."[814] Judge Koroma overwhelmingly agreed with the advisory opinion and emphasized his view that the wall did annex part of the land. He stated that, "first and foremost, the construction of the wall has involved the annexation of parts of the occupied territory by Israel, the occupying Power, contrary to the fundamental international law principle of the non-acquisition of territory by force."[815]

Judge Awn Shawkat Al-Khasawneh of Jordan chose to comment on his views pertaining to the treatment of the Green Line, an issue directly affecting his country, Jordan. He felt that:

> Attempts at denigrating the significance of the Green Line would in the nature of things work both ways. Israel cannot shed doubts upon the title of others without expecting its own title and the territorial expanse of that title beyond the partition resolution not to be called into question.[816]

Al-Khasawneh believed that "ultimately it is through stabilizing [Israel's] legal relationship with the Palestinians and not through constructing walls that its security would be assured."[817] Turning to the subject of *erga omnes* and the obligations of other States, he added that, "the discharge of international obligations including *erga omnes* obligations cannot be made conditional upon negotiations."[818]

The general criticism of Israel, even by those Judges dissenting from all or part of the advisory opinion, for its failure to fully participate in the proceedings and provide needed information in defense of its position, on factual and legal grounds beyond jurisdiction, appears to have adversely impacted Israel's position and resulting in the various conclusions expressed in the advisory opinion.

CHAPTER EIGHT:
Lack of Jurisdiction for the International Court to Issue an Advisory Opinion

To further explain the importance of the jurisdictional issue, why it was so important and why the International Court of Justice erred in determining that it had jurisdiction to issue the advisory opinion, it is worth noting the following points and analysis.

In its broadest meaning, "jurisdiction" refers to "the power of the court to decide a matter."[819] Article 36(6) of the ICJ Statute entitles the Court to determine whether it has jurisdiction to give an advisory opinion. Over the objection of 30 countries, including the US, Israel and the European Union, the International Court of Justice determined that it had jurisdiction to render the advisory opinion

Despite the Court's determination, there are strong arguments against the Court having accepted jurisdiction in this particular case. First, the procedures by which the issue reached the Court and the methodology employed by the General Assembly to garner an advisory opinion from the ICJ are in violation of the UN Charter. The question, and the circumstances from which it arose, were in the purview and jurisdiction of another branch of the United Nations, namely the Security Council, which remained seized of the matter (S/RES/1515, November 19, 2003). Second, the question posed was not a legal question satisfying the essential elements necessary for issuance of an advisory opinion.

I. Jurisdiction Lacking Because of Procedural Defects

The case of Israel's Security Fence reached the Court in a procedurally defective manner. The Court has repeatedly stated, quite clearly, that it is "a precondition of the Court's competence that the advisory opinion be requested by an organ duly authorized to seek it under the Charter, that it be requested on a legal question, and that, except in the case of the General Assembly or the Security Council, that question should be one arising within the scope of the activities of the requesting organ."[820] The General Assembly's request for an advisory opinion was ultra vires, beyond the power of the 10th Emergency Special Session and/or the General Assembly, because the Security Council was seized of the matter, meaning the Security Council was still considering the matter at the time the General Assembly acted. In contradiction to what the Court stated, there was no failure by the Security Council to act, which would justify action taken through a General Assembly Emergency Session.

Commentators have recognized that "the Court's practice throughout its history" clearly demonstrates the Court's presumption towards viewing requests for advisory opinions by the General Assembly and the Security Council as being intra vires or within their power to give.[821] In effect, it follows that "allegations [by parties] of ultra vires in regard to actions taken by the two political organs [the Security Council and General Assembly] are difficult to sustain."[822]

As the principal judicial organ of the United Nations, there should be no reason for the Court to feel compelled to accept such a presumption or to refuse to pass judgment on the legality of procedures taken by UN organs. In the UN system, there exists no principle of separation of powers comparable to that found, for example, in the US Constitution. Indeed, the ICJ has not shied away from expanding its ability to hear controversies. The ICJ's lack of judicial restraint is alarming and worthy of greater examination. Indeed, it is inexplicable why the Court chose to proceed given the procedural defects within the General Assembly's process in bypassing the Security Council and directly requesting an advisory opinion.

1. The Security Council Declared in Resolution 1515 that the Issue was Before it so the General Assembly was Barred from Taking Action on the Issue

Although the General Assembly has some powers over issues of international peace and security, secondary to those of the Security Council, it does not have the authority to infringe on the powers specifically delegated to the Security Council. For instance, the Security Council has the power to enforce its own decisions on international peace and security. The General Assembly, however, does not.[823] Additionally, international law and applicable UN principles dictated that while the Security Council was still considering the matter, the General Assembly was barred from acting.

The United Nations convenes in (1) a General Assembly forum where each member state, along with invited observers, participate in debating and addressing issues of public policy as they relate to international peace and security; and (2) a Security Council where permanent and selected member states address these issues of policy and other resolutions of significance, as the Council deems appropriate. These two organs are the bodies within the United Nations responsible for working toward and maintaining international peace.

The General Assembly is comprised of representatives of all the UN member states. Its purpose is to discuss and provide recommendations on international issues. Article 10 of the UN Charter has conferred on the General Assembly competence relating to any question or matter within the scope of the UN Charter.[824] Article 11 of the UN Charter gives the General Assembly competence to consider the general principles in the maintenance of international peace and security.[825] Article 13 of the UN Charter provides that the General Assembly shall initiate studies and make recommendations for the purpose of encouraging the progressive development of international law and its codification.[826] These general powers are constrained by the General Assembly's obligation to avoid circumventing the powers that are given exclusively to the Security Council and denied to the General Assembly. The General Assembly, either on its own or in combination with the International Court of Justice, has the authority to decide what measures are to be employed to maintain or restore international peace and security. Any attempt to do so is a perversion of the United Nations system as that responsibility is expressly reserved unto the Security Council.

By contrast, the Security Council has the power and granted authority to adopt resolutions which enforce its decisions on international peace and security. Moreover, it can take actions to ensure that affected States are in compliance with its decisions. In particular, the Security Council has exclusive powers to decide what measures are to be employed to maintain or restore international peace and security.[827] According to Article 12 of the UN Charter, when the Security Council is seized of a matter, "the General Assembly shall not make any recommendation with regard to that dispute or situation unless the Security Council so requests."[828] This means that the UN Charter prohibits the General Assembly from making "recommendations" on international security disputes where the issue is before the Security Council.

The United States, Russia, the European Union and the United Nations, acting as a "Quartet," adopted the Roadmap for Peace in the Middle East to govern negotiations between Israel and the Palestinian Authority. The Roadmap was formally ratified and adopted on November 19, 2003 by the Security Council's binding Resolution 1515.[829] This resolution simply and pointedly endorses the Roadmap and calls on all parties to fulfill their obligations there under. Although in the Roadmap there is no mention of the terrorism prevention security fence, the West Bank is never called the "Occupied Palestinian Territory" nor is Israel ever referred to as "an Occupying Power," There is no question that the action of the Security Council in endorsing the Roadmap constituted an action on a matter of international peace and security, to wit, the Arab-Palestinian-Israeli Conflict that, were it any other issue, would neither have been considered for action by the General Assembly nor accepted for review and issuance of an advisory opinion by the ICJ.

In Resolution 1515, enacted just three weeks prior to the General Assembly's vote to request the advisory opinion, the Security Council declared that it was "seized of the matter."[830] This resolution was the only Security Council resolution passed relating to the Arab-Palestinian-Israeli conflict after the security fence's construction began.

In its advisory opinion, the Court opined that there has been an "increasing tendency over time for the General Assembly and the Security Council to deal in parallel with the same matter concerning the maintenance of international peace and security."[831] Based on this tendency, it held that this "accepted practice of the General Assembly, as it has evolved, is consistent with Article 12, paragraph 1, of the Charter."[832] International law scholars, in addition to many of the ICJ panel judges in their separate opinions, questioned the advisory opinion's assertion that the practice of simultaneous action has become customary international law and the applicable facts and law dictate to the contrary.

2. There was No Failure to Act by the Security Council nor was there a Security Council Referral that would Justify Action under the Uniting for Peace Resolution

General Assembly Resolution 377 A (V), known as the "Uniting for Peace Resolution," provides a mechanism by which the General Assembly may consider a matter immediately and make appropriate recommendations for collective measures if:

> The Security Council, because of lack of unanimity of the permanent members, fails to exercise its primary responsibility for the maintenance of international peace and security in any case where there appears to be a threat to the peace, breach of the peace, or act of aggression.[833]

The General Assembly's decision to hold an Emergency Special Session to address the construction of the security fence was not justified because, just three weeks prior to the General Assembly vote to request the advisory opinion, the Security Council declared itself "seized of the matter" in Resolution 1515.[834] The Security Council had just taken action and could not be characterized to have failed to exercise its primary responsibility for the maintenance of international peace and security on the issue. Additionally, this Emergency Special Session of the General Assembly was without any legal basis because it was called to address issues, including the request for an advisory opinion, which had not been previously raised directly before the Security Council. And since the issue had not yet been raised before the Security Council, there could be no "inaction" of the Security Council upon which the General Assembly could properly rely as a predicate to justify its request to the ICJ for the advisory opinion.

Article 11(2) of the United Nations Charter directs the General Assembly to refer to the Security Council those issues of international peace and security that require "action" be taken. The request to the International Court of Justice for an advisory opinion is a form of action. In this case, since the General Assembly did not refer the request for an advisory opinion to the Security Council, the request to the ICJ was invalid and should have been forthwith rejected by the Court. There was no comparable Security Council resolution. In fact, on October 14, 2003, the Security Council did not adopt a draft resolution addressing Israel's terrorism prevention security fence. The United States vetoed the resolution because it "failed to address both sides of the larger security context of the Middle East, including the devastating suicide attacks that Israelis have had to endure over the past three years."[835] However, the Security Council next proceeded to adopt the Roadmap, an action that encompassed the entire conflict, not just the security fence. Nevertheless, the General Assembly voted to petition the ICJ to render its advisory opinion on the question presented. The Court then, in its advisory opinion, used overly-formalistic and convoluted reasoning to conclude that the Security Council had not taken action because it "neither discussed the construction of the wall nor adopted any resolution in that connection" during the specific time of the Emergency Special Session.[836]

To be clear, the timeline is thus: On October 14, 2003, the Security Council rejected a draft resolution concerning Israel's security fence. Weeks later, on November 19, 2003, the Security Council adopted the Roadmap for Peace in resolution 1515 (2003). Thereafter, in November 2003, the General Assembly convened and approved its request for an Advisory Opinion. In its advisory opinion, the Court concluded that by December 8, 2003, the Security Council had not "reconsidered the negative vote of 14 October 2003" and thus, "during that period, the Tenth Emergency Special Session was duly reconvened and could properly be seized, under resolution 377 A (V)."[837]

The Court should have acknowledged that both actions by the Security Council, i.e., its initial rejection of the draft resolution on the security fence and then its groundbreaking decision to adopt the Roadmap for Peace in resolution 1515, constituted significant actions by the Security Council on the subject of the Arab-Palestinian-Israel conflict thereby making the Emergency Special Session inappropriate and unjustified. Had the Court given deference to that analysis, it would have, as it should have, declined jurisdiction over the request for the advisory opinion.

3. The General Assembly Acted Ultra Vires and Usurped the Security Council's Authority

By requesting the advisory opinion when only the Security Council had the authority to act, the General Assembly interfered with and illegally usurped the Security Council's authority. The *South West* Africa advisory opinion of 1971 serves as a useful guide. There, the ICJ was asked, "What are the legal consequences for States of the continued presence of South Africa in Namibia notwithstanding Security Council resolution 276(1970)?"[838]

In form, both the South West Africa question and the question on the security fence are similar. Both questions relate to legal consequences.

In the *South West Africa* advisory opinion, the Court gave the following answers:

1) The continued presence of South Africa in Namibia being illegal, South Africa is under an obligation to withdraw its administration.

2) State Members of the United Nations are under an obligation to recognize this illegality and to refrain from any acts or dealing with South Africa implying recognition of the legality of, or lending support or assistance to the South African presence in Namibia.[839]

Obviously, when looking at the question posed by the General Assembly, it is clear from the face of the language that it wanted the Court to deem the terrorism prevention security fence illegal and to state that Israel is obligated to demolish it. Moreover, they also saw the presentation of the issue to the Court as a political opportunity to ask member States of the United Nations to recognize such illegality and to refrain from any acts or dealings with Israel that might imply recognition or support of the construction or maintenance of the fence.

The question posed by the General Assembly and the potential resulting answer are just the type of determination the Security Council is granted the exclusive authority to make under Chapter VII of the UN Charter. It corrupts the UN system and renders it ineffective for the Court to determine, based on a request by the General Assembly and no involvement by the Security Council, that a member State is under a legal obligation to do something particular on matters of peace and security, constituting a derogation of the powers of the Security Council and an inappropriate usurpation by the General Assembly, condoned by the ICJ. Surely, the ICJ would not have permitted such an inane circumvention were it any issue other than the Arab-Palestinian-Israeli conflict. It was almost as if the Court could not help itself ... could not resist the opportunity to become involved in the issue.

Moreover, the ICJ only has authority to reply to the General Assembly's question with a procedural answer in the form of a non binding advisory opinion to the General Assembly. The consequences arising from the construction of the terrorism prevention fence is a substantive question involving peace and security that must be decided by the Security Council. The Court could provide substantive advice on legal consequences to the Security Council, if requested to do so by the Council. Otherwise, it cannot and should not have responded to the General Assembly itself as to the "legal consequences relating to the "wall."

The action by the General Assembly during the 10th Emergency Special Session was beyond its authority and was a dangerous breach of the balance of powers between the Council and the Assembly, as envisaged by the UN Charter. This power grab could serve as a precedent for similar actions in future conflicts where the General Assembly wishes to bypass the Security Council. There is little doubt that enforcement of the Court's decision on matters of international peace and security rests with the Security Council. But, when the Security Council has not asked the question, and has made no prior determination of illegality or opposition to the security fence's construction, any Court advisory opinion on the issue becomes little more than an empty and improper exercise and should be viewed in that context. It is an affront to the Security Council and its exclusive powers over matters of international peace and security and to the very sovereignty of the State of Israel, which is committed to the Roadmap as adopted by the Security Council.

II. the Jurisdictional Grants of the ICJ Statute were Not Met

The ICJ has jurisdiction to hear cases in two specific circumstances. First, the Court may hear contentious cases. These are cases where two UN member states are in dispute over an issue of international law and both states request a hearing before the Court and agree to abide by its ruling. Article 36 of the Statute of the International Court of Justice prohibits contentious issues from being brought before the Court without the consent of all parties. Second, the Court has no jurisdiction to render an advisory opinion "on any legal question" except when a proper body of the United Nations itself makes such a request. In this case, the only proper body to so request was the Security Council; not the General Assembly. Accordingly, neither of these jurisdictional grants applied here.

1. There was No Consent by Member States for Contentious Case Jurisdiction

This contentious case's lack of consent by all parties involved and the fact that there were not even two "state" parties in the case prevented the ICJ from asserting jurisdiction under Article 36.

Article 34 of the UN Charter instructs that, "only states may be parties in cases before the Court."[840] Indeed, the ICJ affirmed its inability to settle disputes by non-states when it unanimously concluded on December 15, 2004 that because the former Yugoslavia was not a member of the UN when it initiated the action, the Court lacked jurisdiction to resolve whether Serbia and Montenegro had legal claims against NATO countries that participated in the 1999 intervention in Kosovo.[841] As in that case, here, Palestine, which only had organizational observer status at the UN at the time the request for an advisory opinion was made, and as it was not a member-state, the action, by definition was not between two state parties. The PA, which is represented by the PLO at the United Nations has only recently had its status upgraded to be that of a non-member state observer and neither the Palestine Liberation Organization nor the Palestinian Authority, which has recently changed its name to the "State of Palestine" is as yet a sovereign State Party to the Statute of the International Court of Justice.

The International Court of Justice has a specific mandate with regard to contentious cases—resolving legal disputes between two "states" that voluntarily submit to its jurisdiction. Israel, a member state of the United Nations, did not consent to resolve the question presented before the Court. Thus the ICJ could not and should not have considered the issue as an international dispute properly before the Court. In 1923, in the Eastern Carelia case, the Permanent Court of International Justice, a predecessor to the current ICJ, declined to render an advisory opinion requested by the League of Nations. The dispute was between Finland and Russia, but Russia was not a member of the League of Nations. That Court applied the fundamental principle that no State can, without giving its consent, be compelled to submit its disputes with other States to any kind of judgment or opinion by the Court. The consent of all parties is, and always has been, an indispensable jurisdictional requirement in contentious cases.

2. There was No Legal Question Which Is Required For Advisory Opinion Jurisdiction

Article 102 of the Court's rules limits the ICJ's authority to issue advisory opinions to legal questions. In practice, however, the Court has yet to deem any question presented to it as a non-legal one. It has liberally interpreted what it means to be a "legal question" to mean almost any question, including questions where matters of a political nature, often vague and abstract, predominate. Compounding this definitional problem is the absence of an international consensus on what defines a legal question within the ICJ context.

This existence of an ICJ jurisdictional limitation that is bereft of any meaning is disconcerting. The jurisdictional requirement of a legal question should have some teeth. In the case at hand, the ICJ did not possess jurisdiction to render an advisory opinion. The question presented was vague and legally uncertain in addition to concerning a dispute that did not involve two consenting states.

A Jurisdictional Requirement Without Meaning?

The history of the International Court of Justice illustrates that its jurisdiction to render advisory opinions has been limited to legal questions. This, however, has become a constraint without much meaning. The International Court of Justice has roots in the Permanent Court of International Justice ("PCIJ"), which was established by the League of Nations in 1922. Article 14 of the Covenant of the League of Nations gave the Permanent Court of International Justice authority not only to resolve international disputes among parties but also to render advisory opinions on "any dispute or question" referred to it by the other arms of the League of Nations.[842]

Although the PCIJ operated successfully for a time, the outbreak of World War II in 1939 signaled the effective cessation of operations. Its role, however, was not forgotten.[843] In 1945, a judicial committee convened in San Francisco, California to create the United Nations Charter and plan for the future of the PCIJ. The San Francisco Conference officially created a new Court—the International Court of Justice—and the committee drafted the Court's statute based on the pre-existing Statute of the PCIJ.[844]

Compared with its predecessor, the ICJ Statute limited the scope of subject matter that the Court could consider for advisory opinions. Where the PCIJ could render an advisory opinion on "any dispute or question," the latter Statute, still in effect today, limits the permissible subject matter for ICJ advisory opinions to only questions of law.[845] While it appears that the drafters meant to constrain the Court's subject matter jurisdiction under the Statute, in practice, the Court has chosen to consider a large range of questions as legal issues. In fact, as mentioned previously, the Court has never constrained its own authority pursuant to the Statute and ruled that a question presented to it was non-legal.

The Court has adopted the principle that "the question would have a legal character if it were framed in terms of law and raised problems of international law, even if it had political or factual elements."[846] Indeed, "the Court's practice has consistently illustrated that it has "always been willing to answer questions placed before it, even if the questions were intermixed with political and factual issues or even if the drafting of the request was unclear."[847] It is clear from ICJ precedent that neither the political nature of a question nor its abstract nature are sufficient to render a question non-legal and make it outside the scope of the Court's jurisdiction.

Indeed, the Court has stated that the presence of political elements in a question are "in the nature of things, [and as] is the case with so many questions which arise in international life, does not suffice to deprive it of its character as a legal question and to deprive the Court of a competence expressly conferred on it by its Statute."[848] Nor does the Court feel that unduly abstract questions strip it of jurisdiction, insisting that any assertion that the Court should not deal with a question couched in abstract terms is "a mere affirmation devoid of any justification."[849] The Court left little doubt of its opinion of its authority when it bluntly stated, "the Court may give an advisory opinion on any legal question, abstract or otherwise."[850]

The Meaning of "Legal Question" within Realist/Idealist Debate

What is a legal question? According to Charles de Visscher, a former judge at both the Permanent Court of International Justice and the International Court of Justice, a legal question concerns "any problem susceptible of receiving an answer based in law."[851] However, as former ICJ Judge Hardy Cross Dillard noted, "the notion that a legal question is simply one that invites an answer 'based on law' appears to be question-begging and it derives no added authority by virtue of being frequently repeated."[852] Neither the UN

Charter nor the ICJ Statute define what is a "legal question" or what constitutes a non-legal question. This ambiguity remains.

To try to determine the meaning of the term "legal question," one must understand that the term stands within a larger theoretical debate between idealists and realists about the proper function and scope of international law. International relations scholar Hans Morgenthau contrasted the two opposing views: "Whereas the idealist believes in 'abstract principles' and attempts to reeducate people to be better, the realist sees the world and its inhabitants for what they really are, and formulates policies that will 'work with those forces, not against them.'"[853]

Idealists favor a view that "human nature is, for the most part, morally good" and "humankind's bad behavior can be altered positively through the intervention of morally correct institutions."[854] Idealists suggest that there is "no objective standard for distinguishing between legal and political questions." Thomas J. Bodie, an international relations specialist, explained this view:

> The greatest voice in this school, that of Hersch Lauterpacht, suggested this was so, not simple because it was too hard to find the division, but more because international law was such that it did not admit of any division. International law should be viewed as a complete body of law, one with no gaps (as has been argued by so many others). The result is that there are no disputes to which international law cannot be applied. This position would be echoed forcefully later by Rosalyn Higgins.[855]

Idealists believe that all international disputes are susceptible to legal answers whereas realists believe that international law does not provide answers to all disputes, especially those of a political nature.

Morgenthau and Bodie both address the realist belief that people are self-interested and the "world is one 'of opposing interests and of conflict among them.' States are just larger expressions of this principle, and the overriding interest for a state is its security."[856] In regards to the legal/political dichotomy, Bodie explained that:

> The realist is cognizant of the importance of international law in some issue areas, and is even appreciative to a point. After all, it is in every state's interest that international intercourse be predictable. Rules create predictability and lessen the chance for conflict in

a great many areas such as economic trade, diplomatic exchange, movement of people across borders and the like. Having said that, however, the realist would suggest that law has its limits in the international arena. Remembering that states can be the only judges of their own interest, it can be seen that in some instances, states will not be able to surrender their decision-making processes to a third party such as an adjudicative body. The realist definitely sees a difference between legal and political issues.[857]

Currently, the realist view is the position most often adopted and used by states, especially developed nations.[858] That is, "with only a few exceptions, states have proven themselves unwilling to completely and unwaveringly entrust all disputes to international third party dispute resolution."[859] On the other hand, the International Court of Justice adopts the idealist position. Bodie asserts:

> Among scholars in the field [and states], realism, and its inherent conclusion that there are limits to juridical power in the international arena, is the theoretical position chosen most often... this no longer defines the position of the International Court of Justice. The preponderance of realism among the scholarly community only serves to highlight the position of the Court, which... is idealist.[860]

In addressing the Court's authority, Bodie bluntly concludes "the International Court of Justice does not see itself bound by considerations of political context, and it will not in the future. What has emerged is a more activist Court."[861]

The written submissions and oral statements submitted by the various states and entities during the advisory proceedings on the security fence reflected this realist/idealist divide, with developed states favoring realist views and developing states and entities proceeding based upon idealist views. In her discursive analysis of the various submissions to the ICJ on the security fence, Michelle Burgis, international law specialist and attorney, found:

> Third World States tended to demonstrate greater reverence for the Court and its formal function. At the same time, however, they supported the work of the UNGA and viewed the resolution requesting an Advisory Opinion as indicative of international public opinion. Thus, the spheres of international politics and international law were distinguished in such submissions, but were also seen as interdependent and inclusive of Third World States.[862]

Regarding developed states, Burgis observed:

For First World States unsupportive of the Court's jurisdiction, international law tended to garner more formal engagement, as evidenced by less inflammatory language. International law was regarded as being of only limited use in international life. The broader goals discussed by Third World States, such as self-determination and bringing an end to colonialism were overlooked in most First World submissions and negotiations were contrasted with international law to indicate a clear demarcation between legal and political spheres.[863]

The Textual Interpretations of "Legal Question"

The debate surrounding what a "legal question" is for purposes of ICJ advisory opinion jurisdiction can be seen in relation to what a "legal dispute" is for purposes of ICJ contentious case jurisdiction. It is reasonable to extrapolate the meaning of "legal" from the contentious case context and apply it to "legal" within the advisory opinion context because the term appears twice in the same document without being fully explained or distinguished. Despite and in some respects because of the lack of a given definition, it is reasonable to conclude that the drafters intended for the term "legal" to have the same definition in both locations of the same document. To add further support to the contention that "legal" should be defined the same as it is for "legal disputes," Article 102(2) of the ICJ Rules states that in its advisory proceedings, "the Court shall also be guided by the provisions of the Statute and of these Rules which apply in contentious cases to the extent to which it recognizes them to be applicable."[864]

The importance of the term "legal dispute" is derived from Article 36(2) of the Statute. Article 36(2) allows member states the option of accepting the jurisdiction of the Court as compulsory...

> in all *legal disputes* concerning (a) the interpretation of a treaty; (b) any question of international law; (c) the existence of any fact which, if established, would constitute a breach of an international obligation; (d) the nature or extent of the reparation to be made for the breach of an international obligation.[865]

Edward Gordon, retired international law professor and attorney, has explained that within the contentious case context "opinion is divided . . . over whether the words 'legal disputes' are merely descriptive of the enumerated categories [of Article 36(2)] or [whether the terms] qualify them in some restrictive way."[866]

The first interpretation holds that the term "legal dispute" describes the categories listed in Article 36(2). By extension, a legal question would be a question that concerns any of the four aforementioned broad categories. Certainly, this liberal interpretation includes a large range of questions.

The second interpretation holds that the term "legal dispute" qualifies or limits the Court's jurisdiction. That is:

> Those who regard the phrase as a qualification of the Court's compulsory jurisdiction contend that it constitutes a coded reference to a distinction between international controversies that are and ones that are not properly justiciable, in the sense of being suited to judicial resolution or, more specifically, to resolution by the Court pursuant to commitments undertaken in advance within the framework of a regime of compulsory adjudication.[867]

This interpretation would mean that questions that are not "legal" are then not suited to judicial resolution since Article 36(2) only refers to "legal" disputes. Thus, following this more reasonable interpretation, when the Court is determining whether a question is a "legal dispute" with compulsory jurisdiction, the Court would consider "limitations... that derive indirectly from the intrinsic character of certain claims, from the nature of the Court as an adjudicative institution, or from qualities inherent in international law or international relations."[868]

This narrow interpretation of "legal," as applied to a "legal question," is more persuasive because it recognizes the existence of non-justiciable questions and appropriate limits on jurisdiction. Moreover, there would be little reason to draft a jurisdictional limitation without any meaning.

It quickly becomes apparent that these observations are quite similar to an analysis of the Court's discretionary considerations about propriety.[869] International law scholar Shabtai Rosenne has noted that:

> It is believed that as far as concerns the international judicial process, the difference between the Court's declining to render an advisory opinion on the ground that the question put is not a legal one, and its declining to render the opinion in exercise of its judicial discretion, is largely one of formulation and of judicial technique rather than one of substance.[870]

There is No Legal Question Because the Dispute Does Not Concern Two States

The ICJ's authority to give advisory opinions upon request by the General Assembly or another authorized international organization is limited to advisory opinions "on legal questions actually pending between two or more States."[871] Contrary to the requirements of Article 102(2) of the Court's Rules, the issue of the terrorism prevention security fence built by Israel involves only one state—Israel. Israel was not and is not engaged in a legal dispute with any of the states that instigated the resolution. It does, however, have a terrorism problem that emanates from neighboring territorywhich is not territory of another sovereign state universally recognized as such under international law. It is this security problem that prompted the Government of Israel to take specific steps to protect its population while it concurrently explores its diplomatic and legal solutions. One can anticipate, and the PLO has made clear its intention to do so, that now that Palestine has been granted "non member state" status, it will seek full state status at the Court in order to press its claims against Israel; and will likely do the same at the International Criminal Court, if permitted to do so, to press claims against Israel and Israeli Defense Force personnel. Such actions by Palestine will be a two edged sword, making her equally liable for all acts of terrorism and other wrongs supported or committed by the Palestinians. However, at the time of issuance of the advisory opinion, it is clear that Israel did not consent and Palestine was not a state. Nor has the UN Security Council declared her to be a state.

There is No Legal Question Because the Question was Legally Uncertain

General Assembly's Resolution A/RES/ES-10/14, requesting the ICJ to "urgently render an advisory opinion" on the legal consequences arising from the construction of the wall, also fails to meet the Article 102(2) requirements because the question posed by the General Assembly was vague and legally uncertain.

In its submission to the Court, the Israeli government claimed that "the question referred to the Court [was] uncertain in its terms with the result that it is not amenable to a response by the Court."[872] It argued that a legal question must be reasonably specific and legally certain. Article 65(2) of the Statute requires "an exact statement of the question upon which an opinion is required." Based on this, Israel, citing past ICJ cases to support its contention, asserted that "it is not possible to decipher with reasonable certainty the legal meaning of the question."[873]

Israel argued that there was uncertainty over whether the question asked the Court "to find that the construction of the fence is unlawful, and then to give its opinion on the legal consequences of that illegality," or whether it asked the Court "to assume that the construction of the fence is unlawful and then to give its opinion on the legal consequences of that assumed illegality."[874] The differences are significant. The first question was highly politically sensitive, Israel contended, and if "the General Assembly had wanted the Court's opinion on this highly complex and sensitive question, it would expressly have sought such an opinion."[875] Israel urged the Court not to reformulate the question,

As for Israel's second interpretation of the question that assumes illegality, Israel said:

> If the Court were to proceed on the basis of an assumption of illegality, the resulting opinion could have no practical value. As follows from the Western Sahara case, the function of the Court is to give an opinion once it has come to the conclusion that the question put is relevant and has a practical and contemporary effect, and is not devoid of object or purpose. These requirements cannot be considered satisfied if the question is simply asking the Court to give its opinion on the basis of an assumption, i.e., the assumed illegality of the construction of the fence. The resulting opinion could not assist the General Assembly in the proper exercise of its functions. It would also be a source of wider confusion.[876]

Given the uncertainty of the nature of the question asked and the significant difference between the two interpretations, Israel argued that the Court should not establish its jurisdiction by modifying or improving on the question presented to it. That is, the Court's charge was to answer the question "as put to it, not to seek to reformulate the question," and "in the absence of a reasonably certain legal question for it to answer, the Court cannot establish its jurisdiction by augmenting the question before it."[877]

Despite Israel's position, the ICJ determined that the General Assembly's question as referred to it was a legal question, concluding that it had "been framed in terms of law and raises problems of international law; [and that] it is by its very nature susceptible of a reply based on law; indeed it is scarcely susceptible of a reply otherwise than on the basis of law."[878]

In giving its advisory decision, the Court explained that the Court is not deprived of jurisdiction merely because of a "lack of clarity in the drafting of a question... Rather, such uncertainty will require clarification in interpretation, and such necessary clarifications of interpretation have frequently been given by the Court."[879] Instead of interpreting the vagueness and poor wording of the question as a limit on its authority, it used the characteristics as a license to redraft the question it would answer

The Court did not consider the inherent danger of reformulating the question(s) to suit itself when it gave its advisory opinion. It neglected to take note that while the Court is the principal judicial organ of the UN, it does not represent the collective intentions of UN Member States in the same ways that the Security Council or General Assembly do. Rosenne perhaps explained it best:

> The experience which has been attained since 1946 has shown that the process by which a decision to request an advisory opinion is reached, is not conducted with as much care as is desirable. This has thrown upon the Court the unusual duty, too often, of framing the request, in guise of interpreting it, so that it conforms with the terms of the Statute. But the Court cannot substitute itself for the collective intention of the States represented in the organ making the request.[880]

In reformulating and reading into the General Assembly's request, the Court substituted its own intentions to consider and decide for the collective intentions of the member states in the General Assembly who requested the advisory opinion, and notwithstanding the lack of consent by Israel, an affected member-state, to the Court's consideration of the question(s) presented. Such actions threaten the nature of the Court as an adjudicative institution and harm its judicial integrity.

Conclusion

It is clear that the Court has stretched the meaning of "legal question" to its broadest capacity. At this point, it is hard to conceive of any matter that the Court would not consider as a legal question. In so doing, the Court ignored the language in its own enabling Statute that limits its authority and did so in order to maximize its jurisdiction. The inadequacy of the separation of powers and checks and balances doctrines within the UN system resulted in the Court holding itself relatively free to do this without repercussion. However, it does not follow that this practice is prudent. In the view of many states, an overly expansive ICJ advisory opinion jurisdiction is reflective of a judicially active Court that is unwilling to accept limits on its power and assumes that the law can resolve almost any international problem. This could lead to an unintended consequence where states ultimately reject the ICJ as a forum for international legal dispute resolution because of its unwillingness to limit or restrain itself to only questions properly before it.

It is true, as Rosenne says, that "contemporary legal doctrine is to a great extent averse to accepting the proposition that the law cannot provide an answer to any question properly put to it."[881] However, while the law can provide a great many useful answers, it is neither the proper, preferred nor the most effective tool for long-term conflict resolution in the international political arena. Indeed, the political sphere is better suited to resolving international conflicts and disputes, and this certainly includes the controversy regarding Israel's security fence, as reflected in the Court's concluding language urging the parties to essentially return to and engage in a political process and to convene direct negotiations to resolve their long standing differences and achieve a just and hopefully near-term resolution to the Arab-Palestinian-Israeli Conflict.

CHAPTER NINE:
The Impropriety and Dangers of the International Court of Justice's Issuance of the Advisory Opinion

The permissive language of Article 65 of the Statute of the Court grants the International Court of Justice the authority to decide, based on the circumstances of a case, whether it will answer or decline a request for an advisory opinion. Even if the subject posed in the request is a legal question that the Court is fully competent to answer, it may nonetheless decline to do so if aspects of the case make the exercise of jurisdiction improper and inconsistent with the Court's judicial function unless compelling reasons exist. Former President of Israel's High Court Aharon Barak has described judicial discretion as "the power the law gives the judge to choose among several alternatives, each of them lawful."[882] Despite the Court's repeated pronouncements of its discretionary authority, it has rarely exercised this discretion. Michla Pomerance, international law scholar, criticized the Court's repeat pronouncements of its discretionary power when he said "its statements were never more than meaningless mantras, which gained nothing in persuasiveness by their frequent repetition."[883]

Rosenne has observed two general principles that guide the Court in its discussion of its discretion:

> The first is the principle originally laid down in the Eastern Carelia case that the Court, being a Court of justice, cannot, even in giving advisory opinions, depart from the essential rules guiding its activity as a Court. The second, which is peculiar to the present court, is that since the Court is a principal organ of the United Nations, it is under a duty to co-operate with other organs; consequently, a

> request for an advisory opinion should not in principle be refused, and only compelling reasons should lead the Court to refuse to give the requested opinion.[884]

In the particular case concerning the request for an advisory opinion on the security fence, the Court's exercise of jurisdiction was inconsistent with the Court's judicial function. There are a number of compelling reasons why the opinion should not have issued.

I. The ICJ's Actions were Improper in Light of Its Judicial Function

The Court explained in the Western Sahara case that "the International Court of Justice, like the Permanent Court of International Justice, has always been guided by the principle that, as a judicial body, it is bound to remain faithful to the requirements of its judicial character even in giving advisory opinions."[885] However, on only one instance, in the Status of Eastern Carelia case, did the ICJ's predecessor take the position that it "should not reply to a question put to it."[886] In Eastern Carelia, the PCIJ determined that it should not reply to the question because:

> The very particular circumstances of the case, among which were that the question directly concerned an already existing dispute, one of the States parties to which was neither a party to the Statute of the Permanent Court nor a Member of the League of Nations, objected to the proceedings, and refused to take part in any way.[887]

The PCIJ Court focused on two factors that indicated that it would be contrary to the Court's judicial character to proceed: (1) the absence of consent to the adjudication of a legal dispute, and (2) the lack of sufficient evidence before the Court preventing it from making determinations on underlying facts.

The ICJ's Actions were Improper in Light of the Absence of Party Consent to Adjudication of Legal Dispute

The importance of the principle of consent, and the need for it if the Court is to proceed judicially, was first expressed by the PCIJ in the *Eastern Carelia* case. The ICJ then, in the *Western Sahara* case, elaborated further on the relevance of consent, explaining that "the consent of an interested State continues to be relevant, not for the Court's competence, but for the appreciation of the propriety of giving an opinion."[888] The Court went on to describe a situation in which a party's lack of consent should influence the Court in its discretion to refrain from giving an advisory opinion. The Court said:

> In certain circumstances, therefore, the lack of consent of an interested State may render the giving of an advisory opinion incompatible with the Court's judicial character. An instance of this would be when the circumstances disclose that to give a reply would have the effect of circumventing the principle that a State is not obliged to allow its disputes to be submitted to judicial settlement without its consent.[889]

Applying the PCIJ and ICJ criteria to the security fence advisory opinion request and whether the Court acted properly in issuing the advisory opinion turns on three integral elements, each requiring analysis: the existence of a bilateral dispute, the lack of consent and the resulting circumvention of the fundamental requirements for contentious cases. Based on the Court's own past criteria, the Court should have exercised its discretion to refuse to issue the advisory opinion.

The Existence of a Bilateral Dispute

It is clear from looking at the history and current realities of the Arab-Palestinian-Israeli conflict that a dispute between Israelis and Palestinians still exists, particularly regarding to the security fence. In addition, conflicts still remain with respect to unresolved core issues between the parties.

As a preliminary matter, the term "dispute" should not be read narrowly to require the existence of a prior or contemporaneous case before the International Court of Justice. It is apparent from reading both the UN Charter and the ICJ Statute that the term 'dispute' is used "almost indiscriminately, in reference to a wide range of international differences, without apparent regard to intended or likely modes of settlement."[890] International law scholar Edward Gordon demonstrated this point when he said:

> The Charter uses "dispute" in Articles 1, 2, 12, 32, 33, 34, 35, 36, 37, 38 and 52, for example, only once in specific reference to matters coming before the Court. The Statute generally uses "case" when speaking of a matter upon which the Court is called upon to render judgment.[891]

Thus, any contention that there existed no "dispute," as it is used within the greater context of 'whether a party consented to adjudication of a legal dispute,' because there was no contemporaneous case before the ICJ involving the State of Israel and the Palestinians, is without merit.

The General Assembly asked the Court to give its opinion on a matter that was and remains clearly "in dispute" between the Palestine Liberation Organization, its Palestinian Authority and Israel, a dispute which legally could not be brought before the Court under its compulsory jurisdiction. In its submission, Israel pointed out particular language within the documents the Secretary-General sent to the President of the Court on December 8, 2003 that clearly evidences and indeed acknowledges the existence of a dispute.[892] Such existence of a dispute necessarily denies the Court the right of judgment.

The language showing the existence of a dispute is clear. For one, "resolution A/RES/ES-10/14 firmly places the advisory opinion request within the very context of the ongoing Israeli-Palestinian dispute."[893] Secondly, the Secretary-General's report contained two annexes, one submitted by the Government of Israel and that submitted by the Palestine Liberation Organization, which summarized each of their respective legal positions on the issue. And third, "the 'Summary legal position of the Palestine Liberation Organization' which forms Annex II to the Secretary-General's report is apparently based on a self-serving and clearly biased legal opinion provided by the PLO for the purposes of the report."[894]

Israel also argued that the dispute over the security fence was part of the greater overall Arab-Palestinian-Israeli Conflict—which itself is a lengthy dispute between Israel and the Arab countries; and further between Israel and the Palestinians.[895] Thus, the disagreement is not one of "mere differences of views on legal issues which have existed in practically every advisory opinion," as the Court noted in regards to the dispute in the *Namibia* case.[896] Instead, to give the advisory opinion would be "substantially equivalent to deciding that dispute." That is, the opinion would be "substantially equivalent" to adjudicating the particulars of the legal dispute between Israel and the Palestinians that was pending "as to the legality of the fence." Thus, in violation of its governing principles "the Court could not avoid deciding significant elements of the broader ongoing dispute between Israel and 'Palestine',"[897] a matter to which Israel did not consent and which was within the purview of the Security Council not the General Assembly.

The Lack of Consent

Once the adjudicative nature of the Court's opinion in deciding the particular legal dispute between Israel and the Palestinians is understood, it is easy to comprehend why each party's consent to the issuance of an advisory opinion is necessary. If a situation that gives rise to an advisory opinion request has characteristics of contentious cases, then the interested parties should be afforded the procedural protections that are fundamental to contentious cases, one of which is consent to adjudication without which the Court could not and should not have determined to proceed.

The Court in *Western Sahara* made clear that it is not proper to give an advisory opinion when it "would have the effect of circumventing the principle that a State is not obliged to allow its disputes to be submitted to judicial settlement without its consent."[898] Here there exists a particularized legal dispute between the two parties where the advisory opinion, if granted, would result in what is substantially equivalent to a judicial edict (although non-binding in this case) as to a contentious issue between the two parties. This is why Israel's lack of consent, being an interested party, is relevant and should have been determinative as to the contention that the Court was not espousing its "judicial character" when it chose to accept jurisdiction, over Israel's objection, and proceeded to render the advisory opinion in spite of said objection and the further fact that the Security Council was seized of the matter.

Israel clearly at no time consented to have the Court adjudicate the issue of the fence or any other matter in dispute. Israel, which is a State party to the *Statute* by virtue of being a member of the United Nations, opposed the request for an advisory opinion and never accepted the compulsory jurisdiction of the Court. Israel's lack of consent to jurisdiction is evident from, among other things, "(a) the absence of any optional clause declaration" (Israel withdrew its declaration of acceptance to the ICJ's compulsory jurisdiction in 1985), which is the year of the infamous UN Conference to Assess and Approve the Status of Women, held in Nairobi, which became a hate-filled UN Conference focused on Israel, "(b) reservations made by Israel to compromissory clauses in multilateral treaties" (Israel has not accepted compulsory jurisdiction of the Court in any multilateral treaty since 1975), which is the year of the adoption of the infamous Zionism is Racism UN Resolution, and "(c) the different mechanisms of dispute settlement that have been accepted by Israel, including in particular the dispute settlement arrangements in the Israel-PLO agreements," none of which included nor contemplated, nor conferred the right of dispute resolution by the International Court of Justice.[899]

The Advisory Opinion Request Circumvented the Fundamental Protections Required for Contentious Cases

Having established that the situation surrounding the security fence had all of the elements of a contentious case, the Court then should not have allowed the General Assembly to bypass the consent requirement fundamental to contentious cases, but should have returned the request for an advisory opinion back to the General Assembly noting that the General Assembly was depriving its member, the State of Israel, its inherent right to decline to participate in an adjudication that clearly affects its reputation as a nation-state as well as its rights.

Rosenne echoed these underlying concerns when he cautioned that "although the advisory jurisdiction opened up new ways of access to the Court, its existence should not be taken to authorize the surreptitious introduction of compulsory jurisdiction to decide concrete disputes between States by devious means."[900] He urged:

> A cautious attitude, both upon organs authorized to request advisory opinions, and upon the Court, because of the practical danger that, in the guise of an advisory opinion, the Court may be asked to make a judicial settlement of a case without the express or implied consent of the States concerned.[901]

The General Assembly's use of the ICJ advisory opinion procedure to get the issue of the security fence to reach the Court was a devious attempt by anti-Israel members of the General Assembly to bypass the fundamental principle, enshrined in Article 36 of the ICJ's Statute, that contentious issues can only be brought with the consent of the parties to the dispute. Pomerance succinctly captured the issue when he noted that the "positive wisdom underlying the *Eastern Carelia* precedent was ignored in this case, despite the pro forma reiteration of that precedent's continued relevance to the issue of propriety and the need to avoid back-door compulsory jurisdiction."[902]

The Court's Use of 'UN Interest in a Dispute' Circumvented Contentious Case Requirements

In its advisory opinion, the ICJ also circumvented the need for Israel's consent by asserting the United Nations' general interest in the Arab-Palestinian-Israeli conflict and in the security fence itself in meeting the predicate requirements. The ICJ said, "given the powers and responsibilities of the United Nations in questions relating to international peace and security, it is the Court's view that the construction of the wall must be deemed to be directly of concern to the United Nations."[903] The answer begged the question.

ICJ Judge Higgins highlighted the Court's maneuver to assert and retain jurisdiction when she noted in her book, *Problems and Process*, that the Court "has shown that it will rather robustly preserve its right to provide advice to authorized requesting organs" when they have "important tasks to perform."[904] The Court ignored the existence of the ongoing bilateral dispute and Israel's lack of consent in favor of the United Nations interest in the dispute. Because it's nearly impossible to conceive of a dispute scenario before the ICJ where the United Nations would not have an interest or important task to perform, this justification by the Court further widens the door for the ICJ to issue future advisory opinions practically without limitation.

Furthermore, framing the dispute between Israelis and Palestinians as a general issue of interest to the UN circumvents the need to fulfill the consent requirement and overextends the permitted advisory procedure, resulting in potentially dangerous consequences.

International law scholar Ignaz Seidl-Hohenveldern began to voice his concerns about the consequences of enlarging the advisory opinion practice, as far back as 1974, when he said that the ICJ

> had not prevented States from being indirectly arraigned in this way without their consent. The [PCIJ] had quite reasonably declined, in the Eastern Carelia case, to render an advisory opinion on a dispute in which the Soviet Union, a non-Member State at that time, was covertly impleaded. But in a long line of advisory opinions, from the interpretation of the peace treaties right up to the Namibia advisory opinion, the ICJ had placed states in the dock without their consent. Compulsory jurisdiction certainly appears desirable, yet *de lege lata* the ICJ could surely never intervene without the voluntary submission of the States. This enlargement of the advisory opinion machinery could only lead to disrespect of the Court's decisions.[905]

The United States voiced similar concerns in its submission to the ICJ on the security fence issue and opposed the Court exercising jurisdiction in this matter:

> The Court should give due regard to the principle that advisory opinion jurisdiction is not intended as a means to circumvent the rights of States to determine whether to submit their disputes to judicial settlement. As the Court itself recognized, this principle is important to preserve the independence and sovereign rights of States and to maintain the appropriate judicial character of the court in an advisory opinion context.[906]

The Court's enlargement of the advisory opinion practice by casting issues as within the UN's general interest erodes the principle of consent. This threatens to undermine the legitimacy of the Court's opinions and diminish the credence of and compliance with those opinions. As the late international legal scholar Leo Gross once remarked, "the United Nations now has at its disposal an effective procedure for requesting advisory opinions but not a procedure for effective advisory opinions."[907]

ICJ Actions Improper in Light of the Absence of Factual Record

The State of Israel had the absolute right to decline, in fact to refuse, to participate in and dignify proceedings it believed to be improper and indeed illegal; proceedings that were on their face biased and typical of the one country-one vote constant and consistent adversity Israel has encountered at the United Nations for many decades. The politicization at the United Nations of all things related to Israel allowed the General Assembly to violate all applicable principles and overwhelmingly vote to request the advisory opinion. Without Israel's consent, the ICJ should not have accepted jurisdiction; and once accepted over Israel's objection, it is clear that Israel had the right to decline to participate in the proceedings. The Court, however, has noted the absence of evidence or factual record offered by Israel or on her behalf. While Israel submitted a written statement on the Court's jurisdiction and the propriety of hearing the case, Israel chose not to submit evidence addressing the merits or substance of the case. The Court accordingly relied on the UN Secretary-General's report, which did include submissions from the Palestinians. However, neither the UN nor the Court gave any credence to the reasons, well known to both, for the construction of the security fence: to fence out the terrorists in a focused attempt, design and plan by the sovereign State of Israel to protect her people.

Israel's non-submission of evidence or arguments on the substantive merits of the question put before the Court does not excuse the Court's insufficient handling of the facts, the evidence and arguments it was given and the voluminous collateral materials otherwise available to the Court, including the fact-based legal decisions of the Israeli High Court of Justice.

Since there are no "parties" in advisory proceedings, states and organizations act only as amicus curiae (friend of the court) to the Court. It has been rightly pointed out that "Israel was under no obligation to file any pleadings with the Court, written or oral, let alone address particular factual issues in those pleadings."[908] Unlike a contentious case, "where the failure of a party to defend its case may lead the Court to find in favor of the claimant state...no such provision applies to the advisory context."[909] The Court should not have permitted any negative inference as a result of Israel's non-submission of substantive evidence. Instead, the Court had the obligation to utilize more diverse and independent factual sources, beyond just the Secretary General's report, and engage in more thorough fact-finding and factual analysis prior to issuing its advisory opinion.

Moreover, Israel contended that the advisory opinion "question requires the Court to speculate about essential facts and make assumptions about arguments of law."[910] It argued, based on the PLO's summary legal position, that the Court should have to consider "factual issues going to the military necessity of the fence" and "proportionality of the construction of the fence, including factual issues going to the question of whether the requirements of proportionality can more likely be met by different means including different routing of the fence."[911] The Court should also have had to make:

> (a) an assessment of the security threat faced by Israel, which would in turn require an assessment of the nature and scale of terrorist attacks, the continuing nature of the threat, and the likely nature and scale of future attacks; (b) an assessment of the effectiveness of the fence to address the security threat relative to other available means; (c) an assessment of the motives behind the construction of the fence; (d) an assessment of the routing of the fence, including an assessment of whether the routing was justified by military necessity so far as concerns individual sections of the fence; (e) an assessment of the specific nature and extent of the construction, including an assessment of whether these aspects were justified by military necessity so far as concerns individual sections of the fence, to cover, for example, the issue of whether there was a justification on grounds of military necessity for those short sections of wall; (f) an assessment of the specific nature of the threat to the Israeli population at different sections of the fence; (g) in the light of the claim that the requirements of proportionality can better be met by different routing of the fence, an assessment of the relative threat arising as a result of such different routing and of whether the requirements of military necessity could thus be satisfied.[912]

Israel also asserted that the Court would have to speculate on portions of the fence that were not yet built. Israel was right. The speculation factor poisoned the Court's position, as it assumed facts neither ripe nor before it.

The United States, in its written statement to the Court, "suggested that an advisory opinion is 'ill suited' to the application of principles of law to particular factual situations without the participation by an interested state which could provide the Court with necessary pertinent information."[913]

A number of the judges in the case, in their separate opinions, also pointed out that the evidentiary record was seriously lacking in substantial detail, that it failed to adequately present the Israeli side, and that it was unbalanced.[914] Indeed the Court's lack of evidence caused it to make conclusions without fully developing its reasoning. Just as Judge Buergenthal observed in his critical dissent, the Court's findings cannot be well founded under international law without a thorough examination of facts and evidence. This was not undertaken by the Court, which results in a serious deficiency in the analysis and opinion, a serious lack of credibility for the Court and a dangerous precedent.

II. Compelling Reasons Not to Have Issued an Advisory Opinion on Israel's Security Fence

It has been noted that the "judicial policy of the Court in exercising its advisory jurisdiction can be summed up in its tendency to respond affirmatively to requests unless there are 'compelling reasons' to decline."[915] In the case of Israel's security fence there were, without any doubt, most compelling reasons for the Court to decline to issue an advisory opinion.

The ICJ's Actions were Improper and Damaging in Light of The Roadmap–Then and Now

The political issues brought before the ICJ should have been addressed by the Quartet and the parties themselves, in accordance with the Roadmap. The Roadmap was created and accepted by the parties to the dispute, in coordination with the Security Council (among others), as a response to the underlying political realities that had developed in the aftermath of the Camp David negotiations of August 2000 and the subsequent launching by the Palestinians of the Second Intifada, which killed and maimed innocent persons. The fundamental principles underlying the Roadmap and its implementation, already accepted by the parties to the conflict, include:

(1) an immediate end to violence and terrorism;

(2) democratic reform of the PA;

(3) progressive Israeli withdrawal from areas occupied since September 28, 2000; and

(4) negotiation as the basis upon which an independent and viable Palestinian state can be established.[916]

Notwithstanding the parties' prior agreement to be bound by the terms and governing principles of the Roadmap, the PLO and the Palestinian Authority have continuously refused and/or failed to perform its responsibilities under the Roadmap. In particular, the PLO/PA have refused and/or failed to undertake "visible efforts on the ground to arrest, disrupt, and restrain individuals and groups planning violent attacks on Israelis anywhere" while also refusing/failing to undertake "sustained, targeted, and effective operations aimed at confronting all those engaged in terror and the dismantlement of terrorist capabilities and infrastructure."[917] It is within the context of these grave failures to act that Israel, to protect her citizens, commenced to construct the terrorism prevention security fence. It was and remains the PLO/PA's decision to abandon its responsibilities under the Roadmap and its strategic choice to use terror and the threat of terror as a continuing means to achieve its political objectives that has directly resulted in Israel's need to complete construction of the fence for the protection and welfare of her citizens.

Although it is claimed that Israel also failed to fully comply with her Roadmap responsibilities, in particular those restricting Israel from building homes and settlements on the West Bank, it is ludicrous and inane to cite home building as a justification for terror and the threat of terror.[918] In sharp contrast to the Palestinian violations, however, these new Israeli residences neither injure nor kill any human being and can be removed at any time an agreement is reached to do so. The loss of life resulting from Palestinian terrorism is irreversible.

The State of Israel has repeatedly pronounced the terrorism prevention security fence to be a temporary measure that does not create a final border. Israel has clearly stated at the Security Council and elsewhere that it hopes the very construction of the security fence will, because of its function, render itself unnecessary. Based on the "success" of a similar fence Israel constructed to protect its citizens from Gaza-based terrorists, Israel anticipates that the security fence will continue to thwart terrorist activity, hopefully resulting in relative calm and the opportunity for a resumption of meaningful negotiations.[919]

The purpose of the terrorism prevention security fence is fully consistent with one fundamental principle of the Roadmap: putting an end to terror and violence. Instead of accepting the PA's *de facto* refusal to negotiate under the Roadmap, notwithstanding its acceptance of the Roadmap, Israel has (to borrow terms from the Anglo common law of contracts) chosen to mitigate its losses and secure an alternative means of performance. Moreover, Israel remains committed in word and deed to the Roadmap. Prime Minster Sharon, in an attempt to advance the Roadmap and resume negotiations, appealed to the Palestinian people and its leadership and said:

> It is not in our interest to govern you. We would like you to govern yourselves in your own country; a democratic Palestinian state with territorial contiguity in Judea and Samaria. . . . The Roadmap is the only political plan accepted by Israel, the Palestinians, the Americans and a majority of the international community. We are willing to proceed towards its implementation: two states – Israel and a Palestinian state – living side by side in tranquility, security, and peace."[920]

Contrary to what is alleged by the PLO/PA and its supporters, the construction of the terrorism prevention security fence does not create new 'facts on the ground.' To adopt another analogy from the Anglo common law of property, Israel – by its own accord – lacks the *animus possidendi* (intention to possess) that is required to successfully assert a proprietary right to any part of the disputed territory under the law of 'adverse possession,' which could, theoretically, have resulted from the construction of the security fence.[921] Furthermore, as noted elsewhere, Israel has repeatedly demonstrated, in the context of negotiated settlements with Egypt (Sinai), Jordan (the Jordan Valley), and more recently, Lebanon, that it has the ability and the willingness to relocate forces, equipment, fences and border as part of a bilateral agreement or even unilateral withdrawal.[922]

Moreover, Israel's courts have repeatedly ordered the rerouting of the fence, most recently in its opinion issued in December 2012.

The principle of negotiation underpinning the Roadmap obligates the PLO/PA to negotiate any deviations from the Roadmap's plan according to the Roadmap's own established process and precedent. The PLO/PA cannot credibly unilaterally decide that an essential goal of the Roadmap, the cessation of terror and violence, is no longer applicable to it or to Israel, the parties to the conflict. However, in failing to fulfill its obligation to take sustained and decisive action against terror, that is exactly what the PLO/PA have done and continue to do. Rather than take the difficult but necessary steps the Roadmap requires of it, the PLO/PA has essentially and regrettably abandoned its obligations as further evidenced by its recent application to the United Nations to upgrade its status, notwithstanding the requirement of the Roadmap for "negotiation as the basis upon which an independent and viable Palestinian state can be established." The measures Israel has been forced to impose to obtain what it bargained for and is entitled to under the Roadmap, namely, the safety of its citizens, are both fair and necessary in light of the PLO/PA's abdication of its responsibilities. The PLO/PA cannot unilaterally amend the terms of that agreement; rather, it is bound in such circumstances, as a matter of law, to return to the negotiating table within the parameters of the Roadmap.

As concluded by the Supreme Court of Canada in *Reference re Secession of Quebec* when it addressed agreements concerning the governance of fundamental relationships between members of a federation formed through negotiation:

> refusal of a party to conduct negotiations in a manner consistent with constitutional principles and values would seriously put at risk the legitimacy of that party's assertion of its rights, and perhaps the negotiation process as a whole. Those who quite legitimately insist upon the importance of upholding the rule of law cannot at the same time be oblivious to the need to act in conformity with constitutional principles and values, and so do their part to contribute to the maintenance and promotion of an environment in which the rule of law may flourish.[923]

The Security Council continues to endorse the Roadmap as the solution to the Israeli-Palestinian conflict and calls on the parties "to fulfill their obligations under the Roadmap in cooperation with the Quartet and to achieve the vision of two States living side by side in peace and tranquility."[924] The PLO/PA, along with Israel, must heed this call. It cannot unilaterally decide that it is not bound by the terms and guiding principles underlying the Roadmap. The ICJ should have deferred to the Roadmap as the guiding principles and simply declined to hear or advise on the matter. A significant group of states, including the United States, Switzerland, Uganda and Italy (on behalf of the European Union and newly acceding EU states), stated in the General Assembly that they opposed the request for an advisory opinion because it went directly against the Roadmap and the wishes and actions of the Security Council. The position of the Security Council has been clear. It unanimously endorsed the Roadmap in Resolution 1515 and it has repeatedly called for resolution of the conflict via direct negotiations in accordance with Resolutions 242 (1967) and 338 (1973).

Israeli Foreign Minister Silvan Shalom and US Secretary of State Colin Powell concluded, following reports of the ICJ's ruling that fifty-six countries, including Afghanistan and Cameroon, would be allowed to testify against the Israeli terrorism prevention security fence, that if the Palestinians can win in the court of world opinion, they would not have any incentive to pursue the Roadmap peace plan. They were right. The PLO and the PA have declined to meaningfully participate under the Roadmap ever since the Court's decision. The United States submitted a written statement to the Court reaffirming that it opposed the proceedings as it had from the outset. While at the General Assembly, the US stated that:

> While our policy on the fence is clear and President Bush said that Israel... should not prejudice final negotiations with the placement of walls and fences, the resolution requesting an ICJ opinion would undermine rather than encourage direct negotiations between the parties to resolve those differences. This is the wrong way and the wrong time to proceed on this issue.[925]

Indeed, following the ICJ opinion, the Palestinian Observers, Farouk Kaddoumi and Nasser Al-Kidwa, during the 59th session of the UN General Assembly, subsequently confirmed their rejection of the peace process outlined in the Roadmap. Both expressed their desire for a final determination of the status issues of the Israeli-Palestinian conflict, arguing that a negotiations process would chip away at the role of the UN and the international community. These statements were made despite Canadian Ambassador Allan Rock's calls to the Assembly for the UN to take a more active role in encouraging resolution of the conflict through negotiations.[926] The Palestinians' desire for UN involvement is not surprising given that the General Assembly, during each session, has continued to pass approximately its legendary anti-Israel resolutions, as it did once again in the recent 2012 session of the General Assembly.

The PLO and the PA clearly believe they are better off with pronouncements from the UN than they would be negotiating with Israel. If they truly wanted to reach an agreement as to borders, security, refugees and Jerusalem, they would already have done so. Their preferred option, however, has been to malign Israel in public; seek legal pronouncements against her; and seek upgraded status as a non-member state at the UN, incorrectly deeming the General Assembly resolution upgrading its status as the equivalent of "statehood," which under international law, it is not; and thereby bypassing the negotiation process on the essential issues. Without an agreement as to clear and defined borders, for example, they do not qualify under international law to become a member state at the United Nations as they are not a sovereign nation entitled to such membership, which can only be granted by the Security Council.

Israeli Ambassador to the UN Daniel Gillerman addressed the Palestinian Observers' rejection of the Roadmap, calling for international support of the negotiations process and reminding those assembled that peace could be attained "not in New York or Geneva ... but in Ramallah and Jerusalem." In doing so, he underscored Israel's continued dedication to the peace process:

> If the international community is serious about taking advantage of the opportunity before us, it is not enough to encourage and empower those committed to peace. We must also confront those opposed to it. We must show the same urgency and determination in combating these forces as they do in pursuing their hateful agenda. Without that, moderates in the region – be they in Iraq, the West Bank or elsewhere in the Middle East – have no chance to succeed. Without that we will record yet another missed op-

portunity on the road to peace. This is no time for complacency or false equivalencies. Treating those engaged in terror and those determined, under difficult conditions, to respond to it as though they were moral equals is not amoral – it is immoral. We remain hopeful that the circle of peace in the Middle East can be widened, and Israel is, as always, ready to reach a genuine and lasting peace with all its neighbors.[927]

Israel's position on direct negotiations has remained unchanged for a decade: it has repeatedly and continuously stated its willingness to sit at the negotiating table without precondition. It seeks only a willing partner to the discussions. The more, however, the UN rewards the Palestinians for their refusal to negotiate peace under the Roadmap, the prospects for a permanent and lasting secure peace drift away.

The success of the parties behind the initiative to get the ICJ to issue an advisory opinion itself undermined and damaged any prospect of meaningful comprehensive negotiations under the Roadmap.

The ICJ Should Not Have Intervened in a Political Question Controversy

The question of the security fence represents a political controversy between parties who have not yet agreed to actual borders between their respective territories. Although the political nature of a question and the political motives behind it do not prohibit the Court's ability to hear a case jurisdictionally, they should be taken into consideration by the Court when, in its discretion, it determines whether to hear a case.[928]

The Court's discretionary power over whether or not to issue an advisory opinion on a political controversy should not be confused with the US constitutional principle that "political questions" are not justiciable. A "political question" doctrine, like that found in United States constitutional jurisprudence, does not exist in the ICJ context. Indeed, according to Eugene Rostov, the "classic American definition of the political question is that of Chief Justice Marshall in *Marbury v. Madison*, [5 US 137, 165-66 (1803)], where he said that no court had jurisdiction over a matter committed by the Constitution or the laws to the discretion of the political branches of the government."[929] Edward Gordon points out that in *Baker v. Carr*, 369 US 186, 210-211 (1962), the "United States Supreme Court indicated that this doctrine is primarily a function of the separation of powers, a structural feature the International Court does not share."[930]

Nonetheless, there are strong reasons why the ICJ should have refrained from giving the opinion on the political controversy surrounding the security fence. International law scholar Ibrahim Wani has advocated for an international political question doctrine:

> The most compelling argument for an international political question doctrine is based on prudential considerations. To paraphrase Justice Felix Frankfurter, the International Court of Justice, lacking either the power of the purse or of the sword, needs to choose its battles carefully in order to maintain its integrity. The political question doctrine can be handy in avoiding politically controversial disputes and those that cannot be effectively resolved. This is not because there anything inherently political about the disputes but rather simply as an expression of the Court's sense of its practical limitations.[931]

Indeed, Wani recognized that there exists "state practice, and believes that states will ignore the World Court if too great an interest is at stake."[932]

Here, the advisory opinion amounted to a declaration of policy in the face of a framework that already existed and was already in place under the aegis of the Security Council, to wit, the Roadmap. The General Assembly, in passing Resolution 10/14, had already condemned Israel's security fence. As Ambassador Gillerman said "Could there be a more obvious abuse of [the General] Assembly and of the advisory opinion procedure, than for the Assembly to pretend to ask for guidance from the Court on an issue with respect to which it has already determined its response?"[933]

As Israel's High Court of Justice, which regularly considers and adjudicates petitions brought by or on behalf of Palestinians living in the disputed territories, has wisely observed with respect to the role of the judiciary in the peace process:

> A judicial determination, which does not concern individual rights, should defer to a political process of great importance and great significance. Such is the issue before us: it stands at the centre of the peace process; it is of unrivalled importance; and any determination by the court is likely to be interpreted as a direct intervention

therein . . . The petitioners have the right to place a 'legal mine' on the court's threshold, but the court should not step on a mine that will shake its foundations, which are the public's confidence in it.[934]

Accordingly, the ICJ should not have allowed itself to be used nor shall it have injected itself, to quote the Supreme Court of the United States, as a "vehicle for the vindication of the value interests of concerned bystanders."[935]

The purpose of the General Assembly's request was to put political pressure on the government of Israel and to attempt to establish a predicate upon which Israel could be held out for public ridicule and as a springboard for other assaults upon Israel's standing as a nation-state of the world—it was not to resolve an issue of international law. International law scholar Helmut Steinberger explained that "even if advisory opinions do not create a juridical obligation, experience confirms that they are used as a means of exerting pressure against States..."[936] Former United States Ambassador to the United Nations John Danforth pointedly summed up the political nature of the situation when he said:

> If there is to be a solution to the tragedy of the Middle East, it must be political... entailing the agreement by both parties to a reasonable compromise. The judicial process is not the political process, and the International Court of Justice was not the appropriate forum to resolve this conflict.[937]

Without question, the ICJ should have recognized the political question controversy before it and refused to hear the case.

The ICJ Should Not Have an Opinion because the Security Council Rejected the Proposed Request

In October of 2003, the UN Security Council reviewed and rejected a proposed resolution that pronounced the construction of the terrorism prevention security fence by the government of Israel illegal under international law.[938] The Security Council has been called the center of the United Nations system and, as Rostov has pointed out, "its overriding responsibility for keeping the peace necessarily subordinates all the other agencies of the organization to its authority."[939] The General Assembly was required to, and should have, deferred to the Security Council's authority in this area and not hijacked the issue through the submission to the Court of its own request. The UNGA did so in a determined attempt to further its own expansive agenda and in an attempt to secure an adverse ruling against Israel, even though advisory in nature. They pursued this avenue knowing that it would be used and cited in a continuing effort to assault Israel by all means – on the ground, in the court of public opinion and in venues that would simply forget or ignore that such opinion was advisory and not binding. Over time, the opponents of Israel believe, the cumulative effect of assaults upon Israel will win over world public opinion, not only for the purpose of establishing Palestinian statehood, but moreover for the purpose of weakening Israel and seeking to reclaim from her all land deemed "Palestine" without regard to the historical legitimate rights, truth and factual basis of the thousands of years of Israel's existence in Judea and Samaria.

In the absence of General Assembly deference to the Security Council's authority, the ICJ should have shown its own restraint particularly as the Security Council had already refused to declare Israel's construction of the security fence illegal.[940] Among other reasons, the Council's refusal was premised on the imbalance in the language and the content of the proposed resolution, which failed to address (or even mention) the terrorism and security threats that necessitated the construction of the terrorism prevention security fence.US Ambassador John Negroponte pointed out in his statement to the Security Council that that the resolution was "unbalanced" and that it "failed to address both sides of the larger security context of the Middle East, including the devastating suicide attacks that Israelis have had to endure over the past three years."[941] He explained that:

> A Security Council resolution focused on the terrorism prevention barrier does not further the goals of peace and security in the region. We believe that all resolutions on Israeli-Palestinian peace should reflect the kind of balance of mutual responsibilities embodied by the Quartet's Roadmap. That draft resolution did not do so.[942]

The General Assembly's resolution on the same issue, its request for an ICJ advisory opinion, was an attempt by the forces behind the failed Security Council draft resolution to circumvent the

UN's established procedure and obtain from the ICJ a political declaration (under the guise of legal opinion) that the Security Council itself refused to give. Consequently, the ICJ's declaration has the potential to be used in the future by the Palestinian leadership to attempt to deprive Israel of its right to defense, to shield itself from any legal responsibility for sponsored or supported terrorist acts against Israeli citizens and to justify its failure to implement the steps required by the Roadmap's peace plan. The Security Council was clear in its refusal to issue a resolution that would effectively single out Israel by scrutinizing its security measures and ignore the Palestinians failure and refusal to cease support for, and in fact put a stop to the ongoing acts of terrorism, being the failures that actually necessitated Israel's security measures. The ICJ advisory opinion amounted to a political declaration that directly contradicted the Security Council's decision not to pass such a resolution and the Court should never have permitted the General Assembly to act to override the judgment of the Security Council on this issue.

While it is widely recognized that political activity is heavily biased against Israel within the General Assembly, particularly on Middle East issues, involving the ICJ in such a political question crosses a new and alarming threshold.[943]

The Continued Legitimacy of The United Nations as a Neutral Mediator and Monitor Under the Roadmap and in Future Conflicts is Threatened by the Misuse of the Process

The partisan initiative behind the request for the advisory opinion has also threatened the UN's role as a neutral mediator and monitor of Middle East peace.

Article 96 paragraph (a) of the UN Charter provides that, "the General Assembly or the Security Council may request the International Court of Justice to give an advisory opinion on any legal question."[944] Article 18 of the UN Charter dictates the procedural requirements for issues of peace and security, "Decisions of the General Assembly on important questions shall be made by a two-thirds majority of the members present and voting. These questions shall include: recommendations with respect to the maintenance of international peace and security..."[945] Rule 86 of the UN General Assembly Rules of Procedure explains that "for the purposes of these rules, the phrase "members present and voting" means members casting an affirmative or negative vote. Members which abstain from voting are considered as not voting."[946] In regards to the ICJ, Article 65 of the ICJ Statute states, "the Court may give an advisory opinion on any legal question at the request of whatever body may be authorized by or in accordance with the Charter of the United Nations to make such a request."[947]

Clearly, a resolution proposed and passed in an emergency session of the General Assembly that relates to the legal consequences of Israel's security fence qualifies as a "recommendation with respect to the maintenance of international peace and security" that requires a vote by a two-thirds majority of the members present and voting. In this case, although the procedural requirement of having a two-thirds majority was determined to have been technically achieved, in reality it did not amount to an actual majority and clearly not a two thirds majority of the Member States of the United Nations. This is because out of the 191 UN Member states, only 98 of the members were included in the total of those voting on the ICJ referral, with 93 countries either abstaining or not present. Of the 98 present and voting, 90 countries supported the resolution, which shows that only 90 of the 191 total UN member states were supportive of the referral to the ICJ, being a factor that should further have been taken into consideration by the Court which should have declined to review the matter and to issue an opinion.[948]

According to Rosenne:

> The principle underlying the advisory competence is that a qualified international intergovernmental organ, and not an individual State or group of States, may ask the Court for an advisory opinion on legal questions, that opinion itself not constituting per se a "decision" with which anyone is legally bound to comply.[949]

Here, in a partisan effort, and simply put, a group of states allied with the PLO managed to get enough anti-Israel votes together (i.e. 90) to pass the resolution requesting the advisory opinion. Rosenne pointed out that the effect of the majority voting system essentially means that future requests for advisory opinions may be made despite strong opposition or refusal to participate by the disputing parties. Rosenne asserts that this result affects the consensual basis for jurisdiction:

> The fundamental departure from the unanimity rule for voting embodied formerly in the Covenant of the League implies the possibility, under the Charter, that a request for an advisory opinion may be made despite the opposition of States closely concerned with the substance of a question or that, because of the system of majority votes, the views of a minority upon the nature of the legal question are not adequately reflected in the terms of the request. Here, as a result of the operation of the Charter, the way is opened for further attrition of the consensual basis of the Court's jurisdiction, which has already been attenuated in the contentious cases.[950]

Despite the fact that it could significantly affect the weight of an advisory opinion on a conflict or dispute, the fact that a large number of states did not support the referral resolution was not a factor in the Court's determination to proceed. Rosenne recognized this approach by the Court, which has "not regarded opposition [by Member States] to the request as an obstacle to its giving the requested opinion."[951] Instead, Rosenne alludes to the possibility that the Court's lack of consideration may be why advisory opinions have not, in general, become more crucial in the resolution process: the lack of consideration "may be one of the factors which has prevented the Court's advisory work from becoming a decisive element in the political evolution of a given issue."[952]

The ICJ should have acknowledged the partisan nature of the vote and considered the inherent dangers in its issuance of its advisory opinion.

The International Court of Justice's Status In Future Conflict Resolutions is Damaged

The fact that the Court chose to answer a question on the rights and wrongs of a specific conflict situation, when the question was presented by the parties on the side of the conflict that had the most General Assembly votes, but without the issue having been referred by the Security Council, or with their support, means that there is now the potential for many more such questions to be asked, not just about Israel, or the security fence, or other aspects of the Arab-Palestinian-Israeli conflict, but about every conflict or question where the General Assembly decides by vote to interfere and refer to the Court for an advisory opinion. The decision to answer biased one-sided questions—where the Court is asked to judge the legality of the behavior of only one side of the conflict and agrees to do so—could result in the Court being dragged into many conflicts, in a non-neutral way, which does not necessarily advance the interests of peace and security and indeed may prove contrary to the pursuit of the very goal(s) it seeks to resolve.

Legal bodies, doing either too little or too much, can significantly harm international justice. Judicial overreaching is a serious cause for concern. Attempts to extend the doctrine of universal jurisdiction for criminal prosecution to a level beyond international recognition have led to backlash and retrenchment. For example, a negative result of the Spanish and Belgian efforts to extend the reach of universal criminal jurisdiction is that they have fueled opposition to the International Criminal Court and hampered its development.[953]

This form of judicial overreaching poses a similar danger for the International Court of Justice. The nature of any political dispute is that one side in the dispute is more popular than another. It is axiomatic that today at the United Nations, the Palestinian cause musters many supportive votes, without regard to the need to resolve the essential issues between the parties, issues that cannot be decided nor imposed by the United Nations, while the Israeli position has comparatively less political support except among mostly democratic allies who respect the rule of law. The Arab-Palestinian-Israeli conflict is long standing and deeply rooted. It cannot be decided by a popularity contest. And in that regard, the comparative political position and standing of Israel among member states at the United Nations is not a justification for the Court to involve itself squarely in the middle of the conflict which, notwithstanding the Court's opinion, can and only will be resolved by the parties themselves albeit with the assistance of key players playing differing roles. Any resolution will require a convergence of forces committed to achieving a direct result between the parties, for only the parties can commit themselves to a better future for their nations and their peoples.

In the aftermath of the ICJ advisory opinion, Harvard law professor Alan Dershowitz further explained why the ICJ should have refused to answer the General Assembly's request. Comparing the ICJ to a Mississippi Court in the 1930s, he analogized:

> The all-white Mississippi court, which excluded blacks from serving on it, could do justice in disputes between whites, but it was incapable of doing justice in cases between a white and a black. It would always favor white litigants. So too the International Court of Justice. It is perfectly capable of resolving disputes between Sweden and Norway, but it is incapable of doing justice where Israel is involved, because Israel is the excluded black in that court–indeed, when it comes to most United Nations organs. A judicial decision can have no legitimacy when rendered against a nation that is willfully excluded from the court's membership by bigotry.[954]

Moreover, this is not the first case where the Court's partiality has been called in question. Regarding the *Military and Paramilitary Activities in and against Nicaragua* contentious case:

> Critics argue that the Court's summary dismissal without a hearing of El Salvador's request to intervene in the jurisdictional phase of the case and the Court's issuance of preliminary orders directed primarily against the United States rather than both parties indicate that the Court does not always treat states appearing before it fairly.[955]

In this situation, because the Court became involved in a political dispute without the consent of a party to that dispute, it has risked and damaged its own legitimacy and the cause of international justice itself. The ICJ should have considered the question in its broader context, the context of the wars in the Middle East and Israel's struggle for survival in the face of opposing armies and the constant threat of terrorism and annihilation. The construction of the terrorism prevention security fence is a direct response to the PLO and PA and Palestinian terrorist organizations long standing and ongoing war of terror against the State of Israel.

The Court undermined its own existence by allowing itself and in fact actively agreeing to be used for the purpose of achieving one party's political objectives.

The Court itself proceeded to take sides and in so doing legitimized the very ill-defined one-sided debate that belonged in another forum and not before the International Court of Justice for advice and opinion.

Peace is, of necessity, a reciprocal affair. It is impossible to have peace if only one side wants peace, if only one side is prepared to lay down its arms and accept a settlement. For the General Assembly to ask and the Court to answer questions about the culpability of only one side in the Middle East conflict, the entire process ignored the need for reciprocity by both sides.

An opinion that sets out only one party's legal obligations de-contextualizes the acts of that party from the overall conflict. Although setting out the legal obligations of both sides is not necessarily the best way to achieve peace, it is at least a positive contribution. It might make sense to hold that, legally, each side should engage in certain behavior. Security Council and General Assembly resolutions have called on Israel to engage in certain acts, but which are highly dependent on the Palestinians and neighboring Arab States being willing to live at peace with Israel. It was wrong of the Court to advise on, and essentially pre-judge, such an important issue in isolation and without considering the mutual legal obligations on the other side as well.

Any decision or action by an international organization, including the International Court of Justice, that seeks to impose a solution or a condition on Israel undermines the previously approved, agreed upon and already established diplomatic channel or process between Israel and the Palestinians and disrespects the actual purview and decisions of the Security Council itself. Moreover, by rendering a decision on this specific case, the Court has created precedent that may encourage future negotiators, in this situation and others, to seek an opinion from the ICJ in lieu of conflict resolution by direct negotiations.[956]

In shamelessly seeking to politicize the ICJ and bring a subject of dispute before the Court in its advisory capacity, the sponsors of this resolution risked and have caused serious harm to the reputation, independence, and authority of the principal judicial organ of the United Nations. Such cynical abuse of the advisory opinion procedure, in violation of its basic preconditions and its intended purpose, has set an extremely dangerous precedent, and only encourages further use of the ICJ as a political weapon by any party to a political conflict who can garner enough votes from enough states to pass a resolution of referral, framed in its own way, and designed to achieve leverage and control over the end result.[957]

Prospects for Continued Negotiations Between Israel and the Palestinians are Dim and the Legitimacy of the Political Process is in Danger

The UN Charter calls on all States to pursue in good faith the peaceful settlement of disputes.[958] In that context, the Court should have considered the potential negative effects the advisory opinion would have on the prospects for continued negotiations. Unfortunately, however, as Michla Pomerance has explained, the "likely aftermath and practical harm of judicial intervention also failed to induce any hesitation on the part of the Court.[959] Addressing the Court's lack of consideration of the negative effects resulting from giving the opinion, he said:

> Nowhere was there any indication of concern that an opinion upholding the Palestinian view would harden the position of those leaders who, in defiance of the numerous previous commitments to seek negotiated solutions to the conflict and spurn terrorism, were regularly inciting suicide bombers to continue to target innocent men, women, and children at work, at play and at prayer.[960]

Pomerance went on to criticize the ICJ's response regarding "the irrelevance of political motives, political contexts, and political implications was formalistic and formulaic, and bolstered by easily available earlier formulaic responses regarding challenges to the "legal" nature of the questions posed."[961]

We have seen how legal wrangling over rights and wrongs in the International Court of Justice has done nothing to move the parties towards negotiation leading to conflict resolution. By casting the issues in the form of right and wrong, each side necessarily becomes entrenched in its own position. Attitudes become hardened. Just as litigation often moves the parties away from a negotiated settlement in the initial stages, the likelihood that the dispute between the par-

ties will only be further embittered as a result of the Court considering and answering the question is itself a compelling reason why
the question should not have been answered at that time and in that
manner or forum. Indeed, the decision of the International Court of
Justice has done no good, but rather much harm, to the relationship
between the PLO, the PA and Israel.

In the 1950 advisory opinion on the *Interpretation of Peace Trea-*
ties with Bulgaria, Hungary and Romania, the International Court of
Justice agreed to comply with the General Assembly's request for
an advisory opinion despite the opposition of all three concerned
States—Bulgaria, Hungary and Romania. In doing so, the Court
made sure to note that it was only considering the applicability of a
procedure for the settlement of disputes and it was not pronouncing
on the merits of these disputes. This reasoning implies that the Court
may well have refused to answer the request if it had been asked to
pronounce on the merits of a dispute amongst the States concerned.
However, in the case at hand requesting an advisory opinion on
the terrorism prevention security fence, there is no doubt that the
Court was asked to pronounce on the merits of a core dispute between Israel and the PLO/Palestinian Authority. The reasoning from
the *Interpretation of Peace Treaties with Bulgaria, Hungary and Romania*
opinion militated against the ICJ answering the question.

The ICJ in the *Western Sahara* case also agreed to comply with
the General Assembly's request for an advisory opinion, this time
on the legal status of the Western Sahara, despite the objections of
Spain. There was a dispute between Spain and Morocco on the at-
tribution of the territorial sovereignty of the Western Sahara. In
agreeing to render an opinion pursuant to that request, the Court
observed that the purpose of the reference was to assist the General
Assembly in its own functions of decolonization and not to bring
before the Court a dispute between States. Moreover, the Court acknowledged that Spain's legal position could not be compromised
by the Court's answer to the questions submitted. It is clear that the
Court would have declined to answer the question asked if the answer could have compromised the legal position of Spain in any
way.

Again, this certainly did not hold true with regard to the General Assembly's request for an advisory opinion on Israel's terrorism prevention security fence. There is no question that Israel's future legal position could be compromised by applications of the Court's advisory opinion, which is exactly what the Palestinians intended to accomplish. The Court became the willing accomplice.

The ICJ Failed to Exhibit Judicial Restraint—and Failed Justice

The fact that the present Court has never declined to issue an advisory opinion reflects a Court lacking in judicial self-restraint. Judicial restraint is "a philosophy of judicial decision-making whereby judges avoid indulging their personal beliefs about the public good and instead try merely to interpret the law as legislated and according to precedent."[962] It stands for the general proposition that "courts are not the best arenas for community policy-making and community problem-solving, with the correlative proposition that not all matters lend themselves to postulated neutral, third party, judicial settlement or arbitrament."[963] Edward McWhinney has explained that, "theoretically at least, the Court's discretion is almost unlimited."[964] In practice, however, the "ICJ has never once—despite repeated affirmations of its discretionary right to decline to give an opinion—exercised that right."[965]

Michla Pomerance has assailed the Court's pervasive lack of restraint as "driven... by a 'duty to cooperate' doctrine gone awry" meaning that the:

> Court's status as a 'principal organ' and, moreover, as the 'principal judicial organ' of the United Nations spawned a judicial "duty-to-cooperate" doctrine that entailed overlooking and overcoming jurisdictional difficulties that stood in the way of maximal cooperation with the organization's political organs.[966]

Moreover:

> It also meant, less obviously but more seriously still, that the Court would increasingly apply an expansive 'UN law' rather than state-consent-based positive law; that it would be inclined to rubber-stamp UN practices, however questionable; and that it would tend to obliterate the admittedly undefined, but not therefore insignificant, line between the political and the legal.[967]

Rather than pursue judicial restraint the Court has pursued "judicial aggrandizement."[968]

Thomas Bodie, drawing upon the work of Edward McWhinney, suggested after the Court's 1966 decision in *South West Africa Phase Two* that the ICJ turned from exercising judicial restraint to judicial activism. He explained that:

> Prior to 1966, the adherence to a more positivist philosophy constrained the justices of the ICJ from defining "legal questions' expansively. Conversely, the post-1966 Court could be viewed as more activist. In other words, it would be seen as more willing to use itself not so much as a tribunal for textual interpretation, but rather as a vehicle for progressive *change* through interpretation. As opposed to being a separate entity, aloof, and with objectives different from those of the rest of the international machinery, it should now be considered as just an alternative route for states to use in pursuit of purposes and principles of the UN described in Articles 1 and 2 of the Charter.[969]

Bodie highlighted McWhinney's suggestion that the Court is moving "in the direction of Naturalism, with its greater reliance on general principles of law and the higher good of more equitable outcomes" and "beyond positivism, with its greater reliance on textual interpretation."[970] In a later work, McWhinney observed that:

> The furthest step that the International Court has taken in the direction of a judicial activist role was probably in the *Lockerbie* case in 1992, in which, in the course of deciding upon a request for provisional measures, it ruled that a Security Council "decision" under Chapter VII of the UN Charter must prevail over any State obligations under the Montreal Convention of 1971 (on the Suppression of Unlawful Acts against the Safety of Civil Aviation).[971]

Restraint in seeking legal answers to political controversies is a prudent policy for both the General Assembly and the ICJ. In *The Advisory Function of the International Court of Justice 1946-2005*, in which the advisory opinion on the security fence case features prominently, Mahasen M. Aljaghoub wrote, "the requesting for and giving of an advisory opinion is a collective coordinated process involving more than one organ or part of the [UN] Organization. Consequently, each must be mindful of the need for some degree of restraint."[972] Aljaghoub went on to suggest that the UN General Assembly and the Security Council should exhibit some restraint in their readiness to request an advisory opinion from the ICJ and that the ICJ should demonstrate more restraint, asserting:

> The genuine need for legal advice must be the only motive for requesting advisory opinions, but the Court must always be mindful of the need to protect its judicial character and not to sacrifice its independence in order to satisfy the interests of the requesting organ.[973]

UN Member States and scholars alike have recognized that courts safeguard their judicial integrity by exercising discretion in choosing the cases they will hear; especially when significant facts and circumstances indicate they should not hear a case. Lack of judicial restraint can have implications on the legitimacy and relevance of the Court's advisory function and its advisory opinions, not to mention lack of respect for the Court's substantive opinions.

Following the ICJ's controversial 1984 decision on jurisdiction in the *Nicaragua* case, the US State Department voiced its concern over the Court's lack of self-restraint and its effect on the advisory function:

> We are profoundly concerned also about the long-term implications for the Court itself. The [Court's] decision ... represents an overreaching of the Court's limits, a departure from its tradition of judicial restraint, and a risky venture into treacherous political waters. We have seen in the United Nations, in the last decade or more, how international organizations have become more and more politicized against the interests of the Western democracies. It would be a tragedy if these trends were to infect the International Court of Justice.
>
> The Court would do well to reexamine less timorously the positive legacy of the advisory function bequeathed by the League of Nations and the PCIJ and act in accordance with some of its own rhetorical doctrines (to which to date it has only paid lip service) concerning its discretion to refuse to answer inappropriate requests.[974]

The State Department urged the Court to use more discretion in protecting the judicial integrity of the ICJ in its advisory role. Thomas Bodie echoed these reservations:

> In other words, on some occasions, the timing is not right. The courts must pick their fights carefully, lest they look bad in the public's eyes. Those holding this position recognize that the courts have no real power to enforce their decisions. They cannot afford to have a decision ignored, or they would lose the moral strength they carry.[975]

Referring specifically to the advisory opinion on Israel's security fence, Michla Pomerance cautioned that the Court's handling of the case "may well serve to resuscitate and reinforce the early anxieties that surrounded the World Court's advisory function and its potential for abuse, anxieties that were expressed most vocally in the United States in the interwar decades."[976]

A healthy dose of judicial restraint by the ICJ especially the refusal of requests for advisory opinions when it is appropriate to decline would strengthen the advisory opinion mechanism. And although the Court has historically been reticent to refuse a request for an advisory opinion, the Court needs to recognize that judicial restraint is essential for any independent judicial body and that it should practice restraint when justice is greater served by deference than by activism.

In this case, the pursuit of peace has been damaged and therefore justice has been denied.

CHAPTER TEN:
Issues, Questions and Dangers

The Fourth Geneva Convention and the Israeli Terrorism Prevention Security Fence

One of the grounds listed in the General Assembly's Resolution A/RES/ES-10/14 requesting the ICJ's advisory opinion was the Fourth Geneva Convention of 1949 relative to the Protection of Civilian Persons in Time of War. However, since Palestine was not at the time of the advisory opinion and has not, as of yet, been recognized as a sovereign member state by the Security Council, notwithstanding the recent passage by the General Assembly regarding upgrading its status to non-member state observer status, the question remains as to whether any of Israel's past actions regarding the Palestinian Territories fall under the Convention.[977]

In spite of this contention, the Court concluded that the Palestinian Territories was similar enough to foreign state territory to justify the Court's application of the Convention, but, on the other hand, not similar enough to validate Israel's assertion of self-defense against armed attack. Sean D. Murphy, renowned international law and foreign relations law professor and scholar and former State Department official, addressed this contradiction, stating:

> The Court considered the West Bank and Gaza Strip as sufficiently close to being territory of a foreign state for purposes of applying the Fourth Geneva Convention, noting that the territory was part of Jordan at one time and that Jordan and Israel were parties to

the Geneva Conventions when the 1967 armed conflict broke out. Yet the Court refrained from regarding this territory as sufficiently close to being the territory of a foreign state for purposes of applying a different treaty, the UN Charter, to which Jordan and Israel were also parties as of 1967. Only with respect to the jus ad bellum argument does Palestine's formal position as a non-state seem to become a dispositive factor for the Court.[978]

The Court's double standard to benefit the Palestinians underscores the excessiveness of the Court's judicial activism and one-sided application of the law against Israel.

Even if one were to assume that the Convention is applicable; it still does not prohibit the construction of a security fence. Article 27 of the Convention states:

> Protected persons are entitled, in all circumstances, to respect for their persons, their honour, their family rights, their religious convictions and practices, and their manners and customs. They shall at all times be humanely treated, and shall be protected especially against all acts of violence or threats thereof and against insults and public curiosity . . . *However, the Parties to the conflict may take such measures of control and security in regard to protected persons as may be necessary as a result of the war.* [979]

The security fence is a necessary measure of control and security within the parameters of Article 27 of the Geneva Convention.

The Convention does not prohibit the relocation of a civilian population as long as it is necessitated by security concerns and civilians are not forced to relocate outside the boundaries of the state in which they reside. Article 49 addresses when relocation is allowed:

> The Occupying Power *may* undertake total or partial evacuation of a given area if the security of the population or imperative military reasons so demand. Such evacuations may not involve the displacement of protected persons outside the bounds of the occupied territory except when for material reasons it is impossible to avoid such displacement. Persons thus evacuated shall be transferred back to their homes as soon as hostilities in the area in question have ceased.[980]

Additionally, Article 53 makes clear that the destruction of property is allowable if it is necessary for military operations. It says:

> Any destruction by the Occupying Power of real or personal property belonging individually or collectively to private persons, or to

the State, or to other public authorities, or to social or cooperative organizations, is prohibited, except where such destruction is rendered absolutely necessary by military operations.[981]

As is clear, the increasing number of deadly terrorist attacks on Israeli soil was the sole reason and justification for the construction of the fence. The relocation of the civilian population and any destruction of property were "necessary" and "imperative" military measures that had to be taken to carry out Israel's justified construction of the terrorism prevention security fence.

Israel's Inherent Right to Self-Defense and the ICJ's Interpretation of Self-Defense in the Advisory Opinion

The advisory opinion effectively redefines the ways in which countries under terrorist attack are able to defend themselves. The Court blindly held that "Israel cannot rely on the right of self-defense or on a state of necessity" to justify the construction of the fence as a security measure.[982] In this context, the Court's interpretation of "self-defense" is alarming and unprecedented; and should be rejected not only because it does not have the force of law but also because it literally makes no sense.

The ICJ's Interpretation of Article 51 of the UN Charter in the Advisory Opinion on Israel's Security Fence

Article 51 of the UN Charter acknowledges that member states possess the inherent right to self-defense "if an armed attack occurs."[983] The ICJ's interpretation of this right, however, was limited to instances where the attack is by one state against another. Upon analyzing the Court's opinion, Sean Murphy found that it contained "no analysis of why Article 51 was restricted to armed attacks by states even though . . . analysis was merited."[984] Australian Middle East specialist Leanne Piggott agreed with Murphy's conclusion and asserted that the Court's distinction between an armed attack by a state and a non-state is critical in the on-going struggle against international terrorism.[985]

The Court's interpretation results in the creation of a ludicrous safe haven for terrorists and those who support acts of terrorism by pretending to place a wide range of armed attacks by non-state actors beyond the purview of a state's right to self-defense. Steven Lu-bet wrote that the result of the ICJ's disturbing logic has the danger of meaning that "The United States (and other countries) could not fully exercise the right to self-defense against Al-Qaeda terrorists, since they do not represent a state any more than Hamas does."[986] The ICJ opinion, in essence, ignores the violent and murderous armed attacks upon the Israeli people by Palestinian terrorists from the West Bank, from Gaza, inside Israel and in the area of the Is-raeli towns and villages built since 1967, putting people's lives in danger and allowing the Palestinian leadership to self-justify their heinous support and/or blind eye to Palestinian terrorism as if lives on the other side of the fence line do not matter. The opinion utterly disregards the rights of the civilians in those areas, no matter their religion or nationality, to live free of terrorist attack and essentially adopts and potentially encourages the continuation of illegal Pales-tinian justification of terrorism as freedom fighting.

The Court further applied a double standard in how it treat-ed the Palestinians. It gave Palestine the equivalent benefits of state status, even before the UN General Assembly granted her "non member state observer" status, and without the Security Council having granted the PLO state status as a sovereign state member of the UN, which the US has made clear it would veto absent an agree-ment between the parties, but refused to require state accountability by the PLO/PA for terrorist attacks emanating from the territory:

> The Court was unwilling to regard Palestine as a "state" for purpos-es of Article 51, which is consistent with the fact that Palestine is not a member of the United Nations. However, in its treatment of Pal-estine throughout the proceedings (allowing it to make written and oral submissions) and in much of the jus in bello analysis, the Court appears to regard Palestine as the functional equivalent of a state.[987]

The Court somehow curiously and illogically concluded the Pal-estinian Territories are not sufficiently foreign territory to make a terrorist attack emanating from them an armed attack by a foreign state, but they are sufficiently foreign territory for them to be subject to the Geneva Convention.

Scholars, jurists and governments have all criticized the Court's interpretation of self-defense in its advisory opinion. In her separate opinion, Judge Higgins decried the lack of detailed analysis within the Court's reasoning when it explained why Israel could not invoke self-defense in relation to the security fence. She "expected that an advisory opinion would have contained a detailed analysis, by reference to the texts, the voluminous academic literature and the facts at the Court's disposal."[988] In the *Congo v. Uganda* case, Judge Simma commented directly on the Court's interpretation of self-defense in the security fence opinion:

> Such a restrictive reading of Article 51 might well have reflected the state, or rather the prevailing interpretation, of the international law on self-defence for a long time. However, in the light of more recent developments not only in State practice but also with regard to accompanying *opinio juris*, it ought urgently to be reconsidered, also by the Court. . . . Security Council resolutions 1368 (2001) and 1373 (2001) cannot but be read as affirmations of the view that large-scale attacks by non-State actors can qualify as "armed attacks" within the meaning of Article 51.[989]

Citing to Judge Kooijmans' separate opinion, Simma explained further that:

> if armed attacks are carried out by irregular forces from such territory [where there is an almost complete absence of governmental authority] against a neighbouring State, these activities are still armed attacks even if they cannot be attributed to the territorial State, and, further, that it 'would be unreasonable to deny the attacked State the right to self-defense merely because there is no attacker State and the Charter does not so require so' (*ibid.*).[990]

The Court's imprecise and unexplained interpretation may have lasting implications. Sean Murphy addressed a few, noting that:

> At best, the position represents imprecise drafting, and thus calls into question whether the advisory opinion process necessarily helps the Court "to develop its jurisprudence and to contribute to the progress of international law." At worst, the position conflicts with the language of the UN Charter, its travaux préparatoires, the practice of states and international organizations, and common sense.[991]

The Court's Historical Limitations on its Interpretation of Self-Defense

The Court has historically interpreted the right to self-defense against asymmetrical warfare by non-state armed groups narrowly under the Charter. In the case of the construction of the wall, as well as in "*Nicaragua v. United States, Oil Platforms...* and *Democratic Republic of Congo v. Uganda* cases, the Court all but denied such a right, at least absent some overwhelming number of incidents."[992] Following the Court's decision in the *Nicaragua* case, the US State Department criticized the Court's views on self-defense, stating that:

> The Court's decision raises a basic issue of sovereignty. The right of a state to defend itself or to participate in collective self-defense against aggression is an inherent sovereign right that cannot be compromised by an inappropriate proceeding before the World Court.[993]

Since the establishment of the Court, the United States has taken issue with the Court's limited reading of self-defense.

Israel's Self Defense—Within the UN Charter

The language of Article 51 does not contain the qualification that an armed attack must emanate from a state, as summarily asserted by the Court, but it does speak of the "right of self-defense by a 'Member of the United Nations' against an armed attack, without any qualification as to who or what is conducting the armed attack."[994] Article 51's language is "silent on who or what might commit an armed attack justifying self-defense."[995] In his dissent, Judge Buergenthal acknowledged this fact, explaining that Article 51 "does not make its exercise dependent upon an armed attack by another State."[996] Using standard methods of statutory interpretation, Murphy concluded that "the 'ordinary meaning' of the terms of Article 51 provides no basis for reading into the text a restriction on who the attacker must be. Reading the language in context leads to the same conclusion."[997] The Court's decision to impose a restriction was not supported by the clear meaning of the words used in the Charter.

Israel's Self-Defense—Beyond the UN Charter

As the Court itself has recognized, "Article 51 did not create a right of self-defense, rather, it preserved an inherent right of self-defense, one that existed in customary international law prior to enactment of the Charter in 1945.[998] Murphy noted correctly that the

ICJ has repeatedly asserted this definition of self-defense: that a full understanding of self-defense requires a look at customary international law in order "to ascertain the full content of Article 51."[999] The Court's determination that "the principles of necessity and proportionality apply" to self-defense under Article 51 relies upon "the existence of those principles in customary international law, since they do not appear anywhere in the text of Article 51."[1000] And yet, the Court ignored its precedent when it chose to limit the availability of self-defense as a response to attacks only by states.

Under customary international law, as warfare has changed, so have interpretations of Article 51. The world has come to recognize a right to respond to threats and perceptions of attack before an actual attack occurs:

> In a number of cases, most notably the Cuban Missile Crisis of 1962 and the Six Day War of 1967 in the Middle East, the world community decided in effect that the language of article 51 about 'armed attack' was inapt, and that 'the inherent right of individual and collective self-defense' extended to threats and perceptions of attack as well as to the actual occurrence of an armed attack. As Elihu Root once wrote, international law does not require a state to wait before exercising its right of self-defense until it is too late to defend itself.[1001]

The right to self-defense has been repeatedly interpreted broadly to include ever-changing warfare and threats to national security. This interpretation has included and should continue to include the right to self-defense against acts of terrorism. The United States has argued quite often for "a broadened understanding of the Article 51 right, contending, for example, that it should be construed to permit 'self-defense' in a range of circumstances in which an armed attack neither has occurred nor is imminent."[1002]

Israel's Self-Defense in the Age of Terrorism

Security Council Resolutions 1368 and 1373, adopted shortly after the September 11, 2001 terrorist attacks against the United States, permit a State to use force to defend against non-state terror organizations.[1003] Despite the far reaching application of these resolutions, the ICJ held that Israel's failure to "claim that the attacks against it are imputable to a foreign State" denied Israel the inherent right to self-defense, as if the terrorist attacks were of no meaning nor legal significance to the Court.

Following the issuance of the ICJ's advisory opinion, the Security Council adopted Resolution 1566 in October 2004 that defined and condemned terrorism and reaffirmed a country's right to defend against terror. While this resolution essentially may effectively repudiate the advisory opinion's interpretation of self-defense, thus justifying Israel's construction of the security fence as self-defense, its definition of terrorism may prove to be limiting in that the offense must be previously outlawed in order for self-defense to be justified.[1004] This means that, in an incomprehensible application of the advisory opinion according to the UN, the suicide bombings and other tactics used by Palestinian terrorists may by some inane reasoning and justification be considered by the ICJ or some as an unconscionable but permissible means of resistance, further applying the "freedom-fighting" rationale to otherwise heinous and murderous conduct. This shocking and unacceptable result must be rejected by all nations who have respect for the rule of law; because it cannot be, under any circumstances, that suicide bombings and other attacks upon civilians anywhere can ever be countenanced or acceptable.

Nevertheless, the ICJ's fatally defective opinion has widespread implications for all states that wish to preserve the right to self-defense. The severely biased, prejudiced and limiting nature of the opinion mandates states to reject the ruling.

Israel's Security Fence is a Legal and Effective Measure of Self-Defense

Because of the PLO/PA's failure to satisfactorily perform under the Roadmap, Israel, as a sovereign nation state, has the right and authority under international law to take proportional measures to defend and secure itself and its citizens. Israel is not precluded from erecting a terrorism prevention security fence on or around the territory in question to affect its legitimate right to self-defense precisely because the territory does not belong to another sovereign nation state. Only established borders, recognized in international law, and accepted by the parties to the dispute can determine what territory belongs to Palestine and what to Israel. And, that determination is essential for Palestine to be deemed a sovereign nation state member of the United Nations. As the ICJ so aptly noted in *The Legality of the Threat or Use of Nuclear Weapons* advisory opinion of July 8, 1995, "the Court cannot lose sight of the fundamental right of every State to survival, and thus its right to resort to self-defense, in accordance with Article 51 of the Charter, when its survival is at stake."[1005] Yet, in relation to Israel, the Court lost sight of the fundamental right of the State of Israel to her right to resort to self-defense and her right and obligation to defend her people and those visiting or living within her sovereign territory.

The terrorism prevention security fence is a temporary, proven, necessary and non-violent measure that was adopted in accordance with international and local law to defend the people of Israel against a continued campaign of terrorism which killed hundreds of innocent civilians.[1006] As long as the Palestinian leadership continues to rely upon its inaction on the most basic obligations to fight terrorism, and to self-justify its support or blind eye to terrorism, there is simply no alternative for Israel but to take its own measures to provide and assure self-defense. Indeed, the Palestinian terrorism strategy and applications are the only reason for the construction of the terrorism prevention security fence – as soon as the terror ends, the fence will no longer be necessary.[1007] Israel's use of a terrorism prevention security fence as a means to defend itself and its citizens is a non-violent form of protection; neither Israel nor any nation-state should be forced by the ICJ to leave their people vulnerable to terrorist attacks that can be avoided by the application of proper security measures.

Israel's Use of Land, Restriction on Movement and Rights to the Land through the Effluxion of Time

Fences, by their very nature, restrict movement. Accordingly, fences when constructed create legal issues regarding the use of land, limitations on movement, and rights to the land through the effluxion of time. It should come as no surprise that the terrorism prevention security fence has faced criticism with respect to all three of these issues.

1. Does Israel have the right to make use of the land on which the terrorism prevention security fence rests?

Unlike land within Israel or on the Green Line, land within the West Bank is not directly subject to Israeli law and control, except its administrative or military control pending entry into a full peace agreement that addresses said lands, which have been characterized as "occupied territory." The authority and responsibility of Israel should be viewed in the context of both applicable international law and construed in accordance with the Roadmap.

The General Assembly's Resolution A/RES/ES-10/14 (A/ES-10/L.16) lists the Fourth Geneva Convention of 1949 as one of the grounds for the ICJ's advisory opinion.[1008] Palestine's lack of recognition as a sovereign state at the time of the rendering of the opinion means that Israeli measures towards the Palestinians do not fall under the authority of the Convention.

However, the provisions of the Convention most directly implicated in the building of the terrorism prevention security fence are:

Article 3, which prohibits "violence to life and person" of civilians,[1009]

Article 27 which provides that: "Protected persons... shall be protected especially against all acts of violence or threats thereof ...[1010]

Article 53 which provides that:

Any destruction by the Occupying Power of real or personal property belonging individually or collectively to private persons, or to the State, or to other public authorities, or to social or cooperative organizations, is prohibited, except where such destruction is rendered absolutely necessary by military operations.[1011]

And Article 64, which provides that:

The Occupying Power may, however, subject the population of the occupied territory to provisions which are essential to enable the Occupying Power to fulfill its obligations under the present Convention, to maintain the orderly government of the territory, and to ensure the security of the Occupying Power, of the members and property of the occupying forces or administration....[1012]

If Israel is deemed to be an "occupying power" on the West Bank, the Convention imposes upon the Government of Israel both the right and the obligation to take steps necessary to prevent violence and ensure security on both the West Bank and, *a fortiori*, within Israel itself. In the UN Report of the Secretary-General dated November 24, 2003 (A/ES-10/248) (the "SG Report"), the legal position of the Palestine Liberation Organization provided that:

> Israel has a right to undertake certain limited measures in cases of strict military necessity and to protect its legitimate security interests . . . [but that such necessity and interests] can more likely be met by building the Barrier within Israeli territory or even on the Green Line.[1013]

There are a number of Israeli citizens, however, who live both near and on the West Bank. The PLO/PA cites to Israeli citizens living on the West Bank as a significant obstacle to long-term peace. The status of these Israeli citizens and the ultimate location of their residences, and the actual border line (as distinguished from the Green Line) are precisely the issues the Roadmap addresses. Hence, an agreement cannot possibly be reached without completing the preliminary steps of ending violence and directly negotiating terms of such an agreement.

For the terrorism prevention security fence to serve its primary safety goal, it must separate Israeli citizens from terrorists seeking to infiltrate Israel and those areas where Israeli citizens presently reside. As such, it must necessarily run through territory on the West Bank. The specific path chosen by the Government of Israel for the terrorism prevention security fence has been established exclusively for security purposes. The path can and will be modified and, as necessary, relocated by order of the Israeli courts or to a permanent borderline after conclusion of a written agreement between Israel and the PLO/PA.

Israel seeks to balance two current aims: to maximize the effectiveness of the terrorism prevention security fence and minimize its environmental, social and economic impact.[1014] Israel's former Minister of Internal Security and current Minister of National Infrastructure, Uzi Landau, has expressed the difficulty in balancing these dual aims:

> We are sorry that some Palestinian families are cut off from their fields. We have tried to provide a reasonable solution for this: providing gates throughout the length of the fence. But even with these gates, there will be inconvenience for certain families. We had

> to weigh this inconvenience against seeing Israeli families blown
> to bits if the fence is not built. Faced with these two alternatives,
> which is morally more compelling?"[1015]

It is the role of Israel's High Court of Justice to evaluate whether the
Government of Israel has succeeded in balancing these goals, not the
role of the International Court of Justice; and certainly not without giving deference to Israel's highest court, particularly as the Israeli High
Court of Justice is one of the most esteemed judiciaries in the world.

2. Does Israel have the right to restrict access?

The security fence arises out of the judgment that, in the circumstances, the most effective way of limiting violence is to physically separate the Israelis from those who want to attack, maim
and kill her people. As such, the security fence's *raison d'etre* is the
restriction of access from one side to another. Because Israelis reside within parts of the West Bank and immediately adjacent to it,
the terrorism prevention security fence must necessarily restrict
access between parts of the West Bank itself. And to be effective,
access must be restricted particularly between the security fence
and those portions of the West Bank to the East of the security
fence (the "Adjacent West Bank.") There have been limitations,
sometimes severe, to residents on both sides of the security fence.
Residents in the area of the fence have been cut off from services
that they need in the West Bank. Residents on the West Bank have
been cut off from what they wish to access in the area without
going through some security precautionary measures as preconditions of such access.

Without diminishing the suffering that such limitations impose on Arab Palestinians living in both the area and the Adjacent West Bank, such difficulties are a foreseeable cost and consequence resulting from the PLO/PA's failure to combat terror and
end violence. Since it is a given that restrictions are a necessary
consequence of the terrorism perpetrated upon Israel and her
people, necessitating the security fence, the discussion should
focus more on what the restrictions are and whether they are
reasonable, proportional and necessary given the circumstances,
not whether or not they are permitted as a matter of abstract law

unconnected in its application to the realities of the situation on the ground.

The Convention does not speak directly to the issue of limiting movement within an occupied territory. Article 49 prohibits, as a general matter, the forced relocation of persons in the territory. Article 49, however, also provides that an:

> occupying Power may undertake total or partial evacuation of a given area if the security of the population or imperative military reasons so demand . . . The Occupying Power undertaking such transfers or evacuations shall ensure, to the greatest practicable extent, that proper accommodation is provided to receive the protected persons, that the removals are effected in satisfactory conditions of hygiene, health, safety and nutrition, and that members of the same family are not separated.

Therefore, assuming that the security fence's limitation on movement constitutes a partial evacuation, the onus is then on Israel to make sure that such restrictions are diminished to the fullest extent possible while still achieving the primary purpose of safeguarding Israel against terrorism.

Israel has taken significant steps to minimize such restrictions and limitations. Again, whether Israel has succeeded in minimizing these restrictions and limitations are determinations that Israel's High Court of Justice was considering at the time the ICJ accepted jurisdiction over issuing the advisory opinion. It was inappropriate for the ICJ to review and opine on this issue while the Israeli High Court already had the very issue under review and inappropriate for the ICJ not to give deference to the highest court with competent jurisdiction over the questions. In fact, one must ask, would the ICJ have imposed its view on an issue pending before the courts of any other law abiding country other than Israel while the very matter was being considered by that court? The answer is clearly NO. Nor would any country operating under the rule of law tolerate such interference by the ICJ.

3. Will the restriction of access give Israel greater right to the Seam Zone than it had immediately prior to the erection of the terrorism prevention security fence?

Security Council Resolution 242 (S/RES/242 (1967)) emphasizes a basic feature of modern international law, namely, the "inadmissibility of the acquisition of territory by war." When there has been no boundary agreement between parties to a dispute, when both parties reject a particular boundary, and when neither party acts to treat the boundary as a *de facto* frontier, there can be no suggestion that such boundary acquires a permanent legal character by the mere passage of time. No "fact on the ground" can change this basic reality.

The PLO/PA have rejected any suggestion that the terrorism prevention security fence defines or ought to define a future border between Israel and a Palestinian nation that may be permanently established as a sovereign state on the West Bank and in Gaza. Israel has similarly rejected any such conclusion. Therefore, it is clear that the terrorism prevention security fence cannot form the basis of any future border between the two peoples unless they, themselves, agree to make it so.

By selecting November 29th, the day on which the original Partition Resolution was adopted in 1947 as the day when the PLO and PA appealed to the UN for upgraded non-member state observer status, and the January 2013 executive order of the PA changing its name to the "State of Palestine" has been interesting political theatre designed to translate wishes to reality while ignoring the essential requirements in international law for establishment of a state. These requirements include the essential term of borders and the required approval of the Security Council. The PLO and PA would like to believe that a UN General Assembly resolution can impose borders such as those of 1967 or even 1948 or 1947 as the borders of its state. Perhaps one can expect their next move to be an application through the General Assembly for the General Assembly to request a new opinion of the ICJ as to setting borders, totally seeking to bypass the purview of the Security Council and abrogating all of its obligations under the Roadmap.

The practice of One country: One vote at the General Assembly is inapplicable in creating a recognized member-nation-state at the United Nations, as such determinations can be made only by the Security Council. Neither the General Assembly nor the International Court of Justice can create sovereign state status for the PLO or the PA.

CHAPTER ELEVEN:
Omissions and Errors Equal Injustice

The International Court of Justice's advisory opinion is woefully deficient due to glaring omissions and errors for what it does not say.

The Advisory Opinion Omitted Facts Regarding Palestinian Terrorist Attacks Against Israel

Neither the question referred to the Court nor the lengthy resolution made any reference whatsoever to the factors that led to the necessity for the measure, which, if included, could have enabled the Court to more adequately and fairly address the issue. It is outrageous that both the question and the resolution omitted any real discussion of Palestinian terrorism, suicide bombers, missile attacks, Israel's right of self-defense, the failure of the Palestinian leadership to take any measures to prevent terrorism or the institutionalized glorification by the PLO and the PA of terrorists as martyrs, heroes and the teaching of hatred toward Israel in Palestinian schools and by leaders of the PLO/PA.

The ICJ advisory opinion completely ignored the role of the Palestinian terrorist attacks that caused the necessity for the security fence in the first place. As Israeli Ambassador Dan Gillerman said, "the barrier between Israelis and Palestinians is not the security fence, but the terrorism that made it necessary."[1016] As Israel set forth in its Written Statement to the Court, the security fence is for security purposes only and does not affect legal or political boundaries.

Indeed, Judge Kooijmans of the Netherlands explained Israel's purpose in his separate opinion when he said:

> The construction of the wall is explained by Israel as a necessary protection against the latter category of acts which are generally considered to be international crimes. Deliberate and indiscriminate attacks against civilians with the intention to kill are the core element of terrorism which has been unconditionally condemned by the international community regardless of the motives which have inspired them.[1017]

The Court briefly acknowledged Israel's assertion that the "sole purpose [of the terrorism prevention security fence] is to enable it to effectively combat terrorist attacks launched by the West Bank."[1018] It also recognized Israel's guarantee that the security fence would have no impact whatsoever on legal or political boundaries within the territory. And yet, even though the Court recognized these facts, at the same time it ignored them. In a scathing dissent, Judge Buergenthal of the United States noted that:

> to reach [the] conclusion [that the fence violates international law] . . . without having before [the Court] or seeking to ascertain all relevant facts bearing directly on issues of Israel's legitimate right of self-defence, military necessity and security needs, given the repeated deadly terrorist attacks in and upon Israel proper coming from the Occupied Palestinian Territory to which Israel has been and continues to be subjected, cannot be justified as a matter of law. The nature of these cross-Green Line attacks and their impact on Israel and its population are never really seriously examined by the Court, and the dossier provided the Court by the United Nations on which the Court to a large extent bases its findings barely touches on that subject.[1019]

It is quite astonishing and a gross injustice that the 600-page dossier that UN Secretary General Kofi Annan submitted to the Court made no mention of UN Resolution 1373, which condemns terrorism, nor of UN Resolution 1515 which adopts the Roadmap nor according to Judge Buergenthal, did it even barely touch on the subject of the terrorist attacks against Israel and her people which necessitated the construction of the security fence. According to Judge Buergenthal, both the question referred to the Court and the Court's lengthy response wholly ignored crucial facts and failed to make any reference whatsoever to Palestinian terrorism, suicide bombers, Israel's right of self-defense, the failure of the Palestinian leadership to take any measures to prevent terrorism, the institutionalized glorification of terrorists as heroes and martyrs or any of the other factors leading to the security fence's necessity. These are all issues that, if considered, would have enabled the Court to address the question much more adequately and properly. It is actually astonishing that the Court knowing from public and UN sources of the terrorist attacks upon Israel, which were front page news during the Second Intifada, chose to ignore the actual facts on the ground and issue what is clearly an esoteric academic and foolish opinion, neither based in fact nor applicable law, nor considering agreements of the parties, the violations by the Palestinians and the efforts by Washington and other governments to get the PLO and the PA to stop incitement and terrorism.

It was incumbent on the ICJ, in providing an advisory opinion on the "legal consequences" of the construction of the terrorism prevention security in disputed territory over which Israel has administrative control and jurisdiction, to maintain vigilant regard for the fundamental principles of international law and justice upon which the United Nations is rooted and to recognize the rights of the Israeli people to be secure and free from terror. As the Security Council itself made clear in Resolution 1377, "acts of terrorism endanger innocent lives and the dignity and security of human beings everywhere, threaten the social and economic development of all States, and undermine global stability and prosperity."[1020] The prescient words of US President George W. Bush are both apt and worthy of careful deliberation:

> I can understand the deep anger and anguish of the Israeli people. You've lived too long with fear and funerals, having to avoid markets and public transportation, and forced to put armed guards in kindergarten classrooms. The Palestinian Authority has rejected your offered hand and trafficked with terrorists. You have a right to a normal life. You have a right to security...[1021]

The Court's failure to address terrorism and the realities faced by democracies seeking to combat it within the opinion makes the opinion shortsighted and doomed to irrelevancy. For Yehudah Mirsky, former US State Department Special Advisor in the Bureau of

Democracy, Human Rights and Labor, the Court's failure or refusal to opine on the appropriate response to the real threats and attacks that Israel faces on the ground divorces the opinion from reality and undermines the Court's credibility. Mirsky addressed these concerns when he noted that:

> the ICJ's ruling that Israel must unilaterally remove the wall (though to which border is never made clear) and forfeit any claim to self-defense against terror emanating from the territories in the absence of a Palestinian sovereign, undermines rather than strengthens international legality, by unmooring it from concrete realities on the ground, and using it to undermine a functioning, if flawed, democracy in its struggles with determinedly anti-democratic enemies.[1022]

The opinion gives no guidance on how to deal with terrorism because the Court chose to ignore the entire issue as if it was not a factor. How myopic and indeed shocking that the Court would compromise its responsibilities and principles in favor of weighing into political questions involving peace and security within the sole purview of the Security Council and the parties themselves.

By contrast, the dissenting judges in the advisory opinion and the Israeli High Court in its *Beit Sourik* opinion on the security fence, "actually give democracies meaningful guidance on how to bring their actions into conformity with international law."[1023] As Mirsky rightly noted, "we do those principles [of human rights] no service by failing to recognize the inescapably political dimensions of international human rights institutions and of domestic regimes' own acceptance of, and accountability towards, those very principles."[1024]

Once the ICJ decided that the question referred to it for an advisory opinion raised justiciable issues, the Court should have then considered those issues in their historical and political context. The Court should have specifically referenced the Roadmap and the various Security Council Resolutions that call upon the international community to take sustained and comprehensive action against terrorism and against those who facilitate the commission of acts of terror.[1025] The Court should have taken notice of the now well-established fact that the disputed territory, the West Bank, is home to numerous terrorist groups and cells; but also to law abiding Israeli and

Palestinian citizens seeking good lives for their families, prosperous business endeavors and the right to enjoy freedom and democracy under the rule of law, free of terrorist attack. It also should have taken notice of the fact that the West Bank is a repository of violent activity directed against, *inter alia*, the State and people of Israel. President George W. Bush acknowledged this fact in his June 24, 2002 Rose Garden speech given in the midst of the Second Intifada where he outlined a vision of two states living side by side in peace and security.[1026]

The Advisory Opinion Omitted Facts Regarding Israel's High Court of Justice Opinion on the Security Fence and the Role and Responsibility of the Israeli Judiciary's Continual Legal Review of the Security Fence

Although Israel's High Court of Justice issued its *Beit Sourik Village Council v. Government of Israel* decision (*"Beit Sourik* opinion") prior to the ICJ advisory opinion, which afforded the ICJ more than ample time to consider it, the ICJ Justices failed to address the decision at any point. Adequate safeguards existed to provide aggrieved residents on either side of the terrorism prevention security fence with access to justice without the need to resort to the ICJ. Moreover, as legal scholar Yuval Shany put it, "Display of inter-judicial comity could have improved coordination between the two parallel proceedings, facilitated recourse by one tribunal to the decisions of the other and invited mutual deference to their findings."[1027]

Since the ICJ refused to refrain from hearing the question on the security fence and to give deference to the issue being heard before Israel's High Court of Justice, the ICJ should have given real consideration to the HCJ's findings. Indeed, the fact that there were "differences in the identity of parties, in the scope of issues at hand and in the applicable law" made it a theoretical possibility that the two separate cases could be heard in both courts, simultaneously, without necessary judicial conflict.[1028] Once the ICJ erroneously accepted jurisdiction, it was not required for "any of the two courts to stay proceedings, to defer to the jurisdiction of the other court... or to accord [claim preclusion] to the decisions of its counterpart (especially given that the opinion of the ICJ is formally non-binding)."[1029] However, it was wrong for the ICJ to not consider the HCJ's extremely relevant judgment. Quite to the contrary; they were duty bound not only to do so but, moreover, to give deference to the Israeli court's jurisdiction and the applications of its decision.

Given the Israeli High Court's expertise at in-depth fact-finding and its knowledge of details on the ground that are relevant to each segment of the fence and its legality, the ICJ could have substantially benefited from the information contained in the Israeli High Court opinion. Yuval Shany, international law professor and scholar, has suggested that, based on the principle of comity, "both tribunals should have conducted their proceedings in a way which facilitates cross-fertilization: The ICJ should have incorporated and relied on the factual analysis of the HCJ and the latter on the legal analysis of the ICJ."[1030] He pointed out the importance of respecting the authority of other judicial systems and suggested that "comity might require... courts to accord due consideration to the decisions of other courts and tribunals."[1031] Stressing the importance, he called "upon courts to accord deference to the authority of other courts belonging to different legal systems.[1032] By ignoring the relevant and respected decision of the HCJ, the ICJ trivialized the importance of comity between nations and judicial bodies. The ICJ missed an opportunity to improve the detail and depth of its evidence and to bolster the opinion's credibility and deficiencies by ignoring the Beit Sourik decision of the Israeli High Court as if it neither existed of was relevant; a gross error by the ICJ.

The *Beit Sourik Village Council* Opinion

On June 30, 2004, the Israel High Court ordered that the terrorism prevention security fence be rerouted to minimize the negative effects on Palestinians living adjacent to the fence's anticipated path. In doing so, however, the Israel High Court affirmed the fence's security purpose and legitimized its construction under applicable law.

The Israel High Court identified the government of Israel's purpose in deciding to construct the security fence, noting that Israel has "emphasized, numerous times, that 'the fence... is a security measure. Its construction does not express a political border, or any other border...[it] is a security measure for the prevention of terror attacks and does not mark a national border or any other border.'"[1033]

After reviewing all of the evidence before it, the Court decided that the IDF had the authority to erect the fence, but that the authority to do so stemmed from security considerations alone. The Court understood and recognized the fence's impact on the local residents and determined that only the grave need for safety allowed the construction of the fence. In explaining why the grave need for security was the only justification for the construction of the fence, and its qualifying limitations the Court said:

> Indeed, the military commander of territory held in belligerent oc-
> cupation must balance between the needs of the army on one hand,
> and the needs of the local inhabitants on the other. In the frame-
> work of this delicate balance, there is no room for an additional
> system of considerations, whether they be political considerations,
> the annexation of territory, or the establishment of the permanent
> borders of the state.[1034]

The Court made clear to the government of Israel that the route of the fence, in accordance with the Court's mandate, may only take security concerns into consideration, for if any other considerations played a role, the fence would be illegal. The Court noted that the military commander "cannot order the construction of the separation fence if his reasons are political. The separation fence cannot be motivated by a desire to 'annex' territories to the state of Israel. The purpose of the separation fence cannot be to draw a political border."[1035]

The Israel High Court used the principle of proportionality as a standard to balance Palestinian humanitarian considerations against military necessities and did not hesitate in ruling that portions of the fence had to be rerouted.[1036] For example, in considering the section of the fence surrounding the high mountain range of Jeb-
el Muktam (Order Tav/104/03; Order Tav/103/03; Order Tav/84/03
—The Western Part of the Order), the Court concluded:

> Our answer is that the relationship between the injury to the local
> inhabitants and the security benefit from the construction of the
> separation fence along the route, as determined by the military

commander, is not proportionate. The route undermines the delicate balance between the obligation of the military commander to preserve security and his obligation to provide for the needs of the local inhabitants. This approach is based on the fact that the route which the military commander established for the security fence -- which separates the local inhabitants from their agricultural lands -- injures the local inhabitants in a severe and acute way, while violating their rights under humanitarian international law.[1037]

Addressing the impact of the fence on the surrounding population, the Court found:

The injury caused by the separation fence is not restricted to the lands of the inhabitants and to their access to these lands. The injury is of far wider a scope. It strikes across the fabric of life of the entire population. In many locations, the separation fence passes right by their homes. In certain places (like Beit Sourik), the separation fence surrounds the village from the west, the south and the east. The fence directly affects the links between the local inhabitants and the urban centers (Bir Nabbala and Ramallah). This link is difficult even without the separation fence. This difficulty is multiplied sevenfold by the construction of the fence.[1038]

The Israeli Court recognized that, "the task of the military commander is not easy" and advised the commander that he must "delicately balance between security needs and the needs of the local inhabitants."[1039] Despite the fact that the Court was "impressed by the sincere desire of the military commander to find this balance, and his willingness to change the original plan in order to reach a more proportionate solution…[the Court was] of the opinion that the balance determined by the military commander is not proportionate."[1040] Despite the fact that the terrorism prevention security fence was in accordance with Israeli and international law, the Court ruled that the fence's negative impact on the lives of those Palestinians living in the planned route of the fence required some rerouting, despite the decreased protection it would afford Israelis.

The Israeli Court found that the third test, the proportionality requirement, was not satisfied for each section of the fence or for the fence as a whole and ordered the military to conduct "a renewed examination of the route of the fence, according to the standards of proportionality that we have set out."[1041]

Unlike the ICJ, the HCJ recognized that full compliance under international law must take into consideration all of the factors of the situation because "at the end of the day, a struggle according to the law will strengthen her power and her spirit. There is no security without law. Satisfying the provisions of the law is an aspect of national security."[1042]

As a final note, the Israeli Court reflected on how democracy and the rule of law require the delicate balancing between the need for the fence as well as the need to protect the local residents. It made clear that it was aware that "in the short term, [its] judgment will not make the state's struggle against those rising up against it easier," however:

> This is the destiny of a democracy—she does not see all means as acceptable, and the ways of her enemies are not always open before her. A democracy must sometimes fight with one arm tied behind her back. Even so, a democracy has the upper hand. The rule of law and individual liberties constitute an important aspect of her security stance. At the end of the day, they strengthen her spirit and this strength allows her to overcome her difficulties.[1043]

Only a fence built upon the rule of law has and will grant security to the state and its citizens. Only a fence route based on the path of law, will lead the state to the security so yearned for.[1044]

The Effect of the *Beit Sourik* Opinion

Major Gil Limon, who served as legal adviser for Judea and Samaria and was responsible for security affairs from 2002 to 2005, has described how the *Beit Sourik* decision impacted the military's planning of the fence route and how it forced the military to re-evaluate the route, taking better account of its impact on the local Palestinians. Addressing the additional considerations that he had to examine in deciding the route, he said:

> In the decision, the Court made a new calculus, which took into account the damage caused by the fence. For the first time, the Court looked at what was behind the fence—the lives of those people [living] behind the fence. We now [had to take into account] the obstacles to freedom of movement and the impact on [the Palestin-

ians'] way of life. . . . We knew before to minimize direct damages, we also learned to minimize indirect damages. After the decision, we found a new route that was less problematic for the Palestinians and still achieved our security needs.[1045]

Despite the increased difficulties that the *Beit Sourik* opinion imposed on the military in its defense of Israel, Prime Minister Ariel Sharon announced his intent to comply with the Court's ruling and rejected the idea of enacting a special law to contradict it. Only a true democracy, committed to freedom, respect and the rule of law would take such a position, even in the face of adversity. Accordingly, Israel's Ministry of Defense complied with the High Court of Justice's decision and planned a modified route of the fence, which was implemented after Prime Minister Sharon and the Israeli cabinet approved it.[1046]

Indeed, in the later 2005 *Alfei Menashe* opinion, the Court recognized that the Israeli government, in response to its *Beit Sourik* decision, intensified the "constant and continual process of analysis and improvement" that had been taking place since the security fence's construction first began.[1047] The Court observed further that the planning of future phases of construction was altered and, in some necessary cases, the routes of the existing sections were changed.[1048] The Court found that not only did the new route alleviate burdens on Palestinians by ensuring that fewer Palestinian neighborhoods were directly affected by the security fence, it also provided for numerous passageways to allow people and goods to pass through the fence instead of around it.[1049] Secretary-General Kofi Annan, who had often criticized Israel's building of the security fence, praised the Israeli High Court of Justice's decision in *Beit Sourik* as "courageous and bold."[1050] But the world took little notice.

The *Alfei Menashe* Opinion

After the ICJ's advisory opinion was released, the Israeli High Court issued its second ruling ("*Alfei Menashe* opinion") on the petitions pending before it.[1051] The September 2005 decision again employed the principle of proportionality to analyze the parties' concerns and found that the fence in Alfei Menashe was disproportionately burdensome on Palestinians. The High Court therefore ordered the Israeli government to reroute the security fence to minimize the harm caused to Palestinians living in the affected area.[1052]

In doing so, the Israel High Court reiterated the need to consider the impact of the terrorism prevention security fence in small segments, rather than the impact of the fence as a whole, as the ICJ did in its advisory opinion. While analyzing the impact of the ICJ advisory opinion on Israeli jurisprudence, the Israel High Court found that the ICJ based its ruling on a completely different factual record than it had before it in the *Beit Sourik* decision.[1053] The ICJ based its judgment only on the complaints of the Palestinian residents and never took into consideration Israel's security needs. In contrast, the Israel High Court's decision properly took facts from both sides into account and used the proportionality principle to come to a fair and unbiased resolution.[1054] In a remarkable demonstration of impartiality, the HCJ refused to place blame on the ICJ for its "severe oversight," meaning the ICJ opinion's lack of consideration of Israel's security needs, and instead performed an objective comparison of the facts before the ICJ and those before the Israeli High Court in *Beit Sourik*.[1055] Moreover, the HCJ recognized that the ICJ opinion was merely advisory and that, because of the extraordinary difference in the factual records before each court, the ICJ advisory opinion did not bind the Supreme Court of Israel.[1056] IIsrael, giving deference to the ICJ, although undeserved, took the proper legal route in giving deference that the ICJ itself neglected to provide in declining to give deference to the Israeli courts.

Additional Israeli High Court Orders

As time has progressed, the Israeli High Court and the Israeli government have continued the process of evaluating and rerouting the security fence's path. On April 30, 2006, the Israeli cabinet decided to change the route of the Security Fence in several areas to comply with the Israeli High Court decisions.[1057] Interim Prime Minister Ehud Olmert described the changes as "very important" and emphasized that the Security Fence should be completed as "quickly as possible" since it is a "crucial element in the war against Palestinian terror."[1058] This statement by Prime Minister Olmert, who replaced Prime Minister Sharon after he became gravely ill, is quite telling: the mindset of the leadership of Israel across the political spectrum recognized Israel's need, right and obligation to complete construction of the Security Fence for defensive purposes. This is a right guaranteed under the UN Charter to all nation-states.

In further demonstration of the strength of Israel's democracy, two months later in June 2006, the Israel High Court ordered the government of Israel to remove a two-mile stretch of the security fence around Tzofim, a settlement near the West Bank town of Qalqilya, and reroute it to accommodate Palestinians in the area. The Court "lambasted the state for having concealed the fact that the original route of the fence, east of Tzofim, was dictated not by security considerations, but by the settlement's expansion plans."[1059]

In November 2006, however, the High Court ruled that the West Bank security fence route in the Bir Naballah area north of Jerusalem was legal and based on security considerations.[1060] The fence near Bir Naballah is part of the "Jerusalem envelope," the section of the security fence surrounding Jerusalem. It was also decided that, "the first section would separate Givat Zeev and Ramallah, while the second would come between Jerusalem and Ramallah."[1061] In explaining the delicate balance the military must maintain when deciding on the route, outgoing High Court President Aharon Barak wrote:

> The Military Commander has to weight conflicting options. Maximal defense of security is meant to be bound to immeasurable harm to Palestinian residents, and abstention from harming Palestinian residents is meant to greatly threaten security. The solution to this conflict is not a matter of all or nothing. The solution is in finding a balance between the conflicting interests.[1062]

The *Bil'in Village Council* Opinion

In a later September 2007 case between the Bil'in Village Council and the Government of Israel a panel of three judges on the Israeli High Court unanimously ruled that the planned route of the security fence in the Bil'in area must be reconsidered. They determined that the route of the fence was based on the inappropriate consideration of the defense of a future Israeli settlement and ordered a mile-long section of the security fence near the West Bank town of Bil'in to be redrawn and rebuilt in a "reasonable period of time."[1063] The ruling stated that because of the military command-er's plan for of the "'East Mattityahu' neighborhood, and the deci-sive weight which the military commander granted the defense of this future neighborhood, difficulty arises regarding the legality of the route that takes that consideration into account."[1064] To minimize the damage to the residents from the construction of the fence, the Court required the government of Israel to plan an alternative route on state lands rather than Palestinian lands wherever possible and leaving specific areas, including lands designated for a new Jew-ish neighborhood, outside the barrier. Quite importantly, the Israeli High Court emphasized that the route of the security fence must be created for security purposes, not to expand settlements, and the Court ordered the Respondents to "reconsider the current route, and examine the possibility of an alternate route that is not based upon defending phase B of 'East Mattityahu.'"[1065]

The Israeli High Court's Ongoing Role Overseeing the Route of Fence

The display of judicial independence the Israeli High Court of Justice espoused in the *Beit Sourik*, *Alfei Menashe*, *Bil'in Village Coun-cil* and recent *Battir* opinions reconfirms the propriety of the Israeli judicial system as the sole adjudicator of the ongoing disputes re-lated to the security fence. Although such independence in the face of the terrorist attacks suffered by all Israelis is quite remarkable, for the Israeli Court, this type of showing is not unusual.

On December 15, 2008, the Israeli High Court ordered the Israeli government to obey its original *Bil'in Village Council* ruling with no further delay and to map out a route for the fence that meets the criteria set out in the ruling.[1066] Numerous petitions concerning the security fence remain outstanding with the Israeli High Court.

In December 2012, the Israeli High Court issued its most recent opinion in a case involving Battir, where according to Joel Green-berg reporting in The Washington Post, the planned barrier route, including 500 yards of concrete wall, would "cut through the valley, scarring a rare surviving landscape of naturally irrigated terrace agriculture dating back thousands of years. It would also separate villagers from about one-third of their cultivated lands, which would fall on the other side of the barrier."[1067] In response to petitions by villagers and the environmental group Friends of the Earth Middle East, according to Greenberg, Israel's Supreme Court "gave the Israeli defense ministry 90 days to come up with an alternative to the planned wall that would take into account 'the unique character of the area' around Battir."[1068]

In his reporting, Greenberg commented that "In its ruling – a rare intervention by the Supreme Court in the barrier project – the court urged security officials to reconsider 'the nature of the divider and security arrangements' in the sensitive zone, which is a candidate for designation as a UNESCO World Heritage Site." Interestingly, Israel's Nature and Parks Authority, an Israeli government body, sided with the petitioners in court, according to Greenberg, saying "the barrier would create 'a wound in the ancient landscape' and 'cut the farmers off from their lands, leading to the destruction of the ancient farming culture.'" Greenberg reported that Gideon Bromberg, Israeli Director of Friends of the Earth Middle East, stated "We're not against a security barrier in principle, but we're against building it in a cultural landscape site that requires protection."[1069]

Greenberg aptly reported in his *Washington Post* article, "The defense ministry argued that completing the barrier in the Battir area would close a gap south of Jerusalem, protecting the city from possible terrorist attacks and shielding train tracks running on the Israeli side of the boundary. The ministry said steps had been taken to minimize the project's impact on the farming terraces around the village." Greenberg continued "Under the armistice agreement signed in 1949 after Israel's war of independence, the farmers of Battir, it what was then the Jordanian-controlled West Bank, were allowed to continue cultivating village land that remained on the Israeli side of the ceasefire line. In return, they committed not to harm the Israeli train route between Jerusalem and Tel Aviv that runs along the boundary by their village. The agreement has stood for decades, married only by isolated instances of stone-throwing, mostly during the first Palestinian uprising that erupted in the late 1980s."[1070]

Akram Bader, the mayor of Battir, "said that several years ago, students at the local school, which lies next to the tracks, rode the train to Jerusalem by special arrangement with the Israeli railroad company. 'We teach them that the train is a friend, not an enemy,' he said." Greenberg quotes Bader in his forthright statement, deserving of applause: "We take care of the border because we know we will be safe if Israel has security..."[1071]

Conclusion

Except for one collateral reference in a separate opinion, nowhere in its advisory opinion does the International Court of Justice mention the Israel High Court's Beit Sourik 2004 ruling nor does the ICJ give any deference to the court of competent jurisdiction, the Israeli High Court being actively involved in fairly reviewing, and adjudicating, issues; as the Israeli High Court has continued to prove since the issuance of the faulty ICJ opinion. Does anyone think that if this were India and not Israel that the ICJ would not have deferred to the courts of India to complete their due process? It is astonishing and a gross error that the International Court of Justice, which was advised of the High Court of Justice opinion prior to issuing its advisory opinion, chose to ignore it.

The Court's similar refusal to acknowledge the terrorist attacks which the Israelis have endured, making self-defense necessary for survival, as well as the opinion issued by Israel's High Court of Justice, points further towards the bias in its judgment. As Judge Kooijmans states, "the Court could and should have given more explicit attention to the general context of the request in its Opinion."[1072] The ICJ's condemnation of Israel's actions, taken only in light of the humanitarian considerations of the Palestinian people, was thus formulated on false and outdated information and based upon the same bias which Israel has long experienced, and continues to endure to this day, in its dealings generally with and at the United Nations.

The Advisory Opinion Omitted the Standard of Proportionality as a Counter Terrorism Measure

The ICJ opinion completely ignored the question of whether

the construction of a security fence was a proportionate counter-measure against the scourge of violent terrorist attacks emanating from the neighboring territory. Although it is a measure of self-defense implemented by the military and standing within a military framework, it is also a passive countermeasure that decreases the need for aggressive measures.

As Thomas Franck, international law professor and specialist, has pointed out, "the right to respond to an unlawful provocation with nonmilitary countermeasures is specifically recognized in the International Law Commission's *Draft Articles on State Responsibility*," which requires "that the countermeasures withstand the test of being proportionate to the actual injury caused."[1073]

With the Draft Articles allowing a right to respond to an initial illegal act, it "situates lawful countermeasures in the context of the right to self-help."[1074] Franck explains that the rule of proportionality, however, qualifies what types of countermeasures are legal. Under international law, for a countermeasure to be legal, the initial provocation must have been unlawful and the countermeasure must be proportional to the initial provocation.[1075] The ICJ failed to address any of these important elements during its brief self-defense analysis.

The Meaning of Proportionality

Customary international law dictates that all measures of self-defense must be proportionate to the actual injury caused. In evaluating the proportionality of self-defense measures such as the security fence, we start from the understanding that, as renowned human rights expert Michel Rosenfeld describes "both liberty and security are social goods, and the pursuit of one sometimes comes into conflict with the realization of the other."[1076]

The cost from the burden imposed on liberty must be weighed against the resulting benefit in terms of security (the threatened social good). International law, as well as governments and their branches, devise methods to cope with threats, which include passive and active defensive measures. For Rosenfeld, it is the judiciary's responsibility to determine:

Whether implementation of such measures is compatible with maintaining a suitable equilibrium between the two social goods involved, by weighing the benefits the measures in question confer on one social good against the costs that such measures impose on the other social good.[1077]

"Proportionality concerns the means employed to achieve permissible ends." To be legal, it "requires a 'fit' between means and ends."[1078] That is:

When some important collective objective justifies limitation of some [legal] right, the permissible intrusion on that right should be the minimum possible consistent with achieving the objective. A perfect fit is achieved when the right-restricting means to a permissible end are neither over-inclusive—they restrict no one who does not threaten achievement of the relevant end—nor under-inclusive—they do not fail to restrict those who would otherwise frustrate achievement of the aforesaid end.[1079]

Rosenfeld describes the three factor legal test for proportionality:

The first factor of proportionality involves balancing, but it is balancing on a scale that is weighted in favor of constitutional rights. The second factor is likely to include comparisons of costs and benefits of alternative means to the same end, but these are unlikely to involve straightforward balancing in as much as they relate to tradeoffs between restrictions on liberty and restrictions on equality for purposes of achieving something else, such as, in the cases that concern us here, security... In the last analysis, proportionality analysis comprises measuring, 'fitting,' comparing and balancing in relation to normative standards or values that transcend proportionality itself. [1080]

Under this analysis, whether the construction of the security fence is legal depends on whether it is a proportional response to the illegal acts of terrorism committed against Israel.

Proportionality and the International Court of Justice

The ICJ has applied the doctrine of proportionality in the past, adjudicating claims arising out of the Reagan Administration's support for the Contras in Nicaragua, and again, in rendering a second opinion about whether, as a countermeasure, Ugandan troops could be deployed on the territory of the neighboring Congo Republic as a countermeasure to deal with insurgents operating in Uganda from bases in the Congo. [1081] In the *Legality of the Threat or Use of Nuclear*

Weapons, Advisory Opinion, the Court directly addressed the standard of proportionality:

> The submission of the exercise of the right of self-defence to the conditions of necessity and proportionality is a rule of customary international law. As the Court stated in the case concerning *Military and Paramilitary Activities in and against Nicaragua (Nicaragua v. United States of America)*: there is a "specific rule whereby self-defence would warrant only measures which are proportional to the armed attack and necessary to respond to it, a rule well established in customary international law" (*I. C. J. Reports 1986*, p. 94, para. 176). This dual condition applies equally to Article 51 of the Charter, whatever the means of force employed.[1082]

Missing in the ICJ's security fence opinion, however, was any analysis using the proportionality doctrine as applied in previous cases and decisions, and hereby visiting a gross injustice upon Israel..

However, the ICJ did briefly address the question of necessity. Without delving into facts or explaining its reasoning, the Court noted that necessity "requires that the act being challenged be 'the only way for the State to safeguard an essential interest against a grave and imminent peril.'"[1083] Without any in depth analysis, the ICJ proceeded to conclude that it was "not convinced that the construction of the wall along the route chosen was the only means to safeguard the interests of Israel against the peril which it has invoked as justification for that construction."[1084] Denying credence to Israel's necessity arguments is a gross miscarriage of justice.

The Proportionality Analysis in the Israeli High Court's *Beit Sourik* Decision

In its decision in *Beit Sourik*, the Israeli High Court proved adept at utilizing proportionality analysis. Its review of military-tactical decisions has been lauded for demonstrating, as Franck says, "an exemplary capacity to apply the principle of proportionality to complex military and logistic facts that are not the normal fare of adjudication."[1085] The Israeli High Court zeroed in on the issue of its stringent tests as to proportionality in its *Beit Sourik* decision:

> The key question before us is whether the route of the separation fence is proportionate. The question is: is the injury caused to local inhabitants by the separation fence proportionate, or is it is pos-

sible to satisfy the central security considerations while establishing a fence route whose injury to the local inhabitants is lesser and, as such, proportionate?[1086]

The Israel High Court applied the principle of proportionality to balance Palestinian human considerations against Israeli military necessities and ended up determining that portions of the security fence were causing, in its judgment, disproportionate injury to the local Palestinian population. Different than the failed analysis of the ICJ, this decision was made without denying or belittling Israel's pressing security context.[1087] Further proof of the High Court's applied tests is seen in the *Battir* case, as the measure was not just injury to the local Palestinian population but also to the cultural fabric of the ancient lands.

The Israeli High Court explained the three-factor test for proportionality in *Beit Sourik* as:

> First, does the route pass the "appropriate means" test (or the "rational means" test)? The question is whether there is a rational connection between the route of the fence and the goal of the construction of the separation fence.

> Second, does it pass the test of the "least injurious" means? The question is whether, among the various routes which would achieve the objective of the separation fence, is the chosen one the least injurious.

> Third, does it pass the test of proportionality in the narrow sense? The question is whether the separation fence route, as set out by the military commander, injures the local inhabitants to the extent that there is no proper proportion between this injury and the security benefit of the fence. According to the "relative" examination of this test, the separation fence will be found disproportionate if an alternate route for the fence is suggested that has a smaller security advantage than the route chosen by respondent, but which will cause significantly less damage than that original route.[1088]

Whether the fence's route is proportional "varies according to local conditions."[1089] Thus, the Court examined each individual military order specific to the particular part of the fence that was disputed by the petitioners from west to east, in addition to examining the whole fence disputed by the petitioners.[1090]

In *Beit Sourik*, the Court first found that the route of the fence passed the appropriate means test. It heard testimony on the professional expert opinions of members of the Council for Peace and Security as well as from the IDF, both of which expressed divergent views on the best route for the fence based on security considerations. In its "examination of the contrasting military considerations in this case," the Court, in accordance with its "long-held view," gave "special weight to the fact that the commander of the area is responsible for security" and found that petitioners did not carry their burden of convincing "us that we should prefer… [the] opinion of members of the Council for Peace and Security over the security stance of the commander of the area."[1091]

In explaining its decision to give greater weight to the testimony of the commander who is on the ground, it said, "we are dealing with two military approaches. Each of them has military advantages and disadvantages. In this state of affairs, we must place the expert opinion of the military commander at the foundation of our decision."[1092] Citing to its decision in *Amira v. Defense Minister*, the Court acknowledged that when it has "no well founded knowledge of its own, who speaks for those actually responsible for the preservation of security in the administered territories… shall benefit from the assumption that his professional reasons are sincere" and the opposing party must show "very convincing evidence… to negate this assumption."[1093] The High Court found the first test satisfied for each section of the fence and for the fence as a whole. It found that there was a rational connection between the route chosen for the fence and the fence's ultimate goal of protecting Israeli citizens.

Second, the Israeli Court found the fence route to be proportional as determined by the military commander under the second test. The route the military commander chose, when compared to the other possible route options, caused the least damage to the local population while still achieving the level of safety the fence needed to provide. The Israeli Court could not answer whether the route suggested by the members of the Council for Peace and Security, while causing less injury to the local population, would still satisfy the fence's essential security objective. Therefore, based on its "determination that we shall not intervene" in the military commander's position unless convincing evidence exists against it, the Israeli

Court, "determined that there is no alternate route that fulfills, to a similar extent, the security needs while causing lesser injury to the local inhabitants."[1094] Even though the Israeli Court's "long-held view" accords deference to the military commander's opinion, the Israeli Court still made sure to conduct a thorough review, using an objective legal standard, of his analysis on "the proportionality between the military consideration and the humanitarian consideration."[1095] This review included an assessment of "the severity of the injury caused to the local inhabitants by the route decided upon by the military commander."[1096] The Israeli Court concluded the second test was satisfied for each relevant section of the fence and for the fence as a whole.

Third, the Israeli High Court found that the fence's route did not meet the proportionate means test (or proportionality in the narrow sense), in which the administrative authority must weigh "whether the injury caused to the local inhabitants by the construction of the separation fence stands in proper proportion to the security benefit from the security fence in its chosen route."[1097] The Court explained that it is not enough to just satisfy the second test of whether the route chosen is the "proper and most moderate means for achieving the objective," the IDF "must also weigh the benefit reaped by the public against the damage that will be caused to the citizen by this means" and "must ask itself if, *under these circumstances*, there is a proper proportion between the benefit to the public and the damage to the citizen."[1098] This balancing act, weighing costs against benefits, must be "made against the background of the general normative structure of the legal system, which recognizes human rights and the necessity of ensuring the provision of the needs and welfare of the local inhabitants, and which preserves 'family honour and rights.'"[1099] Applying this analysis, the Israeli Court ruled that the balance was not met; the "relationship between the injury to the local inhabitants and the security benefit… as determined by the military commander, is not proportionate."[1100] The Israeli Court evaluated the evidence it had before it and, explaining why the route chosen was not proportionate, said:

> The gap between the security provided by the military commander's approach and the security provided by the alternate route is

minute, as compared to the large difference between a fence that separates the local inhabitants from their lands, and a fence which does not separate the two.[1101]

The Israeli Court held that when the fence's construction results in separating local residents from their lands, the military commander must ensure that the residents are able to access their lands.

Conclusion

Using proportionality analysis, the Israeli High Court analyzed complicated tradeoffs between competing social goods: security and liberty. It considered in detail the facts and evidence surrounding the security fence's construction. In conducting this analysis, it has capitalized on a long history of proportionality analysis in international law. Applying the law, the HCJ made the difficult decision holding that the route chosen caused too much harm to local Palestinians, proportionally to the detriment of the Israeli military's considerations and the requirement to provide for the safety of Israeli citizens. This decision demonstrated the HCJ's ability to be impartial and exemplified why all facts must be considered if a court is to make a fair and balanced judgment. The fact that the ICJ chose to ignore and not address proportionality or apply the particular facts and security risks faced and considered by the Israelis further undermines the advisory opinion's credibility and legitimacy and has led to injustice in the International Court of Justice.

The Advisory Opinion Omitted Facts Regarding Other Countries' Fences and Barriers

The ICJ ignored other unilaterally constructed security fences in its consideration of the Israeli fence. Respected researcher and writer David Makovsky noted the irony that "three countries—India, Saudi Arabia, and Turkey—condemned Israel at the UN General Assembly and voted to refer the Israeli terrorism prevention security fence to the ICJ for an advisory opinion even though they had themselves built barriers in areas contested by their neighbors."[1102] India built a 460-mile barrier in the contested Kashmir to halt infiltrations supported by Pakistan. Saudi Arabia built a sixty-mile barrier along an undefined border zone with Yemen to halt smuggling of weaponry. Turkey built a barrier in an area that Syria claims as its own.[1103] In August 2004, shortly after condemning the Israeli security fence at the United Nations, "the EU put out tenders for companies to construct a European separation fence to prevent migration into the EU from countries excluded from it."[1104] Another instance is UN Secretary General Ban Ki-Moon's home state, South Korea, which is protected from the North Koreans by a "concrete border wall, supplemented with security measures including a buffer zone covered with more than a million land mines, and backed by 37,000 US troops."[1105]

Israel's security fence is certainly not the first security fence of its kind nor will it be the last.[1106] Fences have similarly been built in Cyprus (1974) to separate Turks from Greeks and in Northern Ireland in 1921 to create a physical separation between Catholics and Protestants in Belfast ("peace line"). The United Nations itself began construction of a security barrier in 1991 to protect Kuwait from Iraq.[1107]

In March 2008, Egypt announced that it would build a stone and concrete wall about ten feet high to stop people from Gaza from illegally entering Egypt's borders, as they did when Gaza-based militants blew up the previous barrier in January 2008.[1108] In mid-2009, Egypt began construction of an underground barrier 80 meters from the Gaza border. The proposed barrier is projected to span nearly 10 kilometers (six miles) and runs 15-30 meters below ground.[1109] Egypt's barrier is also aimed at preventing terrorists and smugglers from continuing to utilize the numerous tunnels that run beneath the Gaza border region with Egypt.

Egypt's decision to construct the barrier inflamed relations with the terrorist group Hamas, which administers Gaza. That barrier, in contrast to Israel's security fence, resulted in little international pressure on the Egyptian government to halt construction.

The fence line between Egypt and Israel is being bolstered to stop terrorist infiltrators into Israel. Similarly, the line Israel and Syria is being fortified to protect Israel's northern border.

Moreover, the US is expanding its own fence near the California border between the US and Mexico for border control and homeland security purposes.[1110] Like Israel's terrorism prevention security fence, the effectiveness of the California fence has been proven:

> In the 1990's [before the fence's construction in 1997], the Border Patrol apprehended an average of 500,000 illegal border crossers a year in the San Diego sector, representing half of all apprehensions along the entire 2,000-mile border with Mexico. Last year, the total was 138,000.[1111]

Even within the United States, a fence has been built to separate Prince George's County, Maryland from Washington, DC in order to combat problems of drug dealing.[1112]

As is evident, there are many examples of unilaterally constructed security fences all over the world. One such historically heralded barrier is the Great Wall of China ... built for ancient security purposes. Walls have been built around ancient cities for protection, some with moats. None, however, have faced the level of international criticism and unfair bias and discrimination that Israel's terrorism prevention security fence has endured.

Chapter Twelve:
In the Aftermath of the
Advisory Opinion

An ICJ advisory opinion is technically non-binding. Nevertheless, the Court's role as the "principal judicial organ," established by the UN, dictates that it might well have a strong effect on international disputes. Dutch Judge Pieter Kooijmans acknowledged this in his separate opinion when he wrote, "an advisory opinion is brought to the attention of a political organ of the United Nations and is destined to have an effect on a political process."

Assessing the potential impact of the ICJ opinion, Israeli Attorney General Menachem Mazuz reported to Prime Minister Ariel Sharon that:

> It is hard to exaggerate the negative ramifications the International Court ruling will have on Israel on many levels, even on matters that lie beyond the separation fence. The decision creates a political reality for Israel on the international level that may be used to expedite actions against Israel in international forums, to the point that they may result in sanctions.[1113]

The International Court of Justice recognized its own substantial influence when it declared, "The authority and prestige of the Court attached to its advisory opinions and… here the organ or agency concerned endorses that opinion, that decision is as it were sanctioned by international law."[1114] Former Secretary-General Kofi Annan also addressed the influence of a non-binding advisory opinion when he emphasized the need to "heed and pay attention to the Court's decision; even though it is not enforceable, it has some moral bearing on what [the Israelis] do."[1115]

277

It is clear that the improperly decided and issued advisory opinion will serve as fodder for those who seek to bash Israel on a daily basis.[1116] Alan Dershowitz describes in his book, *The Case for Peace,* how differing international opinion-makers have utilized the ICJ advisory opinion in two ways: either to legitimize Israel's security fence or condemn Israel's security fence. Dershowitz demonstrates his point by comparing an article that accuses Israel of de-facto annexation, published in the Nation in July 2004, with one that draws a comparison to the peace lines of Belfast erected by the British Army.[1117]

The ICJ opinion goes well beyond the authority of the ICJ and interferes with Israel's rights as a sovereign nation-state. It goes so far as to call for action by other States and asserts its "view that the United Nations, and especially the General Assembly and the Security Council, should consider what further action is required to bring to an end the illegal situation" resulting from the construction of the terrorism prevention security fence. It addresses the legal duties of other States when it warns that all countries "are under an obligation not to recognize the illegal situation resulting from the construction of the wall and not to render aid or assistance in maintaining the situation created by such construction."[1118] Anyone who considers this to be a legal opinion, and not a political one, is blind to justice.

The opinion not only ignores the Palestinians' role in and responsibility over Israel's need to construct the terrorism prevention security fence in the first place, it also advises Israel to cease construction and make reparations. In Israel's Ambassador to the UN Dan Gillerman's words, the ICJ has "put the people who are trying to prevent terror and the victims of terror in the dock, rather than the terrorists themselves."[1119] And what about requiring the Palestinian Authority to stop the terrorist infiltration into Israel? "There is after all, one straightforward measure that would lead to the removal of the fence–and it is not more resolutions adopted in UN halls," as Ambassador Gillerman explained. He asserted that:

> It is, simply put, for the Palestinian side to abandon terror as a strategic choice and comply once and for all with its obligations to fight terrorism and incitement. As controversial as the fence may be, one

issue is beyond controversy: the terrorism that made the fence necessary is not only a grave violation of international law, it is the enemy of the Israeli and Palestinian peoples, and its eradication is an indispensable step to lasting peace.[1120]

The ICJ advisory opinion was rendered at approximately 3:00 p.m. on July 9, 2004 at The Hague. As Judge Rosalyn Higgins of the United Kingdom predicted in her separate opinion, the PA leadership immediately took steps to politicize the advisory opinion through the Arab Group at the United Nations. She recognized that:

> The request is not in order to secure advice on the Assembly's decolonization duties, but later, on the basis of [the Court's] opinion, to exercise powers over the dispute or controversy. Many participants in the oral phase of this case frankly emphasized this objective.[1121]

On the following Monday, July 12th, the Arab states called for the 10th Emergency Special Session of the UN General Assembly to convene to consider its draft resolution that required mandatory application of the ICJ advisory opinion and demanded Israel's compliance.[1122] The draft resolution also called for Switzerland, keeper of the Fourth Geneva Convention, to hold a meeting of all parties to the Convention to assure that the Convention's mandate, which in part prohibits participants from "building settlements on land they acquire through the use of force" in times of war, was being followed.[1123]

By the next day, the UN General Assembly had announced its intention to resume a meeting of its 10th Emergency Special Session to consider the Arab Group's resolution and on Friday, July 16th, the Emergency Session reconvened.[1124] Nasser Al-Kidwa, the Palestinian UN observer, expressed the Arab Group's intention to focus its efforts on the 25 nation European Union (EU), for the purpose of obtaining widespread support for the draft resolution.[1125]

John Danforth, then United States Ambassador to the United Nations, immediately condemned the resolution to the General Assembly, emphasizing that "the claims of each side must be accommodated, or there can be no agreement."[1126] Calling the resolution "not balanced" and "wholly one-sided," Ambassador Danforth pointed out that it never "mention[ed] the threat terrorists pose to

Israel. It follows a long line of one-sided resolutions adopted by the General Assembly, none of which has made any contribution to peace in the Middle East."[1127]

Turning his attention to Article 51 of the UN Charter, Ambassador Danforth criticized the ICJ's interpretation:

> The Court opinion, which this resolution would accept, seems to say that the right of a State to defend itself exists only when it is attacked by another state, and that the right of self-defense does not exist against non-state actors. It does not exist when terrorists hijack planes and fly them into buildings, or bomb train stations, or bomb bus stops, or put poison gas into subways. I would suggest that if this were the meaning of Article 51, then the United Nations Charter could be irrelevant in a time when the major threats to peace are not from states, but from terrorists.[1128]

On Tuesday evening, July 20th, the General Assembly, after debate and much inter-governmental negotiation, passed a modified resolution by a majority of 150 to 6, with 10 abstentions and 25 member states absent. The United States voted against the resolution.

The General Assembly Resolution ES 10/15 called upon Israel to comply with the advisory opinion issued by the International Court of Justice.[1129] Although the resolution, like the ICJ advisory opinion, is non-binding, it is, nevertheless, an additional inappropriate and politicized concrete effort to attempt to force Israel to dismantle the security fence. It is yet another harsh example of what Ambassador Gillerman termed, a "virtual reality... An alternate world in which there is but one victim and one villain, in which there are Palestinian rights but no Palestinian responsibilities, in which there are Israeli responsibilities but no Israeli rights."[1130]

Israel has made clear that the terrorism prevention security fence is, firstly, saving lives, and secondly, stopping terrorists. Because of this, Israel has also made it clear that, despite the ICJ advisory opinion, Israel will not dismantle the fence.[1131] Israel has continued to stress, however, that it will relocate the security fence if ordered to do so by its own court, the Israeli High Court of Justice.[1132] In keeping with this assurance, Prime Minister Sharon received cabinet approval on February 20, 2005 to reroute the security fence.[1133] The Israeli cabinet action passed 20 to 1 and complied with the *Beit Sourik* ruling of the High Court of Justice by relocating the planned route closer to the West Bank boundary in order to mitigate hardships to Palestinians living in the area.[1134] The changed route dramatically reduced the percentage of West Bank land on the Israeli side of the security fence from 15 percent to 7 percent.[1135] At this same meeting, Sharon received cabinet approval for his Disengagement Plan.[1136]

Interestingly, one of the ten states to abstain from voting for the General Assembly resolution adopting the ICJ opinion was Uganda, which sponsored the original "Zionism is Racism" resolution at the United Nations in 1975 which attempted to deny Israel its right to exist. As the *Jerusalem Post* put it, Resolution ES 10/15, while stopping just short of making this straightforward assertion, in essence, is different only in "degrees of baldness."[1137] The *Jerusalem Post* explained its comment saying, "The 1975 resolution said Israel has no right to exist. The 2004 resolution says Israel has no right to defend itself, *except* on terms agreeable to the international community generally and the Palestinians particularly, which is tantamount to no defense at all."[1138]

New language was added to the Arab Group's UN resolution during the course of debate and negotiation, calling for both the Palestinians and Israelis to comply with their obligations under the Roadmap and recognizing Israel's right to self-defense.[1139]

The Palestinian Authority expressed its delight at the passing of the resolution through its representative, Nasser Al-Kidwa, who announced that the PA's next step was to take the measure to the UN Security Council. Al-Kidwa said, "The debate is completed. It is now time for implementation and compliance, and at a later stage for additional measures."[1140]

The adoption of Resolution ES 10/15 was a clear accomplishment by the Palestinian and Arab leadership in their continued attempts to ostracize, criticize and demonize Israel. Ambassador Gillerman reacted to the resolution with indignation, stating, "It is simply outrageous to respond with such vigor to a measure that saves lives and respond with such casual indifference and apathy to the ongoing campaign of Palestinian terrorism that takes lives. This is not justice but a perversion of justice."[1141]

Following the passage of the General Assembly Resolution, the foreign ministers of the Non-Aligned Movement (NAM), a group of more than 100 nations representing approximately two-thirds of the UN, met on August 17-19 for their 2004 Summit in Durban, South Africa and issued a "Declaration on Palestine."[1142] The NAM Declaration, like the resolution and the ICJ advisory opinion, was non-binding. Nonetheless, it further politicized the situation in the aftermath of the advisory opinion by calling for sanctions and boycotts against Israel and advising UN member states to:

> Undertake measures, including by means of legislation, collectively, regionally and individually, to prevent any products of the illegal Israeli settlements from entering their markets consistent with the obligations under International Treaties, to decline entry to Israeli settlers and to impose sanctions against companies and entities involved in the construction of the wall and other illegal activities in the Occupied Palestinian Territory, including East Jerusalem.[1143]

Among other things, the NAM Declaration condemned Israel's construction of the security fence and Israel's right to self-defense.[1144] It referred to the findings in the ICJ opinion as "authoritative" and demanded that Israel stop construction on its terrorism prevention security fence, adhering to the ICJ view that the fence "violate[s] the Palestinian people's freedom of movement and the right to work, to health, to education and to an adequate standard of living."[1145] In yet another one-sided attempt within the UN to impose unjust and undeserved sanctions on Israel, including "preventing" any products of the illegal Israeli settlements from entering their markets; the NAM Declaration called for required acts, imposed only upon the State of Israel, and ignored any Palestinian obligations under the Roadmap.

Meanwhile, Israel formulated an Action Plan to present to the 59th UN General Assembly that outlined its priorities for the upcoming session and emphasized its dedication to the Roadmap. Israel declared that it:

> Hopes that member states will reject further escalation and resolutions on the issue. Our hope is that the Middle East agenda of the UNGA [(UN General Assembly]) will stop the biased anti-Israel activity and will reemphasize the essential immediate steps the two

sides have to take: ending terror and violence, and encouraging the Disengagement Plan and the Roadmap process. It is our hope that these steps will lead to the renewal of the dialogue toward a solution between the parties.[1146]

Israel's expression of hope was for naught. The 59th session and subsequent sessions of the UN General Assembly each have passed numerous anti-Israel resolutions, some of which reference the ICJ advisory opinion.

During the 60th session, just five days after the Israeli Court issued the *Alfei Menashe* opinion and despite Israel's rerouting of the fence in light of the *Beit Sourik* ruling, the Quartet commented on the security fence. It noted:

With concern the route of the Israeli separation barrier, particularly as it results in the confiscation of Palestinian land, cuts off the movement of people and goods, and undermines Palestinians' trust in the Roadmap process as it appears to prejudge the final borders of a Palestinian state.[1147]

Subsequent acts at the United Nations throughout the years, pushed and promoted by the PLO/PA as part of its plan for seeking statehood but for the additional purpose of maligning Israel and holding her out to be an apartheid racist criminal state, as seen through actions and statements from Durban in 2001, through the ICJ process and continuing to the present day is a true hijacking of justice that is most disturbing and must be rejected by all governments who respect law and equity. Appreciating the inappropriateness of the resolution, the United States indicated that it would use its veto power against any Security Council resolution designed to make the Advisory Opinion binding or to thwart Israel in her defense against terrorism, just as it did when vetoing the original Security Council resolution to request the ICJ Advisory Opinion on October 14, 2003.[1148]

The UN Security Council, the General Assembly, UN Agencies and Israel

As of February 2013, the United Nations Security Council itself has not passed a resolution implementing or even mentioning the ICJ's advisory opinion on Israel's security fence, nor has it passed any resolutions mentioning Israel's security fence. One attempt was made in February 2011 that consisted of a Palestinian-backed draft resolution denouncing Israel's settlement policy as an illegal obstacle to peace efforts in the Middle East. The US used their veto power to block the resolution.

However, the advisory opinion has been cited in numerous UN General Assembly Resolutions.[1149] In December 2006, by a recorded vote of 162 in favor to 7 against, the UN General Assembly passed a resolution to establish a Register of Damage arising from the construction of Israel's security fence.[1150]

Former UN Secretary-General Kofi Annan and current Secretary-General Ban Ki-Moon, among others, have referred to the advisory opinion as support for the notion that Israel should dismantle its security fence.[1151] In November 2008, the Secretary-General stated that the Assembly should ask for the Council's assistance in putting into practice the ICJ's advisory opinion on the security fence.[1152] The advisory opinion has also been cited in UN Reports, frequently in Committee meetings, and by representatives of member states in UN forums.[1153]

On July 9, 2009, on the fifth anniversary of the advisory opinion, the PLO and the PA called upon the UN, the United States, and the entire international community to "put pressure on Israel" to remove the security fence.[1154] Palestinian Prime Minister Salam Fayyad's cabinet asserted at the end of the meeting that:

> The court's decision that was adopted by the UN General Assembly establishes that the fence and the settlements, including east Jerusalem, are not legal... We demand that the UN Security Council and secretary general take action for Israel to uphold the court's decision.[1155]

UN officials marked the anniversary of the opinion by renewing their calls for the dismantling of Israel's security fence. At an international conference at The Hague on the ICJ's advisory opinion, Richard Falk, Special Rapporteur on the situation of human rights in the Palestinian territories occupied since 1967, proclaimed, "Tear down that wall, Mr. Netanyahu."[1156] The UN High Commissioner on Human Rights, Nava Pillay, called on Israel to "act in accordance with the advisory opinion of the ICJ" and noted that:

Five years after the ICJ issued its Advisory Opinion, the situation has not improved. Israel continues to disregard the views of the ICJ, and the Wall remains under construction. Since the ICJ Advisory Opinion, about 200 kilometers have been constructed, bringing the total amount constructed to 413 kilometers—60% of the planned 709 kilometre long route.[1157]

Additionally, the Office of the UN High Commissioner on Human Rights called on the Israeli Government to "comply with the Advisory Opinion of the ICJ and dismantle the Wall... and make reparation for all damage suffered by all persons affected by the wall's construction." It also called for an:

> End to the current regime of restriction of movement within, to and from the [Occupied Palestinian Territories], in order to ensure that Palestinian residents are able to exercise their rights, including their right to freedom of movement, right to work, right to education, and right to the highest attainable standard of health.[1158]

Likewise, the West Bank branch of the Office of the UN High Commissioner demanded that Israel dismantle the fence and pay reparations to Palestinians who suffered damages, calling the fence "but one element of the wider system of severe restrictions on the freedom of movement imposed by the Israeli authorities on Palestinian residents of the West Bank."[1159]

On February 1, 2013, the *New York Times* reported on a UN Human Rights Council Report accusing Israel of violating international law and committing war crimes by creating and maintaining settlements in the West Bank, calling upon Israel to halt settlement activity and withdraw all settlers.

The Policies of the United States in the Aftermath of the ICJ's Advisory Opinion

Speaking before more than 100 heads of state, heads of government and foreign ministers at the opening of the UN General Assembly on September 21, 2004, President Bush appealed to the Arab states to "end incitement in their own media, cut off public and private funding for terrorism, and establish normal relations with Israel."[1160] Reinforcing this point, US Ambassador John Danforth sent a letter to all Permanent Representatives of Missions to the United Nations outlining the United States' principal objectives for the 59th General

Assembly.[1161] Ambassador Danforth listed "Reducing Middle East Resolutions" as one of the five US aims, calling the resolutions "unbalanced" and advocating for the abolition of four UN bodies, which the United States considered "biased against Israel."[1162]

Later, the US vetoed Algeria's attempt to pass a resolution within the Security Council condemning Israel's defensive operations in Gaza. Ambassador Danforth criticized the Security Council's anti-Israel activities, characterizing them as "acts as the adversary of the Israelis and cheerleader to the Palestinians."[1163] While vetoing the resolution, Ambassador Danforth highlighted Israel's inherent right to self defense, noting that "until the Palestinians and those claiming to act in their name stop their use of indiscriminate acts of terror, Israel will likely continue to track down the terrorists wherever they may hide…"[1164]

The US House of Representatives passed House Resolution 713 in response to the "unjust decision at the Hague" that asserted that the ICJ "violated many of its own rules of jurisdiction where it ordinarily would have recognized the authority of the Supreme Court of Israel to decide such matters."[1165] The resolution, "deploring the misuse of the International Court of Justice by a majority of the United Nations General Assembly for a narrow political purpose," was meant to show America's support for Israel's right of self-defense and its dedication to the Roadmap.[1166] It placed the ICJ advisory opinion in proper perspective—as an opinion which must be rejected as biased, prejudiced, and ignorant of the truthful situation in which Israel finds herself.

Unlike the ICJ advisory opinion and the many one-sided resolutions adopted in the United Nations, the House Resolution acknowledged:

(1) the "three-year campaign of terror [endured by the Israeli people] that has included suicide bombings, snipers, and other attacks on homes, businesses, and places of worship and has resulted in the murder of more than 1,000 innocent people since September 2000;"

(2) Israel's right to self-defense against not only other nations but also that, as acknowledged by "United Nations Secu-

rity Council Resolution 1373 (2001), relating to international cooperation to combat threats to international peace and security caused by terrorist acts, and statements by representatives of other countries at that time, make clear that Article 51 of the United Nations Charter applies to self-defense against actions by terrorist groups against the civilian population of any country;" and

(4) the true defensive purpose, temporary nature, and the legitimate and proven results of the security fence.[1167]

The July 2004 Congressional Resolution also recognized the procedural weaknesses in the General Assembly's referral of the ICJ opinion and the impropriety of the ICJ's exercise of jurisdiction. It specifically included (1) the failure by the General Assembly to obtain a majority vote of member nations for its referral of the request for an advisory opinion to the ICJ; (2) the objection of numerous member States to the ICJ's exercise of jurisdiction; and (3) the decision of Israel's High Court of Justice on June 30, 2004 and the Government of Israel's expressed intention to adhere to the High Court's ruling.[1168]

The House predicted that the Palestinians and other anti-Israel groups would attempt to:

> use the ICJ's advisory judgment to advance their positions on issues committed to negotiations between the Israelis and Palestinians by advancing resolutions in the United Nations General Assembly, the Security Council, or elsewhere calling for the removal of the barrier and for the imposition of sanctions to force Israel to comply with the advisory judgment...[1169]

Specifically, the House's July 2004 Resolution:

(1) reaffirms its steadfast commitment to the security of Israel and its strong support of Israel's inherent right to self-defense;

(2) condemns the Palestinian leadership for failing to carry out its responsibilities under the Roadmap and under other obligations it has assumed, to engage in a sustained fight against terrorism, to dismantle the terrorist infrastructure, and to bring an end to terrorist attacks directed at Israel;

(3) calls on Palestinians and all states, in the region and beyond, to join together to fight terrorism and dismantle ter-

rorist organizations so that progress can be made toward a peaceful resolution of the Israeli-Palestinian conflict;

(4) deplores--

A) the misuse of the International Court of Justice (ICJ)) by a plurality of member nations of the United Nations General Assembly for the narrow political purpose of advancing the Palestinian position on matters Palestinian authorities have said should be the subject of negotiations between the parties; and

B) the July 9, 2004 advisory judgment of the ICJ, which) seeks to infringe upon Israel's right to self-defense, ;including under Article 51

(5) regrets the ICJ's advisory judgment, which is likely to undermine its reputation and interfere with a resolution of the Palestinian-Israeli conflict;

(6) commends the President and the Secretary of State for their leadership in marshaling opposition to the misuse of the ICJ in this case;

(7) calls on members of the international community to reflect soberly on

A) the steps taken by the Government of Israel to) mitigate the impact of the security barrier on Palestinians, including steps it has taken by order of its High Court of Justice, without being required to do so by the ICJ; and

(B) the damage that will be done to the ICJ, to the United Nations, and to individual Israelis and Palestinians, by actions taken under color of the ICJ's advisory judgment that interfere in the Roadmap process and impede efforts to achieve progress toward a negotiated settlement between Israelis and Palestinians; and

(8) urges all nations to join the United States in international fora to prevent the exploitation of the ICJ's advisory judgment for political purposes.[1170]

A few months after the ICJ's advisory opinion was released, the US Senate unanimously approved the 2005 Foreign Operations Appropriations bill, which appropriated funds to Israel for use in military and economic assistance. The bill expressed the United States' continued support for Israel in its struggle to defend herself against the Palestinian acts of terror and the anti-Israel efforts within the United Nations. Among other things, it called on American officials to block the one-sided resolutions within the UN condemning Israel's defensive actions.[1171]

In the wake of Israel's Disengagement from Gaza, an International Relations subcommittee of the US House of Representatives called a hearing to assess the post-pullout situation in Gaza. Subcommittee members expressed frustration at Abbas' approach to the PA's responsibilities.[1172] Assistant Secretary of State David Welch said "overall Palestinian Authority performance to date has been far from satisfactory." Representative Ileana Ros-Lehtinen, R-Fla., chair of the subcommittee, recognized that "lawlessness within the Gaza Strip and continued attacks against Israel has characterized the Palestinian response to disengagement…"[1173]

During "Operation Cast Lead," Israel's response to the 2008 rocket launchings from Gaza, the US Congress stressed its unwavering support of Israel's right to defend itself from attack. On January 8, 2009, the US Senate passed a bipartisan resolution, sponsored by Senate Majority Leader Harry Reid and Senate Minority Leader Mitch McConnell, which "Recognized the right of Israel to defend itself against attacks from Gaza and reaffirm[ed] the United States' strong support for Israel in its battle with Hamas, and supporting the Israeli-Palestinian peace process."[1174] The resolution expressed its support and commitment to "the welfare, security, and survival of the State of Israel as a Jewish and democratic state with secure borders" and again recognized Israel's "right to act in self-defense to protect its citizens against acts of terrorism."[1175] The US House of Representatives passed a similar resolution on January 8, 2009.[1176]

In 2011 Prime Minister Netanyahu appeared before a Joint Session of Congress, and received acclaim and applause for his sober explanation of the security challenges Israel was continuing to face from Hamas on her Southern border with Gaza; from Hezbollah on her northern border with Lebanon; with Syria on the north; and in facing the difficulties posed by the failure and refusal of Mahmoud

Abbas on behalf of the PLO and the PA to return to the negotiating table as envisioned under the Roadmap.

Addressing the United Nations in September 2011 and again September 2012, Prime Minister Netanyahu made it clear that the UN was truly treating Israel with a gross disregard for her rich history, culture, ancestral presence and rights in ancient Israel, contributions to society, commitment to democracy and human rights and her unwavering desire to achieve a final peace agreement with the Palestinians without preconditions.

In response to the November 2012 Hamas launching of rockets from Gaza, the Obama Administration fully supported Israel's right to defend herself in Operation Pillar of Defense. On November 18, 2012, the White House released a statement from President Obama which read, in part that

> The precipitating event here...that's causing the current crisis... was an ever-escalating number of missiles; they were landing not just in Israeli territory, but in areas that are populated. And there's no country on Earth that would tolerate missiles raining down on its citizens from outside its borders. So we are fully supportive of Israel's right to defend itself from missiles landing on people's homes and workplaces and potentially killing civilians. And we will continue to support Israel's right to defend itself." "Israel has every right to expect that it does not have missiles fired into its territory. If that can be accomplished without a ramping-up of military activity in Gaza, that's preferable; that's not just preferable for the people of Gaza, it's also preferable for Israelis....If we're serious about wanting to resolve this situation and create a genuine peace process, it starts with no more missiles being fired into Israel's territory." (*White House*)

And at the United Nations, the US has stood shoulder to shoulder with Israel, including threatening a veto of Palestine's application for full membership as a member state at the United Nations and voting against Palestine's November 29, 2012 successful bid for upgraded status as a non-member state observer.

The Measures Taken in the Aftermath of the ICJ Advisory Opinion Reflect a Reality in Which an Advisory Opinion is No Longer Just an Opinion

Subsequent to its receiving upgraded status at the UN, an emboldened Palestine has continued and renewed its calls for sanctions against Israel, calling for boycotts and renewing focus on the security fence as a de facto border. Israel has responded with announcements to expand planning for construction of homes in East Jerusalem and the corridor between Jerusalem and Maale Adumim. Palestine has threatened new legal attacks on Israel in various forums, including the International Criminal Court ("ICC"). The 2013 UN Human Rights Council Report will serve as a vehicle for the Palestinians to invoke the jurisdiction of the ICC, particularly Article 8 of the ICC Statute, the Chapter on war crimes. Surely, the advisory opinion of the ICJ will be cited in support of the next assaults upon Israel.

There is no question that the advisory opinion has had a substantial affect on Israel, enough to question whether the non-binding nature of an opinion has been compromised by the external results it causes. For instance, immediately following the opinion, the General Assembly passed Resolution ES 10/15 that called upon Israel to comply with the opinion. The PLO Representative to the UN also claimed that the opinion ended the debate and asserted that "it is now time for implementation and compliance, and at a later stage for additional measures."[1177] The NAM Declaration demanded Israel stop construction and the Secretary-General expressed his desire to put the opinion into practice. The General Assembly passed additional resolutions citing to the advisory opinion as authoritative.

How has this affected Israel? There is the constant threat of individual states imposing sanctions on Israel for the construction of the security fence, including the threat of arrest on war crime charges and acts against humanity for Israelis who have participated in the construction of the barrier. Opponents have said the US could "deduct expenses involved in the barrier's construction from the loan guarantees it had extended to Israel."[1178] However, the US, which recognizes the need and right of Israel to defend her people is highly unlikely to adopt any action adverse to Israel's interest relating to the security barrier. It is, however, expected that the issue of the security barrier will become an issue raised by human rights groups on college campuses and in public venues as evidence of apartheid and separation and, furthermore, as Israel's obstacle to peace. Furthermore, when linked to the claims that the settlements violate international law, Israel's opponents feel emboldened.

The EU is Israel's largest trading partner and imposed trade measures could be destructive on Israel.[1179] The EU has already shown its inclination to impose measures against Israel, "in the context of the latter's control over the West Bank and Gaza Strip."[1180] The EU has focused on goods coming from Israeli communities/settlements in the West Bank. Most recently, the Palestinian Authority has called for a full boycott on all goods manufactured not only in the Israeli communities/settlements on the West Bank but on all goods and services from all areas occupied by Israel outside the 1967 lines. Renewed talk of a Palestinian unity government in between Fatah and Hamas, hosted by Egypt, raises interesting questions about the future of relations between Israel and the Palestinians as Hamas' leader Meshal has called for Israel to be removed from all of Palestine, referring to all land between Jordan and the Mediterranean.

The issue of the security fence and the ICJ opinion has not diminished but rather remains in the arsenal of those opposed to Israel and her policies. A possible consequence of the advisory opinion being cited by courts in various countries is its long term effect on customary international law. Israel's High Court of Justice is "widely viewed as an independent and professional judiciary that is committed to the rule of law."[1181] As part of its practice, it has established that customary international law is automatically adopted as Israeli law, unless it is inconsistent with Knesset-enacted statutes.[1182] Customary law is created through custom and usage and there are many elements of an ICJ advisory opinion that demonstrate the opinions ability to become customary and binding. As we have seen, the opinions are often thought of as "an authoritative statement of the law."[1183] And, "past experience shows that they have considerable impact on the evolution of international law."[1184] Accordingly, the opinion could, as time continues, become viewed by some as binding in the context of having become accepted as customary international law. If that situation arises, the Israeli High Court of Justice could be put in a difficult situation: whether it should violate its general policy of adopting customary law.

Steadfast in its defense of Israel's sovereignty, in its various decisions on Israel's terrorism prevention security fence, Israel's High Court, the most respected and law-abiding court in the Middle East's only democracy, has ruled after full consideration, analysis and review that Israel is neither required to abide by the ICJ advisory opinion nor to take down the fence nor should it do so absent security arrangements that will properly protect Israel and her citizens.

The government of Israel has made clear that it will comply with Israeli High Court of Justice rulings, which do have the force of law. The US has continued to support this position. In fact, the US stands so strongly on this issue it has stated that should the Security Council attempt to make the opinion binding, the US would again use its veto power.

A Few Hopeful Signs that the Law-Abiding World Will Recognize Israel as a Respected Member and Acknowledge Her Right and Obligation to Defend her Citizens

There have been a few positive signs that some within the world community recognize Israel's right to build the terrorism prevention security fence in self-defense or in the very least indications that acknowledge the impropriety of the ICJ's advisory opinion. Plans by then PLO representative Nasser Al Kidwa to propose a further resolution threatening Israel with sanctions if it did not comply with the ICJ opinion were reportedly met with disdain by senior diplomats of major European Union countries who argued to Al Kidwa that "the issue of the separation fence in the UN forum has been exhausted, and must now move on to the political level in discussions between Israel and the Palestinian Authority."[1185] European Union diplomats have also reportedly expressed "growing dissatisfaction . . . over what they regard as the almost automatic opposition to Israel that is evident in the General Assembly and in many of its resolutions."[1186]

The UN General Assembly held a Special Session on January 24, 2005 to commemorate the 60th anniversary of the liberation of the Nazi concentration camps at Auschwitz. This meeting was especially historic, as it marked the first commemoration of the Holocaust by the General Assembly. This was the first time the UNGA convened a Special Session at Israel's initiative.[1187] The PLO was granted official observer status for the session and a number of Arab countries supported the calling of the Special Session.[1188] A number of Ambassadors from Arab countries participated in the session, which included addresses by Foreign Ministers from countries such as Germany and France.

Foreign Minister Silvan Shalom of Israel addressed the General Assembly and highlighted the continuing need to recognize the Holocaust:

> The lessons of the Holocaust are crucial today for [several reasons, one being] because today once again we are witnessing, against Jews and other minorities, that the same process of delegitimization and dehumanization, that paved the way to destruction. Let us not forget. The brutal extermination of a people began, not with guns or tanks, but with words, systematically portraying the Jew – the other – as less than legitimate, less than human. Let us not forget this, when we find current newspapers and schoolbooks borrowing caricatures and themes from the Nazi paper *Der Sturmer*, to portray Jews and Israelis.

> And finally these lessons are crucial today, because once again, we are witnessing a violent assault on the fundamental principle of the sanctity of human life . . . . For the Nazis, the destruction of one human being, or of a hundred, a thousand, six million, was of no consequence. It was just a means to an evil end.

> Today, again, we are pitted against the forces of evil, those for whom human life – whether the civilians they target, or their own youth who they use as weapons – are of no value, nothing but a means to their goals. Our sages teach us that "He who takes a single life, it is as if he has taken an entire world." No human life is less than a world. No ideology, no political agenda, can justify or excuse the deliberate taking of an innocent life.[1189]

The Foreign Ministry of Israel sponsored an exhibit entitled "Auschwitz—the Depth of the Abyss" in the main entrance hall of the United Nations. The exhibit featured the Auschwitz Album which displays visual evidence of the extermination process inside Auschwitz-Birkenau.[1190]

At the opening of its 60th session on September 15, 2005, Prime Minister Ariel Sharon addressed the UN General Assembly.[1191] Sharon's speech, which followed Israel's withdrawal from Gaza, received a positive reception which in prior years would have been unthinkable.[1192] Sharon reported that world leaders approached him in the halls of the UN, including some from Islamic countries, to congratulate him on following through with the Disengagement Plan.[1193]

The UN has held an annual Holocaust commemoration each January since then, most recently on January 27, 2013, International Holocaust Remembrance Day at the UN. Israel has been accepted into additional UN bodies and her Ambassador has chaired sessions at the UN. including serving as Vice President of the UNGA. While the UN Human Rights Council has continued to treat Israel as a pariah as evidenced by its late January 2013 report on Israel's settlements, Israel has expanded its working relationships with various UN representatives from countries throughout the world.

At the September 2012 address by Prime Minister Netanyahu to the UN General Assembly, this author was seated in the gallery. Iran's Foreign Minister attended the address delivered by PLO Chairman Mahmoud Abbas, after which he exited the Assembly hall with his delegation prior to Prime Minister Netanyahu's address. Only one representative was left at Iran's official table. When Prime Minister Netanyahu was introduced by Israel's Ambassador to the UN Ron Prosor to address the General Assembly, this author observed only one person stand and leave the Assembly hall: the representative of Iran. During his address, Prime Minister Netanyahu was clear in demonstrating that the real threat to the world is not Israel, but the nuclear intentions of the Islamic Republic of Iran. Displaying a diagram of a bomb, Prime Minister Netanyahu used a bold red marker to draw a clear red line to demonstrate the unacceptability of a nuclear capable Iran. The simplicity of the message received world press attention and strong applause from the delegates seated.

During his address, Prime Minister Netanyahu made it plainly clear that he and the Israeli government consider it to be their primary obligation to defend the people of Israel.

CHAPTER THIRTEEN:
The Victims

T
he key element missing from almost every discussion or argument about the security fence is the recognition that the heart of the debate is about people and their protection—that they be safe and secure in their homes, on buses and in restaurants, that they be free to walk in shopping areas, that children will be safe and that every member of society can enjoy the freedom to which they are entitled as a matter of right.

The security fence exists because of the victims, both those who have died or been maimed and those who are threatened with or at risk of future harm. The Arab-Palestinian-Israeli conflict is not a new reality for Israelis. Many have endured the conflict throughout their entire lives. And many victims of past acts of terrorism have lost or had their lives altered forever.

The fact that the International Court of Justice gave no regard to the victims is beyond conscience, beyond acceptability, beyond reason and without justice. It is important to remember these victims so that we recognize the full extent of the danger faced by future victims. These victims have taught Israel that it must protect and defend her citizens to ensure that they do not become the victims of the future.

The efforts to demonize and delegitimize Israel over her insistence on protecting her citizenry are vicious and motivated by hate, not by the pursuit of a common peace. The international community must take measures to counteract this anti-Semitic activity which threatens Israelis in their homes, cities, places of worship and in their daily lives. Simply put, Israel's construction of the security fence is necessary but not enough. Protecting future victims requires full recognition of all of those who have been lost. Recognizing past threats and attempts at the annihilation of the Jewish people as well as threats to annihilate the State of Israel since her establishment in 1948 must be viewed in the contemporary context of continued attacks by Israel's opponents acting under the guise of freedom fighting.

The hateful words about Israel from Abu Mazen of the PLO; the hateful words about Israel from Ahmadinejad of Iran; the hateful words about Israel from Khaled Meshal of Hamas; the hateful words about Israel from Hassan Nasrallah of Hezbollah; the hateful words from Holocaust deniers; the hateful words from those who advocate the denial of Israel's right to exist: these words must be denied dignity, denied platforms and denied legitimacy. They must, however, be taken seriously as words indeed matter as they are often precursors to acts of murder, terror and destruction. Future victims deserve protection ... not after they are victims ... but before they become such. In order to avert more victims falling to acts of senseless terror, heinous murder and vicious attacks perpetrated by hate, it is imperative for world leaders to take preventive and affirmative action.

While the International Court of Justice was deliberating at the Peace Palace at the Hague, hearings sponsored by the Dutch Center for Information and Documentation on Israel ("CIDI"), on behalf of Israeli Victims of Terrorism were held in the Old City Hall at The Hague. In the presence of members of the European Parliament, terrorist victims testified and an important resolution drafted by this author, who served as lead counsel at the hearings, was unanimously adopted by those assembled. It stated:

WHEREAS,

Terrorism, murder, suicide and homicide bombings are criminal acts

WHEREAS,

The use of young people as suicide and homicide bombers is unthinkable

WHEREAS,

Israel, a nation state accepted into membership at the United Nations in 1949, has the absolute right to defend herself and the obligation to protect her people

WHEREAS,

The Palestinian Authority has failed and refused to stop her people from crossing into Israel for the purpose of killing and maiming innocent citizens of Israel

NOW, THEREFORE,

Be it resolved and declared at The Hague on this the 24th day of February 2004 that

1. Terrorism and suicide bombings are acts of murder

2. The use of young people in criminal acts is unthinkable and must be stopped

3. Israel has the absolute right and obligation to defend herself and to protect her people

4. Israel has the absolute right and obligation to take all appropriate terrorism prevention security measures to protect her people

5. The Palestinian Authority is obligated to stop her people from crossing into Israel for any and all illegal purposes

6. The Palestinian Authority is obligated to use all monies given to her by the European Union, the United States, the Arab countries and other governments around the world for humanitarian purposes including education, health, and the building of a democracy and not for the funding of terrorist acts

FINALLY,

It is resolved and declared that murder and terrorism must stop.[1194]

The Terrorism Prevention Security Fence Works: It is Necessary to Protect the Victims of the Future

Israel's terrorism prevention security fence and Israel's affirmative acts to defend her citizens must, as a matter of law, be viewed in the context of protecting people from becoming future victims of terrorism. There is no question that the fence has proven highly effective in deterring suicide bombings and other attacks against civilians in Israel as there has been a documented sharp decline in the number of terrorist actions.[1195] IDF statistics show that from 2007 through 2012, the number of terror incidents in the West Bank was reduced by 96 percent.[1196]

The numbers speak for themselves. In 2002, prior to the fence's construction, 457 Israelis were murdered by Palestinian terrorists.[1197] The first phase of the fence was built where approximately 75 percent of suicide bombers attacking targets inside Israel came across the border.[1198] From 2000 to the end of the first segment's construction in July of 2003, 73 attacks were carried out by Palestinian terrorists, resulting in 293 Israelis killed and 1,950 wounded. During the period August 2003 until June 2004, following construction of the fence's first segment, successful terror attacks were reduced to 3.[1199]

Since construction of the security fence began, the number of Israelis murdered or wounded has decreased by 70 percent and 80 percent respectively.[1200] In 2009, the number of Israeli casualties was reduced to 8.[1201] Each lost life, however, is precious and even one death is unthinkable. While this sharp reduction can be attributed to a multitude of efforts, such as the success of Operation Cast Lead, Operation Pillar of Defense and the implementation of the Iron Dome, Palestinian terrorists—by their own admission—have been deterred by the security fence from gaining successful entry into Israel to carry out deadly suicide bombings. They have not, however, stopped trying. In late January 2013, Islamic Jihad terrorists were arrested in the West Bank plotting attacks upon Israel.

More Must Be Done to Stop Terrorism

Unfortunately, the fact that the number of suicide bombings in major Israeli population centers has declined does not mean that the threat is over. The Israeli military and intelligence agencies continue to thwart terrorist attempts and clashes with militants. According to Israel's Ministry of Foreign Affairs, in the years since Operation Cast Lead and prior to Operation Pillar of Defense, Hamas dramatically upgraded its rocket arsenal armed by Iran. Operation Pillar of Defense in November 2012 demonstrated that Hamas and Palestinian Islamic Jihad as well as other terrorist organizations have in their possession "thousands of rockets of various ranges, both standard and homemade, including Fajr 5 rockets (from Iran) which can reach the center of Israel."[1202]

While the number of Israeli casualties has significantly decreased on the whole since 2009, the number is slowly and sadly rising again. An all-time low was reached in 2009 with 2 casualties and 11 injured.[1203] 2010 recorded 5 casualties and 35 injured and 2011 recorded 3 and 81 respectively.[1204] In 2012 there were further increases as a result of Hamas rocket launchings, some of which reached as far as the areas of Tel Aviv and Jerusalem. Iron Dome and Israel's new defense system, David's Sling, reportedly destroyed eighty percent of all rockets launched toward populated areas during Operation Pillar of Defense.

Hezbollah has threatened to bombard Israel with tens of thousands of rockets from Lebanon. These rockets have been reportedly supplied by the Islamic Republic of Iran and the Syrian Arab Republic.

In January 20013, Israeli aircraft reportedly attacked Syrian munitions locations containing convoy of anti tank and anti aircraft missiles bound for Hezbollah in Lebanon, the Palestinians have threatened a Third Intifada. Unrest in the Palestinian Territories continues and it is unclear as to whether or not PLO and PA leaders have the will or the ability to control their own people, particularly in Gaza, which is under the continuing control of Hamas who continues to threaten attacks on Israel.

The security fence can stop people but not rockets. Security threats to Israel and her people continue.

It is essential and morally right that all human rights respecting and freedom-loving countries stand together at the United Nations, in both words and in deeds, to take an affirmative stand against terrorism and against the attempt to deny Israel's right to defend herself and her people. It is essential that the world remember the victims. It is essential that the world stand together against terror in all forms. It is essential that the world determine and collectively enforce measures to provide security for all peoples against those who hate, those who maim and those who murder. There is no justification for such despicable and heinous conduct that threatens or takes the lives of innocent victims.

Chapter Fourteen:
Israel's Battle for Justice in a Dangerous Neighborhood

An increase in terrorism and violence is not the only challenge Israel continues to face. Vicious attacks upon Israel's good name coupled with accusations that she is an apartheid racist criminal state who should be found guilty of war crimes violations have resulted in a negative view toward Israel in certain segments of world public opinion. As Prime Minister Netanyahu stated in his address to the UN in September of 2011:

> It's here year after year that Israel is unjustly singled out for condemnation. It's singled out for condemnation more often than all the nations of the world combined. Twenty-one out of the 27 General Assembly resolutions condemn Israel– the one true democracy in the Middle East.[1205]

The Security Fence's success lies in its physical existence, but it can do nothing to protect against and indeed contributes to negative public opinion and anti-Israel, anti-Zionist and anti-Semitic proclamations and acts throughout the world. The existence of the security fence as a barrier against suicide bombers seeking to carry out their mission of destruction can neither deter nor prevent terrorist leaders who plan, sponsor and support those missions. Despite Israel's unrelenting efforts to attain peace, anti-Israel sentiments within the international community continue to rise. The efforts to demonize and delegitimize Israel and her people are currently at an all time high, fueled largely by the PLO, the PA and their leaders who seem to believe that the realization of their own success is dependent upon the weakening and ultimate destruction of Israel.

The just cause of the Palestinian people in their search for self-determination and the establishment of a sovereign nation-state do not justify the physical, verbal and diplomatic attacks by its leaders on Israel. The just cause of the Palestinians, continually used by Arab governments and leaders for their own purposes, is itself a hijacking of the Palestinian pursuit of true nationhood.

Iranian Supreme Leader Ayatollah Ali Khamenei recently gave a speech during the recent 2012 Non-Aligned Movement (NAM) summit, where he called Israelis "ferocious Zionist wolves who digest the Palestinian people."[1206] Representatives from 120 UN member states attended the summit located in Tehran. UN Secretary-General Ban Ki-Moon was in attendance, and while he later "strongly rejected" the verbal attacks upon Israel, neither he nor any other representative walked out of the summit, protested or otherwise rejected the anti-Semitic statements made.[1207]

The recent increase in efforts to demonize Israel under the auspices of the United Nations cannot be ignored and should not be countenanced.[1208]

Anti-Israel proponents have changed the battlefield to the political arena. This can be seen though the intense lobbying efforts by Arab and Islamic states to successfully define Palestinians as "victims" of Israeli racism. Various political maneuvers displayed at Durban-related conferences demonstrate a new approach to delegitimize Israel, resulting in a declaration that has charged Israel alone—out of all UN member nations—with racism.[1209]

> Arab states at first sought to focus their attention on the defeat of Israel solely through military means, but they soon realized that the political battlefield was as important. The Durban Declaration and the follow-up processes it has spawned are the centerpiece of that political battle. By alleging Israel is racist—which they have done consistently since the mid 70's and the Zionism is racism resolution, Israel becomes a rogue state like apartheid South Africa and a country so vile in its moral character that there is no need to negotiate with it, only to impose upon it the right answers.[1210]

The issues of achieving a "responsible peace" with the Palestinians, as Prime Minister Netanyahu has said, is a primary focus of the Israeli government, as it is for the United States government.

The PLO's application for member state status at the UN asserted that the new Palestinian state would have as its borders those which existed before the 1967 war between Israel and her neighbors, with the Palestinian state to include the West Bank, Gaza, and East Jerusalem, with Jerusalem as its capital.[1211] It was Abbas' hope that the vote would "give legitimacy to their claims to statehood and, possibly, UN membership, while simultaneously boosting Arab and Muslim efforts to delegitimize Israel," while at the same time, unfortunately, undermining the Israeli-Palestinian peace process by "deluding the Palestinians into believing that they need not negotiate with Israel."[1212] However, without direct negotiations, there can be no final agreement to establish a universally recognized State of Palestine.

> Who better to supply those answers [that there is no need to negotiate with Israel] but the emblem of human rights, the United Nations. That is why Durban and the unilateral Palestinian move at the UN go hand-in-hand, a one-two punch. It is, therefore, imperative to point out that Durban and UDI [unilateral declaration of independence] are part and parcel of the rejection of a Jewish state; the racists are masquerading as anti-racists; and the organization that is supposed to protect human rights is run by those who oppose those same rights.[1213]

The deluge of violence and hatred directed toward Israel demonstrate how essential it is for Israel to not only maintain the security fence but for the need for the international community to recognize these factors and take necessary steps to combat them. As Netanyahu made clear in his September 2011 address to the UN:

> The world around Israel is definitely becoming more dangerous. Militant Islam has already taken over Lebanon and Gaza. It's determined to tear apart the peace treaties between Israel and Egypt and Israel and Jordan. It's poisoned many Arab minds against Jews and Israel, against America and the West. It opposes not the policies of Israel but the existence of Israel.[1214]

One only has to look at recent UN and world activities to get an accurate portrayal of the battle that those who favor peace and co-existence face. As Iranian President Mahmoud Ahmadinejad stated at the most recent September 2012 session of the UN General Assembly, instead of working towards a peaceful coexistence, he would prefer the Israeli-Arab conflict to be resolved by voting the "Zionist regime" out of existence.[1215]

Political Maneuvers to Delegitimize Israel Continue

Political maneuvers to delegitimize Israel and undermine the Israeli-Palestinian peace process continue within the UN. Ahmadinejad persisted in his unrelenting anti-Semitic rant at the UNGA calling Israelis the "uncivilized Zionists" and continued to defend his right to deny the Holocaust and "criticize the hegemonic policies and actions of the world Zionism" that have prevented "the world media to freely report and shed light on the realities."[1216]

The 67th Session of the UNGA became a platform for other public anti-Israel pronouncements as well. PA President Abbas described what he called "racist" attacks by settlers on Palestinians in collusion with the Israeli government, untruthfully concluding "that the Israeli government rejects the two-state solution."[1217]

Egypt's fifth President, Mohamed Morsi of the Muslim Brotherhood, also demonstrated his disdain for Israel and support for Palestine, calling for "immediate and significant measures to put an end to colonization, settlement activities, the alteration in the identity of Occupied Jerusalem" and a restoration of the "usurped rights of the Palestinian people."[1218] He called the Security Council an "arrangement agreed upon in an era very different from today's realities" and stated that the "delay in implementing the decisions of international legitimacy" is disgraceful.[1219]

Although only the Security Council can approve a grant of sovereign statehood, the General Assembly adopted, on November 29, 2012, a resolution approving upgraded non-member state observer status for the PLO. This procedure, opposed by the United States, Israel and seven other countries, avoids subjecting the PA to another US veto in the Security Council while still achieving a higher observer status, which is the membership category enjoyed by the Vatican, and which may make Palestine eligible for membership within certain UN specialized agencies and organizations.[1220]

The tactic used by Abbas is designed to portray non-member state observer status as a "validation of their unilateral declaration of statehood and use it to circumvent bilateral negotiations with Israel."[1221] Palestine has also been granted "full-fledged Palestinian representation to UNESCO, the science and culture affiliate of the United Nations."[1222] By executive order, President Abbas has changed the name of the Palestinian Authority to the State of Palestine.

Palestinian membership in UN organizations is expected to be the basis of the next round of political and legal challenges against Israel. For example, the International Criminal Court's 2012 determination that it does not have the authority to investigate Palestinian allegations of crimes allegedly committed by Israel within the territories could be revisited should the Palestinians use their upgraded status as a basis for ICC membership.[1223] The UN Human Rights Council Report invoking reference to the ICC is a further precursor of things to come. On the other hand, the PLO and the PA must necessarily consider whether or not Palestine, in seeking to become a member of the ICC and signing the Rome Statute, will subject itself to war crimes prosecution for sponsoring heinous acts of murder.

The Palestinians may also seek to use their upgraded UN status to return to the International Court of Justice in an attempt to essentially convert a non-binding advisory opinion into a potentially justiciable claim against Israel.

Israel's Battle for Security on the Frontlines of Terror

Among the many serious and contentious problems remaining between Israel and the Palestinians, the core issues of borders, refugees, security and the status of Jerusalem are all likely to fuel more terrorist violence against Israeli civilians. Tawfiq Tirawi, security advisor *to PA President Mahmoud Abbas,* has suggested that Palestinians can only successfully retake Jerusalem by terrorist violence:

> It is impossible for Jerusalem to be restored to us without thousands of martyrs. Anyone who thinks that America will restore Jerusalem to us is mistaken. It will never restore Jerusalem to us. And if it does not give us Jerusalem, how can it possibly give us

the Right of Return? . . . These two symbols require blood, action, efforts, resistance, and Palestinian unity.[1224]

There is little question that the security fence will continue to play an important role in Israel's self-defense and its battle for security on the frontlines of terrorism. There is also no doubt that Israel's ongoing battle for justice at the United Nations will continue.

Conclusion

The State of Israel, as every other sovereign country in the family of nations, has the right and obligation to protect and defend her people. No ruling, resolution or advisory opinion of the International Court of Justice should interfere with any nation's duty to defend her citizens, nor any citizen's right and entitlement to be defended by his or her country. To permit otherwise would not only be a travesty of justice but itself would lead democratic nations and freedom-loving people into an odyssey of the unknown.

Endnotes

Preface

1. "PM: Israel faces the 'Goldstone threat.'" *Jerusalem Post*, December 23, 2009, http://www.jpost.com/Israel/Article.aspx?id=164050.
2. "Speech by PM Netanyahu to a Joint Meeting of the U.S. Congress," Israel Ministry of Foreign Affairs, May 24, 2011, http://www.mfa.gov.il/MFA/Government/Speeches+by+Israeli+lead ers/2011/Speech_PM_Netanyahu_US_Congress_24-May-2011. htm.
3. *Ibid*
4. Stephen Harper, "Canadian PM Harper at Ottawa Conference on Combating Anti-Semitism," November 8, 2010, http://haitiholo-caustsurvivors.wordpress.com/anti-semitism/canadian-pm-i-will-defend-israel-whatever-the-cost-with-video/.

Introduction

5. *Legal Consequences of the Construction of a Wall in the Occupied Palestinian Territory*, Advisory Opinion, 2004 I.C.J. 131 (July 9), http://unispal.un.org/UNISPAL.NSF/0/B59ECB7F4C73BDBC85256EE-B004F6D20.
6. In fact, "never before in the history of the ICJ had so many states, apart from the states directly concerned, objected to the Court's granting an opinion requested of it." Michla Pomerance, "Jurisdiction and Justiciability: A Court of 'UN Law,'" *Israel Law Review* 38 (Winter/Spring 2005): 138.
7. *See* discussion *infra*.
8. Reports on the percentage of the security fence that is currently constructed as a concrete barrier fluctuate. Col. (Res.) Danny Tirza stated in a July 1, 2012 article that "less than 5% of the project is a concrete wall." Col. (Res.) Danny Tirza, "Israeli Security Fence Ar-

chitect: Why The Barrier Had to Be Built," *Al-Monitor*, July 1, 2012. http://www.al-monitor.com/pulse/originals/2012/al-monitor/israe-li-security-fence-architect.html.

Another source reported on April 9, 2012 that the "concrete wall comprises 10 percent of the barrier." Haggai Matar, "The Wall, 10 years on: The great Israeli project," April 9, 2012. http://972mag.com/the-wall-10-years-on-the-great-israeli-project/40683/.

The most updated information available from the Israeli Ministry of Defense is from 2007 which reports that 4 percent of the Separa-tion Barrier is an concrete wall. Eyal Hareuveni, "Arrested Devel-opment, The Long Term Impact of Israel's Separation Barrier in the West Bank," *Btselem*, October 2012. http://www.btselem.org/down-load/201210_arrested_development_eng.pdf.

9. UN SCOR, 6847th meeting, Doc. S/PV. 6847 (Resumption 1), Octo-ber 15, 2012, http://unispal.un.org/UNISPAL.NSF/0/52867621FF064 F5485257A9B004B1DBB; United Nations Meeting for Asia and the Pacific on the Question of Palestine, December. 16-17, 2003, http://unispal.un.org/UNISPAL.NSF/0/1FD0E666F772839585256E4E006 661F2; United Nations, "Bir Nabala Wall: A Devastating Blow to the Palestinian Economy," MA'AN Development Center, Febru-ary 2007, http://www.ochaopt.org/documents/opt_districtprofile_ maan_birnabala_wall_febr_2007.pdf; United Nations, "Apartheid Roads: Promoting Settlements, Punishing Palestinians," MA'AN Development Center, December 2008, http://www.ochaopt.org/ documents/opt_prot_maan_apartheid_roads_dec_2008.pdf; Unit-ed Nations, "Means of Displacement: Charting Israel's colonization of East Jerusalem," MA'AN Development Center, February 2010, http://www.ochaopt.org/documents/opt_prot_maan_MeansofDis-placement_feb_2010.pdf.

Chapter One

10. G.A. Res. 181 (II), UN GAOR, Special Sess., Doc. (A+B), November 29, 1947, http://unispal.un.org/unispal.nsf/0/7F0AF2BD897689B785 256C330061D253.

11. Romans used the term "Palestinia" in an attempt to minimize Jew-ish attachment to the land. "The Philistines", *Jewish Virtual Library*, accessed February. 4, 2013, http://www.jewishvirtuallibrary.org/ jsource/History/Philistines.html.

12. "Jordan," *Jewish Virtual Library*, accessed February 4, 2013, http:// www.jewishvirtuallibrary.org/jsource/arabs/jordan.html.

13. "The UN and Israel: Is the Jewish State Getting a Fair Shake from the World Body?" *FLAME: Facts and Logic about the Middle East*, ac-cessed July, 24, 2012, http://www.factsandlogic.org/ad_74.html.

14. "UN, Israel & Anti-Semitism," *UN Watch*, http://www.unwatch.

org/site/c.bdKKISNqEmG/b.1359197/k.6748/UN_Israel__Anti-Semitism.htm.

15. "Anti-Israel Resolutions at 62nd UNGA," *UN Watch,* http://www.unwatch.org/site/c.bdKKISNqEmG/b.3623963/.

16. The UN has applied the principle of proportionality, meaning that the actions Israel takes to defend her citizens must be proportional to the attacks on her citizens. The UN has said that Israel's attack actions are not proportional to Palestinian attacks. This is not what proportionality means in international humanitarian law. Here, the doctrine of proportionality requires Israel to take action that is proportional to what is necessary to stop the rockets attacks/suicide bombings. So since the rockets are still coming, Israel is not violating the law of proportionality. Allen Hertz, "Proportionality and self-defense," *Jerusalem Post,* December 18, 2012), http://www.jpost.com/Opinion/Op-EdContributors/Article.aspx?id=296497.

Chapter Two

17. It should be noted that there is no firm end date for the Second Intifada, although a ceasefire was reached on November 26, 2006.

18. Intelligence and Terrorism Information Center, "Anti-Israeli Terrorism in 2007 and its Trends in 2008," *Israel Intelligence Heritage & Commemoration Center* (May 2008): 51. http://www.jewishvirtuallibrary.org/jsource/Terrorism/antiisraelterrorism.pdf.

19. Don Radlauer, "An Engineered Tragedy - Statistical Analysis of Casualties in the Palestinian—Israeli Conflict, September 2000—September 2002," International Institute for Counter-Terrorism, November 29, 2002, http://ict.org.il/Articles/tabid/66/Articlsid/443/Default.aspx.

20. UN General Assembly Resolution 57/27 (15 January 2003) declares in part: (1) Strongly condemns all acts, methods and practices of terrorism as criminal and unjustifiable, wherever and by whomsoever committed; and (2) Reiterates that criminal acts intended or calculated to provoke a state of terror in the general public, a group of persons or particular persons for political purposes are in any circumstances unjustifiable, whatever the considerations of a political, philosophical, ideological, racial, ethnic, religious or other nature that may be invoked to justify them.

21. The State of Israel entered into an official peace agreement with Egypt in 1978. The agreement was signed at Camp David by the then President of Egypt, Anwar Sadat, and Israeli Prime Minister Menahem Begin). The State of Israel entered into an official peace agreement with Jordan in 1994. The agreement was signed in Washington by King Hussein of Jordan and Israeli Prime Minister Yitzhak Rabin. Sadat was assassinated subsequent to his reaching

a peace agreement with Israel; Rabin was assassinated subsequent to his reaching agreements with the PLO and subsequently with Jordan.

22. "Israel-PLO Recognition—Exchange of Letters between PM Rabin and Chairman Arafat," Israel Ministry of Foreign Affairs, September 9, 1993), http://www.mfa.gov.il/MFA/Peace+Process/ Guide+to+the+Peace+Process/Israel-PLO+Recognition+- +Exchange+of+Letters+betwe.htm.

23. "The Palestinian National Charter: Resolutions of the Palestine National Council," Israel Ministry of Foreign Affairs, July 1-17, 1968, http://www.mfa.gov.il/MFA/Peace+Process/ Guide+to+the+Peace+Process/The+Palestinian+National+Charter. htm.

24. Maj. Gen. (res.) Doron Almog, "Lessons of the Gaza Security Fence for the West Bank," Jerusalem Center for Public Affairs December 23, 2004), http://www.jcpa.org/brief/brief004-12.htm.

25. "The Agreement on The Gaza Strip and The Jericho Area," Israel Ministry of Foreign Affairs, May 4, 1994, http://www.mfa.gov.il/ MFA/Peace+Process/Guide+to+the+Peace+Process/Agreement+on+ Gaza+Strip+and+Jericho+Area.htm.

26. Lamia Lahoud, "Arafat: No Concessions on Jerusalem," *Jerusalem Post*, August 29, 2000, http://www.cdn-friends-icej.ca/noconsessions.html.

27. "Arafat in Morocco over Jerusalem," *BBC News*, August 27, 2000, http://news.bbc.co.uk/2/hi/africa/899064.stm.

28. In November 1987, Israeli forces entered the Jabaliya refugee camp to apprehend wanted terrorists. The "First Intifada" began on December 8, 1987, in response to an automobile accident between an Israeli and a Palestinian vehicle at the camp, which killed four Palestinians and wounded others. "First Intifada Begins," Israel Defense Forces, http://dover.idf.il/IDF/English/about/ History/80s/1987/0912.htm.
The First Intifada initially consisted of small riots throughout the Gaza Strip and disturbances such as stone throwing, but later escalated to shooting attacks. *Ibid.*
The Israeli Defense Forces shored up their units in Gaza as a result, but the Palestinian terrorist attacks of the First Intifada did not end until 1995. *Ibid.*

29. HCJ 7015/02 Ajuri v. IDF Commander, [2002], elyon1.court.gov.il/ Files_ENG/02/150/070/A15/02070150.A15.pdf.

30. HCJ 2056/04 *Beit Sourik Vill. Council v. Gov't of Isr.*, [2004], http:// www.unhcr.org/refworld/country,,ISR_SC,,ISR,,4374ac594,0.html.

31. *See* discussion *infra*.

32. *See* discussion *infra*.

33. "Breakdown of Fatalities: 27 September 2000 through 1 January 2005," International Policy Institute for Counter-Terrorism, Interdisciplinary Center Herzliya, http://212.150.54.123/casualties_project/stats_page.cfm.

34. Matti Friedman, "Israel Allows Small-Arms Shipment to Abbas," *Washington Times*, September 6, 2008, http://www.washingtontimes. com/news/2008/sep/06/israel-allows-small-arms-shipment-to-abbas/; Mark Lavie, "Israel OKs Arms for Police in West Bank," *Washington Post*, November 21, 2007, http://www.washingtonpost.com/ wp-dyn/content/article/2007/11/21/AR2007112100294_pf.html; "Israel Lets Egypt Ship Arms to Fatah," *Jerusalem Post*, December 28, 2006, http://www.jpost.com/Israel/Article.aspx?id=46209.

35. The Mitchell Report, *Jewish Virtual Library*, May 6, 2001, http://www. jewishvirtuallibrary.org/jsource/Peace/Mitchellrep.html.

36. *Ibid*

37. *Ibid*

38. "The Roadmap for Peace in the Middle East," *BBC News*, April 30, 2003, http://www.jpost.com/Israel/Article.aspx?id=46209.

39. Israel's Disengagement Plan, April 18, 2004, http://www. mfa.gov.il/MFA/Peace+Process/Reference+Documents/ Disengagement+Plan+-+General+Outline.htm. Available at www.mfa.gov.il.

40. *Ibid*

41. "G8 Leaders Welcome Israeli Disengagement Plan," Embassy of the United States in Israel, June 10, 2004, http://www.usembassy-israel. org.il/publish/press/2004/june/061001.html.

42. "Annan: UN Will Help Israel Implement Withdrawal Plan," *Jerusalem Post*, June 11, 2004, http://www.jpost.com/servlet/ Satellite?pagename=JPost/JPArticle/ShowFull&cid=1086934151991.

43. Jeremy Hurewitz, "Viewpoints on a Post-Arafat Middle East," *World Security Network Newsletter*, December 19, 2004, http://www.world-securitynetwork.com/showArticle3.cfm?article_id=10651, (interviewing Barry Rubin, director of the Global Research in International Affairs (GLORIA) Center, co-author of *Yasir Arafat: A Political Biography* and columnist for *The Jerusalem Post* who states that "70 to 80%" of the Israeli population believes they have no Palestinian partner).

44. *Ibid* (interviewing Shlomo Avineri, a professor of Political Science at the Hebrew University of Jerusalem, author of works on Middle Eastern affairs and political theory, and former Director-General of Israel's Ministry of Foreign Affairs).

45. *See Ibid* (quoting Barry Rubin).

46. "In Final Briefing to Security Council, Special Coordinator for Middle East Peace Process Says Need to Act Could Not Be Any Clear-

er," United Nations Information Service, November 15, 2004, http://www.unis.unvienna.org/unis/pressrels/2004/sc8244.html.

47. See Khaled Abu Toameh, "Abbas Denounces 'Zionist Enemy," Jerusalem Post, January 4, 2005, http://www.unitedjerusalem.org/index2.asp?id=537470&Date=1/6/2005.

48. See Ehud Ya'ari, "PeaceWatch #485: Beyond Arafat: Palestinian Politics in the New Era," The Washington Institute for Near East Policy, December 13, 2004, http://www.washingtoninstitute.org/policy-analysis/view/beyond-arafat-palestinian-politics-in-the-new-era.

49. Colin Powell, "Statement of Colin Powell on NBC's Meet the Press," January 2, 2005, http://www.msnbc.msn.com/id/6770575/ns/meet_the_press/t/transcript-jan/#.T_88Vxzk0pE.

50. See "GAZA CITY—Militant groups have agreed to temporarily halt attacks on Israel," Washington Post, January 25, 2005.

51. Ariel Sharon, "Speech of Israeli Prime Minister Ariel Sharon at a summit at the Red Sea Resort in Sharm el-Sheikh, Egypt," February 8, 2005, http://www.jewishvirtuallibrary.org/jsource/Peace/sharon020805.html.

52. Ariel Sharon, "Transcript of Ariel Sharon's speech at Egypt summit," CNN.com, February 8, 2005, http://edition.cnn.com/2005/WORLD/meast/02/08/transcript.sharon/index.html.

53. Ibid

54. Mahmoud Abbas, "Transcript of Mahmoud Abbas' speech at Egypt summit," CNN.com, February 8, 2005, http://edition.cnn.com/2005/WORLD/meast/02/08/transcript.abbas/.

55. "Mideast Cease-Fire Expected Tuesday," CNN.com, February 7, 2005, http://www.cnn.com/2005/WORLD/meast/02/07/mideast/index.html.

56. "Speech of US President George W. Bush Before European Leaders in Brussels, Belgium," New York Times, February 21, 2005, http://www.nytimes.com/2005/02/21/international/europe/21wire-ptex.html?.

57. Ibid

58. "Cabinet Approves Disengagement Plan and Security Fence Route," Israel Ministry of Foreign Affairs, February 20, 2005, http://www.mfa.gov.il/MFA/Government/Communiques/2005/Cabinet+communique+20-Feb-2005.htm.

59. Ibid

60. Ariel Sharon, "Speech of Prime Minister Ariel Sharon before the Conference of Presidents of Major American Jewish Organizations on February 20, 2004," http://www.mfa.gov.il/MFA/Government/Speeches+by+Israeli+leaders/2005/Address+by+PM+Sharon+to+the+Conference+of+Presidents+20-Feb-2005.htm.

61. Greg Myre, "Sharon Gets A Big Lift With Approval of Gaza Pull-

out," *New York Times*, February 22, 2005, http://www.nytimes.com/2005/02/21/world/africa/21iht-sharon.html.

62. *Ibid, see* "Speech of Prime Minister Ariel Sharon before the Conference of Presidents of Major American Jewish Organizations on February 20, 2004," http://www.mfa.gov.il/MFA/Government/Speeches+by+Israeli+leaders/2005/Address+by+PM+Sharon+to+the+Conference+of+Presidents+20-Feb-2005.htm.

63. "Relocation of Residence in the Gaza Strip and Four West Bank Communities Prohibited," *Israel Ministry of Foreign Affairs*, March 20, 2005, http://www.mfa.gov.il/MFA/Government/Communiques/2005/Relocation+of+residence+into+the+Gaza+Strip+prohibited+17-Mar-2005.htm.

64. Amos Harel and Anon Regular, "Israel Hands Over Tul Karm to PA Security Control," *Haaretz*, March 21, 2005, http://www.haaretz.com/news/israel-hands-over-tul-karm-to-pa-security-control-1.153671.

65. *Ibid*

66. Kenzo Oshima, Press Statement of UN Security Council President on Israeli Disengagement From Gaza Strip, SC/8480, August 24, 2005), http://www.un.org/News/Press/docs/2005/sc8480.doc.htm.

67. IDF Spokesman, "Exit of IDF Forces from the Gaza Strip Completed," *Israel Ministry of Foreign Affairs*, September 12, 2005, http://www.mfa.gov.il/MFA/Government/Communiques/2005/Exit+of+IDF+Forces+from+the+Gaza+Strip+completed+12-Sep-2005.htm?WBCMODE=PresentationUnpublishedMinisters+and+Senior+Officials+of+the+31st+Government+of+Israel.

68. *Ibid*

69. Steven Erlanger and Greg Myre, "2 Gaza Synagogues Cleared of Settlers: Israeli Army and Police Move to End Resistance by Most Fervent Protesters," *International Herald Tribune*, August 19, 2005, http://garden.egloos.com/10002538/post/17358.

70. *Ibid*

71. Matthew Gutman, "An Orgy of Looting and Arson," *Jerusalem Post*, September 13, 2005, http://saveisraelcampaign.com/atad/Articles.asp?article_id=6872.

72. Remarks by President [George W. Bush] at Republican Jewish Coalition 20th Anniversary Luncheon, Andrew W. Mellon Auditorium, Washington, DC, September 21, 2005, http://georgewbush-whitehouse.archives.gov/news/releases/2005/09/20050921-1.html.

73. Herb Keinon, "Bush: No More Steps Till Gaza is Quiet," *Jerusalem Post*, September 15, 2005, http://saveisraelcampaign.com/atad/Articles.asp?article_id=6909.

74. Yossi Verter, "Netanyahu Quits Government Over Disengagement," *Haaretz*, August 7, 2005, http://www.haaretz.com/news/netanyahu-

quits-government-over-disengagement-1.166110.

75. *Ibid*

76. Lally Weymouth, "A 'Fateful Step,'" *Washington Post*, September 11, 2005, http://www.washingtonpost.com/wp-dyn/content/article/2005/09/09/AR2005090902458.html.

77. *Ibid*

78. Ariel Sharon, "Speech of Prime Minister Ariel Sharon at the UN General Assembly 60th Session," September 15, 2005, http://www.mfa.gov.il/MFA/Government/Speeches+by+Israeli+leaders/2005/PM+Sharon+addresses+the+UN+General+Assembly+15-Sep-2005.htm.

79. Arieh O'Sullivan, "Mofaz Defends Decision on Synagogues," *Jerusalem Post*, September 13. 2005, http://www.unitedjerusalem.org/index2.asp?id=636535&Date=9/13/2005.

80. *Ibid*

81. *See* Scott Wilson, "Arafat Cousin Who Formerly Led Security Forces in Gaza Shot Dead," *Washington Post*, September 7, 2005, http://www.washingtonpost.com/wp-dyn/content/article/2005/09/06/AR2005090601660.html.

82. "Gaza: Gunmen Set Up Checkpoints," *Ynetnews.com*, September 16, 2005, http://www.ynetnews.com/articles/0,7340,L-3142822,00.html.

83. Middle East Quartet Statement, September 20, 2005, http://www.consilium.europa.eu/ueDocs/cms_Data/docs/pressdata/EN/declarations/86284.pdf.

84. Diane Bahur-Nir and Ali Waked, "'Israel Will Eventually Disappear'," *Yedioth Ahronot*, June 24, 2005, http://www.ynetnews.com/articles/0,7340,L-3111238,00.html.

85. "Commander of Military Wing Women's Unit: 'Our Members Yearn for Martyrdom'," MEMRI Special Dispatch, *MEMRI*, September 8, 2005, http://www.memri.org/report/en/0/0/0/0/0/0/94/1470.htm.

86. *Ibid*

87. *Ibid*

88. Sarah Al Deeb, "Tens of Thousands Gather for Hamas Rally," *Washington Post*, September 14, 2005.

89. "Dealers Smuggle Weapons Into Gaza From Egypt," *New York Times*, September 15, 2005, http://www.nytimes.com/2005/09/15/international/middleeast/15GAZA.html?_r=1&fta=y.

90. Address by Deputy Prime Minister and Minister of Foreign Affairs Silvan Shalom to United Nations 60th General Assembly, September 20, 2005, http://www.mfa.gov.il/MFA/Government/Speeches+by+Israeli+leaders/2005/Address+by+FM+Shalom+to+the+UN+General+Assembly+20-Sep-2005.htm.

91. *See* Lara Sukhtian, "Palestinian Leader Appears Weak, Isolated," *Associated Press*, September 20, 2005, http://www.kibush.co.il/show_

file.asp?num=8572.

92. *Ibid*

93. *Ibid*

94. *Ibid*

95. *Ibid*

96. Speech of President George W. Bush at the National Building Museum, Washington, DC, on Sept. 14, 2005, http://www.imakenews. com/jcrcgw/e_article000459518.cfm?x=b11,0,w.

97. Remarks by the President [George W. Bush] at Republican Jewish Coalition 20th Anniversary Luncheon, Andrew W. Mellon Auditorium, Washington, DC, September 21, 2005, http://georgewbush-whitehouse.archives.gov/news/releases/2005/09/20050921-1.html.

98. Herb Keinon, "Bush: No More Steps Till Gaza is Quiet," *Jerusalem Post*, September 15, 2005, http://www.pressmon.com/cgi-bin/press_view.cgi?id=744357.

99. Middle East Quartet Statement, Sept. 20, 2005, http://www.consilium.europa.eu/ueDocs/cms_Data/docs/pressdata/EN/declarations/86284.pdf.

100. *Ibid*

101. *See* Manfred Gerstenfeld, "The EU Constitutional Crisis and Its Impact on Israel," *Jerusalem Viewpoints* 532 (July 1, 2005): 9. http://jcpa. org/article/the-eu-constitutional-crisis-and-its-impact-on-israel/.

102. *See* Statement by FM Shalom After Meeting with FM Kasuri, Israel Ministry of Foreign Affairs, September 1, 2005.
http://www.mfa.gov.il/MFA/Government/Speeches+by+Israeli+leaders/2005/Statement+by+FM+Shalom+after+meeting+with+Pakistan+FM+Kasuri+1-Sep-2005.htm?WBCMODE=PresentationUnpArab+Work+-+A+poem?DisplayMode=print.

103. Address by Deputy Prime Minister and Minister of Foreign Affairs Silvan Shalom to the United Nations 60th General Assembly, http:// www.un.org/webcast/ga/60/statements/isr050920eng.pdf.

104. Scott Wilson, "Hamas Sweeps Palestinian Elections, Complicating Peace Efforts in Mideast," *Washington Post*, January 27, 2006, http:// www.washingtonpost.com/wp-dyn/content/article/2006/01/26/ AR2006012600372.html.

105. "Palestinians Urge Israel Not to Interfere," *Associated Press*, September 17, 2005, http://www.astandforjustice.org/2005/9/09-17-07. htm.

106. *Ibid*

107. *Ibid*

108. Paul Morro, "International Reaction to the Palestinian Unity Government," Congressional Research Service Report, Congressional Research Service, May 9, 2007, http://www.fas.org/sgp/crs/mideast/ RS22659.pdf.

109. Ruthie Blum Leibowitz, "One On One: 'I Was the Resident Skeptic'," *Jerusalem Post*, February 12, 2009, http://www.jpost.com/Features/FrontLines/Article.aspx?id=132715.

110. *See Ibid*

111. Dina Kraft, "Israel Withdraws From Gaza as Truce Begins, Unsteadily," *New York Times*, November 27, 2006, http://www.nytimes.com/2006/11/27/world/middleeast/27mideast.html.

112. *Ibid*

113. *Ibid*

114. Jeremy M. Sharp, "Lebanon: The Israel-Hamas-Hezbollah Conflict," CRS Report for Congress, September 15, 2006, http://www.fas.org/sgp/crs/mideast/RL33566.pdf.

115. Paul Morro, "International Reaction to the Palestinian Unity Government," CRS Report for Congress, May 9, 2007, http://www.fas.org/sgp/crs/mideast/RS22659.pdf.

116. *Ibid*

117. *Ibid*

118. "A Year Since the Hamas Takeover of Gaza," *Israel Ministry of Foreign Affairs*, June 16, 2008, http://www.mfa.gov.il/MFA/Terrorism-+Obstacle+to+Peace/Hamas+war+against+Israel/A+year+since+the+Hamas+takeover+of+Gaza+-+June+2008.htm.

119. *Ibid*

120. Scott Wilson, "Under Pressure, Palestinian Territories Pull Apart," *Washington Post*, March 10, 2007, http://www.washingtonpost.com/wp-dyn/content/article/2007/03/09/AR2007030902198.html?nav=emailpage.

121. *Ibid*

122. "Israel, Hamas Begin Truce With Both Sides Skeptical," *Bloomberg.com*, June 19, 2008, http://www.bloomberg.com/apps/news?pid=newsarchive&sid=antRN3ZYhjVY&refer=europe.

123. "Quartet," *Haaretz*, July 19, 2012, http://www.haaretz.com/meta/Tag/Quartet?viewAll=LatestArticles&page=1.

124. *Ibid*

125. Middle East Quartet, Statement on the Appointment of Tony Blair as Envoy, June 27, 2007, http://www.jewishvirtuallibrary.org/jsource/Peace/quartet062707.html (numbers added).

126. *Ibid*

127. Middle East Quartet Statement, September 23, 2007, http://www.eu-un.europa.eu/articles/fr/article_7328_fr.htm.

128. *Ibid*

129. The Office of Tony Blair, "Blair Announces Moves to Give Impetus to Palestinian Economy," The Office of Tony Blair, November 19 2007, http://www.tonyblairoffice.org/index.php/news/entry/41/

130. Howard LaFranchi, "Global Donors Exceed Palestinian Expecta-

tions at Paris Conference," *The Christian Science Monitor*, Decemeber 19, 2007, http://www.csmonitor.com/2007/1219/p06s01-woeu.html.

131. *Ibid*

132. Middle East Quartet Statement, December 17, 2007, http://www.consilium.europa.eu/uedocs/cms_data/docs/pressdata/en/declarations/97741.pdf.

133. "Berlin Conference Pledges Security Aid for Palestinians," *AFP*, June 24, 2008, http://www.unitedjerusalem.org/index2.asp?id=1084517&Date=6/24/2008.

134. Tim McGirk, "Tony Blair on Restarting the Middle East Peace Process," *Time*, April 8, 2009, http://www.time.com/time/world/article/0,8599,1889926,00.html.

135. *Ibid*

136. *Ibid*

137. The Office of Tony Blair, "Gaza Needs Larger and More Predictable Transfers of Cash, Says Tony Blair," The Office of Tony Blair, April 7, 2009, http://www.tonyblairoffice.org/quartet/news-entry/gaza-needs-larger-and-more-predictable-transfers-of-cash-says-tony-blair/.

138. The Office of Tony Blair, "Egypt Conference Sees Donors Pledge $4.4billion for Gaza Reconstruction and Development," The Office of Tony Blair, March 2, 2009, http://www.tonyblairoffice.org/quartet/news-entry/egypt-conference-sees-donors-pledge-4.4-billion-for-gaza-reconstruction-and/

139. Middle East Quartet Statement, May 4, 2004, http://www.un.org/News/dh/infocus/middle_east/quartet-comque-4may04.htm

140. Middle East Quartet Statement, September 22, 2004, http://www.un.org/News/Press/docs/2004/sg2091.doc.htm

141. Quartet Envoys Meetings with Israeli and Palestinian Negotiators, United Nations Special Coordinator for the Middle East Peace Process (UNSC), December 14, 2011.

142. Middle East Quartet Statement, April 11, 2012, http://www.un.org/News/Press/docs//2012/sg2182.doc.htm.

143. US Department of State, Announcement of General James Jones as Special Envoy for Middle East Security by Secretary Rice, November 28, 2007, http://merln.ndu.edu/archivepdf/NEA/State/95838.pdf.

144. *Ibid*

145. David Ignatius, "Gen. Jones: Mideast Facilitator on Board," *Washington Post*, December 7, 2008, http://www.realclearpolitics.com/articles/2008/12/gen_jones_can_get_anyone_to_wo.html.

146. *Ibid*

147. US Department of State, "Palestinian Security Forces Training Center Opens," US Department of State, March 17, 2009, http://www.

state.gov/r/pa/prs/ps/2009/03/120446.htm.

148. David Horovitz, "The Enemy is Getting Stronger, But So Are We," *Jerusalem Post*, November 20, 2008, http://www.jpost.com/Features/Article.aspx?id=121263.

149. David Ignatius, "Gen. Jones: Mideast Facilitator on Board," December 7, 2008, http://www.realclearpolitics.com/articles/2008/12/gen_jones_can_get_anyone_to_wo.html.

150. Helene Cooper, "National Security Pick: From a Marine to a Mediator," *New York Times*, November 28, 2008 (quoting David Makovsky of the Washington Institute for Near East Policy), http://www.nytimes.com/2008/11/29/us/politics/29jones.html.

151. Anti-Israeli Terrorism in 2007 and its Trends in 2008.

152. *See* Helene Cooper, "National Security Pick: From a Marine to a Mediator"

153. Scott Wilson, "Under Pressure, Palestinian Territories Pull Apart," *Washington Post*, March 10, 2007, http://www.washingtonpost.com/wp-dyn/content/article/2007/03/09/AR2007030902198.html?nav=emailpage.

154. Anti-Israel Terrorism in 2007 and its Trends in 2008.

155. "The Hamas Terror War Against Israel," *Israel Ministry of Foreign Affairs*, January 1, 2009, http://www.mfa.gov.il/MFA/Terrorism+Obstacle+to+Peace/Hamas+war+against+Israel/Missile+re+from+Gaza+on+Israeli+civilian+targets+Aug+2007.htm.

156. Anti-Israel Terrorism in 2007 and its Trends in 2008.

157. Carol Migdalovitz, "Israeli-Palestinian Peace Process: The Annapolis Conference," CRS Report for Congress, *Federation of American Scientists*, December 7, 2007, http://www.fas.org/sgp/crs/mideast/RS22768.pdf.

158. "Quartet Press Statement," US Dept, of State, November 9, 2008, http://merln.ndu.edu/archivepdf/NEA/State/111664.pdf.

159. S.C. Res. 1850, UN SCOR, 6045th meeting, Doc. S/RES/1850, December 16, 2008, *available at* http://unispal.un.org/UNISPAL.NSF/0/7F7430A137000C4E85257523004CCADF.

160. "Statement Following Adoption of UN Security Council Resolution 1850," *Israel Ministry of Foreign Affairs*, December 16, 2008, http://www.mfa.gov.il/MFA/About+the+Ministry/MFA+Spokesman/2008/Statement_UN_Security_Council_resolution_1850_16-Dec-2008.htm.

161. "Remarks With Quartet Members," US Department of State, December 15, 2008, http://merln.ndu.edu/archivepdf/NEA/State/113219.pdf.

162. *Ibid*

163. "President Bush Meets with President Abbas of the Palestinian Authority," The White House, December 19, 2008, 1:13 PM, http://

merln.ndu.edu/archivepdf/NEA/WH/20080925-5.pdf.

164. "FM Livni Press Conference on IDF Operation in Gaza," *Israel Ministry of Foreign Affairs*, December 31, 2008, http://www.mfa.gov.il/MFA/Government/Speeches+by+Israeli+leaders/2008/FM_Livni_press_conference_IDF_operation_Gaza_31-Dec-2008.htm.

165. *Ibid*

166. Dan Eggen, "Bush Blames Hamas for Starting Gaza Conflict," *Washington Post*, January 5, 2009, 12:40 PM, http://www.washingtonpost.com/wp-dyn/content/article/2009/01/05/AR2009010501150.html.

167. "Operation Cast Lead – Israel Defends its Citizens," Isr. Ministry of Foreign Affairs, accessed September 21, 2012, http://www.mfa.gov.il/GazaFacts/About/Operation-Cast-Lead-against-Hamas.htm.

168. *Ibid*

169. "Security Council Calls For Immediate, Durable, Fully Respected Ceasefire," UN Dept. of Pub. Info., January 8, 2009, http://www.un.org/News/Press/docs/2009/sc9567.doc.htm.

170. "Statement by Ambassador Gabriela Shalev to the UN Security Council," *Israel Ministry of Foreign Affairs*, January 8, 2009, http://www.mfa.gov.il/MFA/Foreign+Relations/Israel+and+the+UN/Speeches+-+statements/Amb_Shalev_UN_Security_Council_8-Jan-2009.htm.

171. Condoleezza Rice, "Remarks at the UN Security Council Session on the Situation in the Middle East," January 8, 2009, http://2001-2009.state.gov/secretary/rm/2009/01/113698.htm.

172. Interview with President Obama, "'This Week' Transcript: Barack Obama," *ABC News*, January 11, 2009, http://abcnews.go.com/ThisWeek/Economy/story?id=6618199&page=2.

173. "Memorandum of Understanding Between Israel and the United States Regarding Prevention of the Supply of Arms and Related Materiel to Terrorist Groups," *Israel Ministry of Foreign Affairs*, January 16, 2009, http://www.mfa.gov.il/MFA/Peace+Process/Reference+Documents/Israel-US_Memorandum_of_Understanding_16-Jan-2009.htm.

174. Robert Wood, "US Welcomes Agreement on Gaza Weapons Smuggling," US State Dept., March 16, 2009, http://www.state.gov/r/pa/prs/ps/2009/03/120436.htm.

175. President Barack Obama, "Remarks by President Obama to the Turkish Parliament," The White House, April 6, 2009, http://www.whitehouse.gov/the_press_office/Remarks-By-President-Obama-To-The-Turkish-Parliament/.

176. "Remarks by President Obama and Prime Minister Netanyahu of Israel in Press Availability," The White House, May 18, 2009, http://www.whitehouse.gov/the_press_office/Remarks-by-President-Obama-and-Israeli-Prime-Minister-Netanyahu-in-press-availability/.

177. Robert Satloff, "The Obama-Netanyahu Meeting: Analysis and Assessment," The Washington Institute for Near East Policy, May 21, 2009, http://www.washingtoninstitute.org/policy-analysis/view/the-obama-netanyahu-meeting-analysis-and-assessment.

178. Dr. Dore Gold, "The US and "Defensible Borders": How Washington Has Understood UN Security Council Resolution 242 and Israel's Security Needs," *Israel's Critical Security Requirements for Defensible Borders: The Foundation for a Viable Peace,* ed. Dan Diker, (Jerusalem Center for Public Affairs, 2011): 52.

179. Dr. Dore Gold, "Preface: Israel's Continuing Requirements for Defensible Borders in a Rapidly Changing Middle East," *Israel's Critical Security Requirements for Defensible Borders: The Foundation for a Viable Peace,* ed. Dan Diker, (Jerusalem Center for Public Affairs, 2011): 6.

180. "Transcript: Israeli Prime Minister Binyamin Netanyahu's address to Congress," *Washington Post,* May 24, 2011, http://www.washingtonpost.com/world/israeli-prime-minister-binyamin-netanyahus-address-to-congress/2011/05/24/AFWY5bAH_story.html (pp. 1-5).

181. Barack Obama, President Obama's 2013 State of the Union Address, *NYTimes.com,* February 12, 2013, http://www.nytimes.com/2013/02/13/us/politics/obamas-2013-state-of-the-union-address.html.

182. "Netanyahu Sworn in as Israel's Prime Minister," *Haaretz,* March 31, 2009, 11:31 PM, http://www.haaretz.com/news/netanyahu-sworn-in-as-israel-s-prime-minister-1.273265.

183. Benjamin Netanyahu, "Why Israel Needs a Fence," *New York Times,* July 13, 2004, http://www.nytimes.com/2004/07/13/opinion/why-israel-needs-a-fence.html.

184. *Ibid*

185. *Ibid*

186. *Ibid*

187. *Ibid*

188. Rebecca Anna Stoil and Jonny Hadi, "PM: We'll Keep Security Fence In Place," *Jerusalem Post,* July 22, 2009, *available at* http://www.imra.org.il/story.php3?id=44679.

189. "Netanyahu: Israel Won't Dismantle West Bank Fence," *Haaretz,* July 22, 2009, 2:06 PM, http://www.haaretz.com/news/netanyahu-israel-won-t-dismantle-west-bank-fence-1.280514.

190. Benjamin Netanyahu, "Prime Minister Benjamin Netanyahu's Speech at AIPAC," May 5, 2009, 8:30 AM, http://www.freerepublic.com/focus/f-news/2244414/posts .

191. *Ibid*

192. "Meshal: Hamas Seeks Palestinian State Based on 1967 Borders," *Haaretz,* May 5, 2009, http://www.haaretz.com/news/meshal-

hamas-seeks-palestinian-state-based-on-1967-borders-1.275412.

193. President Barack Obama and Prime Minister Benjamin Netanyahu, "Remarks by President Obama and Prime Minister Netanyahu of Israel in Press Availability," The White House, May 18, 2009, 1:21 PM, http://www.whitehouse.gov/the_press_office/Remarks-by-President-Obama-and-Israeli-Prime-Minister-Netanyahu-in-press-availability/.

194. *Ibid*

195. Robert Satloff, *The Obama-Netanyahu Meeting: Analysis and Assessment.*

196. *Ibid*

197. "Lieberman: Israel is Changing Its Policies on Peace," *Haaretz,* April 1, 2009, 4:02 PM, http://www.haaretz.com/hasen/spages/1075510.html.

198. *Ibid*

199. Binyamin Netanyahu, "Full Text of Binyamin Netanyahu's Bar Ilan Speech," *Jerusalem Post,* June 14, 2009, *available at* http://www.freerepublic.com/focus/news/2271719/posts.

200. *Ibid*

201. *Ibid*

202. *Ibid*

203. *Ibid*

204. Binyamin Netanyahu, "Transcript of Prime Minister Netanyahu's address to US Congress," www.theGlobeandMail.com, May 24, 2011, http://www.theglobeandmail.com/news/world/transcript-of-prime-minister-netanyahus-address-to-us-congress/article635191/?page=all.

205. Binyamin Netanyahu, "Full Transcript: Netanyahu's 2011 UN Speech," *mwcnews.net*, September 23, 2011, http://mwcnews.net/focus/letters-to-editors/13648-netanyahu-un.html.

206. Binyamin Netanyahu, "Full Transcript: Prime Minister Netanyahu Speech to United Nations General Assembly 2012 (VIDEO)," *www.algemeiner.com*, September 27, 2012, http://www.algemeiner.com/2012/09/27/full-transcript-prime-minister-netanyahu-speech-to-united-nations-general-assembly-2012-video/.

Chapter Three

207. *See generally* United Nations, "Restrictions on Palestinian Access in the West Bank," July 2011, http://www.ochaopt.org/documents/ocha_opt_Area_C_Fact_Sheet_July_2011.pdf

The "Green Line" refers to the 1949 Armistice lines established after Israel's War of Independence in 1948 that serve as an unofficial boundary between Israel and the West Bank. This boundary is recognized by the international community, but is not recognized by

Israel as any official or final border. The territory between the security fence and the Green Line is termed the "Seam Zone" or "Seam Area" or "Seam Line." The Israel Defense Forces (IDF) declared the Seam Zone a "closed military area."

208. *Beit Sourik Vill. Council v. Gov't of Isr.*

209. Col. (Res.) Danny Tirza, "The Strategic Logic of Israel's Security Barrier," Jerusalem Center for Public Affairs, March 8, 2006, http://www.jcpa.org/brief/brief005-18.htm.

210. "Israel's Disengagement Plan: Selected Documents," *Israel Ministry of Foreign Affairs*, last visited July 30, 2012, http://www.mfa.gov.il/MFA/Peace+Process/Guide+to+the+Peace+Process/Israeli+Disengagement+Plan+20-Jan-2005.htm.

211. *Ibid.* Col. Tirza has said, "Around 4,300 of those 7,000 live in the town of Barta'a in the northwest corner of the West Bank." Rafael D. Frankel, "Security Fence Won't Be Done Before '07," *Jerusalem Post*, February 7, 2006, http://www.jpost.com/Israel/Article.aspx?id=12458.

212. *Beit Sourik Vill. Council v. Gov. of Isr.*, at p. 3.

213. Mark Dubowitz, "Fenced In: Israel Draws A Red Line On The Green Line," *National Review Online*, September 9, 2004, http://dubowitz.pundicity.com/4619/fenced-in.

214. Minister Uzi Landau, "The Security Fence: An Imperative for Israel," *Jerusalem Issue Brief*, 3, no. 15, Jerusalem Center for Public Affairs, January 15, 2004, http://www.jcpa.org/brief/brief3-15.htm.

215. Robbie Sabel, "The International Court of Justice Decision on the Separation Barrier and the Green Line," *Isr. L. Rev.* 38 (Winter/Spring 2005): 316.

216. "Israel-Jordan Armistice Agreement," *Israel Ministry of Foreign Affairs*, (April 3, 1949), http://www.mfa.gov.il/MFA/Foreign+Relations/Israels+Foreign+Relations+since+1947/1947-1974/Israel-Jordan+Armistice+Agreement.htm.

217. Robbie Sabel, "The International Court of Justice Decision on the Separation Barrier and the Green Line."

218. *Ibid* at p. 323.

219. *Beit Sourik Vill. Council v. Gov't of Isr.*, at p. 17.

220. *Ibid*

221. David Makovsky, "How to Build a Fence," *Foreign Affairs*, Mar/Apr. 2004.

222. *Ibid*

223. *Ibid*

224. *Ibid*

225. *Ibid*

226. *Ibid*

227. *Ibid*

228. *Ibid*
229. *Ibid*
230. *Ibid*
231. *Ibid*
232. Danny Tirza, "The Strategic Logic of Israel's Security Barrier."
233. David Makovsky, "How to Build a Fence."
234. Danny Tirza, "The Strategic Logic of Israel's Security Barrier."
235. Eric Trager, "Special Policy Forum Report: Understanding the Middle East: A View from Inside the Mossad," The Washington Institute for Near East Policy, May 25, 2006, http://www.washingtoninstitute.org/policy-analysis/view/understanding-the-middle-east-a-view-from-inside-the-mossad.
236. Danny Tirza, "The Strategic Logic of Israel's Security Barrier."
237. *Ibid*
238. *Beit Sourik Vill. Council v. Gov't of Isr.*
239. *Ibid*
240. *Ibid*
241. *Ibid*
242. *Ibid*
243. *Ibid*
244. *Ibid*
245. *Ibid*
246. Scott Wilson, "Touring Israel's Barrier With Its Main Designer," *Washington Post*, August 7, 2007, http://www.washingtonpost.com/wp-dyn/content/article/2007/08/06/AR2007080601661_pf.html.
247. *Ibid*
248. Col (Res.) Danny Tirza, telephone interview with author, April 16, 2009.
249. *Ibid;* Col. (res.) Danny Tirza, "The Influence of Christian Interests in Setting the Route of the Security Fence," Jerusalem Center for Public Affairs, November 1, 2008, http://www.jcpa.org/JCPA/Templates/ShowPage.asp?DBID=1&LNGID=1&TMID=111&FID=443&PID=0&IID=2698.
250. Scott Wilson, "Touring Israel's Barrier With Its Main Designer".
251. *Beit Sourik Vill. Council v. Gov't of Isr.*
252. *Ibid*
253. *Ibid*
254. Danny Tirza, "The Strategic Logic of Israel's Security Barrier."
255. *Ibid*
256. *Ibid*
257. Col (Res.) Danny Tirza, telephone interview with author, April 16, 2009.
258. *Ibid*
259. Freedom House, "Freedom in the World 2012 - Israel," *UNHCR,*

August 31, 2012, accessed September 20, 2012, http://www.unhcr. org/refworld/docid/504494e423.html

260. "Court urges reroute of planned West Bank barrier," *Jerusalem Post*, December 13, 2012, http://www.jpost.com/NationalNews/Article. aspx?id=295854

261. "Israel green agency backs Palestinian farmers on West Bank wall," *Haaretz*, December 12, 2012, http://www.haaretz.com/news/national/israel-green-agency-backs-palestinian-farmers-on-west-bank-wall-1.484381

262. *See* discussion *infra*.

263. Col (Res.) Danny Tirza, telephone interview with author, April 16, 2009.

264. *Ibid*

265. *Ibid*

266. *Ibid*

267 Nir Hasson, "Israel Gearing for Effective Separation of East Jerusalem Palestinians," *Haaretz*, December 23, 2011, http://www.haaretz. com/print-edition/news/israel-gearing-for-effective-separation-of-east-jerusalem-palestinians-1.403034.

268. *Ibid*

269. Danny Tirza, "The Influence of Christian Interests in Setting the Route of the Security Fence."

270. *Ibid*

271. "Special Focus: Barrier Update," Office for the Coordination of Humanitarian Affairs occupied Palestinian Territory, United Nations, July 2011, http://unispal.un.org/pdfs/OCHA_BarrierReport7.pdf.

272. *Ibid*

273. Matt Zalen, "The Way It Came About," *Jerusalem Post*, May 22, 2010, http://www.jpost.com/LocalIsrael/InJerusalem/Article. aspx?id=175960.

274. Scott Wilson, "Touring Israel's Barrier With Its Main Designer."

275. Dan Izenberg, "Barring Palestinians From Highway 443 Prevents Attacks on Israel, Court Hints," *Jerusalem Post*, March 6, 2008, http:// www.jpost.com/Israel/Article.aspx?id=94007.

276. *Ibid*

277. Danny Tirza, "The Strategic Logic of Israel's Security Barrier."

278. Col (Res.) Danny Tirza, telephone interview with author, April 16, 2009.

279. Ethan Bronner, "Palestinians Fear Two-Tier Road System," *www. NYTimes.com*, March 28, 2008, http://www.nytimes.com/2008/03/28/ world/middleeast/28road.html?_r=1&pagewanted=print.

280. Freedom House, "Freedom in the World 2011—West Bank," June 9, 2011, http://www.unhcr.org/refworld/country,,FREEHOU,,ISR,,4 df087491a,0.html.

281. Col (Res.) Danny Tirza, telephone interview with author, April 16, 2009.

282. Benjamin Netanyahu, "Israel's Standing in the United States and Future Israeli-American Relations," Address at the Herzliya Conference, January 22, 2005. For disclosure, it is noted that the author serves as Chair of The Herzliya Conference International Advisory Board.

283. Shaul Arieli, "Remember The Separation Fence?" *Haaretz*, March 29, 2009 http://www.haaretz.com/print-edition/opinion/remember-the-separation-fence-1.273087.

284. *Ibid*

285. Amos Harel, "West Bank Fence Not Done and Never Will Be, It Seems," *Haaretz*, July 14, 2009, http://www.haaretz.com/print-edition/news/west-bank-fence-not-done-and-never-will-be-it-seems-1.279934

286. *Ibid*

287. Amos Harel, "West Bank Fence Not Done and Never Will Be, It Seems."

288. Tovah Lazaroff, "Security Wall Barely Built in Past 15 Months," *Jerusalem Post*, July 9, 2009, http://www.jpost.com/Israel/Article.aspx?id=148065.

289. Shaul Arieli, "Remember The Separation Fence?"

290. Amos Harel, "West Bank Fence Not Done and Never Will Be, It Seems."

291. Yoav Zitun, "Fence on Syrian border Undergoes Major Upgrade," *www.YNetNews.com*, September 13, 2012, http://www.ynetnews.com/articles/0,7340,L-4281021,00.html.

292. *Ibid*

293. Tovah Lazaroff, "Security Wall Barely Built in Past 15 Months."

294. Col (Res.) Danny Tirza, telephone interview with author, April 16, 2009.

295. *Ibid*

296. Shaul Arieli, "Remember The Separation Fence?"

297. Amos Harel, "West Bank Fence Not Done and Never Will Be, It Seems."

298. *Ibid*

299. Shaul Arieli, "Remember The Separation Fence?"

300. *Ibid*

301. Tovah Lazaroff, "International donors fund Bil'in protests, top IDF official in West Bank charges," *The Jerusalem Post*, June 27, 2011, 3.

302. *Ibid*

303. "Special Focus: Barrier Update."

304. Ocha-oPtt, "The Humanitarian Impact of the Barrier," July 2012, *Jews for Justice for Palestinians*, http://jfjfp.com/?p=32548.,

305. Shaul Arieli, "What We Have Learned From the Barrier," July 10, 2012, http://www.haaretz.com/opinion/what-we-have-learned-from-the-barrier.premium-1.450015.
306. Anti-Israeli Terrorism in 2007 and its Trends in 2008.
307. *Ibid*
308. Major Gil Limon, telephone Interview with author, April 17, 2009. Major Limon was the Israeli legal adviser for Judea & Samaria responsible for Security Affairs (2002-2005)..
309. Anthony L. Kimery, "In Israel, Proof that a Security Fence Works," *Homeland Security Today*, February 27, 2008, http://www.hstoday.us/index.php?id=483&cHash=081010&tx_ttnews%5Btt_news%5D=1960.
310. "Security Fence's Effectiveness," *Israel Ministry of Defense*, January 7, 2004, http://www.securityfence.mod.gov.il/Pages/ENG/news.htm#news19; *see also* Mark Dubowitz, "The UN's Court Of 'Justice' Refuses To Draw A 'Red Line' Against Terrorism; Israeli Court Orders Barrier Route Revision," *Washington Post*, September 15, 2005, A26 (noting the "sharp decline in suicide attacks inside Israel" since the fence's construction).
311. Dan Gillerman, Speech of Israeli Ambassador to the UN Dan Gillerman before the 10th Emergency Session of the 58th UN General Assembly, July 16, 2004, *available* at http://www.aish.com/jw/me/48908977.html.
312. "Israel Line," Israeli Consulate, September 28, 2004.
313. "The Anti-Terrorist Fence—An Overview," *Israel Ministry of Foreign Affairs*, http://securityfence.mfa.gov.il/mfm/Data/48152.doc.
314. Mark Dubowitz, "Fenced In: Israel Draws A Red Line On The Green Line," *National Review Online*, September 9, 2004, http://old.nationalreview.com/comment/dubowitz200409090833.asp.
315. Hillel Frisch, "(The) Fence or Offense? Testing the Effectiveness of 'The Fence' in Judea and Samaria," The Begin-Sadat Center for Strategic Studies, Bar-Ilan University, *Mideast Security and Policy Studies* 75 (Oct. 2007): *available* at http://www.biu.ac.il/Besa/MSPS75.pdf.
316. *Ibid*
317. *Ibid*
318. *Ibid*
319. *Ibid*
320. *Ibid*
321. *Ibid*
322. *Ibid*
323. *Ibid*
324. *Ibid*
325. *Ibid*
326. *Ibid*

327. *Ibid*
328. *Ibid*
329. "The Leader of the Palestinian Islamic Jihad Again Admits that the Israeli Security Fence Built by Israel in Judea and Samaria Prevents the Terrorist Organizations From Reaching the Heart of Israel to Carry Out Suicide Bombing Attacks," Intelligence and Terrorism Information Center at the Israel Intelligence Heritage & Commemoration Center, March 26, 2008, http://www.terrorism-info.org.il/ malam_multimedia/English/eng_n/html/ct_250308e.htm.
330. *Ibid*
331. *Ibid*
332. Anti-Israeli Terrorism in 2007 and its Trends in 2008.
333. "IDF Thwarts Attempted Terror Attack Near Gaza Security Fence," *Israel Ministry of Foreign Affairs*, November 12, 2008, http://www.mfa.gov.il/MFA/Terrorism-+Obstacle+to+Peace/ Hamas+war+against+Israel/IDF_thwarts_terror_attack_Gaza_security_fence_12-Nov-2008.htm.
334. Anti-Israeli Terrorism in 2007 and its Trends in 2008. "[Between 2006 and 2008] there was a substantial increase in rocket fire compared with 2001-2005, the years before the disengagement."
335. Hillel Frisch, "(The) Fence or Offense? Testing the Effectiveness of 'The Fence' in Judea and Samaria."
336. Clyde R. Mark, Israel's Security Fences, Separating Israel from the Palestinians, Congressional Research Service Report for Congress, Congressional Research Service, August 1, 2003.
337. Yaakov Katz, "IDF Tightens Security on Jordan Border," *Jerusalem Post*, April 8, 2012, http://www.jpost.com/LandedPages/PrintArticle.aspx?id=99232.
338. Maj. Gen. (res.) Doron Almog, "Lessons of the Gaza Security Fence for the West Bank."

Chapter Four

339. "The Anti-Terrorist Fence — An Overview: A Comprehensive Summary of the Major Issues Concerning the Fence," Gov. of Isr., accessed August 6, 2012, http://securityfence.mfa.gov.il/mfm/web/ main/missionhome.asp?MissionID=45187&.
340. "Israel's Security Fence: Humanitarian Concerns," Isr. Ministry of Defense, http://seamzone.mod.gov.il/Pages/ENG/Humanitarian. htm.
341. "Not All it Seems: Preventing Palestinians Access to their Lands West of the Separation Barrier in the Tulkarm-Qalqiliya Area," June 2004, (citing Order Regarding Defense Regulations (Judea and Samaria) (No. 378) 5730 — 1970, Declaration Regarding Closure of Area No. 20/03 (Seam Area)), http://www.btselem.org/down-

load/200406_qalqiliya_tulkarm_barrier_eng.pdf.

342. *Ibid* (citing Order Regarding Defense Regulations (Judea and Sa-maria) (No. 378) 5730 – 1970, Declaration Regarding Closure of Area No. 20/03 (Seam Area), Sections 3(a) and (b) of the declaration, respectively).

343. *Ibid*

344. *Ibid*

345. "Ground to a Halt: Denial of Palestinians' Freedom of Movement in the West Bank," *B'Tselem*, August 2007, http://www.btselem.org/download/200708_ground_to_a_halt_eng.pdf .

346. *Ibid*

347. "2007 Annual Report: Human Rights in the Occupied Territories Special Report," December 2007, http://www.btselem.org/download/200712_annual_report_eng.pdf.

348. *Ibid*

349. *Ibid*

350. "The Anti-Terrorist Fence - An Overview: A Comprehensive Summary of the Major Issues Concerning the Fence."

351. *.Ibid*

352. *Ibid*

353. *Ibid*

354. *Ibid*

355. Dr. Barry A. Feinstein and Justus Reid Weiner, "Israel's Security Barrier: An International Comparative Analysis and Legal Evaluation," 37 *Geo .Wash. Int'l L. Rev.* 309, 357 (2005).

356. *Beit Sourik Vill. Council v. Gov't of Isr.*, para. 8.

357. *Ibid* para. 32.

358. *Ibid* para. 8.

359. *Ibid* para. 32.

360. *Ibid*

361. "Under the Guise of Security: Routing the Separation Barrier to Enable the Expansion of Israeli Settlements in the West Bank," Joint Report with Bimkom—Planners for Planning Rights, December 2005, http://www.btselem.org/download/200512_under_the_guise_of_security_eng.pdf.

362. *Ibid*

363. "Not All it Seems: Preventing Palestinians Access to their Lands West of the Separation Barrier in the Tulkarm-Qalqiliya Area."

364. *Ibid*

365. *Ibid*

366. "The Anti-Terrorist Fence - An Overview: A Comprehensive Summary of the Major Issues Concerning the Fence."

367. "Israel's Security Fence: Humanitarian Concerns."

368. *Beit Sourik Vill. Council v. Gov't of Isr*, para. 15.

369. *Ibid* para. 32.

370. *Ibid* para. 60.

371. Dr Françoise Jeanson President of Médecins du Monde-France. Dr Ruchama Marton, President of Physicians for Human Rights-Isr.,& Younis Al-Khatib, President of the Palestine Red Crescent Society, *Position Paper on the Health Impact of the Wall*, Médecins du Monde-France, Physicians for Human Rights-Isr. and Palestine Red Crescent Society, February 14, 2005, http://www.doctorsoftheworld.org.uk/resources/news.asp?yy=2005&id=963.

372. M. Barghouthi, J. Jubran, N. Awad, R Al-Faqih, A. Nafe, & S. Khalili, "Health and Segregation II: The Impact of the Israeli Wall on Access to Health Care Services," Health, Development, Information, and Policy Institute, August 2005, http://www.hdip.org/health%20resources/health%20and%20the%20uprising/Health&the-uprising-abst60.htm.

373. Ali Waked, "Pregnant Palestinian Women Forced To Give Birth at Home Because of Fence," *Ynet.com*, December 26, 2007, http://www.ynetnews.com/articles/0,7340,L-3487160,00.html.

374. *Ibid*

375. Dr. Barry A. Feinstein & Justus Reid Weiner, "Israel's Security Barrier: An International Comparative Analysis and Legal Evaluation." (citing Telephone Interview by Agnes Szorenyi with Saad Kahtib, Senior Policy Advisor at the Ministry of National Economy, Ramallah, West Bank) (Apr. 2, 2004).

376. *Ibid*

377. *Ibid* (citing Telephone Interview by Agnes Szorenyi with Saad Kahtib, Senior Policy Advisor at the Ministry of National Economy, Ramallah, West Bank) (Apr. 2, 2004).

378. "Under the Guise of Security: Routing the Separation Barrier to Enable the Expansion of Israeli Settlements in the West Bank."

379. Dr. Barry A. Feinstein & Justus Reid Weiner, "Israel's Security Barrier: An International Comparative Analysis and Legal Evaluation." (citing Telephone Interview by Agnes Szorenyi with Khalid Jaber, Spokesperson at the Palestinian Ministry of Agriculture, Gaza City, Gaza Strip) (Apr. 3, 2004).

380. *Ibid*

381. *Ibid*

382. *Beit Sourik Vill. Council v. Gov't of Israel*, para. 84.

383. "Israel's Security Fence: Humanitarian Concerns."

384. *Ibid*

385. Yehuda Ben Meir & Dafna Shaked, "The People Speak: Israeli Public Opinion on National Security 2005-2007," Institute for National Security Studies (May 2007), http://www.inss.org.il/upload/(FILE)1188302092.pdf.

386. *Ibid*
387. *Ibid*
388. Matthew Gutman, "Israeli Arabs Credit Fence for Newfound Prosperity," *Jerusalem Post*, June 17, 2004, http://www.takeapen.org/Takeapen/Templates/showpage.asp?DBID=1&LNGID=1&TMID=84&FID=648.
389. *Ibid*
390. *Ibid*
391. *Ibid*
392. Kobi Michael & Amnon Ramon, "A Fence Around Jerusalem," The Jerusalem Institute for Isr. Studies (2004), http://jiis.org/.upload/publications/fence_around.pdf.
393. Linda Gradstein, "Israeli Wall Fuels Migration," *Washington Post*, December 10, 2008, http://www.washingtonpost.com/wp-dyn/content/article/2008/12/09/AR2008120902780.html.
394. *Ibid*
395. *Ibid*
396. *Ibid*
397. Kobi Michael & Amnon Ramon, "A Fence Around Jerusalem."
398. Lt. Col. (Ret.) Amir Cheshin, "Impact of the Fence on the Fabric of Life in Jerusalem," Seminar Abstracts: Aspects of the Security Fence, Council for Peace and Security, November 11 2007.
399. Eric Westervelt, "Israeli Settlement Seeks Protection," *National Public Radio*, April 8, 2009, http://www.npr.org/news/specials/2009/israelbarrier/part3.html.
400. *Ibid*
401. "Jewish Settlers Protest the Security Fence," *israelinsider.com*, February 13, 2007, http://web.israelinsider.com/Articles/Politics/10668.htm.
402. Danny Dayan, Chairman of the Yesha Council, "Impact of the Fence on Israeli Fabric of Life," Seminar Abstracts: Aspects of the Security Fence, Council for Peace and Security, November 11, 2007.
403. *Ibid*
404. Foundation for Middle East Peace, "The Separation Barrier Lowered the Price of Apartments in the Territories by 10-15 Percent," Foundation for Middle East Peace (May-June 2006) (citing Feb. 2006 data by *The Marker*, an Israeli business daily.), http://www.fmep.org/reports/archive/vol.-16/no.-3/the-separation-barrier-lowered-the-price-of-apartments-in-the-territories-by-10-15-percent.
405. Naday Shragar, "Most Settlements Lie East of Fence, Most Settlers West," *Haaretz*, August 16, 2007, http://www.haaretz.com/news/most-settlements-lie-east-of-fence-most-settlers-west-1.227537.
406. *Ibid*
407. "Statistics: Settlement Population Outside the Separation Barrier,"

Foundation for Middle East Peace, (May-June 2006), http://www.fmep.org/settlement_info/settlement-info-and-tables/stats-data/settlement-population-outside-the-separation-barrier-1.

Chapter Five

408. Greg Myre, "In the Middle East, Even Words Go to War," *New York Times*, August 3, 2003, http://www.nytimes.com/2003/08/03/weekinreview/the-world-fencing-off-in-the-middle-east-even-words-go-to-war.html?pagewanted=all.
409. *Ibid*
410. Tami Amanda Jacoby, *Bridging the Barrier*, 4 (Hampshire: Ashgate Pub. Co. 2007).
411. Richard Rogers & Anat Ben-David, "Coming to Terms: A conflict analysis of the usage, in official and unofficial sources, of 'security fence,' 'apartheid wall,' and other terms for the structure between Israel and the Palestinian Territories," *GOVCOM.ORG*, August 2010, http://govcom.org/publications/full_list/ben-david_rogers_coming_to_terms_2oct.pdf.
412. For instance, the "Abu-Dis wall is the most photographed segment of the wall." It lies on the outskirts of Jerusalem within close proximity to journalists in Jerusalem. *See* Ami Isseroff, "Facts and Fiction About the Israeli Wall/Fence/Barrier in Jerusalem," *Mideastweb.org*, April 12, 2004, http://mideastweb.org/log/archives/00000242.htm.
413. Tami Amanda Jacoby, *Bridging the Barrier*, 6.
414. Richard Rogers & Anat Ben-David, "Coming to Terms: A conflict analysis of the usage, in official and unofficial sources, of 'security fence,' 'apartheid wall,' and other terms for the structure between Israel and the Palestinian Territories."
415. *Ibid*
416. *Ibid*
417. *Ibid*
418. *Ibid*
419. Eric Boehlert, "Fence? Security Barrier? Apartheid Wall?" *Salon.com*, August 1, 2003, http://www.salon.com/2003/08/01/wall_5/singleton/.
420. *Ibid*
421. Richard Rogers & Anat Ben-David, "Coming to Terms: A conflict analysis of the usage, in official and unofficial sources, of 'security fence,' 'apartheid wall,' and other terms for the structure between Israel and the Palestinian Territories."
422. Greg Myre, "In the Middle East, Even Words Go to War."
423. *Ibid*
424. UN Secretary-General, Letter dated Jan. 11 2005 from the Secre-

tary-General Kofi Annan addressed to the President of the General Assembly, A/ES-10/294 (Jan. 13, 2005), *available* at http://unispal. un.org/UNISPAL.NSF/0/CBE972CE0176733B85256F8E005ADE20.

425. Richard Rogers & Anat Ben-David, "Coming to Terms: A conflict analysis of the usage, in official and unofficial sources, of 'security fence,' 'apartheid wall,' and other terms for the structure between Israel and the Palestinian Territories."

426. *Ibid*

427. *Ibid*

428. *Legal Consequences of the Construction of a Wall in the Occupied Palestinian Territory.*

429. *Ibid*

430. *Ibid*

431. Written Statement of the Government of Israel on Jurisdiction and Propriety Request for an Advisory Opinion from the 10th Emergency Special Session of the United Nations General Assembly on "the legal consequences arising from the construction of the wall being built by Israel," at para.2.7, *www.mfa.gov*, January 30, 2004, http://securityfence.mfa.gov.il/mfm/Data/49486.pdf.

432. "Documentation Centers and Museums," Official Website of the City of Berlin, *www.Berlin.de*, http://www.berlin.de/mauer/museen/index.en.html.

433. *Ibid*

434. "Saving Lives: Israel's Anti-Terrorist Fence – Answers to Questions," *Israel Ministry of Foreign Affairs*, January 1 2004, http:// www.mfa.gov.il/mfa/mfaarchive/2000_2009/2003/11/saving%20 lives-%20israel-s%20anti-terrorist%20fence%20-%20answ.

435. "German Minister Justifies Israeli Barrier," *Deutsche Welle* (Germany), September 14, 2004, http://www.dw.de/dw/article/0,,1327916,00.html.

436. *Ibid*

437. *Ibid*

438. *Ibid*

439. Prof. Gideon Shimoni, "Deconstructing Apartheid Accusations Against Israel," Jerusalem Center for Public Affairs, September 2, 2007, http://jcpa.org/article/deconstructing-apartheid-accusations-against-israel/.

440. *Ibid*

441. B'nai B'rith, "International Delegates Walkout on Ahmadinejad Speech at Durban," Press Release, *B'nai B'rith Int'l*, April 20, 2009, http://www.bnaibrith.org/latest_news/Ahmadinejad_durban.cfm.

442. Tovah Lazaroff, "Delegates Walk Out On Ahmadinejad," *Jerusalem Post*, April 20, 2009, http://www.jpost.com/International/Article. aspx?id=139650.

443. Anne Bayefsky, "Durban Diary, Day One: Ahmadinejad's Ugly Entrance," *New York Daily News*, April 20, 2009, http://www.nydaily-news.com/opinion/durban-diary-day-ahmadinejad-ugly-entrance-article-1.362448.

444. B'nai B'rith, "International Delegates Walkout on Ahmadinejad Speech at Durban."

445. *Ibid*

446. Tovah Lazaroff, "Delegates Walk Out On Ahmadinejad."

447. "Not an Apartheid Wall," *Honestreporting.com*, February 15, 2004, http://honestreporting.com/not-an-apartheid-wall/.

448. "Saving Lives: Israel's Anti-Terrorist Fence—Answers to Questions."

449. Prof. Gideon Shimoni, "Deconstructing Apartheid Accusations Against Israel."

450. Benjamin Pogrund, "Apartheid? Israel Is A Democracy In Which Arabs Vote," *MidEastWeb.org*, (first published in *Focus 40* (Dec. 2005)), http://www.mideastweb.org/israel_apartheid.htm.

451. *Ibid*

452. "Q&A: Israeli Arabs," *www.BBCNews.com*, July 23, 2009, http://news.bbc.co.uk/2/hi/middle_east/8165338.stm

453. "Saving Lives: Israel's Anti-Terrorist Fence - Answers to Questions."

454. "Q&A: Israeli Arabs."

455. "Not An Apartheid Wall."

456. *Ibid*

457. "Saving Lives: Israel's Anti-Terrorist Fence - Answers to Questions."

458. "Not An Apartheid Wall."

459. *Ibid*

460. Gerald M. Steinberg, "Abusing 'Apartheid' for the Palestinian Cause," *Jerusalem Post*, August 24, 2004, http://www.ngo-monitor.org/article/_abusing_apartheid_for_the_palestinian_cause.

461. G.A. Res. 3068(XXVIII), UN GAOR 28th Sess., 2163 plen. mtg, UN Doc. A/RES/3068 (Nov. 30, 1973), *available* at http://dac-cess-dds-ny.un.org/doc/RES./GEN/NR0/281/40/IMG/NR028140.pdf?OpenElement.

462. *Ibid*

463. Prof. Gideon Shimoni, "Deconstructing Apartheid Accusations Against Israel."

464. *Ibid*

465. *Ibid*

466. Benjamin Pogrund, "Apartheid? Israel Is A Democracy In Which Arabs Vote."

467. *Ibid*

468. "The Apartheid Analogy: Wrong for Israel," Anti-Defamation League, *www.ADL.org*, http://www.adl.org/israel/apartheid/confronting_the_apartheid_analogy.pdf.

469. *Ibid*

470. *See Beit Sourik Vill. Council v. Gov't of Isr.*; HCJ 7957/04 Zaharan Yunis Muhammad Mara'abe v. Israel, 58(5) PD 807 *[2005]*, http://www.unhcr.org/refworld/pdfid/4374aa674.pdf; HCJ 8414/05 Abdallah Yassin, Bil'in Vill. Council Chairman v. Israel, [2007], http://elyon1.court.gov.il/Files_ENG/05/140/084/n25/05084140.n25.pdf.

Chapter Six

471. *Beit Sourik Vill. Council v. Gov't of Isr.*

472. *The permit regime in the seam zone: HCJ9961/03*, HaMoked: Center for the Defence of the Individual, *www.Hamoked.org*, accessed August 13, 2012, http://www.hamoked.org/Case.aspx?cID=Cases0099.

473. Yuval Yoaz, "High Court Petitioned Against Fence," *www.Haaretz.com*, December 29, 2003, http://www.haaretz.com/print-edition/news/high-court-petitioned-against-fence-1.110059.

474. An "order *nisi*" is a court order that will become absolute unless the adversely affected party shows the court within a specified time why the order should be set aside. *Supreme Court: "If you cannot provide solutions—the barrier must be moved," www.electronicintifada.net*, May 5, 2004, http://electronicintifada.net/content/supreme-court-if-you-cannot-provide-solutions-barrier-must-be-moved/1644.

475. *Ibid*

476. *See* for example: HCJ 5100/94 Pub. Comm. Against Torture in Isr. v. Gov't of Isr.,53(4) PD 817 [1999]; HCJ 2936/02 Physicians for Human Rights v. The Commander of IDF Forces in the West Bank, 56(3) [2002]; HCJ 3278/02 Center for Def. of the Individual et al v. Commander of IDF Forces in West Bank, [2002]; HCJ 5591/02 Yassin v. Ben David et al, [2002]; HCJ 7015/02 Ajuri et al v. IDF Commander.

477. Justice William J. Brennan, Jr., "The Quest to Develop a Jurisprudence of Civil Liberties in Times of Security Crises," Address at the Law School of the Hebrew University of Jerusalem, December 22, 1987, *available* at http://www.hofstra.edu/PDF/law_civil_hafetz_article1.pdf.

478. S.C. Res. 1515, UN Doc. S/RES/1515, November 19, 2003, http://daccess-dds-ny.un.org/doc/UNDOC/GEN/N03/621/85/PDF/N0362185.pdf?OpenElement.

479. Statement by Dan Gillerman, UN GAOR 58th Sess., 21st plen. mtg. GA/10177, October 20, 2003, http://www.un.org/News/Press/docs/2003/ga10177.doc.htm.

480. UN Charter art. 92.

481. I.C.J. Statute, art. 38, para. 1.

482. Mohamed Shahabuddeen, *Precedent in the World Court* (Cambridge: Cambridge Univ. Press, 1996) 165.

483. Shabtai Rosenne, *The World Court: What it is and How it Works*, 5th ed. (Boston: Martinus Nijhoff Pub., 5th ed. 1995) 106.

484. G.A. Res. 377 A(V), UN GAOR, 5th Sess., 302 plen. mtg., (Nov. 3, 1950), http://www.un.org/Depts/dhl/landmark/pdf/ares377e.pdf.

485. Illegal Israeli actions in Occupied East Jerusalem and the rest of the Occupied Palestinian Territory, UN General Assembly, 10th Emergency Special Sess., http://www.un.org/en/ga/sessions/emergency10th.shtml.

486. G.A. Res. 10216, 10th Emergency Special Sess., UN Doc. A/RES/ES-10/14 (Dec. 12, 2003), http://www.un.org/News/Press/docs/2003/ga10216.doc.htm.

Chapter Seven

487. *Legal Consequences of the Construction of a Wall in the Occupied Palestinian Territory.*

488. Note that the ICJ used the term "wall" to refer to the security fence in its Advisory Opinion. The same term is used in this chapter summarizing the ICJ's Advisory Opinion.

489. Article 51 of the UN Charter reads:

> Nothing in the present Charter shall impair the inherent right of individual or collective self-defence if an armed attack occurs against a Member of the United Nations, until the Security Council has taken measures necessary to maintain international peace and security. Measures taken by Members in the exercise of this right of self-defence shall be immediately reported to the Security Council and shall not in any way affect the authority and responsibility of the Security Council under the present Charter to take at any time such action as it deems necessary in order to maintain or restore international peace and security.

UN Charter art. 51.

490. *Legal Consequences of the Construction of a Wall in the Occupied Palestinian Territory*, at para. 1.

491. Letter from the Government of Israel to the International Court of Justice, December 11, 2003, *Legal Consequences of the Construction of a Wall in the Occupied Palestinian Territory.*

492. *Ibid*

493. *Legal Consequences of the Construction of a Wall in the Occupied Palestinian Territory*, at para. 4.

494. The following states and entities filed written submissions: Guinea, Saudi Arabia, League of Arab States, Egypt, Cameroon, Russian Federation, Australia, Palestine, United Nations, Jordan, Kuwait,

Lebanon, Canada, Syria, Switzerland, Israel, Isr.,Yemen, United States: of America, Morocco, Indonesia, Organization of the Islamic Conference, France, Italy, Sudan, South Africa, Germany, Japan, Norway, United Kingdom, Pakistan, Czech Republic, Greece, Ireland on its own behalf, Ireland on behalf of the European Union, Cyprus, Brazil, Namibia, Malta, Malaysia, Netherlands, Cuba, Sweden, Spain, Belgium, Palau, Federated States of Micronesia, Marshall Islands, Senegal, Democratic People's Republic of Korea.

495. Written Statement of the Government of Israel on Jurisdiction and Propriety.

496. *Ibid*

497. For a discursive analysis of state and entity written submissions and oral statements, *see* Michelle Burgis, "Discourses of Division: Law, Politics and the ICJ Advisory Opinion on the *Legal Consequences of the Construction of a Wall in the Occupied Palestinian Territory*," *Chinese Journal of International Law*, March 2008.

498. Citing Application for Review of Judgment No. 273 of the UN Administrative Tribunal, Advisory Opinion, 1982 I.C.J. 333-334, para. 21, http://www.icj-cij.org/docket/files/66/9419.pdf.

499. *Legal Consequences of the Construction of a Wall in the Occupied Palestinian Territory*, para. 14.

500. Citing *Interpretation of Peace Treaties with Bulgaria, Hungary and Romania*, First Phase, Advisory Opinion, 1950 I.C.J. 71 (Mar. 30), http://www.icj-cij.org/docket/files/8/1865.pdf

501. *Legal Consequences of the Construction of a Wall in the Occupied Palestinian Territory*, para.17.

502. *Ibid*

503. Citing Certain Expenses of the United Nations (Article 17, paragraph 2, of the Charter), Advisory Opinion, 1962 I.C.J. 155 (July 20), http://www.icj-cij.org/docket/files/49/5259.pdf

504. *Legal Consequences of the Construction of a Wall in the Occupied Palestinian Territory*, para. 25.

505. *Ibid*

506. *Ibid* para. 28.

507. *Ibid* para. 27.

508. *Ibid* para. 25.

509. *Ibid* para. 27.

510. Remarks of the Legal Counsel, UN GAOR, 23rd Sess. 3rd Comm., 167th mtg. at 9, UN Doc. A/C.3/SR.1637.

511. *Legal Consequences of the Construction of a Wall in the Occupied Palestinian Territory*, para. 29.

512. To date, ten special emergency sessions have been convened. The Tenth session deals with Illegal Israeli actions in Occupied East Jerusalem and the rest of the Occupied Palestinian Territory, and has

not yet ended, although it has been adjourned and can be resumed at any time by request of member states. *See* UN General Assembly, Emergency Special Sessions, UN General Assembly, http://www.un.org/ga/sessions/emergency.shtml.

513. *Legal Consequences of the Construction of a Wall in the Occupied Palestinian Territory*, para. 30.
514. *Ibid* para. 31.
515. *Ibid* para. 33.
516. *Ibid*
517. *Ibid* para. 34.
518. *Ibid* para. 36.
519. *Ibid*
520. *Ibid*
521. *Ibid* para. 38.
522. *Ibid*
523. Citing *Legality of the Threat or Use of Nuclear Weapons* (I), Advisory Opinion, 1996 I.C.J. 234, para. 14 (July 8), http://www.icj-cij.org/docket/files/95/7495.pdf.
524. *Legal Consequences of the Construction of a Wall in the Occupied Palestinian Territory*, para. 40.
525. Citing Application for Review of Judgment No. 158 of the United Nations Administrative Tribunal, Advisory Opinion, 1973 I.C.J. 172, para. 14 (July 12), http://www.icj-cij.org/docket/files/57/6027.pdf.
526. *Legality of the Threat or Use of Nuclear Weapons* (I), p. 234, para. 13.
527. Certain Expenses of the United Nations; *see* also, for example, Difference Relating to Immunity from Legal Process of a Special Rapporteur of the Commission of Human Rights (I), Advisory Opinion, 1999 I.C.J. 78-79, para. 29 (Apr. 29), http://www.icj-cij.org/docket/files/100/7619.pdf.
528. *Legality of the Threat or Use of Nuclear Weapons* (I).
529. Citing *Interpretation of Peace Treaties with Bulgaria, Hungary and Romania; see* also, for example, Difference Relating to Immunity from Legal Process of a Special Rapporteur of the Commission of Human Rights (I).
530. *Legality of the Threat or Use of Nuclear Weapons* (I), para. 14.
531. *Legal Consequences of the Construction of a Wall in the Occupied Palestinian Territory*, para. 43.
532. Citing Western Sahara, 1975 I.C.J. 25, paras. 32-33 (Oct. 16), http://www.icj-cij.org/docket/files/61/6195.pdf.
533. *Status of Eastern Carelia*, Advisory Opinion, 1923, P.C.I.J., Series B, No. 5 (July 23), http://www.icj-cij.org/pcij/serie_B/B_05/Statut_de_la_Carelie_orientale_Avis_consultatif.pdf.
534. *Legal Consequences of the Construction of a Wall in the Occupied Palestinian Territory*, para. 47.

535. *Interpretation of Peace Treaties with Bulgaria, Hungary and Romania*.
536. *Legal Consequences of the Construction of a Wall in the Occupied Palestinian Territory*, para. 50.
537. Citing G.A. Res. 57/107, UN Doc. A/RES/57/107 (Dec. 3, 2002), http://daccess-dds-ny.un.org/doc/UNDOC/GEN/N02/544/92/PDF/N0254492.pdf?OpenElement.
538. *Legal Consequences of the Construction of a Wall in the Occupied Palestinian Territory*, para. 49.
539. *Legality of the Threat or Use of Nuclear Weapons* (I), para. 17.
540. *Legal Consequences of the Construction of a Wall in the Occupied Palestinian Territory*, para. 53.
541. *Ibid* para. 54.
542. *Ibid*
543. *Ibid* para. 55
544. *Ibid*
545. *Ibid*
546. Citing *Interpretation of Peace Treaties with Bulgaria, Hungary and Romania*, p. 72.
547. *Legal Consequences of the Construction of a Wall in the Occupied Palestinian Territory*, para. 57.
548. *Ibid*
549. *Ibid* para. 59.
550. *Ibid*
551. *Ibid* para. 60; *Legality of the Threat or Use of Nuclear Weapons* (I), para. 16.
552. *Ibid* at 62.
553. *Ibid*
554. *Ibid* at 63.
555. *Ibid*
556. *Ibid* at para. 67.
557. *Ibid* para. 70.
558. Citing *International Status of South West Africa*, Advisory Opinion, 1950 I.C.J. 132 (July 11), http://www.unhcr.org/refworld/country,,ICJ,,ZAF,,4028e9d44,0.html.
559. *Ibid* p. 131. (brackets in original).
560. *Legal Consequences of the Construction of a Wall in the Occupied Palestinian Territory*, para. 70.
561. *Ibid* para. 71.
562. Citing S.C. Res. 62, UN Doc. S/RES/62 (Nov. 16, 1948), http://unispal.un.org/UNISPAL.NSF/0/1A2B613A2FC85A9D852560C2005D4223.
563. Citing Treaty Of Peace Between The State Of Israel and The Hashemite Kingdom Of Jordan, Article VI, para. 8 (Oct. 26, 1994), http://www.knesset.gov.il/process/docs/peace-jordan_eng.htm.

564. *Legal Consequences of the Construction of a Wall in the Occupied Palestinian Territory*, para. 73.
565. S.C. Res. 242, UN Doc. S/RES/242 (Nov. 22, 1967), http://dac-cess-dds-ny.un.org/doc/RESOLUTION/GEN/NR0/240/94/IMG/NR024094.pdf?OpenElement.
566. Citing Israel-Jordan Peace Treaty, Article 3, paras. 1 and 2.
567. *Legal Consequences of the Construction of a Wall in the Occupied Palestinian Territory*, para. 77.
568. Referring to Article 42 of the Regulations Respecting the Laws and Customs of War on Land annexed to the Fourth Hague Convention of October 18, 1907.
569. *Legal Consequences of the Construction of a Wall in the Occupied Palestinian Territory*, para. 78.
570. *Ibid* para. 80.
571. *Ibid*
572. *Ibid*
573. *Ibid*
574. *Ibid*
575. *Ibid*
576. *Ibid* at para. 81.
577. *Ibid*
578. *Ibid* at para. 82.
579. *Ibid*
580. *Ibid* at paras. 81-83.
581. *Ibid* at para. 84.
582. *Ibid* at paras. 84-85.
583. *Ibid*
584. UN Charter Art. 2, para. 4.
585. Citing G.A. Res. 2625 (XXV), UN GAOR 25th Sess., UN Doc. A/8082 (Oct. 24, 1970), http://daccess-dds-ny.un.org/doc/RESOLUTION/GEN/NR0/348/90/IMG/NR034890.pdf?OpenElement.
586. *Legal Consequences of the Construction of a Wall in the Occupied Palestinian Territory*, para. 88.
587. *Ibid* para. 88; Citing *Legal Consequences for States of the Continued Presence of South Africa in Namibia (South West Africa)* notwithstanding Security Council Resolution 276, paras. 52-53, Advisory Opinion, 1971 I.C.J. 31 (June 21, 1970), http://www.icj-cij.org/docket/files/53/5597.pdf; Western Sahara; International Covenant in Civil and Political Rights, art. 1; International Covenant on Economic, Social and Cultural Rights; art. 1.
588. Citing Judgment of the International Military Tribunal of Nuremberg, p. 65 (Sept. 30 & Oct. 1, 1946).
589. *Legal Consequences of the Construction of a Wall in the Occupied Palestinian Territory*, para. 89.

590. *Ibid* para. 90.

591. *Ibid* para. 91.

592. Convention (IV) relative to the Protection of Civilian Persons in Time of War, art. 2, August 12, 1949.

593. *Legal Consequences of the Construction of a Wall in the Occupied Palestinian Territory*, para. 93.

594. *Ibid* para.

595. Expressed in Article 31 of the Vienna Convention on the Law of Treaties of May 23, 1969, p. 331, *Treaty Series* 1155, United Nations.

596. *Legal Consequences of the Construction of a Wall in the Occupied Palestinian Territory*, para. 95.

597. *Ibid*

598. *Ibid*

599. *Ibid*

600. *Ibid*; *Travaux preparatoires*, literally prepatory works, are the records of a negotiation useful in clarifying the intention of treaties and other instruments. Articles 31 and 32 of the Vienna Convention on the Law of Treaties treat the travaux as a secondary method of interpretation, with ordinary meaning as the favored means of interpretation

601. *Ibid* para. 96.

602. *See* G.A. Res. 56/60, UN Doc. A/RES/56/60, December 10, 2001, http://unispal.un.org/UNISPAL.NSF/0/765529CE2510ABC685256B 7200556EFA; G.A. Res. 58/97, UN Doc. A/RES/58/97 (Dec. 17, 2003), http://unispal.un.org/UNISPAL.NSF/0/D6F5D7049734EFFF8525 6E1200677754.

603. *See* S.C. Res. 446, UN Doc. S/RES/446, March 22, 1979, http:// unispal.un.org/UNISPAL.NSF/0/BA123CDED3EA84A-5852560E50077C2DC; S.C. Res. 681, UN Doc. S/RES/681, December 20, 1990, http://unispal.un.org/UNISPAL.NSF/0/E22E504363 6EEE55852560DD00637DF4; S.C. Res. 799, UN Doc. S/RES/799, December 18, 1992, http://unispal.un.org/UNISPAL.NSF/0/D7E-7A668894B0455852560DD0062D041; & S.C. Res. 904, UN Doc. S/ RES/904, March 18, 1994, http://unispal.un.org/UNISPAL.NSF/0/4 690652A351277438525634C006DCE10.

604. *Legal Consequences of the Construction of a Wall in the Occupied Palestinian Territory*, paras 98-101.

605. *Ibid*

606. *Ibid*

607. Citing UN Secretary General, Written Statement in Case of *Legal Consequences of the Construction of a Wall in the Occupied Palestinian Territory* (Request for an Advisory Opinion), Annex I, January 29, 2004.

608. Citing *Legality of the Threat or Use of Nuclear Weapons*, p. 240, para.

25.

609. *Ibid*

610. *Legal Consequences of the Construction of a Wall in the Occupied Palestinian Territory*, para. 106.

611. International Covenant on Civil and Political Rights, art. 2, para. 1.

612. *Legal Consequences of the Construction of a Wall in the Occupied Palestinian Territory*, para. 109.

613. *Ibid*

614. *See* Sergio Euben Lopez Burgos v. Uru., No. 52/79, Merits, UN Doc. CCPR/C/13/D/52/1979, July 29, 1981, http://www1.umn.edu/humanrts/undocs/session36/12-52.htm; Lilian Celiberti de Casariego v. Uru., No. 56/79, Merits UN Doc. CCPR/C/OP/1, July 29, 1981, http://www1.umn.edu/humanrts/undocs/html/56_1979.htm; Montero v. Uru., No. 106/81, Merits, UN Doc. CCPR/C/18/D/106/1981, March 31, 1983, http://www1.umn.edu/humanrts/undocs/session38/106-1981.htm.

615. *Legal Consequences of the Construction of a Wall in the Occupied Palestinian Territory*, para. 109.

616. *Ibid* para. 111.

617. *Ibid* para. 112.

618. *Ibid*

619. *Ibid*

620. Citing Secretary-General, Report of the Secretary-General prepared pursuant to General Assembly resolution ES-10/13, Annex II, UN Doc. A/ES-10/248, November 24, 2003, http://unispal.un.org/UNISPAL.NSF/0/A5A017029C05606B85256DEC00626057.

621. *Legal Consequences of the Construction of a Wall in the Occupied Palestinian Territory*, para. 115.

622. *Ibid*

623. *Ibid*

624. Citing Secretary-General, Report of the Secretary-General prepared pursuant to General Assembly resolution ES-10/13, Annex I, UN Doc. A/ES-10/248, November 24, 2003, http://unispal.un.org/UNISPAL.NSF/0/A5A017029C05606B85256DEC00626057.

625. UN SCOR, 58ᵗʰ yr, 4841 mtg. at p. 10, UN Doc. S/PV.4841, October 14, 2003, http://unispal.un.org/unispal.nsf/60bce917c90afe128525741a005d0910/a95b6a90f821028685256dc000509321?OpenDocument.

626. Citing UN GAOR, Emergency Special Sess., 23ʳᵈ mtg. at p. 6, UN Doc. A/ES-10/PV.23, December 8, 2003, http://unispal.un.org/UNISPAL.NSF/0/A6B42CA0EDCD304385256E15006A76BD.

627. *Legal Consequences of the Construction of a Wall in the Occupied Palestinian Territory*, para. 117.

628. S.C. Res. 242.

629. *Legal Consequences of the Construction of a Wall in the Occupied Pales-*

tinian Territory, para. 118.

630. Israeli-Palestinian Interim Agreement on the West Bank and the Gaza Strip, Isr.-Palestine, Sept. 28, 1995, Preamble, paras. 4, 7, 8; Article II, para. 2; Article III, paras. 1 and 3; Article XXII, para. 2, http://www.unhcr.org/refworld/publisher,ARAB,,,3de5ebbc0,0. html.

631. *See* G.A. Res. 58/163, UN Doc. A/RES/58/163, March 4, 2004, http://daccess-dds-ny.un.org/doc/UNDOC/GEN/N03/504/36/PDF/ N0350436.pdf?OpenElement.

632. *Legal Consequences of the Construction of a Wall in the Occupied Palestinian Territory*, para. 119.

633. Citing Fourth Geneva Convention, art. 49, para. 6.

634. *Legal Consequences of the Construction of a Wall in the Occupied Palestinian Territory*, para. 120.

635. Citing S.C. Res. 446.

636. *Legal Consequences of the Construction of a Wall in the Occupied Palestinian Territory*, para. 121.

637. *Ibid*

638. *Ibid* para. 122.

639. *Ibid*

640. *Ibid* para. 124.

641. Fourth Geneva Convention, art. 47.

642. *Ibid* art. 49.

643. *Ibid*

644. *Legal Consequences of the Construction of a Wall in the Occupied Palestinian Territory*, para. 127.

645. Citing International Covenant on Civil and Political Rights, art. 17, para. 1.

646. Citing International Covenant on Civil and Political Rights, art. 12, para. 1.

647. *Legal Consequences of the Construction of a Wall in the Occupied Palestinian Territory*, para. 129.

648. Citing International Covenant on Economic, Social and Cultural Rights, arts. 6, 7, 10, 11, 12, 13, & 14.

649. *Legal Consequences of the Construction of a Wall in the Occupied Palestinian Territory*, para. 132.

650. *Ibid* para. 133.

651. Citing to United Nations, *The Right to Food*, Report by the Special Rapporteur of the United Nations Commission on Human Rights, Jean Ziegler, Addendum, Mission to the Occupied Palestinian Territories, UN Doc. E/CN.4/2004/10/Add.2, para. 49, October 31, 2003.

652. *Ibid*

653. *Ibid*

654. *Legal Consequences of the Construction of a Wall in the Occupied Pales-*

tinian Territory, para. 133.

655. *Ibid*

656. *Legal Consequences of the Construction of a Wall in the Occupied Palestinian Territory*, para. 134.

657. *Ibid* para. 135.

658. *Ibid*

659. The communication continued as stated:

> This situation constitutes a public emergency within the meaning of article 4 (1) of the Covenant. The Gov't of Israel has therefore found it necessary, in accordance with the said article 4, to take measures to the extent strictly required by the exigencies of the situation, for the defence of the State and for the protection of life and property, including the exercise of powers of arrest and detention. In so far as any of these measures are inconsistent with article 9 of the Covenant, Isr. thereby derogates from its obligations under that provision.

660. *Legal Consequences of the Construction of a Wall in the Occupied Palestinian Territory*, para. 136.

661. *Ibid*

662. *Ibid* para. 137.

663. *Ibid*

664. UN Charter art. 51.

665. Citing UN GAOR, 10th Emerg. Sess., UN Doc. A/ES-10/PV.21, October 20, 2003, p. 6.

666. *Legal Consequences of the Construction of a Wall in the Occupied Palestinian Territory*, para. 139.

667. *Ibid*

668. *Ibid* para. 140.

669. Citing The Gabcikovo-Nagymaros Project (Hung./Slovk.), Judgment, I.C.J Reports 1997, p. 7, September 25, http://www.icj-cij.org/docket/files/92/7375.pdf.

670. Citing The International Law Commission's Articles on Responsibility of States for Internationally Wrongful Acts, art. 25; *see* also The Draft Articles on the International Responsibility of States, former art. 33, slightly different wording in the English text.

671. *Legal Consequences of the Construction of a Wall in the Occupied Palestinian Territory*, para. 141.

672. *Ibid* para. 149.

673. *Ibid*

674. *Ibid* para. 150.

675. Citing *Military and Paramilitary Activities in and against Nicaragua (Nicar. v. US)*,, Merits, Judgment, 1986 I.C.J. 149 (June 27), http://www.icj-cij.org/docket/index.php?sum=367&code=nus&p1=3&p2=3&case=70&k=66&p3=5; United States Diplomatic and Consular

Staff in Tehran (US v. Iran), Judgment, 1980 I.C.J. 44, at 95 (May 24), http://www.icj-cij.org/docket/files/64/6291.pdf; Haya de la Torre (Colom. v. Peru), Judgment, 1951 I.C.J. 82 (June 13), http://www.icj-cij.org/docket/index.php?sum=68&code=haya&p1=3&p2=3&case=14&k=d4&p3=5.

676. *Legal Consequences of the Construction of a Wall in the Occupied Palestinian Territory*, para. 151.

677. *Ibid*

678. *Ibid*

679. *Ibid* para. 152.

680. Citing Factory at Chorzow (Ger. V. Pol.), Merits, Judgment, No. 13, 1928 P.C.I.J. (ser. A) No. 17, at 47 (Sept. 13), http://www.world-courts.com/pcij/eng/decisions/1928.09.13_chorzow1.htm.

681. *Legal Consequences of the Construction of a Wall in the Occupied Palestinian Territory*, para. 153.

682. *Ibid*

683. *Ibid*

684. *Ibid* para. 155.

685. Citing Barcelona Traction, Light and Power Company, Limited, (Belg. v. Spain), Second Phase, Judgment, 1970 I.C.J. 32, para. 33 (Feb. 5), http://www.icj-cij.org/docket/files/50/5387.pdf.

686. Citing East Timor (Port. v. Austl.), 1995 I.C.J. 102, para. 29 (June 30), http://www.icj-cij.org/docket/files/84/6949.pdf.

687. Citing G.A. Res. 2625.

688. Citing *Legality of the Threat or Use of Nuclear Weapons* (I), para. 79.

689. *Ibid*

690. *Legal Consequences of the Construction of a Wall in the Occupied Palestinian Territory*, para. 158.

691. *Ibid* para. 159.

692. *Ibid*

693. *Ibid*

694. *Ibid* para. 160.

695. *Ibid* para. 161.

696. *Ibid* para. 162.

697. *Ibid*

698. *Ibid*

699. The "Dispositif" is the final paragraph of an opinion reciting the Court's conclusions.

700. IN FAVOR: *President* Shi; *Vice-President* Ranjeva; *Judges* Guillaume, Koroma, Vereshchetin, Higgins, Parra-Aranguren, Kooijmans, Rezek, Al-Khasawneh, Elaraby, Owada, Simma, Tomka; AGAINST: *Judge* Buergenthal.

701. IN FAVOR: *President* Shi; *Vice-President* Ranjeva; *Judges* Guillaume, Koroma, Vereshchetin, Higgins, Parra-Aranguren, Kooijmans,

Rezek, Al-Khasawneh, Elaraby, Owada, Simma, Tomka; AGAINST: *Judge* Buergenthal.

702. IN FAVOR: *President* Shi; *Vice-President* Ranjeva; *Judges* Guillaume, Koroma, Vereshchetin, Higgins, Parra-Aranguren, Kooijmans, Rezek, Al-Khasawneh, Elaraby, Owada, Simma, Tomka; AGAINST: *Judge* Buergenthal.

703. IN FAVOR: *President* Shi; *Vice-President* Ranjeva; *Judges* Guillaume, Koroma, Vereshchetin, Higgins, Parra-Aranguren, Kooijmans, Rezek, Al-Khasawneh, Elaraby, Owada, Simma, Tomka; AGAINST: *Judge* Buergenthal.

704. IN FAVOR: *President* Shi; *Vice-President* Ranjeva; *Judges* Guillaume, Koroma, Vereshchetin, Higgins, Parra-Aranguren, Rezek, Al-Khasawneh, Elaraby, Owada, Simma, Tomka; AGAINST: *Judges* Kooijmans, Buergenthal.

705. IN FAVOR: *President* Shi; *Vice-President* Ranjeva; *Judges* Guillaume, Koroma, Vereshchetin, Higgins, Parra-Aranguren, Kooijmans, Rezek, Al-Khasawneh, Elaraby, Owada, Simma, Tomka; AGAINST: *Judge* Buergenthal.

706. *Legal Consequences of the Construction of a Wall in the Occupied Palestinian Territory*, Advisory Opinion, 2004 I.C.J. 131, para. 1 (July 9), (separate opinion of Judge Buergenthal,), *available* at http://www.icj-cij.org/docket/files/131/1687.pdf.

707. *Ibid*

708. Citing Western Sahara, para. 46.

709. Separate Opinion of Judge Buergenthal, para. 1.

710. *Ibid* para. 2.

711. *Ibid*

712. *Ibid* para. 4.

713. *Ibid* para. 3.

714. *Ibid* para. 5.

715. International Law Commission, Articles of Responsibility of States from Internationally Wrongful Acts, art. 21, 53rd Sess., 2001, UN Doc. A/56/49(Vol. I)/Corr.4, http://untreaty.un.org/ilc/texts/instruments/english/draft%20articles/9_6_2001.pdf.

716. Separate Opinion of Judge Buergenthal, para. 5.

717. *Ibid*

718. *Ibid*

719. *Ibid*

720. *Ibid* para. 6.

721. *Ibid*

722. *Ibid*

723. *Ibid*

724. *Ibid*

725. *Ibid*

726. *Ibid*
727. *Ibid* para. 7.
728. *Ibid*
729. *Ibid*
730. *Ibid*
731. *Ibid* para. 8.
732. *Ibid*
733. *Ibid* para. 10.
734. *Legal Consequences of the Construction of a Wall in the Occupied Palestinian Territory*, Advisory Opinion, 2004 I.C.J. 131, para. 2 (July 9), (separate opinion of Judge Higgins), *available* at http://www.icj-cij. org/docket/files/131/1681.pdf.
735. *Legal Consequences for States of the Continued Presence of South Africa in Namibia (South West Africa)* notwithstanding Security Council Resolution 276.
736. Separate Opinion of Judge Higgins, para. 2.
737. *Ibid*
738. *Ibid* para. 3.
739. *Ibid*
740. *Ibid*
741. *Ibid* para. 9.
742. *Ibid*
743. *Ibid* (emphasis added).
744. *Ibid* para. 11; Citing Western Sahara, para. 30.
745. *Ibid*
746. *Ibid* para. 12; Citing Western Sahara, para. 39.
747. *Ibid* para. 12.
748. *Ibid* para. 13.
749. *Ibid*
750. *Legal Consequences of the Construction of a Wall in the Occupied Palestinian Territory*, Advisory Opinion, 2004 I.C.J. 131, para. 2 (July 9), (separate opinion of Judge Owada), *available* at http://www.icj-cij. org/docket/files/131/1691.pdf.
751. *Ibid* para. 2.
752. *Ibid* para. 10.
753. *Ibid*
754. *Ibid*
755. *Ibid* para. 13, (emphasis added by Judge Owada).
756. *Ibid*
757. *Ibid* para. 14.
758. *Legal Consequences of the Construction of a Wall in the Occupied Palestinian Territory*, Advisory Opinion, 2004 I.C.J. 131, para. 15 (July 9), (separate opinion of Judge Kooijmans), *available* at http://www. icj-cij.org/docket/files/131/1683.pdf.

759. *Ibid* (emphasis added by Judge Kooijmans).
760. *Ibid* para. 16.
761. *Ibid*
762. *Ibid*
763. *Ibid* para. 19-20.
764. *Ibid* para. 23; Citing *Legal Consequences for States of the Continued Presence of South Africa in Namibia (South West Africa)* notwithstanding Security Council Resolution 276, p. 128.
765. *Ibid* para. 25-26.
766. *Ibid* para. 26.
767. *Ibid*
768. Separate Opinion of Judge Higgins, paras. 15-16.
769. *Ibid* para. 16.
770. *Ibid* paras. 16-17.
771. *Ibid* para. 15.
772. *Ibid* para. 18, *Dispositif* is a French legal word equivalent in Rule 95(1) of the I.C.J. Rules of Court of 1978 (*I.C.J. Acts and Documents No. 6*) as 'the operative provisions of the judgment'..
773. *Ibid* para. 19.
774. *Legal Consequences of the Construction of a Wall in the Occupied Palestinian Territory*, Advisory Opinion, 2004 I.C.J. 131, p. 249 (July 9), (separate opinion of Judge Elaraby), *available* at http://www.icj-cij.org/docket/files/131/1689.pdf.
775. *Ibid* p. 252. (emphasis added by Judge Elaraby).
776. Separate Opinion of Judge Kooijmans, para. 3.
777. Separate Opinion of Judge Higgins, para. 21.
778. *Ibid* para. 24.
779. *Ibid* para. 23.
780. Separate Opinion of Judge Elaraby, p. 254.
781. *Ibid* para. 255-256.
782. *Ibid*
783. Separate Opinion of Judge Higgins, para. 30.
784. *Ibid*
785. Separate Opinion of Judge Kooijmans, para. 31.
786. Separate Opinion of Judge Higgins, para. 33.
787. Citing *Military and Paramilitary Activities in and against Nicaragua (Nicar. v. US),*, Merits, Judgment.
788. *Ibid* para. 195.
789. Separate Opinion of Judge Higgins, para. 34.
790. *Ibid*
791. *Ibid*
792. *Ibid*
793. *Ibid* para. 35 (parenthesis by Judge Higgins).
794. *Ibid*

795. *Ibid*

796. Separate Opinion of Judge Owada, para. 30; *Legal Consequences of the Construction of a Wall in the Occupied Palestinian Territory*, Advisory Opinion, para. 140.

797. *Ibid* para. 30.

798. *Ibid* para. 30 (emphasis added). Proprio motu means "by his own motion" in Latin.

799. Separate Opinion of Judge Kooijmans, para. 35.

800. *Ibid*

801. *Ibid*

802. *Ibid* paras. 46, 50; Citing Geneva Convention, art. 1.

803. *Ibid* para. 47.

804. *Ibid* para. 44..

805. *Ibid* para. 50.

806. Separate Opinion of Judge Higgins, para. 37.

807. *Ibid*

808. *Ibid* para. 40.

809. *Ibid*

810. Separate Opinion of Judge Owada, para. 22.

811. *Ibid* para. 24; Citing *Legal Consequences of the Construction of a Wall in the Occupied Palestinian Territory*, Advisory Opinion, para. 137.

812. *Ibid*

813. *Ibid* para. 25.

814. Separate Opinion of Judge Elaraby, p. 254.

815. *Legal Consequences of the Construction of a Wall in the Occupied Palestinian Territory*, Advisory Opinion, 2004 I.C.J. 131, para. 2 (July 9), (separate opinion of Judge Koroma), *available* at http://www.icj-cij.org/docket/files/131/1679.pdf.

816. *Legal Consequences of the Construction of a Wall in the Occupied Palestinian Territory*, Advisory Opinion, 2004 I.C.J. 131, para. 11 (July 9), (separate opinion of Judge Al-Khasawneh), *available* at http://www.icj-cij.org/docket/files/131/1685.pdf.

817. *Ibid*

818. *Ibid* para. 13.

Chapter Eight

819. *Black's Law Dictionary*, 6th ed. (1990).

829. Application for Review of Judgment No. 273, para. 21.

821. *Ibid*

822. Mahasen M. Aljaghoub, *The Advisory Function of the International Court of Justice 1946-2005* (Springer 2006), p. 44.

823. UN Charter art. 41 and 42.

824. UN Charter art. 10.

825. UN Charter art. 11.

826. UN Charter art. 13.

827. UN Charter art. 39.

828. UN Charter art. 12.

829. S.C. Res. 1515.

830. *Ibid*

831. *Legal Consequences of the Construction of a Wall in the Occupied Palestinian Territory*, para 27.

832. *Ibid* para 28.

833. G.A. Res. 377 A (V).

834. S.C. Res. 1515.

835. "US Vetoes Syria's Proposed UN Resolution on Israeli Fence," US Dept of State, October 10, 2003, http://www.america.gov/st/washfile-english/2003/October/20031015144513atia0.635647.html#ixzz0K2PafBOd&D.

836. *Legal Consequences of the Construction of a Wall in the Occupied Palestinian Territory*, para. 31.

837. *Ibid*

838. Citing *Legal Consequences for States of the Continued Presence of South Africa in Namibia (South West Africa)* notwithstanding Security Council Resolution 276.

839. *Ibid*

840. UN Charter art. 34, (emphasis added).

841. Legality of the Use of Force (Serbia and Montenegro v. Belgium) Preliminary Objections, 2004 I.C.J. 279, December 15, 2004, http://www.icj-cij.org/docket/files/105/8440.pdf.

842. *See* League of Nations Covenant art. 14, http://avalon.law.yale.edu/20th_century/leagcov.asp.

843. *See* International Court of Justice, http://www.icj-cij.org.

844. *Ibid*

845. *See* League of Nations Covenant art. 14; *compare to* International Court of Justice Statute art. 65.

846. Manhasen M. Aljaghoub, *The Advisory Function of the International Court of Justice 1946-2005.*

847. *Ibid* p. 57.

848. Application for Review of Judgment No. 158, para. 14.

849. *Legality of the Threat or Use of Nuclear Weapons*, p. 236, para. 15.

850. *Ibid* (citing Conditions of Admission of a State to Membership in the United Nations (Article 4 of Charter), Advisory Opinion, 1948 I.C.J. 57, 61 (May 28), http://www.icj-cij.org/docket/files/3/1823.pdf; see also Effect of Awards of Compensation Made by the United Nations Administrative Tribunal, Advisory Opinion, 1954 I.C.J. 51 (July 13),http://www.icj-cij.org/docket/files/21/2123.pdf; and *Legal Consequences for States of the Continued Presence of South Africa in Namibia (South West Africa)* notwithstanding Security Council Resolu-

tion 276, para. 40.)

851. Charles De Visscher, *Theory and Reality in Public International Law,* 2nd ed., Corbett, trans., (London: Oxford University Press, 1968), http://bordesinremedio.blogspot.com/2009/04/icj-advisory-jurisdiction-wall-case.html.

852. Manhasen M. Aljaghoub, *The Advisory Function of the International Court of Justice 1946-2005,* p. 57 (citing Western Sahara, Sep. Op. of Judge Dillard).

853. Thomas J. Bodie, *Politics and the Emergence of an Activist International Court of Justice* (London: Praeger, 1995), 16-17, (citing Hans J. Morgenthau, *Politics Among Nations: The Struggle for Power and Peace,* 5th ed. revised, (New York: Alfred A. Knopf, 1978), http://www.eou.edu/~jdense/morgenthau.pdf).

854. *Ibid* p. 16.

855. *Ibid* p. 85-86.

856. *Ibid* p. 16-17 (citing *Politics Among Nations: The Struggle for Power and Peace*).

857. *Ibid* p. 17.

858. *Ibid* p. 85-86.

859. *Ibid*

860. *Ibid* p. 4.

861. *Ibid* p. 94.

862. Michelle Burgis, *Discourses of Division: Law, Politics and the ICJ Advisory Opinion on the Legal Consequences of the Construction of a Wall in the Occupied Palestinian Territory,* 62.

863. *Ibid*

864. Revised Rules of the Court, 1978 I.C.J. art. 102, para. 2, (emphasis added).

865. International Court of Justice Statute art.36(2), (emphasis added).

866. Edward Gordon, "Legal Disputes Under Article 36(2) of the Statute," *The International Court of Justice at a Crossroads,* ed. Lori Fisler Damrosch, (New York: Transnational publishers, 1987) 183.

867. *Ibid* p. 183.

868. *Ibid* p.184.

869. *See* Chapter 10.

870. Shabtai Rosenne, *The Law and Practice of the International Court,* (Netherlands: Sjithoff-Leyden, 1965), 703.

871. *See* Revised Rules of the Court, 1978 I.C.J. art. 102, para. 2.

872. Written Statement of the Government of Israel on Jurisdiction and Propriety.

873. *Ibid* para. 5.3; *Legality of the Threat or Use of Nuclear Weapons,* para. 95; United States Diplomatic and Consular Staff in Tehran (US v. Iran), Judgment, para. 58; See also Fisheries Jurisdiction Case (Spain v. Can.), Separate Opinion of Judge Oda, 1998 I.C.J. 432, para. 9

(Dec. 4), http://www.icj-cij.org/docket/files/96/7539.pdf.

874. Written Statement of the Government of Israel on Jurisdiction and Propriety.

875. *Ibid* para. 5.5.

876. *Ibid* para. 5.11.

877. *Ibid* para. 5.5.

878. *Legal Consequences of the Construction of a Wall in the Occupied Palestinian Territory*, para. 37.

879. *Ibid* para. 38.

880. Shabtai Rosenne, *The Law and Practice of the International Court*, 756.

881. *Ibid* p. 703.

Chapter Nine

882. Aharon Barak, *Judicial Discretion* (New Haven: Yale Univ. Press, 1989), 7.

883. Michla Pomerance, "The ICJ's Advisory Jurisdiction and the Crumbling Wall Between the Political and the Judicial," 99 *A.J.I.L.* 99 (Jan. 2005): 26, 29.

884. Shabtai Rosenne, *The Law and Practice of the International Court*, 709.

885. Western Sahara, para. 22.

886. *Legal Consequences of the Construction of a Wall in the Occupied Palestinian Territory*, para. 44 (citing Status of Eastern Carelia).

887. *Legality of the Threat or Use of Nuclear Weapons* (I), para. 14.

888. Western Sahara, para. 32.

889. *Ibid* para. 33.

890. Edward Gordon, "Legal Disputes Under Article 36(2) of the Statue," 198.

891. *Ibid*

892. Written Statement of the Government of Israel on Jurisdiction and Propriety, at para. 7.3.

893. *Ibid* para. 7.4.

894. *Ibid* para. 7.6.

895. *Ibid* para. 7.7.

896. *Legal Consequences for States of the Continued Presence of South Africa in Namibia (South West Africa)* notwithstanding Security Council Resolution 276, para. 34.

897. Written Statement of the Government of Israel on Jurisdiction and Propriety, at para. 7.9.

898. Western Sahara, para. 33.

899. Written Statement of the Government of Israel on Jurisdiction and Propriety, at para. 7.11.

900. Shabtai Rosenne, *The World Court: What It Is and How It Works*, 107.

901. Shabtai Rosenne, *The Law and Practice of the International Court*, 756.

902. Michla Pomerance, *The ICJ's Advisory Jurisdiction and the Crumbling*

Wall Between the Political and the Judicial, p. 40.

903. *Legal Consequences of the Construction of a Wall in the Occupied Palestinian Territory*, para 49.

904. Rosalyn Higgins, *Problems and Process: International Law and How We Use It* (Oxford: Clarendon Press, 1995), 201.

905. Discussion, *Judicial Settlement of International Disputes*, Symposium of the Max Planck Institute for Comparative Public Law and International Law (New York: Springer Verlag, 1974), 73-74.
The term *de lege lata* means, *what the law is* (as opposed to what the law ought to be).

906. Written Statement of the United States of America, Request for an Advisory Opinion from the 10th Emergency Special Session of the United Nations General Assembly on "the legal consequences arising from the construction of the wall being built by Israel," at p. 2, January 30, 2004, http://www.icj-cij.org/docket/files/131/1583.pdf.

907. Leo Gross, *The International Court of Justice and the United Nations 369*, 120 Recueil Des Cours 314 passim (1967 I), http://nijhoffonline.nl/book?id=er120_er120_313-440.

908. Sean D. Murphy, "Self-Defense and the Israeli Wall Advisory Opinion: An Ipse Dixit from the ICJ?" *A.J.I.L.* 99 (Jan. 2005): 62, 74.

909. *Ibid*

910. Written Statement of the Government of Israel on Jurisdiction and Propriety, at para. 8.1

911. *Ibid* para. 8.3.

912. *Ibid* para. 8.4.

913. Mahasen M. Aljaghoub, *The Advisory Function of the International Court of Justice 1946-2005*, 98 (referring to Written Statement of the United States of America.)

914. *See* Chapter 8, discussions of Judge Buergenthal's Declaration, and Other Judges' Separate Opinions.

915. Mahasen M. Aljaghoub, *The Advisory Function of the International Court of Justice 1946-2005*, 66.

916. *See* "Performance-Based Roadmap to a Permanent Two-State Solution to the Israeli-Palestinian Conflict," *Israel Ministry of Foreign Affairs*, April 30, 2003, http://www.mfa.gov.il/MFA/Peace+Process/Guide+to+the+Peace+Process/A+Performance-Based+Roadmap+to+a+Permanent+Two-Sta.htm.

917. *Ibid*

918. Barak Ravid, "U.S. condemns Israel's settlement expansion plan in Jerusalem, West Bank," *Haaretz*, November 30, 2012, http://www.haaretz.com/news/diplomacy-defense/u-s-condemns-israel-s-settlement-expansion-plan-in-jerusalem-west-bank.premium-1.481706.

919. During the period of 2001 to 2008, only one suicide bombing attack

had emanated from Gaza. On March 14, 2004, two suicide bombers killed ten people and wounded 16 people in Ashdod. The terrorists "infiltrated into Israel from the Gaza Strip via the Karni Crossing while hidden in a double cell wall installed in a cargo container departing the Gaza Strip to Israel." Additionally, in January 2002, two Hamas terrorists infiltrated the fence facing Keren Shalom and killed four soldiers at the IDF's perimeter base. "2000-2006: Major Terror Attacks," *Israel Ministry of Foreign Affairs*, accessed September 10, 2012, http://www.mfa.gov.il/MFA/Facts+About+Israel/Israel+in+Maps/2000-2004-+Major+Terror+Attacks.htm.

920. Prime Minister Ariel Sharon, Address at Annual Conference of the Herziliya Interdisciplinary Institute, December18, 2003, http://www.c-spanvideo.org/program/184870-1.

921. Adverse possession is "a method of acquiring title to real property by possession for a statutory period under certain conditions, especially a nonpermissive use of the land with a claim of right when that use is continuous, exclusive, hostile, open and notorious." *Black's Law Dictionary*, 2nd Pocket Ed. (2001).

922. *See, e.g.,* Res. of the US Senate 116, a concurrent resolution commending Israel's redeployment from Southern Lebanon, S. Con. Res. 116, 106th Cong., May 23, 2000, http://www.govtrack.us/congress/bills/106/sconres116/text/es.

923. Reference re Secession of Quebec, 2 S.C.R. 217 (1998), http://scc.lexum.org/en/1998/1998scr2-217/1998scr2-217.html.

924. S.C. Res. 1515.

925. *See* "ICJ Says Fifty-Six Arab States Can Testify Against Israeli Fence," *Jerusalem Post*, January 22, 2004.

926. *See* Ambassador Allan Rock, Statement by Canada's Permanent Representative at the UN, November 30, 2004.

927. Dan Gillerman, Statement by Ambassador Dan Gillerman, Permanent Representative of Israel to the United Nations, before the 59th Session of the UN General Assembly, November 30, 2004, http://www.mfa.gov.il/MFA/Foreign+Relations/Israel+and+the+UN/Speeches+-+statements/Statement+by+Amb+Gillerman+at+UN+General+Assembly-+The+situation+in+the+Middle+East+30-Nov-2004.htm.

928. In its Opinion on the *Legality of the Threat or Use of Nuclear Weapons,* the Court noted "the political nature of the motives which may be said to have inspired the request and the political implications that the opinion given might have are of no relevance in the establishment of its jurisdiction to give such an opinion." para. 13.

929. Eugene V. Rostow, "Disputes Involving the Inherent Right of Self-Defense," *The International Court of Justice at a Crossroads,* ed. Lori Fisler Damrosch, (New York: Transnational publishers, 1987), 276.

930. Edward Gordon, "Legal Disputes Under Article 36(2) of the Statute," 202 fn. 63.

931. Ibrahim Wani, "The Future of Compulsory Jurisdiction: Rethinking the Political Question Doctrine After Iran and Nicaragua," *Am. Soc'y Int'l L. Proc.* 80 (1986): 468, 469.

932. Thomas J. Bodie, "Politics and the Emergence of an Activist," *International Court of Justice*, 19.

933. Speech of Israeli Ambassador to the UN Dan Gillerman before the 10th Emergency Session of the 58th UN General Assembly.

934. Bargil et al v. Government of Israel, et al, H.C.J. 4481/91, Reasons released (Aug. 25, 1993), http://www.hamoked.org/files/2011/3850_eng.pdf

935. Valley Forge College v. Americans United, 454 US 464, 473 (1982).

936. Helmut Steinberger, "The International Court of Justice," *Judicial Settlement of International Disputes*, Symposium of Max Planck Institute for Comparative Public Law and International Law (New York: Springer Verlag, 1974), 256-57.

937. John C. Danforth, Speech of US Ambassador to the UN John C. Danforth before the 10th Emergency Session of the UN General Assembly, July 16, 2004.

938. *See* UN SCOR, 58th yr, 4841 mtg..

939. Eugene V. Rostow, *Disputes Involving the Inherent Right of Self-Defense*, 270.

940. UN SCOR, 58th yr, 4841 mtg.

941. *Ibid*

942. *Ibid*

943. *UN, Israel & Anti-Semitism.*

944. UN Charter art. 96, para. (a).

945. UN Charter art 18, para. 2., Rule 86 of the UN General Assembly Rules of Procedure explains: For the purposes of these rules, the phrase 'members present and voting' means members casting an affirmative or negative vote. Members which abstain from voting are considered as not voting. UN Doc. A/520/Rev 15, Rule 86 (1984).

946. *Ibid*

947. I.C.J. Charter art.15, para. 1.

948. G.A. Res. ES 10/14; Warren Hoge, "Remove Wall, Israel Is Told By the UN," *New York Times*, July 21, 2004, http://www.nytimes.com/2004/07/21/world/remove-wall-israel-is-told-by-the-un.html?pagewanted=all&src=pm; See "Delegitimizing Israel: What the Mideast Conflict Has Wrought," noting that during the Security Council proceedings:

> The Singaporean ambassador began by pointing out that he had voted for the Palestinian position on all 17 anti-Isr. Res.s that had

passed in the last UN session. But 'as a small state,' the ambassador explained impudently, 'we rely upon the integrity of international law, of which the ICJ is one of the most important pillars . . . . This should be settled by negotiation among the parties concerned.' Similarly, the Ugandan ambassador said that rather than going to the court, the Roadmap 'should be given a chance.' Res.s that 'condemn one side would only harden attitudes and 'would not serve the cause of peace.' . . . he warned against 'politicizing the court' and accused Res. proponents of 'forum shopping when there is already a mechanism to address the issue.'

Saul Singer, "Delegitimizing Israel: What the Mideast Conflict Has Wrought," *National Review,* January 23, 2004, http://www.national-review.com/articles/209254/delegitimizing-israel/saul-singer#.

949. Shabtai Rosenne, *The World Court: What It Is and How It Works,* 106.

950. Shabtai Rosenne, *The Law and Practice of the International Court,* 756.

951. *Ibid*

952. Shabtai Rosenne, *The World Court: What It Is and How It Works,* 109.

953. For Spain, *see* the Guatemala Genocide Case, 42 I.L.M. 686, February 25, 2003, http://www.asil.org/ilm/ilm033.pdf; and *see* The Peruvian Genocide Case, 42 I.L.M. 1200 (2003), http://www.asil.org/ilm/ilm035.pdf; for Belgium, *see* Belgium's Amendment to the Law of June 15, 1993 (as Amended by the Law of February 10, 1999 and April 23, 2003) Concerning the Punishment of Grave Breaches of Humanitarian Law, 42 I.L.M. 1258, September 2003, http://www.asil.org/ilm/ilm035.pdf.

954. Alan Dershowitz, *The Case for Peace* (New Jersey: Wiley and Sons, 2005), 103.

955. Edith Brown Weiss, "Judicial Independence and Impartiality: A Preliminary Inquiry," *The International Court of Justice at a Cross-roads,* ed.Lori Fisler Damrosch, (New York: Transnational publishers, 1987) 133. (referring to *Military and Paramilitary Activities in and against Nicaragua (Nicar. v. US),* Merits, Judgment, (Order, Declaration of Intervention of the Republic of El Salvador).

956. The Gabcikovo-Nagymaros Project. In this case concerning a dam, the Court refused to render a decision because the two countries had engaged in a diplomatic process, which the Court did not want to undermine.

957. Speech of Israeli Ambassador to the UN Dan Gillerman before the 10th Emergency Session of the 58th UN General Assembly.

958. *See* UN Charter art. 33.

959. Michla Pomerance, *The ICJ's Advisory Jurisdiction and the Crumbling Wall Between the Political and the Judicial,* p. 33.

960. *Ibid*

961. *Ibid*

962. *Blacks Law Dictionary*, 2nd Ed. (2001).

963. Edward McWhinney, *The International Court of Justice and the Western Tradition of International Law,* (Boston: Martinus Nijhoff, 1987), 140.

964. *Ibid*

965. Michla Pomerance, *The Advisory Function of the International Court in the League and UN Eras* (Baltimore: John Hopkins Univ. Press, 1973), 281.

966. Michla Pomerance, *The ICJ's Advisory Jurisdiction and the Crumbling Wall Between the Political and the Judicial*, 27.

967. *Ibid* p. 30.

968. *Ibid*

969. Thomas J. Bodie, "Politics and the Emergence of an Activist," *International Court of Justice*, 62.

970. *Ibid* p. 83.

971. Edward McWhinney, "The International Court of Justice and International Law-Making: The Judicial Activism/Self-Restraint Antinomy," *Chinese J. Int'l L.* 5 (March 2006): 3.

972. Mahasen M. Aljaghoub, *The Advisory Function of the International Court of Justice 1946-2005*, 5.

973. *Ibid*

974. US Department of State, US Withdrawal from the Proceedings Initiated by Nicaragua in the International Court of Justice (Jan. 18, 1985), 24 ILM 246, 248 (1985), excerpted in 79 AJIL 438, 441 (1985).

975. Thomas J. Bodie, "Politics and the Emergence of an Activist," *International Court of Justice*, 18.

976. Michla Pomerance, *The ICJ's Advisory Jurisdiction and the Crumbling Wall Between the Political and the Judicial*, 40.

Chapter Ten

977. The Palestine Liberation Organization, "entrusted with the functions of the Government of the State of Palestine by decision of the Palestine National Council, decided, on 4 May 1989, to adhere to the Four Geneva Conventions of 12 August 1949 and the two Protocols additional thereto." *International Committee of the Red Cross*, accessed September 11, 2012, http://www.icrc.org/web/eng/siteeng0.nsf/html/57JMC7. Nonetheless, "on 13 September 1989, the Swiss Federal Council informed the States that it was not in a position to decide whether the letter constituted an instrument of accession, due to the uncertainty within the international community as to the existence or non-existence of a State of Palestine." *Ibid*

978. Sean D. Murphy, *Self-Defense and the Israeli Wall Advisory Opinion: An Ipse Dixit from the ICJ?*,p. 63 fn. 10.

979. Fourth Geneva Convention art. 27, (emphasis added).

980. *Ibid* art. 49 (emphasis added).

981. *Ibid* art. 53 (emphasis added).

982. *Legal Consequences of the Construction of a Wall in the Occupied Palestinian Territory*, para. 142.

983. UN Charter art. 51.

984. Sean D. Murphy, *Self-Defense and the Israeli Wall Advisory Opinion: An Ipse Dixit from the ICJ?*, 63.

985. Leanne Piggott, "Justices' Ruling Rewrites UN Charter On Self-Defence," *The Australian*, July 12, 2004, http://www.think-israel.org/piggott.selfdefence.html.

986. Steven Lubet, "Lack of Regard Shown For Israel's Security Concerns," *The Chicago Tribune*, July 13, 2004, http://articles.chicagotribune.com/2004-07-13/news/0407130118_1_bombing-in-tel-aviv-israel-requirements-of-national-security.

987. Sean D. Murphy, *Self-Defense and the Israeli Wall Advisory Opinion: An Ipse Dixit from the ICJ?*, p. 63 fn. 10.

988. Separate Opinion of Judge Higgins, para. 23.

989. Armed Activities on the Territory of the Congo (Congo v. Uganda), 2005 I.C.J. 168, para. 11 (Dec. 19), (separate opinion of Judge Simma), *available* at http://www.icj-cij.org/docket/files/116/10467.pdf.

990. *Ibid* para. 12.

991. Sean D. Murphy, *Self-Defense and the Israeli Wall Advisory Opinion: An Ipse Dixit from the ICJ?*, 62.

992. Marshall J. Breger and Marc D. Stern, "Introduction to the Symposium on Reexamining the Law of War," Symposium on Reexamining the Law of War, *Cath. U.L. Rev.* 56 (Spring 2007): 745, 748.

993. U.S. Statement on withdrawal from the case, *Military and Paramilitary Activities in and against Nicaragua (Nicar. v. U.S.)*, Merits, Judgment, (Order, Declaration of Intervention of the Republic of El Salvador).

994. Sean D. Murphy, *Self-Defense and the Israeli Wall Advisory Opinion: An Ipse Dixit from the ICJ?*, 64.

995. *Ibid*

996. Separate Opinion of Judge Buergenthal, para. 6.

997. Sean D. Murphy, *Self-Defense and the Israeli Wall Advisory Opinion: An Ipse Dixit from the ICJ?*, 64.

998. *Ibid*

999. *Ibid*

1000. *Ibid*

1001. Eugene V. Rostow, *Disputes Involving the Inherent Right of Self-Defense*, 270.

1002. Robert J. Delahunty, "Paper Charter: Self-Defense and the Failure of the United Nations Collective Security System," Symposium on

Reexamining the Law of War, *Cath. U.L. Rev.* 56 (Spring 2007): 871.

1003. Written Statement of the Government of Israel on Jurisdiction and Propriety.

1004. *See* S.C. Res. 1566, UN SCOR, 5053rd mtg., UN Doc. S/RES/1566 (2004), http://daccess-dds-ny.un.org/doc/UNDOC/GEN/N04/542/82/PDF/N0454282.pdf?OpenElement.

1005. *Legality of the Threat or Use of Nuclear Weapons* (I).

1006. *See* Barry Rubin, "Op-Ed: Fencing Out the Terrorists," *National Post*, January 26, 2004, A12, noting:

> This [the security fence] is a method that has worked on the perimeter of the Gaza Strip and on the Lebanon border. The technology is so good that other countries, like India, are eager to buy it for their own border defenses.

1007. Speech of Israeli Ambassador to the UN Dan Gillerman before the 10th Emergency Session of the 58th UN General Assembly.

1008. G.A. Res. ES 10/14.

1009. Fourth Geneva Convention art. 3.

1010. *Ibid* art 27.

1011. *Ibid* art. 53.

1012. *Ibid* art. 64.

1013. Secretary-General, Report of the Secretary-General prepared pursuant to General Assembly resolution ES-10/13.

1014. *See Israel's Security Fence: Route, Israel Ministry of Defense,* (last updated April 30, 2007), http://www.securityfence.mod.gov.il/Pages/ENG/route.htm.

1015. Minister Uzi Landau, "The Security Fence: An Imperative for Israel," *Jerusalem Issue Brief*, vol. 3, no. 15, Jerusalem Center for Public Affairs, January 15, 2004, http://www.jcpa.org/brief/brief3-15.htm.

Chapter Eleven

1016. Speech of Israeli Ambassador to the UN Dan Gillerman before the 10th Emergency Session of the 58th UN General Assembly.

1017. Separate Opinion of Judge Kooijmans, para. 5.

1018. Summary of the Advisory Opinion of 9 July 2004, *Legal Consequences of the Construction of a Wall in the Occupied Palestinian Territory* (Request for advisory opinion), Summary 2004/2 (July 9), at 10, http://www.icj-cij.org/docket/files/131/1677.pdf.

1019. Separate Opinion of Judge Buergenthal, para. 3.

1020. S.C. Res. 1377, UN Doc. S/RES/1377, at 2, November 12, 2001, http://daccess-dds-ny.un.org/doc/UNDOC/GEN/N01/633/01/PDF/N0163301.pdf?OpenElement.

1021. President George W. Bush, Speech of President George W. Bush at the Rose Garden, June 24, 2002, http://georgewbush-whitehouse.archives.gov/news/releases/2002/06/20020624-3.html.

1022. Yehudah Mirsky, "The ICJ's Advisory Opinion and International Relations Theory: Human Rights, Democracy, and the Inescapability of Politics; or Human Dignity Thick and Thin," *Isr. L. Rev.* 38 (Winter/Spring, 2005): 358, 376.

1023. *Ibid*

1024. *Ibid* p. 369.

1025. *See, e.g.,* S.C. Res. 1515; S.C. Res. 1377; S.C. Res. 1373, UN Doc. S/RES/1373 (Sept. 28, 2001), http://daccess-dds-ny.un.org/doc/UNDOC/GEN/N01/557/43/PDF/N0155743.pdf?OpenElement; S.C. Res. 1368, UN Doc. S/RES/1368, September 12, 2001, http://daccess-dds-ny.un.org/doc/UNDOC/GEN/N01/533/82/PDF/N0153382.pdf?OpenElement.

1026. Speech of President George W. Bush at the Rose Garden, June 24, 2002.

1027. Yuval Shany, "Examination of Issues of Substantive Law: Capacities and Inadequacies: A Look at the Two Separation Barrier Cases," *Isr. L. Rev.* 38 (Winter/Spring, 2005): 230, 231.

1028. *Ibid* p. 232.

1029. *Ibid*

1030. *Ibid* p. 246.

1031. *Ibid*

1032. *Ibid* p. 245.

1033. *Beit Sourik Vill. Council v. Gov't of Isr.,* para. 28.

1034. *Ibid* para. 27.

1035. *Ibid* para. 27.

1036. *See infra* discussion on proportionality.

1037. *Beit Sourik Vill. Council v. Gov't of Isr.,* para. 60.

1038. *Ibid* para. 84.

1039. *Ibid* para. 85.

1040. *Ibid*

1041. *Ibid*

1042. *Ibid* para. 86.

1043. *Ibid* (Citing HCJ 5100/94 Public Committee Against Torture v. Israel 53(4) PD 817, 845 [1999], *available* at http://elyon1.court.gov.il/files_eng/94/000/051/a09/94051000.a09.pdf).

1044. *Ibid*

1045. Telephone Interview with Maj. Gil Limon, Israeli legal adviser from 2002 to 2005 for Judea and Samaria responsible for security affairs, (Apr. 17, 2009), (text with author).

1046. *See* Matthew Gutman and Hilary Leila Krieger, "PM Approves Revised Fence Route," *Jerusalem Post,* July 7, 2005, http://saveisraelcampaign.com/atad/Articles.asp?article_id=6296; *see also* Etgar Lefkovits, "55,000 Arabs to Be Fenced Out of Jerusalem," *Jerusalem Post,* July 11, 2005.

1047. Mara'abe v. Israel, para. 6.

1048. *Ibid*

1049. *See* Greg Myre, "Jerusalem Barrier to Cut Off 55,000 Palestinians," *New York Times*, July 11, 2005, http://www.nytimes.com/2005/07/10/world/africa/10iht-mideast.html.

1050. United Nations, "Palestinian Authority Should Tackle Crisis Through Reform, Annan Says," *UN News Centre*, July 21, 2004, http://www.un.org/apps/news/printnewsAr.asp?nid=11425 .

1051. Mara'abe v. Israel.

1052. *Ibid*

1053. *Ibid* paras. 59-65.

1054. *Ibid; See* also "Israeli Court Orders Barrier Route Revision," *Washington Post*, September 16, 2005, A26.
Mara'abe v. Israel, paras. 59-65.

1055. *Ibid* para. 65.

1056. *Ibid* para. 74.

1057. "Israel's Security Fence: News Briefs," *Israel Ministry of Defense*, http://www.securityfence.mod.gov.il/Pages/ENG/news.htm#news49.

1058. *Ibid*

1059. Amos Harel, "Israel Finally Agrees to Move Separation Fence at Bil'in," *Haaretz*, July 27, 2008, http://www.haaretz.com/news/israel-agrees-to-raze-part-of-west-bank-separation-fence-1.250659.

1060. Aviram Zino, "Court: Security Fence Route in J'lem Legal," *Ynet.com*, November 26, 2006, http://www.ynet.co.il/english/articles/0,7340,L-3332617,00.html.

1061. *Ibid*

1062. *Ibid*

1063. Isabel Kershner, "Israeli Court Orders Barrier Rerouted," *New York Times*, September 5, 2007, http://www.nytimes.com/2007/09/05/world/middleeast/05mideast.html.

1064. Abdallah Yassin, Bil'in Vill. Council Chairman v. Israel, para. 35.

1065. *Ibid* para. 38.

1066. Tomer Zarchin, "Beinisch Blasts Gov't for Not Moving Fence Around Bil'in," *Haaretz*, December 16, 2008, http://www.haaretz.com/print-edition/news/beinisch-blasts-gov-t-for-not-moving-fence-around-bil-in-1.259590; Dan Izenberg, "Court Rejects New Bil'in Barrier Route," *Jerusalem Post*, December 15, 2008, http://www.jpost.com/Israel/Article.aspx?id=124613.

1067. Joel Greenberg, "West Bank barrier plan threatens ancient farming landscape," *Washington Post*, December 22, 2012, http://articles.washingtonpost.com/2012-12-22/world/36017245_1_barrier-route-separation-barrier-battir.

1068. *Ibid*

1069. *Ibid*

1070. *Ibid*

1071. *Ibid*

1072. Separate Opinion of Judge Kooijmans, para. 4.

1073. Thomas M. Franck, "On Proportionality of Countermeasures in International Law," *A.J.I.L* 102 (October 2008): 715, 738 (Citing Draft Articles on Responsibility of States for Internationally Wrongful Acts, Commentary to Art. 21, para. 4, in Report of the International Law Commission on the Work of Its Fifty-third Session, UN GAOR, 56th Sess., Supp. No. 10, at 43, UN Doc. A/56/10 (2001), reprinted in [2001] 2 Y.B. Int'l L. Comm'n 74, UN Doc. A/CN.4/SER.A/2001/Add.1 (Part 2)).

1074. *Ibid*

1075. *Ibid* p. 763.

1076. Michel Rosenfeld, "Judicial Balancing in Times of Stress: Comparing the American, British, and Israeli Approaches to the War on Terror," Symposium: Terrorism, Globalization and the Rule of Law, *Cardozo, L. Rev.* 27 (March 2006): 2079, 2089.

1077. *Ibid* p. 2089.

1078. *Ibid* p. 2092.

1079. *Ibid*

1080. *Ibid* p. 2093-2094.

1081. Thomas M. Franck, *On Proportionality of Countermeasures in International Law.*

1082. *Legality of the Threat or Use of Nuclear Weapons* (I), para. 41.

1083. *Legal Consequences of the Construction of a Wall in the Occupied Palestinian Territory*, para. 140, (Citing Article 25 of the International Law Commission's Draft Articles on Responsibility of States for Internationally Wrongful Acts).

1084. *Ibid* para. 140.

1085. Thomas M. Franck, *On Proportionality of Countermeasures in International Law*, 742.

1086. *Beit Sourik Vill. Council v. Gov't of Isr.*, para. 49.

1087. Yehudah Mirsky, *The ICJ's Advisory Opinion and International Relations Theory: Human Rights, Democracy, and the Inescapability of Politics; or Human Dignity Thick and Thin*, 367.

1088. *Beit Sourik Vill. Council v. Gov't of Isr.*, para. 44.

1089. *Ibid* para. 49.

1090. *Ibid* para. 48.

1091. *Ibid*

1092. *Ibid*

1093. *Ibid* para. 47.

1094. *Ibid* para. 58.

1095. *Ibid* para. 48.

1096. *Ibid*

1097. *Ibid* para. 59.

1098. *Ibid* (emphasis added) (citing Zamir, "The Administrative Law of Israel Compared to the Administrative Law of Germany," *Mishpat U'Mimshal* 2 (1994): 109, 130).

1099. *Ibid* para. 59 (Referring to Article 46 of the Regulations Respecting the Laws and Customs of War on Land annexed to the Fourth Hague Convention of October 18, 1907).

1100. *Ibid* para. 60.

1101. *Ibid* para. 61.

1102. David Makovsky and Ben Thein, "PeaceWatch #465: Unilaterally Constructed Barriers in Contested Areas," The Washington Institute for Near East Policy, July 8, 2004, http://www.washingtoninstitute.org/policy-analysis/view/unilaterally-constructed-barriers-in-contested-areas.

1103. *Ibid*

1104. Ben Thein, "Is Israel's Security Barrier Unique?" *Middle East Quarterly* (Fall 2004) (citing *Israel Business Arena* (August 12, 2004), http://www.meforum.org/652/is-israels-security-barrier-unique.

1105. Edward Olshaker, "Ban Ki-Moon's Bigotry," *American Thinker*, January 11, 2009, http://www.americanthinker.com/2009/01/ban_kimoons_bigotry.html.

1106. For in depth discussion of other countries' security fences, *see* Barry A. Feinstein and Justus Reid Weiner, "Israel's Security Barrier: An International Comparative Analysis and Legal Evaluation," *Geo. Wash. Int'l L. Rev.* 37 (2005): 309.

1107. *The Case for Peace*, 214.

1108. "Egypt Building Wall Along Sensitive Gaza Border," *Reuters*, March 6, 2008, http://www.reuters.com/article/2008/03/06/us-egypt-border-idUSL064228820080306; David Schenker, "Egypt Builds a Wall, Changes Its Tune on Israel's Barrier," *Weekly Standard*, April 28, 2008, http://www.weeklystandard.com/Content/Public/Articles/000/000/015/010aplyi.asp?pg=1.

1109. "Tension between Egypt and Hamas following the Construction of an Underground Barrier Along the Egyptian-Gaza Strip Border," Meir Amit Intelligence and Terrorism Information Center, Israel Intelligence Heritage & Commemoration Center, January, 15, 2010, http://www.terrorism-info.org.il/en/article/18158.

1110. *See* "Battle Over US-Mexico Border Fence Heats Up," *Foxnews.com*, March 15, 2004, http://www.foxnews.com/story/0,2933,114090,00.html.

1111. John M. Broder, "With Congress's Blessing, a Border Fence May Finally Push Through to the Sea," *New York Times*, A8, July 4, 2005, http://www.nytimes.com/2005/07/04/national/04fence.html?pagewanted=all&_moc.semityn.www.

1112. Jamie Stockwell, "Criminals To Face New Hurdle On D.C.-Prince George's Line," *Washington Post*, January 4, 2005, http://www.washingtonpost.com/wp-dyn/articles/A45674-2005Jan3.html.

Chapter Twelve

1113. Yuval Yoaz, "AG: Hague Fence Ruling May Lead To Sanctions Against Israel," *Haaretz*, August 19, 2004, *available* at http://groups.yahoo.com/group/niag_pal_news/message/115; Professor of International Law Michla Pomerance similarly noted:

> Glaringly unbalanced, the question posed was transparently designed to elicit from the Court the "correct" response, thus enabling the Res.'s sponsors to add "judicial" reinforcement to the earlier political delegitimation of Israel's self-defensive measures. Thereby, a relentless campaign of economic and other pressures against the targeted state could more readily and effectively be pursued in international fora.

Jurisdiction and Justiciability: A Court of 'UN Law.' 138-139.

1114. "How the Court Works," The International Court of Justice, accessed September. 18, 2012, http://www.icj-cij.org/court/index.php?p1=1&p2=6.

1115. "Palestinian Authority Should Tackle Crisis Through Reform, Annan Says," *UN News Centre*, July 21, 2004, http://www.un.org/apps/news/storyAr.asp?NewsID=11425&Cr=palestin&Cr1=.

1116. *See* discussion.

1117. *The Case for Peace*, 100-101.

1118. *Legal Consequences of the Construction of a Wall in the Occupied Palestinian Territory*, para. 146.

1119. Tovah Lazaroff and Melissa Radler, "Gillerman: Dark Day For The United Nations," *Jerusalem Post*, July 15, 2004, *available* at http://palestinename.com/darkday.htm.

1120. Speech of Israeli Ambassador to the UN Dan Gillerman before the 10th Emergency Session of the 58th UN General Assembly.

1121. Separate Opinion of Judge Higgins.

1122. Irwin Arieff, "Arab Nations Want UN To Pressure Israel On Barrier," *Reuters*, July 12, 2004.

1123. *Ibid*

1124. "UN Assembly To Meet Friday In Emergency Session On ICJ Ruling," UN News Service, July 13, 2004, http://www.un.org/apps/news/story.asp?NewsID=11328&Cr=palestin&Cr1=#.UFifgRyLNqU.

1125. Edith M. Lederer, "Palestinians Seek Support On Wall Issue," *Washington Post*, July 16, 2004, *available* at http://www.unitedjerusalem.org/index2.asp?id=465302&Date=7/17/2004.

1126. Speech of US Ambassador to the UN John C. Danforth before the 10th Emergency Session of the UN General Assembly.

1127. *Ibid*

1128. *Ibid*

1129. *See* G.A. Res. ES 10/15, UN GAOR, 10th Emergency Special Sess., UN Doc A/RES/ES-10/15 (July 20, 2004), http://unispal.un.org/UNISPAL.NSF/0/F3B95E613518A0AC85256EEB00683444.

1130. Speech of Israeli Ambassador to the UN Dan Gillerman before the 10th Emergency Session of the 58th UN General Assembly.

1131. Leslie Susser, "World Court Says Security Fence Illegal, But Israel Rejects Opinion," *JTA News*, July 12, 2004, http://archive.jta.org/article/2004/07/12/2922180/world-court-says-security-fence-is-illegal-but-isrel-rejects-opinion.

1132. Ilil Shahar, "Officials Applaud High Court Decision On Barrier," *Maariv International*, July 1, 2003, *available at* http://saveisraelcampaign.com/atad/Articles.asp?article_id=3759.

1133. Greg Myre, "Sharon Gets A Big Lift With Approval of Gaza Pullout," *New York Times*, February 22, 2005, http://www.nytimes.com/2005/02/21/world/africa/21iht-sharon.html?_r=0.

1134. *Ibid*

1135. *Ibid*

1136. *See* discussion.

1137. "Opinion: This Infamous Act," *Jerusalem Post Online Edition*, July 21, 2004.

1138. *Ibid*

1139. Warren Hoge, "Remove Wall, Israel Is Told By The UN"

1140. *Ibid*

1141. "Explanation of Vote by Amb. Gillerman at UNGA," *Isr. Ministry of Foreign Affairs*, July 20, 2004, http://www.mfa.gov.il/MFA/Foreign+Relations/Israel+and+the+UN/Speeches+-+statements/Explanation+of+Vote+by+Amb.+Gillerman+at+UNGA+20-July-2004.htm.

1142. Declaration on Palestine, Non-Aligned Movement, adopted at Non-Aligned Movement's conference in Durban, South Africa on August 17-19, 2004, NAM 2006/Doc.7/Rev. 3, http://nam.gov.ir/Portal/File/ShowFile.aspx?ID=33435c95-3d30-43d8-a057-776836cded68.

1143. *Ibid*

1144. *Ibid*

1145. *Ibid*

1146. 59th United Nations General Assembly Israel's Priorities and Action Plan, Isr. Ministry of Foreign Affairs, August 22, 2004, http://www.mfa.gov.il/MFA/Foreign+Relations/Israel+and+the+UN/Issues/59th+UN+General+Assembly-+Israel+Priorities+and+Action+Plan+Aug+2004.htm.

1147. Middle East Quartet Statement, UN SCOR, 5270th mtg. (AM & PM), UN Doc. SC/8510, September 20, 2005, http://www.un.org/

News/Press/docs/2005/sc8510.doc.htm.

1148. Rachel Pomerance, "Europeans Held The Key As Palestinians Succeeded In Pressing Barrier Case At UN," *JTA*, July 21, 2004, *available at* http://saveisraelcampaign.com/atad/Articles.asp?article_id=3896.

1149. *E.g.:* G.A. Res. 62/146, UN GAOR 62nd Sess., UN Doc. A/62/PV.76, December 18, 2007, http://daccess-dds-ny.un.org/doc/UNDOC/GEN/N07/472/53/PDF/N0747253.pdf?OpenElement; G.A. Res. 62/108, UN GAOR 62nd Sess., UN Doc. A/62/PV.75, December 17, 2007, http://daccess-dds-ny.un.org/doc/UNDOC/GEN/N07/470/25/PDF/N0747025.pdf?OpenElement;
G.A. Res. 62/84, UN GAOR, 62nd Sess., UN Doc. A/62/PV.65, December 10, 2007, http://daccess-dds-ny.un.org/doc/UNDOC/GEN/N07/468/81/PDF/N0746881.pdf?OpenElement.

1150. G.A. Res. ES 10/17, 10th Emergency Special Sess., UN GAOR, UN Doc. A/ES-10/PV.31, December 15, 2006, http://daccess-dds-ny.un.org/doc/UNDOC/GEN/N06/669/72/PDF/N0666972.pdf?OpenElement.

1151. "Israeli-Palestinian Mistrust Must Be Overcome, Annan Says," UN News Centre, December 15, 2006, http://www.un.org/apps/news/story.asp?NewsID=21005&Cr=palestin&Cr1=; "Israelis and Palestinians Should Accelerate Peace Efforts, Annan Says," UN News Centre, December 13, 2005, *available* at http://electronicintifada.net/content/israelis-and-palestinians-should-accelerate-peace-efforts-annan-says/2276.

1152. "UN Reports Highlight Israeli Infringement of Palestinians' Rights," UN News Centre, November 7, 2008, http://www.un.org/apps/news/story.asp?NewsID=28861&Cr=Palestin&Cr1.

1153. *Id;* "UN Special Committee Calls for New Thinking on Israeli-Palestinian Relations," UN News Centre, October 27, 2005, http://unispal.un.org/UNISPAL.NSF/0/14778A1CECAED82A85250A 80051074F; UN GAOR, 61st Sess., 27th & 28th mtg. (AM & PM) (November 10 2006), *available at* http://www.un.org/News/Press/docs/2006/gaef3167.doc.htm;
"UN Forum on Palestinian Rights Adopts Declaration Urging New System to Protect Civilians," UN News Centre, December 17, 2006, *available* at http://cosmos.ucc.ie/cs1064/jabowen/IPSC/php/art.php?aid=51578; "UN Rights Experts Call on Israel to Remove Barrier on Occupied Palestinian Territory," UN News Centre, August 4, 2005, http://www.un.org/apps/news/story.asp?NewsID=15284& Cr=Middle&Cr1=Palestin#.UFit5hyLNqU; "World Must Persuade Israel to Tear Down Barrier on Palestinian Land – UN Meeting," UN News Centre, March 10, 2005, http://www.un.org/apps/news/story.asp?NewsID=13600&Cr=Middle&Cr1=East#.UFiuAhyLNqU.

1154. Ali Waked, "PA to UN: Pressure Israel to Remove Separation Fence," *Ynet.com*, July 8, 2009, http://www.ynetnews.com/articles/0,7340,L-3743567,00.html.

1155. *Ibid*

1156. "Israel Barrier Must Come Down, UN Rights Expert Says," UN News Centre, July 9, 2009, http://www.un.org/apps/news/story.asp?NewsID=31430&Cr=palestin&Cr1=#.UFivLxyLNqU.

1157. Navanethem Pillay, "OPT; Five Years On, Israel Continues to Disregard the International Court of Justice's Advisory Opinion on the Wall," Statement by the UN High Commissioner for Human Rights, July 9, 2009, http://reliefweb.int/report/occupied-palestinian-territory/opt-five-years-israel-continues-disregard-icjs-advisory.

1158. *Ibid*

1159. "Israel Barrier Must Come Down, UN Rights Expert Says."

1160. President George W. Bush, Speech of President George W. Bush at the UN General Assembly, September 21, 2004), *available* at http://www.presidentialrhetoric.com/speeches/09.21.04.html.

1161. Letter from US Ambassador to the UN John C. Danforth to all Permanent Representatives of Missions to the UN outlining principal objectives for the 59th General Assembly, July 20, 2004.

1162. *Ibid*

1163. Shlomo Shamir, "US To Veto UN Resolution Condemning Israel," *Haaretz*, October 4, 2004, http://www.haaretz.com/news/source-us-to-veto-un-resolution-condemning-israel-1.136455.

1164. Explanation of vote by US Ambassador to the UN John C. Danforth on the Resolution addressing the situation in the Middle East, in the Security Council, UN GAOR, 59th Sess., 5051st mtg., UN Doc. s/PV.5051, October 5, 2004, http://unispal.un.org/unispal.nsf/1ce874ab1832a53e852570bb006dfaf6/71b641b86bad4a2f85256f25004fc005?OpenDocument.

1165. H.R. 713, 108th Cog. (2004), (statement of Representative Michael Pence on July 14, 2004, introduced by Rep. Pence, Berkley, and Ros-Lehtinen), http://www.gpo.gov/fdsys/pkg/CREC-2005-07-26/pdf/CREC-2005-07-26.pdf.

1166. H.R. Res. 713, 108th Cong., July 15, 2004, http://www.govtrack.us/congress/bills/108/hres713.

1167. *Ibid*

1168. *See Ibid*

1169. *See Ibid*

1170. *Ibid*

1171. Foreign Operations, Export Financing, and Related Programs Appropriations Act, H.R. 4818, 108th Cong., September 23, 2004, http://www.gpo.gov/fdsys/pkg/PLAW-108publ447/pdf/PLAW-108publ447.pdf.

1172. Barry Schweid, "D.C. Gives Palestinian Authority Low Grade," *Associated Press*, September 21, 2005.

1173. *Ibid*

1174. S. Res. 10, 111ᵗʰ Cong., January 8, 2009, http://www.gpo.gov/fdsys/pkg/BILLS-111sres10ats/html/BILLS-111sres10ats.htm.

1175. *Ibid*

1176. H.R. Res. 34, 111th Cong., 1st Session, January 9, 2009, http://www.govtrack.us/congress/bills/111/hres34/text.

1177. Warren Hoge, "Remove Wall, Israel Is Told By The UN"

1178. Moshe Hirsch, "The Impact of the Advisory Opinion on Israel's Future Policy: International Relations Perspective," The Hebrew University of Jerusalem, May 17, 2006, 14.

1179. *Ibid*

1180. *Ibid*

1181. *Ibid* p. 18

1182. *Ibid*

1183. *Ibid*

1184. *Ibid*

1185. Shlomo Shamir, "EU Opposed To More Talks On Fence At UN," *Haaretz*, September 15, 2004, http://www.haaretz.com/print-edition/news/eu-opposed-to-more-talks-on-fence-at-un-1.134900.

1186. *Ibid*

1187. *See* "Special Session of UN General Assembly to Mark the 60th Anniversary of the Liberation of the Death Camps," Isr. Ministry of Foreign Affairs, January 16, 2004, http://www.un.org/ga/28special/links.html.

1188. *See* "General Assembly to Convene Special Session Commemorating Sixtieth Anniversary of Liberation of Nazi Death Camps," Monday, 24 January, Press Release, UN Note No. 5913/Rev.1*, Jan. 21, 2005, http://www.unis.unvienna.org/unis/pressrels/2005/note5913.html.

1189. Silvan Shalom, Address of Israeli Foreign Minister Silvan Shalom before the UN General Assembly, January 24, 2005,http://www.mfa.gov.il/MFA/Anti-Semitism+and+the+Holocaust/Documents+and+communiques/Address+by+FM+Shalom+to+the+UN+General+Assembly+Special+Session+24-Jan-2005.htm?WBCMODE=Pr?DisplayMode=print .

1190. *See* "Auschwitz – the Depth of the Abyss' Exhibit Opens at Headquarters on 24 January," UN Press Release, Note No. 5914/Rev. 1, January 20, 2005, http://www.un.org/News/Press/docs/2005/note5914.doc.htm.

1191. *See* Joel Brinkley, "Sharon Tells UN It's Time For Palestinian Peace Steps," *New York Times*, Sept. 16, 2005, http://www.nytimes.com/2005/09/16/international/middleeast/16nations.

html?pagewanted=print&_r=0.

1192. *Ibid*

1193. *Ibid*

Chapter Thirteen

1194. Declaration of those assembled at the Hearings of Victims of Terror in Israel sponsored by the Dutch Center for Information and Documentation on Israel led by Richard D. Heideman and with the participation of Members of the European Parliament (February 24, 2004).

1195. Anthony L. Kimery, "In Israel, Proof that a Security Fence Works."

1196. US Dept. of State, "Country Reports on Terrorism 2011 - Israel, West Bank, and Gaza," July 31, 2012, http://www.unhcr.org/refworld/country,,,,ISR,,501fbcb323,0.html.

1197. "The Importance of Israel's Security Fence," *www.Solve Israel's Problems.com*, February 18, 2012, http://www.solveisraelsproblems.com/the-importance-of-israels-security-fence/.

1198. *Ibid*

1199. *Ibid*

1200. *Ibid*

1201. *Ibid*

1202. "Palestinian Ceasefire Violations Since the End of Operation Cast Lead," *Isr. Ministry of Foreign Affairs*, September 12, 2012, http://www.mfa.gov.il/MFA/Terrorism-+Obstacle+to+Peace/ Hamas+war+against+Israel/Missile+fire+from+Gaza+on+Israeli+ci vilian+targets+Aug+2007.htm.

1203. *Ibid*

1204. *Ibid*

Chapter Fourteen

1205. Israeli Prime Minister Binyamin Netanyahu, Address at the UN General Assembly 66th Session, September 23, 2011, http://togetherwithisrael.wordpress.com/2011/09/23/israel-prime-minister-benjamin-netanyahus-speech-at-the-un-united-nations-full-text-transcript-excerpts/.

1206. Herb Keinon, The NAM Meeting's Chilling Message, www.JPost. com, Aug. 30, 2012, http://www.jpost.com/DiplomacyAndPolitics/ Article.aspx?id=283302.

1207. *Ibid*

1208. *Ibid*

1209. *Ibid*

1210. Benjamin Weinthal, "UN Statehood and Durban III Part of 'one-two punch,'" http://www.jpost.com/DiplomacyAndPolitics/Article. aspx?id=238652.

1211. UN General Assembly 2011: Palestinian Statehood Bid Explained, *www.HuffingtonPost.com*, September 21, 2011, http://www.huffingtonpost.com/2011/09/20/un-general-assembly-2011-palestine_n_972542.html.

1212. James Phillips and Brett Schafer, "How the US Should Respond to the UN Vote for Palestinian Statehood," *www.Heritage.org*, July 6, 2011, http://www.heritage.org/research/reports/2011/07/how-the-us-should-respond-to-the-un-vote-for-palestinian-statehood.

1213. Benjamin Weinthal, "UN Statehood and Durban III Part of 'one-two punch.'"

1214. Israeli Prime Minister Binyamin Netanyahu, Address at the UN General Assembly 66th Session, September 23, 2011, http://togetherwithisrael.wordpress.com/2011/09/23/israel-prime-minister-benjamin-netanyahus-speech-at-the-un-united-nations-full-text-transcript-excerpts/.

1215. "Ahmadinejad: No need for nukes, Israel should be voted away," *www.JPost.com*, September 24, 2012, http://www.jpost.com/Iranian-Threat/News/Article.aspx?id=286034.

1216. *Ibid*

1217. Palestinian President Mahmoud Abbas, Address at the UN General Assembly 67th Session, September 27, 2012, http://www.cfr.org/palestinian-authority/abbas-remarks-un-general-assembly-september-2012/p29168.

1218. Egyptian President Mohammed Morsi, Address at the UN General Assembly 67th Session, September 26, 2012, http://www.whatthefolly.com/2012/09/27/transcript-egyptian-president-mohammed-morsis-speech-at-the-u-n-general-assembly/.

1219. *Ibid*

1220. James Phillips and Brett Schafer, "The US Must Oppose the Palestinian Statehood Amendment," *www.Heritage.org*, September 28, 2012, http://www.heritage.org/research/reports/2012/09/palestinian-statehood-effort-at-the-un-us-must-take-a-strong-stance-against.

1221. *Ibid*

1222. "Abbas at UN blasts Israel as 'racist,' Tamps Down Statehood Bid," *www.JTA.org*, September 27, 2012, http://www.jta.org/news/article/2012/09/27/3108056/abbas-blasts-israel-as-racist-tamps-down-statehood-bid.

1223. James Phillips and Brett Schafer, "The US Must Oppose the Palestinian Statehood Amendment."

1224. Tawfiq Tirawi, Security Advisor to PA President Mahmoud "Abbas: Jerusalem Cannot Be Regained Without Thousands of Martyrs," MEMRI Special Dispatch, *MEMRI*, August 3, 2009, http://www.memri.org/report/en/0/0/0/0/0/0/3539.htm.

Index

A

Abbas, Mahmoud, 12, 18-20, 22, 27-30, 34-36, 41-42, 46, 48, 50, 52, 54, 60, 98, 101, 289-290, 295, 303-305
Abu Marzouq, Mousa, 82
Action Plan, 282
Advisory Function of the International Court of Justice 1946-2005, The, 236
Afghanistan, 221
Ahmadinejad, Mahmoud, 106, 297, 303-304
Al Aqsa Martyrs Brigade, 9, 19, 21
Alfei Menashe, 74, 98, 262, 265, 283
Algeria, 126, 286
Aljaghoub, Mahasen M., 236
Al-Manar, 82
Al-Qaeda, 242
Al-Quds Committee, 15
Al-Sharq, 82
American-Israel Public Affairs Committee (AIPAC), 57
Amira v. Defense Minister, 272
Anata, 88
andal-Walajah, 88
Anglo-Transjordanian Treaty, 140
Annan, Kofi, 26, 102, 254, 262, 277, 284
Annapolis

Conference, 1, 44, 48-49, 58
Process, 48-50, 58
Arab Group, 279, 281
Arab-Israeli Conflict, 5, 7-8, 11, 99
Arab-Palestinian-Israeli Conflict, 21, 129-130, 166-167, 190-191, 194, 206, 209-210, 213, 229-230, 296
Arab Peace Initiative, 12, 49
Arabs
    Arab Israelis, 67, 88, 95, 97, 108, 113, 115
    Arab Palestinians, 8-10, 59, 84, 96, 107, 109
    Nations/states, 5, 11-12, 15, 28-29, 33, 37-38, 64, 102, 141, 163, 210, 232, 279, 281, 285, 294, 298, 302-303
    Territories, 154, 181
Arab Spring, 39
Arafat, Yasser, 12-15, 17-19, 22, 26-27, 29-30, 34, 37, 67, 101, 153
Ariel, 76-77, 97
    Ariel-Kedumim, 76
Arieli, Shaul, 77
Armistice Agreement, 64, 157
Ashkenazi, Gabi, 47
Association for Civil Rights in Israel (ACRI), 117
Auschwitz, 294
Australia, 106

Ayalon, Daniel, 58
Azariya, 72
Azzun Atma, 93

B

Bader, Akram, 267
Baker v. Carr, 224
Balfour Declaration, 66
Bangladesh, 126
Ban Ki-Moon, 106, 275, 284, 302
Bantustans, 108-109
Baqa al-Sharqiya, 143
Barak, Aharon, 207, 264
Barak, Ehud, 14-15, 42, 68
Bar Ilan University, 59
Battir, village of, 73, 265-267, 271
Beer Sheva, 80
Beirut, 39
Beit Sourik, 65, 69, 72, 91, 94, 117,
    256-258, 260-263, 265, 267, 270-
    271, 280, 283
    decision of, 65, 69, 258, 261-263,
    270
Belfast, 275, 278
Belize, 126
Berlin, 43, 100, 103-104
    Berlin Wall, 4, 99-100, 103-104
Bethlehem, 32, 43, 76, 89
Bil'in, 78, 264-265
    Bil'in Village Council Opinion, 264
Birkenau, 294
Bir Naballah, 74, 260, 264
Blair, Tony, 20, 41-44
B'nai B'rith International, 105
Bodie, Thomas J., 199-200, 236-237
Brazil, 119, 125
Brennan, William J., 118
Bridging the Rift, 85
British Mandate, 5, 140-141
Bromberg, Gideon, 266
B'Tselem, 88, 90, 94
Buergenthal, 125, 169, 170-173, 217,
    244, 254
Bulgaria, 234
Burgis, Michelle, 200
Bush, George W., 22-24, 29, 33, 36-
39, 44, 50-51, 101, 118, 221, 255,
257, 285
    Rose Garden speech, 24, 118, 257

C

Cairo, 6
California, 197, 275-276
Cameroon, 221
Camp David, 13-15, 63, 68, 217
Canada, 12, 52, 106, 220
    Supreme Court, 220
Cheshin, Amir, 97
China, 119, 124, 276
Chirac, Jacques, 37
Clinton, Hillary, 53
Clinton, William, 13-15
Center for Information and Docu-
    mentation on Israel (CIDI), 297
Compulsory jurisdiction, 202, 210-
    213
Conference of Government Ex-
    perts, 149
Conference of Presidents of Major
    American Jewish Organiza-
    tions, 31, 105
Conference to Assess and Approve
    the Status of Women, 212
Contentious cases, 119, 135, 137,
    173, 195-196, 201, 209, 211-212,
    215, 229, 231
Convention on the Rights of the
    Child, 150, 152, 157, 159
Council for Peace and Security, 66,
    77, 272
Cuba, 126
Cuban Missile Crisis, 245
Cyprus, 275

D

Damascus, 6, 82
Danforth, John, 225, 279-280, 285-
    286
David's Sling, 300
Dayan, Danny, 97
Dayton, Keith, 44-46, 57
Dead Sea, 85
Declaration on Measures to Elimi-

nate International Terrorism, 10
Declaration on Palestine, 282
Democratic Republic of Congo v. Uganda, 129, 243-244, 269
Denmark, 52
Dershowitz, Alan, 231, 278
Der Sturmer, 294
Dimona, 79, 83
Disengagement Plan, 25-28, 30-31, 33-34, 37, 281, 283, 295
Dispositive/dispositif, 179-180, 182-183, 185, 240
District Coordinating Offices (DCO), 90
Dror, Shlomo, 77
Durban Conference, xv, 105-106, 283, 302-303
Durban Declaration, 302
Durban Review Conference (Durban II), xv, 105-106

E

East Mattityahu, 265
Egypt, 1, 5-6, 11, 23, 29, 32, 35, 38-39, 41, 46-48, 52-53, 64, 82, 125, 146, 180, 219, 275, 292, 303-304
Eilat, 79
Elaraby, Nabil, 125-126, 174, 180, 185
Elkana, 79-80, 143
El-Mouteelah, 70
El Salvador, 231
Erdogan, Tayyip, 47
Erekat, Saeb, 38
Erga omnes, 146, 165, 184-185
Ethiopia, 115
Etzion bloc, 76
European Parliament, 297
European Union (EU), 11, 20, 23, 38-39, 41, 106, 187, 190, 221, 275, 279, 292-293, 298
Exchange of Letters, 12-13, 153

F

Falk, Richard, 284
Farra, Osama al-, 32

Fatah, 19, 21-22, 38, 40-41, 46, 58, 292
Fayyad, Salam, 19, 22, 42, 284
Finland, 196
First Temple, 6
Flotilla, 47
Foreign Operations Appropriations Bill (2005), 288
Foreign Terrorist Organization (FTO), 8, 38
Foundation for Defense of Democracies (FDD), 3, 122
Fourth Geneva Convention, 121, 125, 146-149, 154, 156-157, 159, 165-166, 168, 170, 173, 239, 248, 279
  Article 1, 149, 183
  Article 2, 112, 145, 147-148
  Article 3, 248
  Article 6, 156
  Article 27, 240, 248
  Article 47, 149, 156, 159
  Article 49, 154, 156, 159, 173, 240, 251
  Article 52, 156
  Article 53, 156-157, 159, 240, 248
  Article 59, 156
  Article 64, 248
  Article 154, 146
France, 37, 52, 119, 124, 294
Franck, Thomas, 268, 270
Frankfurter, Felix, 224
Fraser, William, III, 44
French Hill, 96
Friends of the Earth Middle East, 266
Frisch, Hillel, 80-83

G

Gabcikovo-Nagymaros Project (Hungary/Slovakia), 162
Gadhafi, Moammar, 11
Ganim, 31
Gavish, Yishayahu, 32
Gaza, 1, 6-10, 13-16, 18, 20, 22, 24-27, 30--43, 46-47, 50-53, 64, 67, 83-85, 95, 113, 150, 153, 219,

239, 242, 252, 275, 286, 289-290, 292, 295, 300, 303
General Assembly (UNGA), xvi, 2-4, 7-8, 10, 33, 37, 60, 64, 79, 102-103, 107, 119-121, 123, 125-132, 134-139, 141, 145, 149, 153, 161, 166-169, 174-178, 180, 187-195, 200, 203-205, 210-213, 215, 221-222, 224-232, 234-236, 239, 242, 248, 252, 274, 278-288, 291, 293-295, 301, 303-304
   10th Emergency Special Session, 121, 128, 130, 188, 193-194, 279
   59th Session, 221, 282
   67th Session, 304
   Resolution 181, 5-6, 67, 252
   Resolution 377 A (V), 120, 130, 132, 177, 191
   Resolution 2625, 123, 145
   Resolution ES-10/12, 127
   Resolution ES-10/14, 121, 125, 128-129, 177-178, 203, 239, 248
   Resolution ES 10/15, 280-281, 291
   Rules of Procedure, 227
Germany, 52, 102-104, 106, 125, 294
Gilad, Amos, 45
Gillerman, Dan, 27, 79, 222, 224, 253, 278, 280-281
Gilo, 76, 143
Givat Zeev, 264
GOI, 23-24
Golan Heights, 6, 76
Goldstone Report, xv, 8
Gordon, Edward, 201, 209, 224
Gradstein, Linda, 96
Greenberg, Joel, 265-267
Green Line, 61, 63-66, 76, 81, 88-90, 98, 141-144, 149, 157-158, 171-172, 185, 248-249, 254
Gross, Leo, 214
Guillaume, Gilbert, 124
Gush Etzion, 76-77

H

Habla, 89
Hadassah Hospital, 93

Hague, The, xvi, 2, 279, 284, 286, 297-298
   Convention of 1907 (Fourth Hague Convention), 146
   Conventions, 72
   Peace Palace, 297
   Regulations of 1907, 146, 155, 157, 159, 173
      Article 43, 155
      Article 46, 155, 157, 159, 173
      Article 52, 155
      Section II, 146
      Section III, 146, 155
Hamas, 8-10, 18-19, 21-22, 29, 34-41, 43, 46, 48, 50-53, 57-58, 67, 82-83, 95, 242, 275, 289-290, 292, 297, 299-300
Hamastan, 58
HaMoked, 117
Health, Development, Information and Policy Institute, 92
Hebrew University, 107
Hebron Accords, 1, 7, 14
Herzliya Conference, 76
Hezbollah, 9, 21, 34, 39, 82, 289, 297, 300
Higgins, Rosalyn, 125, 174-175, 179, 180-182, 184, 199, 213, 243, 279
Hindi, Ofer, 73
Hitler, Adolf, 47
Holland, 106
Holocaust, xvii, 106, 114, 294-295, 297, 304
   International Remembrance Day, 295
Homesh, 31
Hungary, 162, 234
Hussein, King, 6
Hussein, Saddam, 11

I

IHH, 47
India, 119, 267, 274
Indonesia, 126
Interim Agreement, 14, 153
International Convention on the

Suppression and Punishment of the Crime of Apartheid (ICSPCA), 112-113
Article 1, 112
Article 2, 112
International Court of Justice (ICJ), xvi, 2-4, 56, 65, 102-104, 117, 119-136, 169, 174, 187-190, 192-198, 200-201, 203-210, 212-215, 217, 221, 223-238, 241-242, 245-247, 250-252, 255-258, 261, 263, 267-271, 274, 277-280, 282-283, 285-288, 292-293, 296-297, 305-306
Advisory opinion. *See Legal Consequences of the Construction of a Wall in the Occupied Palestinian Territory*
Roles of, 119-120, 127, 195
Rules, 196, 201, 203
Statute, 187, 195-197, 199, 209, 228
Article 36, 187, 195, 201-202, 213
Article 59, 119-120
Article 65, 126, 133, 204, 207, 228
International Covenant on Civil and Political Rights, 150-151, 158-160
Article 2, 151
Article 9, 157, 159
Article 12, 157, 159-160
Article 17, 157, 160
International Covenant on Economic, Social and Cultural Rights, 150-152, 157, 159
International Criminal Court (ICC), 60, 110-111, 203, 230, 291, 305
ICC Statute, 291
International Law Commission, 170, 268
Articles on Responsibility of States for Internationally Wrongful Acts, 170
Draft Articles on State Responsibility, 268
International Military Tribunal of Nuremburg, 146
International Status of South West Africa, 140
Interpretation of Peace Treaties with Bulgaria, Hungary and Romania, 234
Iran, 7, 9, 11, 21, 34, 39, 57, 106, 295, 297, 299-300
Iraq, 5-6, 11, 222, 275
Iron Dome, 299-300
Islamic Resistance Movement. *See* Hamas
Israel
Declaration of Independence, 64
Foreign Ministry, 294
High Court of Justice (HCJ), 2, 16-17, 65, 73, 75-78, 89-90, 94, 100-111, 115, 117-118, 121, 215, 224, 250-251, 256-258, 261-265, 267, 270-271, 273-274, 280, 286-288, 292-293
Israeli Defense Forces (IDF), 2, 32, 41, 47, 51, 56, 69, 71-78, 83, 89, 91, 110-111, 117-118, 144, 259, 272-273, 298
Knesset, xv, 26, 56, 58, 108, 292
Ministry of Defense, 91, 143, 262
Ministry of Foreign Affairs, 104, 299
Nature and Parks Authority, 266
War of Independence, 5-6, 64
Written Statement to the Court, 253
Italy, 52, 102, 106, 119, 221

J

Jaber, Khalid, 94
Jacoby, Tami Amanda, 99
Japan, 119, 125, 175
Jebel Muktam, 259
Jenin, 45, 92, 96, 143
Jenin Initiative, 45
Jericho, 13, 42, 45
Jerusalem, 1, 6, 9, 13, 15, 33, 35, 42,

44, 52, 54, 58, 69, 70-72, 74, 76, 83, 88, 92-93, 96-97, 110, 114, 141-144, 153-154, 222, 264, 266-267, 291, 300, 303-305

East Jerusalem, 6, 14-15, 21, 26, 52, 60, 74, 88, 96, 98, 121, 125, 139, 142-144, 149, 152, 154, 164, 166, 168, 282, 284, 291, 303

Jerusalem Institute for Israel Studies, 96

Jerusalem Post, 47, 73, 281

Jihad, 9, 19, 21, 35, 45, 52, 82, 299

Joint Understanding, 48-49

Jones, James L., 44-46

Jordan, 1, 5-6, 11, 20, 22-23, 27, 29, 38, 45, 63-65, 70, 84-85, 125-126, 141-143, 146-149, 185, 219, 239-240, 292, 303

Jordan Valley, 6, 143, 219

Judea, 5-6, 16, 63, 66, 70-71, 74, 79-81, 109, 219, 226, 261

Judean Desert, 76

K

Kaddoumi, Farouk, 221

Kadim, 31

Kafr 'Aqab, 88

Kahtib, Saab, 93-94

Karaman, Tawfiq, 96

Karnei Shomron, 76

Kashmir, 274

Kasuri, Khurshid, 37

Kedumim, 76-77

Kerry, John, 54

Khamenei, Ali, 302

Khasawneh, Awn Shawkat Al-, 125, 174, 185

Khirbet Jubara, 78

kibbutzim, 6

Kidwa, Nasser Al, 221, 279, 281, 293

Kollek, Teddy, 97

Kooijmans, Pieter H., 125, 174, 177-181, 183-184, 243, 254, 267, 277

Koroma, Abdul G., 124, 174, 185

Kosovo, 196

Kuwait, 102, 275

L

Landau, Uzi, 63, 249

League of Arab States, 125-126

League of Nations, 135, 140, 146, 196-197, 208, 237

Covenant, 140, 146, 197, 229

Article 22, 140, 146

Lebanon, 5, 7, 9, 11, 39-40, 63, 77, 219, 289, 300, 303

Legal Consequences of the Construction of a Wall in the Occupied Palestinian Territory, xv, 44, 55-56, 123, 212, 221, 227, 231, 239, 242, 246, 248, 253, 256, 262-263, 267, 270, 278-286, 288, 291-293

Legality of the Threat or Use of Nuclear Weapons, The, 136, 247, 269

Libya, 11

Lieberman, Avigdor, 58

Limon, Gil, 79, 261

Litani River, 39

Livni, Tzipi, 49-50

Lockerbie case, 236

Lubet, Steven, 242

M

Ma'aleh Adumim, 70, 74, 76-77

Maariv, 99

Madagascar, 124, 126

Madrid, Spain, 1, 13, 41

Mahajaneh, Abdel Rahman, 96

Makovsky, David, 274

Malaysia, 126

Marbury v. Madison, 223

Marker, The, 98

Mavi Marmara, 47

Mazen, Abu, 22, 30, 50, 101, 297

Mazuz, Menachem, 277

McConnell, Mitch, 289

McWhinney, Edward, 235-236

Mecca Accord, 40

Memorandum of Understanding, 52

Mercaz Ha'Rav Yeshiva, 83

Meshal, Khaled, 46, 58, 292, 297

Mevasseret Adumim, 74
Mexico, 119, 275-276
Middle East Peace Summit, 13-14, 23
Military and Paramilitary Activities in and against Nicaragua (Nicaragua v. United States), 181, 231, 269-270
Ministers' Committee on National Security, 61, 69-70
Mirsky, Yehudah, 255-256
Mitchell, George, 23
Mitchell Report, 23-24
Modi'in, 74
Mofaz, Shaul, 31, 34
Montenegro, 195
Montreal Convention of 1971, 236
Morgenthau, Hans, 199
Morocco, 15, 119, 234
Morsi, Mohammed, 46, 53, 304
Moshavim, 6
Mount Avner, 70
Mubarak, Hosni, 53
Murphy, Sean D., 239, 241, 243-244
Muslim Brotherhood, 304

N

Nablus, 73
Nachman, Ron, 97
Nairobi, 212
Namibia, 174, 176, 178, 193, 210, 214
Nasrallah, Hassan, 297
Negev, 46
Negroponte, John, 226
Netanyahu, Benjamin, xv-xvi, 13-14, 21, 33, 39, 47, 52-60, 68, 75-77, 97, 284, 289-290, 295, 301-303
Netherlands, 52, 125, 177, 254
Neve Dekalim, 32-33
New Zealand, 106, 119
Nicaragua v. United States, Oil Platforms, 237, 244
Non-Aligned Movement (NAM), 282, 291, 302
2012 Summit, 302
NAM Declaration, 282, 291

Northern Ireland, 275
Norway, 52, 231

O

Obama, Barack, xvi, 46, 50, 52-55, 58, 290
Olmert, Ehud, 48, 263
Operation Cast Lead, 8, 41, 43, 50-51, 289, 299
Operation Pillar of Defense, 8, 41, 83, 290, 299-300
Operation Summer Rains, 39
Organization of the Islamic Conference, 102, 126
Oslo Accords, 7, 11-15, 20, 58, 67-68, 84-85
Ottoman Turks, 5
Owada, Hisashi, 125, 174-176, 182-184

P

Pakistan, 37, 274
Palestine Liberation Organization (PLO), xvi, 1, 4, 6, 8-9, 12-16, 18-19, 34, 49, 58, 60, 95, 111, 121, 125, 142, 147, 152-153, 163, 167, 196, 203, 210, 212, 216, 218-222, 228, 231, 234, 242, 246, 249-250, 252-253, 255, 283-284, 290-291, 293-295, 297, 300-302, 304-305
Palestine National Fund, 66
Palestine, State of (Arab), 5-6, 13, 21, 30, 63, 66, 141
Palestinia, 5, 65
Palestinian Anti-Terrorism Act of 2006, 40
Palestinian Authority (PA), 4, 6-9, 12-15, 17-23, 26-27, 30-35, 37-46, 49, 52, 57-59, 62-63, 71, 78, 84, 89, 93-95, 98, 101, 111, 119, 139, 163, 167, 190, 196, 210, 218-222, 231, 234, 242, 246, 249-250, 252-253, 255, 278-279, 281, 283-284, 289-290, 292-293, 298, 300-301, 304-305
Palestinian Investment Conference, 43

Palestinian Legislative Council, 38
Palestinian Liberation Movement,
    147
Palestinian Ministry of Agriculture,
    94
Palestinian National Authority
    (PNA), 13, 100
    Ministry of Foreign Affairs, 100
Palestinian Observers, 24, 221-222
Palestinian Security Forces, 31, 34-
    35, 40, 45
Parra-Aranguren, Gonzalo, 125
Partition Plan, 64
Partition Resolution. *See* General
    Assembly, Resolution 181
Peace Treaty (1994), 157
Peel Commission Report, 66
Peres, Shimon, 67
Permanent Court of International
    Justice (PCIJ), 134-135, 164,
    196-198, 208-209, 214, 237
Petren, Sture, 178
Philadelphi corridor, 32
Piggott, Leanne, 241
Pisgat Zeev, 96
Plan of Partition, 141
Pogrund, Benjamin, 114
Political Question, 134, 167, 223-
    225, 227
Pomerance, Michla, 207, 213, 233,
    235, 238
Portuguese colonies, 129
Powell, Colin, 27, 221
Presidential Guard Training Cen-
    ter, 45
Prevention of the Supply of Arms
    and Related Materiel to Terror-
    ist Groups, 52
Proportionality, 8, 91, 172, 182, 216,
    245, 259-260, 262-263, 268-271,
    273-274
Prosor, Ron, 295

Q

Qabatiya, 45
Qalqiliya, 73-74, 89, 92-93, 144, 264

Qassam rocket fire, 34, 39
Qatar, 121
Quartet, 11, 20, 29, 32, 34, 37-38,
    41-44, 48-49, 119, 190, 217, 221,
    226, 283
    Principles, 44, 48-49
Queria, Ahmed, 22

R

Rabin, Yitzhak, 12-13, 67
Rachel's Tomb, 89
Ramallah, 27, 32, 74-75, 92, 98, 222,
    260, 264
Ramat Shlomo, 54
Ranjeva, Raymond, 124
Reagan Administration, 269
Red Sea, 85
Reference re Secession of Quebec,
    220
Register of Damage, 284
Reid, Harry, 289
Republican Jewish Coalition, 36
Rezek, Francisco, 125
Rice, Condoleezza, 29, 37, 49, 51
Right of Return, 306
Right to Food, 158
Road Map to a Permanent Two-
    State Solution, 48-49, 125
Roadmap to Peace in the Middle
    East, 1, 21, 23-25, 29, 32-37, 44,
    48-50, 53, 58, 63, 86, 118-119,
    121-122, 124, 128, 130-132, 136,
    167, 181, 190, 192-193, 195, 217-
    224, 226-227, 246, 248-249, 252,
    254, 256, 281-283, 286-288, 290
Rock, Allan, 222
Roed-Larsen, Terje, 27
Romania, 234
Rome Statute, 110-111, 305
Root, Elihu, 245
Rosenfeld, Michel, 268-269
Rosenne, Shabtai, 202, 205-207, 212,
    228-229
Rosenthal, Ruvik, 99
Ros-Lehtinen, Ileana, 289
Rostov, Eugene, 223, 225

Route 443, 74-75

Russia, 11, 20, 38, 41, 119, 190, 196

S

Sabel, Robbie, 65

Salam, 70

Salem, 79-80, 143

Samaria, 5-6, 16, 63, 66, 70-71, 74, 79, 81, 89, 109, 219, 226, 261

San Francisco Conference, 197

Sanur, 31

Satloff, Robert, 53, 58

Saudi Arabia, 12, 21, 126, 274

Schily, Otto, 104

Seam Line/Zone, 69-70, 76, 100, 117, 251, 322

Sea of Galilee, 6

Second Intifada, xvi, 1, 10, 15-19, 21-23, 61, 66, 68, 82, 85, 93-94, 118, 217, 255, 257

Second Lebanon War, 39, 77

Second Temple, 6

Security Council, 7, 11-12, 25, 27, 32, 40, 48-51, 104, 111, 118-121, 124-125, 127-132, 138-139, 141-142, 145, 149, 153-154, 159, 161, 166-167, 169, 171-172, 176-178, 183, 187-195, 203, 205, 211, 217-218, 220-222, 224-227, 229, 232, 236, 239, 242-243, 245-246, 251-252, 255-256, 278, 281, 283-284, 286-287, 293, 304

Resolution 237, 149

Resolution 242, 141, 153, 251

Resolution 276, 176, 193

Resolution 298, 142

Resolution 338, 124, 167, 221

Resolution 478, 142

Resolution 1368, 183, 243, 245

Resolution 1373, 183, 243, 245, 254, 287

Resolution 1377, 255

Resolution 1515, 128-132, 167, 192-193

Resolution 1566, 246

Resolution 1701, 40

Resolution 1850, 48

Security Fence, xv-xvi, 1-4, 13, 41, 43, 52, 55-57, 60-63, 65-71, 74-80, 83-89, 93-95, 97, 99-100, 102-104, 111-115, 119, 121, 142, 163, 188, 190-195, 200, 203, 206, 208-210, 212-219, 221, 223-226, 228-229, 231, 234-236, 238-241, 243, 246-257, 260, 262-265, 268-271, 273-276, 278, 280-284, 287, 291-293, 296-298, 300-301, 303, 306

"Apartheid wall," 4, 101, 104-105, 107-110, 114

Comparison to border, 56, 62-64, 69-70, 85, 97, 108-109, 153, 155, 218, 252, 259, 291

Effectiveness, 79-80, 82-84, 299

High Court decisions, 2, 17, 73, 115-116, 258, 262-265, 293

Route of, 2, 62-63, 68, 72-73, 143

"Security barrier," 99-101

"Separation barrier," 99-101, 103

"Separation wall," 3, 100-104, 107, 123

Seidemann, Daniel, 96

Seidl-Hohenveldern, Ignaz, 214

Senegal, 126

Serbia, 195

Shahal Commission, 67

Shahal, Moshe, 67

Shalah, Ramadan Abdallah, 82

Shalev, Gabriela, 51

Shalit, Gilad, 39, 52

Shalom, Silvan, 36-37, 221, 294

Shany, Yuval, 257-258

Sharansky, Natan, 31, 48

Sharm el-Sheikh, Egypt, 43, 48

Sharon, Ariel, 25-26, 28, 31, 33-37, 48, 68-69, 73, 101, 219, 262, 264, 277, 280-281, 295

Shi Jiuyong, 124

Shimoni, Gideon, 107, 113

Sierra Leone, 124

Simma, Bruno, 125, 243

Sinai, 6, 63, 219

Six Day War, 6, 64, 141, 245

Slovakia, 119, 125, 162
Somalia, 119
South Africa, 105, 107-109, 114, 126,
  174, 176, 178, 193, 282, 302
South Korea, 275
South West Africa People's Organi-
  zation (SWAPO), 174
South West Africa Phase Two, 236
Spain, 41, 234
Status of Eastern Carelia, 135, 196,
  207-208, 213-214
Steinmetz Center, 68
Sudan, 7, 102, 126
suicide bombing, 4, 9, 16, 18-19, 21,
  79-80, 82-83, 85, 95, 115, 163,
  246, 286, 298-299
Suppression of Unlawful Acts
  against the Safety of Civil Avi-
  ation, 236
Sweden, 231
Switzerland, 147, 221, 279
Syria, 5-7, 9, 11, 21, 39, 76-77, 102,
  275, 289

T

Tarqumiya, 42
Tayseer, 70
Tehran, 302
Tel Aviv, 52, 54, 67-68, 74, 83, 95,
  266, 300
Third Intifada, 300
Tirawi, Tawfiq, 305
Tirza, Danny, 62, 71, 73-75, 77
Tivon, Noam, 74
Tomka, Peter, 125
trans-Samaria road, 70
Tulkarem, 31, 92
Turkey, 38, 47, 274-275
Tzofim, 264
Tzur, Sa'ar, 78

U

Uganda, 119, 221, 281
Umm el-Fahm, 96
UNESCO World Heritage Site, 266
unilateral declaration of independence (UDI), 303

United Kingdom, 52, 119-120, 125,
  140, 174, 279
  Judicial Committee of the Privy
    Council, 120
United Nations, xv-xvi, 1, 3, 5-8,
  10-12, 17, 19, 21, 23, 25, 29, 30,
  38, 56, 60, 100, 106-107, 119,
  124, 126, 134-135, 138, 145, 160-
  161, 163, 166-167, 169, 171, 175,
  179, 187-190, 193-196, 207, 211,
  213-215, 220, 222, 225, 227-228,
  230-232, 235, 237, 242, 244, 247,
  252, 254-255, 267, 275, 277-279,
  281, 283, 285-286, 288-290, 294,
  298, 300, 302-303, 305-306. *See
  also* General Assembly; Security Council
  Charter, xv, 3, 86, 112, 119, 121,
    123, 127-130, 132-133, 145-146,
    161, 165-166, 169-171, 178,
    182, 187-192, 194-195, 197,
    199, 209, 227-229, 233, 236,
    240-241, 243-244, 247, 264,
    270, 280, 287
    Article 2, 145
    Article 10, 127, 189
    Article 11, 127, 192
    Article 12, 128-129, 177-178,
      190-191
    Article 14, 86, 128-130
    Article 18, 227
    Article 24, 128
    Article 51, xv, 3, 123, 161-162,
      171-172, 181-183, 241-245,
      247, 270, 280, 287-288
    Article 96, 127, 133, 227
    Chapter VII, 194, 236
  Human Rights Council, 7, 295
  Report, 285, 291, 305
  Report of the Secretary-General
    (A/ES-10/248), 249
  UN Observer, 121
United States, 2, 10-12, 17, 20, 22-
  23, 27-28, 36, 40-41, 48, 51-53,
  57, 76, 106, 110, 112, 119-120,
  130, 190, 192, 214, 216, 221, 223,

231, 238, 242, 244-245, 276, 280, 283-286, 288-289, 298, 302, 304
Bureau of International Narcotics and Law Enforcement Affairs, 45
Congress, xvi, 54
Department of State, 9, 24
House of Representatives Resolution 34, 111th Congress, 289
National Security Council, 39
Supreme Court, 118, 224, 225
Uniting for Peace Resolution.
    See General Assembly, Resolution 377 A (V)

V

Vatican, 12, 304
Venezuela, 125
Vereshchetin, Stepanovich, 125

W

Wani, Ibrahim, 224
Washington Institute for Near East Policy, 53
Welch, David, 289
West Bank, 6-7, 9-10, 14-15, 18-22, 24, 26-27, 31, 35, 41, 43, 45-46, 54, 56, 58, 61, 63-64, 67-69, 71, 73-74, 78-79, 81-83, 85-88, 92-94, 96-98, 101, 107-108, 110-115, 141-144, 150, 153, 155, 190, 218, 222, 239, 242, 248-250, 252, 254, 256-257, 264, 266, 281, 285, 292, 299, 303
Western European and Others Grouping (WEOG), 11
Western Sahara, 135, 169, 175, 204, 208, 211, 234
White House, 1, 53, 101, 290
World Conference against Racism, Racial Discrimination, Xenophobia and Related Intolerance, 105
World War I, 140
World War II, 197
Wye River, 1, 7, 13-14

Y

Yemen, 102, 274
Yesha Council, 97

Z

Zahar, Mahmoud Al-, 35-36
Zionism is Racism, 100, 105
    Resolution, 212, 281, 302

About the Author

Richard D. Heideman is a tireless fighter on behalf of the State of Israel and an advocate for victims of terrorism around the world whose human and individual rights have been violated.

Founder of the Washington, D.C. law firm of Heideman Nudelman & Kalik PC, he is licensed to practice before the US Supreme Court and numerous federal and state courts. Heideman serves as lead trial counsel on behalf of American victims of terrorism in claims brought against Libya, Syria, Iran and other organizations and financial institutions accused of providing material support for terrorism. In the past few years, the firm's clients have been awarded Judgments against the Islamic Republic of Iran in the amounts of $1.27 billion and $813 million; and against Syria in the amounts of $601 million, $51 million and most recently a landmark Judgment of $3.58 billion.

A noted public speaker, Heideman has appeared on CNN's "Burden of Proof," "Fox Morning News," CNBC and as legal analyst for WUSA-9, the CBS-TV affiliate in Washington, DC, Reuters and other news organizations, providing commentary and analysis on various civil and criminal matters. He has taught seminars at the Potomac Institute, the Herzliya Conference, the Student Conference on International Law, lectured at the Georgetown University School of Foreign Service Center for Arab Studies, at the International Law Society of the George Washington University Law School and at the

Israel Bar Association, as well as on contemporary topics of interest throughout the world. Heideman twice was elected as President
of B'nai B'rith International and since 2002 has continued to serve
the organization as Honorary President. In 1985, Heideman was an
NGO delegate to the United Nations World Conference on Women;
in 2001 as Head of Delegation to the United Nations World Conference Against Racism in Durban, South Africa; in 2009 as Head
of Delegation to United Nations Durban Review Conference; and
in 2011 as Chairman of the UN Durban 10-year assessment event.
Heideman has participated in meetings at The White House, the
Department of State and with numerous heads of state, prime ministers, foreign ministers and ambassadors around the globe.

Currently Heideman is Chairman of The Israel Forever Foundation, Chair of The Herzliya Conference International Advisory
Board, Chairman of the Jerusalem-based Student Conference on International Law and the Chairman of the United States Holocaust
Memorial Museum Washington Lawyers Committee. He has at
various times served on the Boards of the Anti-Defamation League,
the Jewish Agency for Israel, World Zionist Organization, the American Israel Public Affairs Committee, the World Jewish Congress,
Hillel: The Foundation for Jewish Campus Life and as a Trustee of
the B'nai B'rith World Center in Jerusalem. As a young person he
served as the founding chair of the groundbreaking Kallah international leadership training conference and subsequently served as
the international President (Grand Aleph Godol) of the B'nai B'rith
Youth Organization after which he graduated from the University
of Michigan (BA, 1969), the National Law Center at George Washington University (JD, 1972) and studied at the Hebrew University
Faculty of Law in the Law and Policy Institute Abroad, concentrat-
ing in Legal Aspects of the Middle East Conflict. Heideman is also
former President of the George Washington University Law School
Alumni Association.

In 2001, Heideman received the distinguished Merito de Mayo
decoration by then-President Duhalde of Argentina, having received
the Heritage Award from State of Israel Bonds in 1988 and the Sam
Beber Distinguished Alumnus Award from the B'nai B'rith Youth

Organization in 1999. In 2005 he received the Joseph Papp Racial Harmony Award from the Foundation for Ethnic Understanding.

Heideman lives in Bethesda, Maryland with his wife, Hon. Phyllis Greenberg Heideman, a former Presidential Appointee to the United States Holocaust Memorial Council. They have three daughters, Stefanie Jo Heideman, Dr. Elana Yael Heideman, and Ariana Michal Heideman, as well as three grandsons, Max, Eytam and Noam.